Faith Schools

Is there a role for faith schools in modern society?

For more than a century the English education system has included schools supported by faith communities. That consensus is now under challenge and the recent desire to expand such schools has raised the question of their appropriateness in the plural and diverse society of today. There are strong lobbies to support both further expansion and dilute their membership by ensuring they include children from other faiths or no faith at all.

This book is intended to address the current concerns, questions and interest surrounding the legitimacy, support and intended expansion of faith schools. Divided into five sections, the book includes chapters on:

- The legal frameworks for faith schools and the rights of the child;
- Faith-based schools in the UK, Northern Ireland, France and the USA;
- The impact of faith schools on pupil performance;
- Faith schools, religious education and citizenship;
- Political and research issues.

Faith Schools: Consensus or Conflict? will be of interest to educators, policy makers, researchers and students of education, religion and sociology.

Roy Gardner is Co-ordinator of Advanced Short Courses, Institute of Education, University of London; **Jo Cairns** was formerly Head of Religious Education at the Institute of Education, University of London, and Assistant Director at the Quality Assurance Agency for Higher Education; **Denis Lawton** is Emeritus Professor of Education and formerly Director of the Institute of Education, University of London.

Faith Schools

Consensus or conflict?

Edited by
**Roy Gardner, Jo Cairns
and Denis Lawton**

Routledge
Taylor & Francis Group

LONDON AND NEW YORK

First published 2005
by Routledge
2 Park Square, Milton Park, Abingdon, Oxon, OX14 4RN

Simultaneously published in the USA and Canada
by Routledge
270 Madison Ave, New York, NY 10016

Routledge is an imprint of the Taylor & Francis Group

Transferred to Digital Printing 2006

Typeset in Baskerville by
HWA Text and Data Management, Tunbridge Wells

British Library Cataloguing in Publication Data
A catalogue record for this book is available from the British Library

Library of Congress Cataloging in Publication Data
A catalog record for this book has been requested

ISBN 0–415–33525–6 (hbk)
ISBN 0–415–33526–4 (pbk)

Publisher's Note
The publisher has gone to great lengths to ensure the quality of this reprint
but points out that some imperfections in the original may be apparent

Contents

List of tables and figures   ix
Contributors   xi

Introduction   1
JO CAIRNS, ROY GARDNER AND DENIS LAWTON

PART I
Faith schools: past and present   5

1 **Faith schools now: an overview**   7
   ROY GARDNER

2 **Faith schools and colleges of education since 1800**   14
   BRIAN GATES

3 **The legal framework for faith-based schools and the
   rights of the child**   36
   MARIE PARKER-JENKINS

PART II
Faith schools: for and against   49

4 **Faith schools: can they be justified?**   51
   RICHARD PRING

5 **Are faith schools divisive?**   61
   J. MARK HALSTEAD AND TERENCE McLAUGHLIN

6   Religion and schools – a fresh way forward? A rights-based
    approach to diversity in schools   74
    MARILYN MASON

7   Faith-based schools in the United Kingdom: an
    unenthusiastic defence of a slightly reformed status quo   83
    HARRY BRIGHOUSE

8   Keeping the faith with social capital: from Coleman
    to New Labour on social justice, religion and education   90
    EVA GAMARNIKOW AND ANTHONY GREEN

PART III
Faith schools: in practice   103

9   Perceptions and practices of Christian schools   105
    BART McGETTRICK

10 Learning together: the case for 'joint church' schools   113
    ALAN J. MURPHY

11 Segregation or cohesion: Church of England schools in
    Bradford   122
    RACHEL BARKER AND JOHN ANDERSON

12 Through the looking glass: religion, identity and
    citizenship in a plural culture: from the viewpoint
    of the modern Orthodox Jewish school   138
    LYNNDY LEVIN

PART IV
Faith schools: the experience elsewhere   145

13 Measuring Catholic school performance: an
    international perspective   147
    JAMES ARTHUR

14 Faith schools and Northern Ireland: a review of
    research   156
    TONY GALLAGHER

15 Exclusion or embrace? Faith, social ideals and 'common schooling' in America's public education 166
MICHAEL TOTTERDELL

16 Faith schools in France: from conflict to consensus? 178
CÉCILE DEER

PART V
Faith schools: the way forward 189

17 Faith schools and communities: communitarianism, social capital and citizenship 191
JOHN ANNETTE

18 The impact of faith schools on pupil performance 202
IAN SCHAGEN AND SANDIE SCHAGEN

19 Faith schools, religious education and citizenship 213
JOHN KEAST

20 Continuing personal and professional development and faith schools 222
ROY GARDNER AND JO CAIRNS

21 Faith schools: some political issues and an agenda for research 242
DENIS LAWTON AND JO CAIRNS

Index 257

Tables and figures

Tables

2.1	Proportions of regular churchgoers in the 1851 Census	15
8.1	Catholic schools: educational achievement, social class, gender and faith exclusivity	98
11.1	Social disparity in four wards in the Bradford Metropolitan area	124
11.2	Ethnic breakdown of secondary school pupils in Bradford, 2002	126
11.3	Distribution by ethnic background of pupils in secondary schools in Bradford LEA	127
12.1	Examples of curricular extensions of traditional orthodox concepts	143
14.1	Denominations of pupils by school type in 2001/2, primary, secondary and grammar schools only	161
14.2	Denominations of pupils in integrated schools in 1998/9 and 2001/1	162
18.1	National value-added datasets	203
18.2	Pupils and schools with different religious affiliations in KS3–GCSE dataset	204
18.3	The impact of faith schools at GCSE	205
18.4	Faith schools in context at GCSE	208
18.5	The impact of faith schools on GCSE results, by LEA	208
18.6	The impact of faith schools at Key Stage 3	209

Figures

18.1	Total GCSE scores vs KS3: religious and non-religious schools	206
18.2	Average GCSE scores vs KS3: religious and non-religious schools	206
18.3	English GCSE scores vs KS3: religious and non-religious schools	207

Contributors

John Anderson is Co-Director of Education for the Diocese of Bradford; previously he was Principal of the College of St Mark and St John, Plymouth, after working in many countries and institutions, including the University of Nairobi and the University of Sussex.

John Annette is Professor of Citizenship and Lifelong Learning and Dean of the Faculty of Continuing Education at Birkbeck College, University of London. He is also Chair of the CSV's Council for Citizenship and Learning in the Community.

James Arthur is Head of Educational Research at Canterbury Christchurch University College and has written widely on Catholic schools.

Rachel Barker was Religious Education Adviser to the Diocese of Bradford and is now a member of staff of RE Today.

Harry Brighouse is Professor of Philosophy and Affiliate Professor of Educational Policy Studies at the University of Wisconsin, Madison. He is author of *School Choice and Social Justice* (Oxford University Press, 2000) and of numerous articles on topics in political philosophy, education policy and meta-ethics.

Jo Cairns was Head of Religious Education, Institute of Education, University of London, and Assistant Director at the Quality Assurance Agency for Higher education.

Cécile Deer is currently Research Fellow at the Department of Economics, Oxford University, and is College Lecturer at Balliol College. She has published extensively on education including *Higher Education in England and France Since the 1980s* (Symposium Books, 2002).

Tony Gallagher is Professor of Education in Queen's University Belfast. In recent years he has carried out research on the effects of selective education and on religiously integrated education. His research interests include the role of education in ethnically divided societies.

Roy Gardner is Co-ordinator for Advanced Short Courses, Institute of Education, University of London.

Eva Gamarnikow is Lecturer in Sociology and Human Rights in the School of Educational Foundations and Policy Studies at the Institute of Education, University of London, where she is Course Leader for the MA in Social Justice and Education.

Brian Gates is Professor of Religious and Moral Education in the Division of Religion and Philosophy at St Martin's College, Lancaster. He is Chair of the RE Council of England and Wales and on the Editorial Board of *The Journal of Moral Education*.

Anthony Green is a Lecturer in Sociology in the School of Educational Foundations and Policy Studies at the Institute of Education, University of London, where he is Course Leader for the MA Sociology of Education.

J. Mark Halstead is Professor of Moral Eduation and Associate Dean (Research and Enterprise) at the University of Plymouth. He has written widely on multicultural education and spiritual and moral education.

John Keast is a consultant for RE and citizenship. From 1996 to 2003 he was RE officer, then Principal Manager for RE, citizenship, and personal, social and health education at the Qualifications and Curriculum Authority. He has also been an OFSTED inspector, LEA adviser and RS examiner.

Denis Lawton is Emeritus Professor of Education and formerly Director of the Institute of Education, University of London.

Lynndy Levin is a doctoral researcher at the Institute of Education, University of London. She is also Lead Researcher for the Jewish Aids Trust project in supporting the development of sex and relationship education in Jewish schools in Britain.

Marilyn Mason is Education Officer of the British Humanist Association. She used to teach English and Philosophy; her role now includes advising parents and teachers, writing and speaking about humanism and education, and co-ordinating BHA education policies and campaigns.

Bart McGettrick is Professor of Education at the University of Glasgow, and a member of the Council of the International Federation of Catholic Universities. He is currently Chairman of the Schools Commission for the Holy Land.

Terence McLaughlin is Professor of Philosophy of Education at the Institute of Education, University of London. He has a particular interest in the philosophical aspects of matters of educational principle, policy and practice relating to faith schools in liberal democratic societies.

Alan J. Murphy is Director of the Catholic School Leadership MA programme at St Mary's College, Twickenham. Previously he was headteacher of St Edward's joint Roman Catholic–Church of England VA comprehensive school in Poole, Dorset.

Marie Parker-Jenkins is Professor of Education at the University of Derby. She has worked abroad in a number of multi-cultural settings, and has a particular interest in issues of social justice with reference to ethnicity and gender.

Richard Pring recently retired as Professor of Educational Studies and Director of the Department of Educational Studies, University of Oxford. He is currently a Director of the Nuffield Review of 14–19 Education and Training.

Ian Schagen is Head of the Statistics Research and Analysis Group of the National Foundation for Educational Research (NFER).

Sandie Schagen is a Principal Research Officer in the Department of Evaluation and Policy Studies at the National Foundation for Educational Research (NFER).

Michael S. Totterdell is Director of the Institute of Education, Manchester Metropolitan University. He has worked with schools government agencies and non-government organisations in the UK and abroad to develop collaboration partnership models of teacher education.

Introduction

Jo Cairns, Roy Gardner and Denis Lawton

Nearly 30 years ago, the distinguished educationalist from Northern Ireland, John Greer, addressed a conference on religion in the following way:

> Schools are communities of human beings undergoing education …This I take to imply the development of the ability to judge between alternative patterns of interpretation and claims to truth, and is bound to lead to a critical evaluation of society and forms of religion which are found in society.
>
> (Greer 1975: 29)

Our book is about just that. First the recognition that each school, faith or non-faith, is different in its mission, culture and practices because each is a community of human beings committed to the fostering of learning in ways that will prepare young adults to take their individual place in an increasingly complex and unstable world. How we as a society judge which educational cultures and practices are best suited to this task will ultimately depend on our particular stance towards religion and faith in that society and, in particular, its role in our public spaces. Whether we, as a diverse, plural and multi-faith society, can, or indeed should, reach agreement on this particular issue is a matter for further speculation.

Faith Schools: Consensus or Conflict? attempts to present a balanced debate and evaluation of the issues involved in the continuing and expanded provision of faith-based education in our present society. It arose initially from the proceedings of a conference held at the Institute of Education, University of London, to discuss the implications of the White Paper, *Schools Achieving Success* (DfES 2001). Many of the participants sought a way of widening participation in this debate and also a means of securing a sustained engagement with the issues. The book is offered as a contribution to achieving those aims. As such it is derived from the following principles on which the conference was based:

- the need both to respect and confront the historical context of policies attached to faith-based schools in the United Kingdom (UK);
- to understand faith and schools as contested and complex concepts both in the UK and overseas;
- to articulate the conditions which a school's learning culture should satisfy to develop competent, mature adults for our diverse, plural and increasingly global society;
- to encourage a culture of systematic research into faith-based education and to provide means of modelling excellence in the sector through developing the capacity of faith-

based schools to speak for themselves to all stakeholders and engage in ongoing comparative analysis;
- to provoke and support a continuing conversation about faith-based schools consistent with the rules and ideals attached to living in a liberal democratic community.

The book is divided into five parts.

Part I – Faith schools: past and present

This section seeks to introduce the particular issues and concerns which have arisen both in education and in the wider community as a result of the government's decision at the beginning of the twenty-first century to sponsor faith schools at this particular time in the cultural, social and economic life of the country. The historical foundations on which such a scheme is built are set out, including some long-term perspectives on the place of religion in education in England, and explanations are offered as to why not all faith communities are playing on a level field as this new initiative begins. Finally, the section explores the legal frameworks in which this initiative is situated and examines the rights of parents and children in the choice and manner of the education of our young people today.

Part II – Faith schools: for and against

As a society we find it difficult to agree about which of the nomenclatures, such as secular or postsecular, modern or Christian, plural or postmodern, we wish to ascribe to our present culture. Such bandying of words by politicians, journalists, philosophers and sociologists arises from a very real tension felt across our society about our individual and our communities' roles and status. This section attempts to set out what may be considered as reasoned and worthwhile arguments to justify or condemn the existence of faith schools at a time not only of personal and communal uncertainty about identity but of very real division about the role of religion in the public and private lives of our citizens. Finally those major themes of 'inclusiveness', 'social justice' and 'social capital', promoted by politicians and many others as means of achieving a fair and just society, are examined against the prospect of the expansion of faith schools.

Part III – Faith schools: in practice

The section begins with an exploration of some typologies of faith schools based on particular characteristics and clusters of characteristics currently exhibited in schools in the UK and throughout the world. This helps to situate the wide-ranging examples of some recent approaches and practices within faith schools. There is an example of an initiative to bring two faith communities together in the formation of a 'joint school'. In another example, an evaluation is made of the specific approaches taken by a faith community through partnerships as it sought to strengthen the impact of its schools in meeting the challenges and opportunities of serving severely economically deprived children in areas marked out by religious and ethnic tensions and violence. The section ends with an analysis of the critical reflective processes with which a faith school must engage in the area of citizenship education to reflect both its own educational needs, beliefs and values and those of the state, and considers the impact of each on the other.

Part IV – Faith schools: the experience elsewhere

This section offers perspectives on the critical questions surrounding the place of faith in education culled from diverse national experiences across the world.

It begins by looking at the complex challenges of evaluating faith schools' performance through consideration of whether it is possible to measure Catholic school performance from an international perspective. Up to now, research has been at local and national levels, focusing on what can be measured in outcomes, with examination of the 'religio-philosophical' effect seriously missing. There is then a critical examination of the American culture of apparent ambivalence towards religion in the public realm and the consequences for American pluralism. Crucial issues related to spiritual and 'immaterial equity' are raised in relation to a society's practice of fairness and democracy in its theoretical structures. The section then appraises the experience of faith and schools in Northern Ireland from the first half of the nineteenth century through the last 30 years of political violence, the development of separate schools and the measures taken by schools to promote reconcilia-tion and tolerance. It challenges the view that a common system of mass education is always the best vehicle for social integration, since this is often based on assimilationist principles in which minority identities are either denied or discouraged in favour of a fictive cultural homogeneity. The last part of this section examines the case of how the French educational system has evolved in relation to faith schooling in recent years. It shows that, from a historically grounded, 'culturally' specific situation of antagonism, the secular state sector and the religious private sector have developed forms of 'complementarities' which have led to an unprecedented level of mutual tolerance.

Part V – Faith schools: the way forward

With the upsurge in questions of identity in our currently fragmented society, combined with the Department for Education and Skills (DfES) sponsorship of new models of faith schools and faith-based community action, this section begins with a consideration of the policy dilemmas faced both by central government and the faith communities when introducing citizenship education. Has the introduction of citizenship education become an excuse for the DfES not to take forward a pressing concern in the teaching of religion in schools, namely the development of national guidelines for a religious education curriculum? To what extent are the assumptions from communitarian theory and social capital theory used by politicians and central policy makers in accord with the actual role of faith schools in providing social capital, community cohesion and active citizenship? Should education be freed from the hands of politicians? For a genuine conversation to take place in response to these and other related questions, the section closes with a call for hard information. After setting out the results of a project which examined the impact of faith schools on pupil performance, it looks forward to a strategic approach to research into faith schools: namely, one of models of self-researching schools, supported through programmes of continuing personal and professional development, able to speak for themselves, combined with independent and critical analysis of the impact of faith in education through projects sponsored by national policy and research institutions.

References

Greer, J. (1975) 'Opening Conference of Religion in Ireland, 31 January', *International Journal of Comparative Religious Education and Values*, 7(1), Summer 1995: 26.
DfES (2001) *Schools Achieving Success*, Norwich: Stationery Office.

Part I

Faith schools

Past and present

1 Faith schools now

An overview

Roy Gardner

The White Paper *Schools Achieving Success* (DfES 2001a) called for the expansion of faith-based education in England and Wales. The conditions set out were financially generous and sought only a contribution of 10 per cent from governing bodies in the development of their schools. At the same time, the White Paper called for a new approach to admissions policies in faith-based schools, seeking a goal of inclusiveness by setting a target of 20 per cent non-faith pupils in the school's composition. In so doing the government could be said to be responding positively to the religiously plural and ethnically diverse population which constitutes our society in the twenty-first century. On the other hand, those who seek inclusivity as the overriding characteristic of state-supported education argue that a continuation of the nineteenth-century historic settlement between the Christian churches and state-supported education is itself the major cause of increased sectarianism and social fragmentation in our multi-faith but secular society.

The extent of religious identification and diversity is shown by the census figures of 2001. Just over three-quarters of the population identified themselves as religious, with 15.5 per cent saying they had no religion and 7.3 percent not answering the question. At the same time just under a third of English state-funded schools had a religious foundation, educating 23 per cent of all pupils. According to the *Guardian*, of the 7,000 state-funded faith schools, 4,716 were Church of England, 2,108 were Roman Catholic, a small number were Methodist, there was one Greek Orthodox, one Seventh Day Adventist, 32 Jewish, four Muslim and two Sikh. These figures underline the fact that in the United Kingdom (UK) we have a multiplicity of religious and non-religious life stances. What they do not indicate is whether we have a political, educational or religious consensus about the place of religion in full-time compulsory education.

The 1870 Education Act established state education by supplementing the existing Christian voluntary provision. A means was found of funding those existing religious schools and establishing new forms of schools to ensure elementary education for all. The place and teaching of religion in all types of schools was then regulated by the same Act. The 1902 Education Act consolidated the settlement and the 1944 Education Act continued in this tradition. It was only in the 1980s with the drive towards a national curriculum for all schools that real tensions arose in the settlement and real fears grew in the Christian communities that their historic right to determine the make-up of their schools' populations and their curriculum was under threat from the state. Then, in 2001, the government in its *Schools Building on Success* firmly pledged to sponsor the extension and provision of faith-based schooling. As the Archbishops' Council (2001: 3) argued: 'Today there is full state provision and the purpose of the Church in education is not simply to provide the basic education needed for human dignity.'

The time is therefore right to question the purpose not only of the Christian Churches in education but also the place of other religions and life stances, too.

At issue is whether the purpose of education is to induct children and young people into a prescribed way of life chosen by parents and/or religious leaders or to socialize children and young people into the norms of society in general, a matter discussed fully by Durkheim (1986).

In England, the state from 1870 had chosen to sponsor a dual system of education, and even by 1944 the state was still not prescribing a set curriculum for all schools operating within that dual system; religious education remained the one statutory subject. Interestingly, too, Harry Judge (2001: 237) has also pointed out that, by 1991, at a time when the New Labour Party was emerging, signs of traditional Labour hostility to denominational schools was disappearing. In that year, when Tessa Blackstone, Labour Party spokesperson in the House of Lords, speculated about the desirability of all maintained schools becoming secular, other Labour peers hastened to make it clear that such a revolution was no part of official Labour policy.

The question of the purpose the Labour Party attached to faith-based schooling in the years leading to its election victory in 1997 remains difficult to pin down. Here Judge refers to a letter to the *Church Times* (ibid: 237) from the politician responsible for developing the Labour Party portfolio on education as saying:

> [a Labour government] will undoubtedly wish to restore the important partnership between central government, local government and the Churches which underpinned the 1944 Act. However, it would be unrealistic … to put the clock back to 1944. It cannot be assumed that church schools that have felt the need to give up their voluntary-aided status in return for 100 per cent funding would have, or would even wish to have, voluntary-aided status restored.

Clearly then the government was interested in partnership with the churches as one of a number of sponsors of different categories of schooling. That policy indication and the subsequent White Paper of 2001 make little or no effort to differentiate between the different types of faith and religious groups which may choose such partnerships in return for generous funding. Also no effort was made to coax individual schools going forward for such state support to articulate the place they understood religion to occupy in education within our present diverse and mainly secular society. Nor were questions asked about the different roles religion and faith do/might play in individual schools. In that way, the Archbishop of Canterbury's recent comment (*The Times*, 12 September 2003) about young people to a conference of Church of England headteachers may be similarly applied to the government's lack of clarity in the matter of sponsoring an extension of faith-based schools:

> I don't think I'm the only person to have struggled with groups of teenagers, trying to get them to articulate values that really matter to them, to discover that practically the only thing they will agree in voicing is the importance of tolerance – usually seen as an incurious co-existence, even a bland acceptance of mutual ignorance and non-understanding, in the name of not passing judgment.

Despite the Blair's government's emphasis on standards as the main criterion for judging between schools it seems content to permit a dual system of sorts to continue, alongside numerous other partnership-based alternatives to 'bog-standard' schools. As yet it does not seem ready to move to a situation where state provision for education is stripped down to a legal state framework concerned only to enforce certain core standards and an adequate examination system. Schools could then present an unambiguous offering of their purpose and values in education to their parents, pupils and local communities. Those that were faith based could take on the challenge to offer an alternative mode of education to those 'without a spiritual ethos', which, the Archbishop of Canterbury (as above, *The Times*) has claimed, risk generating 'individualism, functionalism and ultimately fragmentation'. In that scenario the richness and diversity of the education system might then be complemented by a state partnership based on responsibilities proper to the state and each educational institution.

In part, the difficulty in addressing the question of whether the existence of faith-based schools is a source of consensus or of conflict in our society arises from a very peculiar English problem. It is that highlighted by Michael Hastings at a lecture at the Royal Society of Arts (RSA) (RSA, 28 January 2003) in which he pointed out that in England we now have a situation in which different faith communities have sought to become integrated into a nation which itself lacks a faith identity of its own. He argued:

> When faith issues are at the forefront of people's thinking, whether that is about matters of behaviour, or ideas of belief, or about constitutional issues such as the role of the church or the monarch's relationship to the church or the constitution of the nation, there is no clarity about the way we should go.

This is not an excuse for vague or muddled policy-making. Nonetheless this lack of a common national faith identity is often ignored in discussion at national and local levels to the detriment of clear policy decisions. Already the issues which have arisen from the extension of faith-based schooling indicate a failure to get to grips with the huge cultural and social differences in the political and educational climate between 1870, 1944 and those of the present day. At the same time, confusion marks much debate about the purpose of faith and religion in education in our society, which is increasingly characterised and shaped by the plurality of its beliefs and cultures and the multiple identities of its citizens. Faith and religion shape not only a national identity but the belief systems of communities as well as those of individuals. To what extent can faith communities in their state-sponsored schools set about answering the questions set out by Hastings according to their own dispositions and preferences alone? Should they not also respond to them against criteria embedded in the boundaries of inclusiveness and multiple identity which both implicitly and explicitly underpin and shape the purpose of our current general state education?

Indeed, imprecision and a failure to engage with the more fundamental aspects of the challenges and outcomes of faith-based schooling often arise from a non-recognition that the very concepts of 'faith' and 'school' are themselves complex and contested. Sociologists and philosophers have identified, for example, the following typologies of religion, which can each be found in our plural culture today (Heelas and Woodhead 2000: 2–3):

- religions of difference
- religions of humanity
- spiritualities of life.

Further, a recent survey conducted by the Institute of Jewish Policy Research (IJPR 2003) points out the consensus and 'dissensus' among certain types of London Jews, who for the purpose of the survey were asked to identify themselves into three sociological categories of 'belief: their attitudes and opinions'; 'belonging: their membership, attachments, participation'; and 'behaviour: actions and answers to certain questions'. Not only does the survey provide a rich source of information about the bases for likely consensus and 'dissensus' among a particular diverse religious group, it also points up the diversity in belief, belonging and practice among any religious community in Britain today. As one leading researcher into faith communities has commented (Jackson 1997: 202): 'When I meet a person from a religion I do not meet someone who relates straightforwardly to a whole cumulative tradition.'

Complex and contested concepts demand a response from policy makers which is at once consistent with the concept's intellectual and ethical seriousness and its epistemological influence in our plural society. To take one example, schools are required (DfEE/QCA 1999: 11, 47) to promote the diverse value systems which operate among their pupils and to give them equality within spiritual education. One researcher has recently pointed out that the requirement for spiritual education should apply differently to faith-based schools for two reasons (Pinner 2003):

- faith-based schools have axiological threads woven into their philosophical fabric in the form of defined value systems;
- faith-based schools catering for religiously homogenous populations need to promote their pupils' spiritual education within their own religiously oriented frameworks.

For our society, which covets its democratic institutions and way of life, can schools bring about the development of a common good as well as fulfilling the needs of the children and young people they serve? In a state education system which provides for the existence of faith-based schools alongside community schools, can we find a common learning culture which fosters inclusiveness, equality and social justice?

Is it not viable and necessary for each type of school to incorporate the three fundamental liberal democratic values described by Halstead (1996: 18) as:

1. individual liberty (i.e. freedom of action and freedom from constraint in the pursuit of one's own needs and interests);
2. equality of respect for all individuals within the structures and practices of society (i.e. non-discrimination on irrelevant grounds);
3. consistent rationality (i.e. basing decisions and actions on logically consistent rational justifications)?

With such values, could not each school 'explore the meanings of religion, secularisation, pluralism and citizenship in an epistemologically open way'? For Robert Jackson (1997: 126), if schools could achieve this they would be developing the competence in children and young people to move '... between the different arenas and perspectives of religious and modern plurality'. Skeie (1995: 27–9) has argued that this would mean that children become 'subjects in their own culture' representing traditions and working with pluralism rather than against it.

Some would, however, argue that in fact it is only faith-based schools that can effectively provide the spiritual aspect of education demanded by current legislation. In *The Way Ahead* (Archbishops' Council 2001: 3), the Church of England has argued that the purpose of the church in education is to 'offer a spiritual dimension to the lives of young people, within the traditions of the Church of England, in an increasingly secular world'. Here there is a strong case for evaluating the use of language in educational policy making.

There is a real danger of state education policy language in our present dual system 'borrowing' the language of the churches and other religious groups to explain away a direction or aim which it seeks for education. Hence the need for restraint and clarity when examining what is intended by 'spiritual education' and 'mission' in policy documents. Some would argue that the definitions of the spiritual suggested in, for example, Office for Standards in Education (OFSTED) Handbooks are a shorthand for discussing those characteristics of human beings which formal education should foster. Similarly, the use of 'mission' in almost evangelical prose suggests that it is the role of each school to have a vision of its responsibilities and goals arising from its own beliefs and values. Yet there are surely common educational visions which most schools share, whatever their particular culture or ethos. On the other hand, the Archbishop of Canterbury (*The Times*, 12 September 2003), in his speech to the conference of Anglican headteachers, felt it important to point to 'a real tension in educational thinking between those whose concern is primarily, almost exclusively, with imparting skills to individuals and those who understand education as something that forms the habits of living in a group'.

All of this serves to underline the importance of critically examining the language and values behind statements which support the expansion of faith-based schools. It is important that there is a genuine sharing of arguments and research about the significant educational differences and values which are offered by schools operating as either community schools or faith-based ones. Richard Pring (Chapter 4, this volume) has suggested that arguments for and against faith-based schools need to address the following key concepts:

- educational aims and the promotion of a valued form of life;
- the autonomy of the child and the promotion of a particular creed;
- indoctrination and notions of rationality.

In relation to the autonomy of the child, we might wish to couple Pring's concerns with the advice of Hirst and Peters (1970: 31–2), when they argued that ideals such as autonomy are 'vacuous unless people are provided with forms of knowledge and experience to be critical, creative and autonomous with'. They (ibid: 32) continued: 'Autonomy, or following rules that one has accepted for oneself, is an unintelligible ideal without the mastery of a body of rules on which choice can be exercised.'

The challenge which exercised our state education system over the last 30 years has been how best to encourage children from widely different social, ethnic and religious backgrounds to learn from a curriculum which has not overly changed since the 1902 Education Act. When, for example, the preamble to the 1988 Education Act called for education in personal, moral, spiritual and social development, the detailed national curriculum failed to meet in detail such fine aspirations. Individual schools, some faith-based, others standard-maintained/community schools, sought to work with the curriculum in innovative ways to meet the children's needs, despite failures within the central curriculum. The question to be addressed to both community and faith-based schools is whether they are satisfied that they are operating a curriculum which does justice to preparation for living in the twenty-first century. For all schools are facing the opportunities and tensions which our society presents: the fragmentation and violence experienced particularly in northern cities; the call in the Education Act of 2000 for education to contribute to an inclusive society; the disappointment experienced by many from the outcomes of the national curriculum and its processes; the inclusion of citizenship education in the school curriculum; and the increasing possibility of a national framework for religious education. We must ask alongside our schools, therefore:

- How do we best incorporate the opportunities and challenges experienced by all living in England today into the content and learning outcomes of our school curricula?
- Which people and which experiences do children and young people need to meet and have in order to be able to think critically and 'manage on their own'?
- How can the experience of formal education best complement the home and community experiences of all children and young people in so diverse a society?

Our final concern must be to ask whether the government has paid due attention to the messages and outcomes which the initiative to expand faith-based school provision through the measures outlined in *Schools Building on Success* will offer to our diverse society and its multi-identity citizens. Stewart Sutherland (Sacks and Sutherland 1996: 47) has suggested that the degree of pluralism which characterises our society gives rise to the following questions:

1   What are the conditions for the functioning of a society that is plural in character?
2   What in such a society are the conditions of civil liberty?

Sutherland argued that very close to the heart of these questions is the relationship between particular forms of economic strength in a society and the prospects for the acceptance of tolerance and therefore pluralism. He (ibid: 47) illustrates this point in the following way:

> There are clear implications in this for schools in relationship to shaping the curriculum – for example, in identifying what depth of understanding of aspects of these interactions and also of the diversities of cultures present in any community is a precondition of the practice of toleration by the citizens of the future. Equally important, however, is how such awareness on the part of staff and governors of schools informs the ethos, structure and institutional practice of those schools.

Any justification for faith-based schools must surely lie in how in practice individual schools respond to Sutherland's questions and conditions for pluralism. A real and present danger must be that the current government initiative makes no such demands and, indeed, does not even invite faith schools to justify, in a wider public conversation, the contribution they are making to young people's understanding of the place of religion in education and society in general and to the growth and development of those young people as they study in particular schools.

What then are the characteristics of schools which cause 'human flourishing' (ibid: 48) in a pluralist society and how are these different from those of other schools? As Tony Gallagher argues in Chapter 14 (this volume):

> Plural societies are faced with a dilemma: whether they should operate plural schools, within which all or most identities are acknowledged and recognised, or a plurality of schools, in which minorities are accorded the right to their own schools.

That dilemma in England has brought about the present initiative which is the subject of our book. It is a policy that both deserves consideration and demands a continuing conversation about its consequences.

References

Archbishops' Council (2001) *The Way Ahead: Church of England Schools in the New Millennium*, London: Church House Publishing.

DfEE/QCA (1999) *The National Curriculum Handbook for Primary/Secondary Teachers in England*, London: DfEE/QCA.

Durkheim, E. (1986) *Moral Education: A Study in the Theory and Application of the Sociology of Education*, New York: Free Press.

DfES (2001a) *Schools Achieving Success*, Norwich: Stationery Office.

DfES (2001b) *Schools Building on Success: Raising Standards, Promoting Diversity, Achieving Success*, Norwich: Stationery Office.

Halstead, J.M. (1996) 'Liberal values and liberal education', in J.M. Halstead and M.J. Taylor (eds) *Values in Education and Education in Values*, London: Falmer.

Heelas, P. and Woodhead, L. (2000) *Religion in Modern Times: An Interpretive Anthology*, Oxford: Blackwell.

Hirst, P. and Peters, R. (1970) *The Logic of Education*, London: Routledge and Kegan Paul.

IJPR (2003) *Secular or Religious? The Outlook for London Jews*, London: David Graham IJPR.

Jackson, R. (1997) *Religious Education: An Interpretive Approach*, London: Hodder and Stoughton.

Judge, H. (2001) *Faith based Schools and the State*, Oxford: Symposium Books.

Pinner, H. (2003) Unpublished research paper, London.

Sacks, J. and Sutherland, S. (1996) 'The Victor Cook Memorial Lecture', University of St Andrews, Centre for Philosophy and Public Affairs.

Skeie, G. (1995) 'Plurality and pluralism: a challenge for religious education', *British Journal of Religious Education*, 17(2): 84–91.

2 Faith schools and colleges of education since 1800

Brian Gates

Thirty years ago it might have been predicted that the involvement of the churches in schools, as in the education and training of teachers, had little future except to be part of a quaintly remaindered past. The logic would have been inescapable for legislators. The acid tides of secularisation were corroding the Christian heartlands of the nation. Education had no need of any religious hypothesis. The proportion of pupils being taught in church schools had fallen dramatically. Many Church Colleges of Education had already closed or been amalgamated out of distinctive existence. It was only a matter of time before a promised educational millennium would demonstrate that the nation had at last outgrown all talk of religious sponsorship.

A century before that, in a very different context, similar voices might have predicted that the future of education would become independent of religious sponsorship. Atheism was no longer the silent whispering of a few. Developments in the natural sciences were undermining faith, and not only in its literal forms. Far from being dependent on religion, moral sense provided grounds for questioning it. The varieties of Christian denominations were compounded by the religious diversity within empire and beyond. The public funding of education for all was an eminently sensible prospect without need of religion.

There are those who would still stand by such predictions, albeit over a delayed time frame. However, few can now justify the folly of pretending that this is the necessary evolutionary outcome for a participatory democracy. It was not so in 1802, any more than in 1902 or 2002. There is much in the past that the predictions overlooked. There is much in the future that would have been lost if they came to be. The missing ingredients will emerge in the course of this historical overview. For good and ill, their capacity to challenge routine expectations is not in doubt.

For the purposes of this chapter, the two centuries since 1800 have been divided into three periods. Following some initial characterisation of the religious context for each period, special attention is given to school provision and funding, and to teacher education and training. Within these, the main focus is on the voluntary sector and the parts of the churches and other faith communities involved in public educational provision.

1803–69: The predominance of Christian voluntary provision

Context

These were years of restrictions on child labour, the abolition of slavery and of factory reform. The conflicting Christian polities and loyalties which inflamed the English Civil

War still persisted, but radical and utilitarian reformers alike were less obviously inspired by Christian conviction. Democratisation took another step forward with the Reform Act of 1832 – one million people were now qualified to vote.

Overall, the Church was nationally normative for public institutional life, for the rhythms of the annual calendar and for individual rites of passage. Even without the inclusion of 'occasional conformists', the majority association was with the Church of England (CofE). It had its critics for social arrogance and corruption, as in *The Extraordinary Black Book* (Wade 1832) which called for its abolition, but in both its Evangelical and High Church wings it aspired to be socially inclusive and serve the poor. The Free Church (FC) denominations were known as Dissenters and included principally Baptists, Congregationalists, Methodists, Presbyterians, Quakers and Unitarians. Until recently, most Roman Catholics (RCs) had come from families remaining loyal to their pre-Reformation heritage, but numbers were significantly strengthened by Irish immigration, especially during the Potato Famines.

Religion, which is always a final boundary marker for what matters most in life, was expressed through its institutional expressions, fertile ground for protectionism. Dissenters and RCs were subject to restrictions on registering births, marriages and churchyard burials, and on attending university. The restrictions applied equally to Jews, but were insufficient to discourage continuing immigration, especially from Eastern Europe, and during years of persecution large numbers arrived in Hull, and thence to Leeds, Manchester and Liverpool. The largely Sephardic community, now joined by Ashkenazis, had itself become well established. Some Jews were more religiously observant than others; short of blasphemy, most were ready to demonstrate their loyalty to the establishment. Even so, service as a member of parliament was denied until 1858, when the Christian specification of the oath of office was finally amended.

Avowed atheists and secularists, as well as more hesitant agnostics, became more widely heard during this period. Though those engaged in science and technology had not over-whelmingly abandoned religion, evolutionary biology and geology were seen as challenging Biblical truth. So too was critical study of the Bible. All this came to wider note from within the churches themselves, from more generalised impressions, and from more strident critiques. Books such as *Essays and Reviews* (Wilson 1860) publicised debates such as that between Wilberforce and Huxley, and the work of George Eliot, as both novelist and translator of the works of Feuerbach and Strauss, all illustrate the changing intelligence of faith. And, as in George Holyoake's adoption of a preacher's mantle in Cheltenham, atheists were courageous to blaspheme.

The religious demography of the period as documented in the 1851 Census of regular churchgoing, as interpreted by Horace Mann, is shown in Table 2.1. Such was the Establishment's anxiety regarding the high level of churchgoing amongst Nonconformists that no further religious question was permitted in any subsequent census – until 2001.

School provision and funding

In common with civilisations and cultures worldwide, in Christendom, too, religion and education have had a close association (Newsome, 1961). This is the direct consequence

Table 2.1 Proportions of regular churchgoers in the 1851 Census

Church of England	Free Church	Roman Catholic	Jews	Total population
29.5% (5,292,551)	25.3% (4,536,264)	2.1% (383,630)	0.3% (6,030)	17,927,609

of a popular desire to ensure that the meanings, which matter most in life, are effectively shared and passed on to succeeding generations. More open versions of this priority are attentive to 'secular' aspects of knowledge as well as explicitly 'religious' ones, since all study is a God-given pilgrim's trail. For others, the trail itself requires tight control if the learner is not to stray.

So pre-1870 educational provision in England and Wales derived its primary sponsorship from the institutional churches and individual charitable acts and foundations, most of which acknowledged some Christian inspiration. This was true of the cathedral, grammar and public schools from previous centuries but these reached only a minority of children. The more determined drive during the nineteenth century to extend this opportunity continued to be church led, but two different perspectives on the question of ownership and responsibility for the provision came into direct tussle.

The view from within the established Church was that the education of all children was desirable. This was not unanimously held, however, especially amongst those who benefited from employing children, and there were anxieties as to how it could be afforded. Influential taxpayers recognised the advantage of their contributing to local charity schools rather than some large-scale national provision. The thinking of the leadership is reflected in the foundation of the National Society for Promoting the Education of the Poor in the Principles of the Established Church (known also as the National Society, or NS) in 1811. The prime challenge was how to provide elementary education to the masses presently deprived of it. The solution would be a school in every parish throughout the land; parish boundaries were such that no-one would be left outside the care of one parish or another. Subsequent national surveys show how local clergy often took on this initiative whole-heartedly, with or without the benefit of special donations. The inclusion of the fourth 'R' of religion, alongside the other three (reading, writing and arithmetic), was simply assumed as right. It took the form of the Bible, catechism and prayer book services.

The second view was denominationally more open and is clearly articulated in the foundation in 1814 of the British and Foreign School Society for the Education of the Labouring and Manufacturing Classes of Society of Every Religious Persuasion (BFSS), which drew on the pioneering work of the Quaker Joseph Lancaster.[1] This preferred schools that were not specific to one denomination, although Scripture and general Christian principles would be part of the general curriculum. Most dissenting churches favoured such an approach, along with liberal Anglicans and some RCs and Jews.

Although there were also exponents of a third view, which favoured schools with no reference at all to religion, represented by the Central Society of Education (1836), they were a tiny minority. Arguably, it was the tussling between the other two that delayed the introduction of a fully comprehensive school system funded by public taxation. There was also a real fear that it would be wrong to give governments the means of 'dictating opinions and principles to the people' (so Lord Brougham in his evidence given to the Parliamentary Committee) (Maclure 1965: 40). Instead, beginning in 1833, annual grants towards school provision were given to each of the Societies, in proportion to their own respective funding bases. The NS, having a more extensive network, received more. From 1846 similar grants were given (subject to agreement to the reading of Scripture) to Baptists and Congregationalists, from 1847 to Wesleyan Methodists and to the Catholic Poor School Committee, and in 1853 (subject to the reading of at least part of the Bible) to the Manchester Jewish community.

The NS and CofE Bishops resisted the introduction of a 'conscience clause' that would have enabled children of Dissenters to attend its schools without fear of religious offence. Similarly, no alternative to the Authorised Version of the Bible would be considered acceptable, and that delayed the granting of aid to RC schools. Accordingly, the continuing offence in 'single school' areas was underlined in the 1861 Report of the Newcastle Commission. In the Archbishop of Canterbury's 'concordat' with the government in 1840, he conceded 'inspection rights', but not their say in who was appointed to that role; the principle was later extended to the other churches. The CofE left an individual school's management in the discretion of local vicars and head teachers. The same was initially true in RC schools but that responsibility was pulled back into episcopal control.

Teacher education and training

Much learning of how to teach has come by imitation and related critical reflection. At the beginning of the eighteenth century, self-conscious attention to this apprenticeship process was already being pursued by Quakers at their school near Pontefract. In 1805 Joseph Lancaster, also a Quaker, combined monitorial teaching with residential training of superintendents at his Borough Road Free School. Success was recognised in a formal Teacher's Certificate. Andrew Bell, his contemporary, was encouraged by the Bishop of Newcastle to develop a comparable training scheme in the north-east, and shortly thereafter in central London. The two models were endorsed respectively by the BFSS and NS.

Teacher training in this vein continued piecemeal as the dominant model until the mid-1830s, when the first government grants were made to support and extend provision. As with children's education, that for teachers was denominationally contentious and, in spite of attempts to create one in 1839, this prevented the endorsement of any Normal College. The establishment lobby gave priority to CofE training places; Dissenters and Secularists objected. Accordingly, there were to be grants (initially for buildings but by 1846 for maintenance as well) for a range of residential colleges. By the mid-1840s there were 20 CofE colleges, quickly to be followed by a smaller number of Congregational, Methodist and RC ones. By 1859 the average annual government grant to colleges had risen to 70 per cent.

Several characteristics stand out in this provision. First, it was patchy in availability, affected by such factors as variations in diocesan leadership, local town politics and relative wealth for voluntary endowments. Second, at its best it combined genuine love of learning with the nurturing of professional skills that would enable sharing that love of learning with children, but this was not consistently the case and the length and depth of training were very mixed. Third, as in school provision, issues of denominational allegiance and ownership were too easily divisive.

Alongside the colleges, the main source of teacher supply continued to be those trained on the job as pupil-teachers. The arrangements for such apprenticeships were centrally regularised in 1845, with no enrolments under 13, but thereafter with grants to the schools and mentors. Their instruction included religious education (RE), in all kinds of school. Their success was marked by the award of a Queen's Scholarship which enabled them to go on to training college. The preponderance of CofE schools and colleges made the issue of training opportunities all the more contentious.

Prompted by the findings of the Newcastle Commission, the 1862 Revised Code of Regulations for administration of grants was designed to improve the overall quality of education, whilst driving down costs, by the introduction of performance indicators. The consequences included, for schools, the employment of less well-qualified teachers, and, for colleges, fewer and less able applicants, less attention to personal academic development, and a heightened divide between college and university, which would persist for over a century. Intentionally or otherwise, having highlighted the degree of dependence on state funding, which had been induced in previous decades for both schools and teacher training, the need to resolve the tension between voluntary and state provision could not be ignored for much longer.

1870–1943: The partnership of church and state in the 'Dual System' of educational provision

Context

The interdependence of the national church with the state remained strong during the second half of Queen Victoria's reign and, in spite of the subsequent impact of two World Wars, that continued to be the case, at least in England. In contrast, FC Dissent brought about disestablishment of the church in Wales – almost in 1895, and finally so in 1914. This was perceived within Wales as a sign of Christian vitality. Although social attitudes and patterns of religious belonging were changing, in both England and Wales the churches were an intrinsic feature of physical and emotional landscapes.

For some, the optimism and confidence at its height towards the turn of the century was totally blown away by the horrors of the First World War. The sense of futility and waste as conveyed by returning soldiers or conjured by the war poets took the shine off any easy faith and a reported mood of desperate gaiety in the interwar decades may have reflected this. Though unwelcome, for many, the Second World War engaged a sense of greater moral purpose and patriotism, and even Christian service.

The different Christian denominations retained their relative popularity, in spite of the hopes of some that they would fade away. In the 1920s and 1930s an ecumenical momentum began to build. Reports from the overseas missionary field boosted self-confidence back home. Working-class parishes, the Friends Ambulance Brigade and the Salvation Army were all reminders that the church had many faces. And limited Jewish immigration continued.

School provision and funding

At the start of this period, it was entirely feasible to envisage that educational provision might move from being so significantly tied in with religious associations. Church and State could have made their separate arrangements, as in other countries. That this did not happen was based on a combination of economic realism, institutional convenience and a political predisposition to enjoy religious company in spite of its irks.

Forster's Bill, as enacted in 1870, addressed the need for a national strategy that would guarantee elementary education to every child and in a way that would be affordable and acceptable to the many sectional interests. Although church interests saw children's nurture and learning as a right and responsibility shared with parents, they themselves had not been able to make such universal provision. The state would now draw on public taxation to fund schools managed by locally elected, and interdenominationally representative, School Boards. Church schools would continue to receive a maintenance grant of up to 50 per cent[2], but once the system was in place there would be no new building money. In the new board schools the Cowper–Temple clause ensured that there would be no learning of denominationally specific catechetical formulae. Moreover, in every school receiving public funding there was the conscience clause which, without any detriment, would permit parents to withdraw children and teachers to withdraw themselves from any religious instruction. Neither would school inspection monitoring effectiveness any longer be denominationally controlled.

If anyone thought that this would lead to an immediate replacement of church schools by board schools, they were quickly proved wrong. Many within the FCs, in the BFSS tradition, did take the considered theological view that publicly funded schools serving local communities made separate church school provision superfluous. Not so most Anglicans and virtually all RCs. In the half year allowed before districts were authorised to bring forward the creation of new schools, both churches moved with great alacrity to plan as many as they could. The NS raised £10 million over the next decade (compared with £15 million over the previous half century) and put in 2,000 building grants. Another 500 requests came from RCs or the FC. In 15 years, CofE schools leapt from 6,382 to 11,864, and RC schools from 350 to 892. In that same period, children attending voluntary schools doubled to 2 million.[3]

The costs of sustaining such provision were formidable. Knowingly or not the churches had overreached themselves. Already in 1884 a newly formed interdenominational Voluntary Schools Association was lobbying against the unfair financial advantages enjoyed by board schools, with both local and central government rates and taxes to draw on. Four years later, as a result of reviewing the working of the 1870 Act, the Cross Commission recommended funding for the 'secular' curriculum in church schools, but this was not fully followed through until the Balfour Act of 1902.

Surprising though it may now seem, when not actually required by law, RE was virtually universal in board schools. Apparently, exposure to the Bible and related moral teaching was generally favoured and opt-outs on the part of individuals or institutions were rare. Far more contentious were the religious presuppositions associated with the voluntary schools, CofE to some extent and RC much more so. In the CofE schools their religious instruction always involved the catechism and simple prayer, alongside some Bible teaching – and there were withdrawal rights and local discretion. Even so, many FC parents felt they could not easily claim exemption for their children.[4] RC schools were centrally controlled by the bishops and their RE was denominationally very specific. Accordingly, to non-Catholics they were more 'suspect'.

This came to a head in the debates surrounding the 1902 Balfour Bill. The 1870 Act had required 28 days of debate; this one needed 59 – largely on the religious clauses. Inside and outside Parliament there was outcry against 'Rome on the rates'. Nevertheless, the outcomes were significant. Borough and county councils became local education authorities (LEAs), with authority over school boards and the 'secular' curriculum of voluntary schools. The LEAs provided grants for school maintenance. Denominationally specific teaching could be requested, but at the same time teachers were to be appointed regardless of denominational allegiance. In return for the right to provide denominational teaching in church schools, the buildings had to be provided by the denominations.

By now the sharply different understandings of conscience were apparent. Dissenters and Doubters were clear that no pupil or teacher should be faced in school with any expectation of conformity to religious belief or ritual. CofE schools were expected to heed this, and to facilitate convenient arrangements for withdrawal. RC schools, whilst having the same obligation in law, had far fewer subscribers who were not baptised than was the case in the middle of the previous century, when the school might be open to the poor more generally. This tendency to focus on the RC family of faith is also illustrated by two other developments. First, in response to the greater abundance of jobs in CofE or board schools, there was active discouragement from bishops for RC teachers to teach in any other school. Second, a canon was introduced in 1917, which expressly forbade anyone from a Catholic family to attend a non-RC school, or risk excommunication. The ecclesiastical prerogative could not have been clearer than in the 1927 Encyclical *Divini illius magistri*:

> (to be a fit place for Catholic students) it is necessary that all the teaching and the whole organisation of the school, and its teachers, syllabus and textbooks in every branch, be regulated by the Christian spirit, under the direction and maternal supervision of the Church ... and this in every grade of school.
>
> (Gibbons 1963: 60)

The embeddedness of CofE and RC schools within the state's educational provision made it difficult to deny them economic support from the public purse; the Encyclical was not alone in highlighting the principle of distributive justice. Uneasiness, both from outside (teacher unions and politicians) and between the different churches, over the existence and terms of any funding for church schools was as strong in the 1930s as it had been in 1870 or 1902. But since 1902, the scale of the education industry had grown enormously. Then it had been mainly elementary schools; now there were many additionally or separately providing for seniors, and the leaving age had risen to 14+ in 1918. The cost implications were enormous. Faced with the prospect of a 15+ school leaving age, the 1936 Education Act authorised building grants of up to 75 per cent for new denominational 'Special Agreement' senior schools. CofE interests were in balanced local arrangements, as appropriate between local authority and church schools, including some transfer of pupils between the two and agreed forms of RE in both. They submitted proposals for *at least* 230 new schools (Louden 1984). RC interests were in achieving new senior schools sufficient to meet the needs of the Catholic community, and 289 schools were proposed, plus additional places in Liverpool.

Although CofE and FC views on education were not identical, by the mid-1930s, mutual distrust had largely gone, but could still flare up. Thus, the NS, now recognised in both England and Wales as the Church's Central Council for RE, could even state its appreciation of the BFSS.[5] The practice of producing a syllabus, which was locally agreed with denominational representatives, also became quite popular, initially in Cambridgeshire in 1924, then in seven other counties by 1930. At the same time, the attempt by the Archbishop of Canterbury to extend the building grants agreed for senior schools to elementary schools would have destroyed the spirit of that new relationship, had it not been withdrawn.

Teacher training

In spite of the more systematic underwriting of education by the 1870 Act, no comparable provision was made for teacher education and training. Instead, the existing position was permitted to hobble along, with a combination of apprentice pupil teachers, and the limited number of training colleges (TCs), mainly but not exclusively church related. In 1901 the proportions of student places available were: 25 per cent Methodist, BFSS or non-Denominational, 6 per cent RC and 69 per cent CofE (McGregor 1991: 86).

However, change had to come. Of the church colleges which did exist, most were poorly endowed and suffered from their limited funding base, having had no grants since the 1850s. During the 1880s and 1890s several more were founded (e.g. Maria Grey, Stockwell, Saffron Walden), but alongside them were rather more that were non-denominational colleges (e.g. Froebel, Edge Hill and Charlotte Mason) or new teacher training departments of universities – 16 by the turn of the century. These last were day colleges and clear rivals to the previously dominant two-year residential model. Even then, there was still a massive mismatch between those qualifying for entry as Queen's scholars (6,000) and the actual numbers of places available (3,732) and only around a quarter of all teachers had actually been 'college trained'.

The 1902 Act followed up proposals from the earlier Cross Report by empowering LEAs to support TCs. One immediate consequence of the expansion of LEA places was that by 1906 not all places at denominational TCs were being filled. Accordingly, the Board of Education decreed, to the delight of the FCs, that if they wished to receive grant aid they would no longer be permitted to retain their previous practice of using denominational criteria to control their admissions. Following CofE and RC representations, hard to comprehend a century later, this was amended to permit priority in recruitment of up to half the student body by denominational allegiance.[6]

Church colleges were from now on in an increasingly more competitive environment. They had lost their monopoly on residential experience. They were poor relations to university departments in providing training for secondary teaching. And they were also more economically vulnerable than LEA TCs, whose costs from 1926 onwards were shared out across the LEAs. CofE economies led to amalgamations and closures – continually feared, and occasionally realised, in 1916 (St Mark and St John combined as 'Marjons') and again in 1937 (Brighton, Peterborough and Truro). Even so, on the eve of the Second World War, the church-related colleges outnumbered LEA ones 63 to 28.

1944–2002: Dual system – death and rebirth

Context

The rate and extent of social and economic change during this period are hard to exaggerate. Emerging from the grimness of the Second World War, there was the optimism at home of the welfare state and abroad of an empire becoming the Commonwealth. Mobility by road, rail and air, or vicariously through television, began to stretch horizons. The experience is now compounded by the internet, multi-channel television and mass tourism. What it means to be family has become more varied. Extended families now include more 'step' links or breaks. Childhood and adolescence for half the population is now experienced differently from 'going home to Mum and Dad'. Whereas at the start of the period, the housing shortage was for young families wishing to live apart from parents, now it is because more are living singly.

In respect of religion, these have been decades of secularisation. For the first two decades of the period, the normative frame of reference was labelled in Christian terminology. Forenames on forms (Christian), the naming ceremony for children (Christening), Spring Bank Holiday (Whitsuntide), Sunday school/closings/best all took this for granted, but no longer is this so. Churchgoing has declined steadily to less than 10 per cent; so too the percentage of church weddings. Virtually simultaneous with these changes, the National Anthem disappeared from the cinemas and nightly television, and patriotic identity and loyalty became blurred. By some this shift was seen as a delayed realisation of truths that had been self-evident to the educated and scientific minded since at least the last century: society had become post-Christian.

These decades have also involved ethnic, cultural and religious diversification. At the start of the period, except for very small numbers, the society was largely white. Anglo-Jewry was robust and largely self-contained, with the negative stereotype for Jew still blatant in common speech and dictionaries. Large-scale Commonwealth immigration from the Caribbean in the 1950s and from India and Pakistan during the 1960s, plus more recent asylum seekers, has now created a much richer diversity. In religious terms, this feature is often termed 'multi-faith'. As the 2001 Census confirms, the Jewish minority has now been joined and numerically exceeded by Muslims, Hindus, Sikhs, Buddhists and people of other faiths, amounting to 6.5 per cent in England and 1.5 per cent in Wales, most of whom were born there.

It would be wrong, however, to conclude that the term 'Christian' no longer has any different significance in England and Wales than do other religious allegiances or secularist perspectives. Before the law there is (or ought to be) religious freedom and equality. Overnight, however, the landscape and townscape will not lose their churches and cathedrals. Moreover, the 2001 Census exposed a startling 70 per cent self-ascription of Christian identity. Even allowing for the lower percentages amongst those under 40, it cannot be dismissed as 'social conformity'. Instead it has to be seen, perhaps like the crowds at the Golden Jubilee, as signalling that loyalties, identities and fundamental belief systems do run far deeper than outward appearance conveys.

Those belief systems are variously expressive of 'faiths', the term now being used for a distinct category of schools. It is a term which, like 'spiritual', generally carries more cachet than religion/religious, which is perceived as harder edged and institutionally oriented. All of these words refer to that area of deepest meanings, of closest approximations to what is recognised as good and true, in the midst of life and death. Often, but not always, there is a God-ward reference. The writings of a CofE bishop in the 1960s opened up conversations between the thinking of academic theologians, too easily confined within a select circle, and a wider public. His brother pointed to some parallel links in individual religious experience and on the part of artists.[7] More recently, Grace Davie (1994) has characterised the current religious condition as 'believing without belonging'.

What is clear is that the current context, in which both the schools and the education and training of teachers are set, is facing questions of human meaning which are just as far reaching, just as theologically loaded, as those which were being asked in 1800. In what ways have the Faith Schools and Colleges been developing during this period as effective companions for this challenge?

School provision and funding

During the parliamentary debates on the 1944 Education Act, war was still shaking foundations, the Commons Chamber quite literally had been blitzed. Both in the preparatory reports of the previous three years and now during the debates themselves, there was a heightened sense of the need to get things right for the benefit of society as a whole. Moral and spiritual concerns were fundamental, and RE was singled out. It was seen as having two component aspects: the teaching part – religious instruction (RI) – and the assembling part – collective worship (CW). This key role was envisaged throughout the dually maintained system.

That partnership of church and state in together providing for the nation's educational needs now became further entrenched as a result of the Act. The generosity of public funding was stretched to 50 per cent of any new building costs, as well as all maintenance. Church schools, however, were now distinguished by two categories: voluntary aided and controlled. In the latter, 100 per cent building costs would also be covered, as in what would now be called 'county maintained schools'. RI would be in accord with an LEA-created Agreed Syllabus, as produced by locally representative church leaders, professional teaching interests and elected politicians. As distinct from the county and controlled schools, the voluntary aided category left more to the discretion of the churches. In CofE schools, that discretion was lodged with the headteacher and chair of managers, and commonly came to involve following, but supplementing, the local Agreed Syllabus. In RC schools, the RE was in accord with an episcopally agreed national syllabus and very much concentrated on introducing children to the Catholic community of faith.

During the course of the next 30 years, the proportion of building costs which could be claimed by the churches from the public purse was increased by successive Acts as follows: in 1959, 75 per cent; in 1967, 80 per cent; and in 1974, 85 per cent. The arrangement was confirmed in the 1988 Education Reform Act and most recently (2001) the proposed percentage has risen to 90.

When the two different categories of church school were introduced, both R A Butler, the Minister of Education, and William Temple, the Archbishop of Canterbury, were expecting that the dioceses and local trustees of as few as 500 of the 9,000 CofE schools would opt for voluntary aided status, as making both economic and educational sense. They were wrong. The figures were nearer one third. [8] The responses from the FCs for their remaining schools was definitely to prefer the 'controlled' arrangement. By contrast, all RC schools were kept as 'voluntary aided'. [9] This preference also applied to the Jewish schools.

In subsequent decades, there have been further fluctuations in numbers. Many of the CofE primary schools have been amalgamated or closed as too small. Though far fewer in number overall, some new CofE secondary schools have been opened and yet more are projected. Far fewer RC primary schools have been closed, rather more built, along with more secondary schools, for which there was a major building programme. In dramatic contrast to the position in 1870, there are now more RC voluntary aided schools than CofE, testimony at least to the commitment and sacrifice on the part of the Catholic community.

Although some degree of public accountability has existed since the beginning of public education, the Office for Standards in Education (OFSTED) and Welsh equivalent Arolygiaeth Ei Mawrhydi Dros Addysg A Hyfforddiant yng Nghymru/Her Majesty's Inspectorate For Education and Training in Wales (ESTYN) inspection regimes and reporting requirements have been more systematically pursued since the 1992 Education Act (revised 1996). Two complementary inspections were required of voluntary aided schools: a 'Section 9' (11 in 1996) inspection covering the National Curriculum and other aspects such as Equal Opportunities and Health and Safety, plus a 'Section 13' (23 in 1996) inspection covering the RE under the control of the governors and foundation bodies. The CofE 'Section 9' inspections are carried out under guidance from the NS, and the RC school inspections under guidance from the Bishops, supported by material from the Catholic Education Service. Equivalent inspections in Jewish schools have been supported by guidance from the Board of Deputies of British Jews (Keiner 1996). Faith schools, in common with all other maintained schools, feature in school performance tables, measured by national criteria.

It is often overlooked that the terms of the dual system as elaborated in 1944 provided for a link for the churches with county schools. Their association is not confined to church schools any more than the link with the state is confined to county schools. Local managers/governors in church schools comprise either one- or two-thirds LEA appointments depending on whether or not the school is voluntary controlled or aided. [10] The Agreed Syllabus Conference comprises four panels: teachers, politicians, CofE and other denominations (last extended in 1988 to other locally represented religions). To avoid a fall-back on the Secretary of State, they are required to agree. These local syllabuses have carried force of law in both county/community and voluntary controlled church schools from 1944.

After 1988 they played an equivalent role in RE (now changed from RI) as the National Curriculum did in other subjects. In other words, from 1944 the churches, and from 1988 the other religious communities as well, have had a part in providing an official and normative reference point for RE for the overwhelming majority of children. At the same time, CofE schools and dioceses commonly take note of the local Agreed Syllabus in devising the RE for voluntary aided settings. Furthermore, the 1988 Act deliberately located RE as fundamental to the entire curriculum, more basic than and prior to the National Curriculum.

It is the logic of faith, the spiritual energy by which people live, to warrant attention in public education. Within the dual system, 'faith schools' are particularised ways of working with that equation. Their design was not constitutionally intended to usurp the complementary attention to the grounding in faith in LEA-maintained schools.

Teacher training

Between 1944 and the end of the 1960s, the balance of provision of teacher education and training shifted decisively away from being predominantly church sponsored. The story subsequently includes the churches maintaining some significant involvement with this provision, but attention to RE, as more generally to understanding faith, within this 'voluntary sector' has been given variable priority. At the same time, it became increasingly ignored by the other providing agencies, universities, polytechnics, colleges and, most recently, school-centred Initial Teacher Training.

The supply of teachers at the end of the war needed urgent replenishment, if it was to meet the challenges of both the 15+ school-leaving age and secondary school reorganisation. Accordingly, an Emergency Training programme was introduced in 1945, beginning with new colleges in Alnwick, Coventry and Watford and rising to 53 in all. A few, including Trent Park, continued, but most were run down by the end of five years. Following a recommendation in the McNair Report, some order was brought to the chaos of 100+ teacher training institutions, by the creation in 1947 of 13 Area Training Organisations (ATOs) in England and one in Wales to co-ordinate provision. The universities retained their separate training departments/institutes, but they also became hubs for the ATO clusters of colleges, both LEA and voluntary.

Government funding of 50 per cent was guaranteed for the church colleges for new building and plant improvement. Whilst a welcome parallel to what was given to voluntary aided church schools, the 100 per cent (ratio 2:3, LEA:central government) for LEA colleges explains their expansion, an extra 19 in the two years 1946–8. By the early 1950s, there had been no new CofE or FC colleges, whereas LEA colleges now numbered 76. However, four new RC colleges had been opened, bringing their total to 13. The restrictions against denominational preference in student recruitment remained at 50 per cent; this was less of an issue in RC colleges where for the most part there was little competition from non-RCs applying for places.

The need for co-ordination of the CofE involvement in teacher training was reflected in the creation of the Council of Church Training Colleges in 1944 and subsequent policy papers brought to the Church Assembly. It made no attempt to change the autonomous foundations of the individual colleges, but saw them as the collective responsibility of the

CofE in educating men and women with a Christian vision (not tied to one denomination) of teaching the nation's children.

Expansion brought major changes throughout the 1960s. Extension of course length from two to three years in 1960 (even to a four-year Bachelor of Education (BEd) following the *Robbins Report* in 1963), coupled with the effects of a higher birth rate, led to an eight-fold increase in the government's allocation of student teacher numbers, bringing it to 80,000 by the end of the decade. The CofE took up the challenge, increased its intakes generally and opened two new colleges (in Canterbury and Lancaster) but even with the increase in government grant to 75 per cent it struggled to retain the high proportion of trainee places which it had previously enjoyed. By 1973 it was providing only one in six of all qualifying teachers. Simultaneously the Catholic Training Colleges Advisory Committee, established in 1958, steered the expansion of student places to be commensurate with the need for teachers in RC schools, amounting to one in 10.

Change of a different order kicked in with the *James Report* (1972) with its mention of a widening higher education role for the colleges, and shortly thereafter the White Paper *Education: A Framework for Expansion*, which highlighted the dip in the birth rate and promoted both diversification and rationalisation. The position was set out starkly in *Circular 7/73*: student teacher numbers were to be virtually halved. It further emerged that government intended to increase the proportion entering teaching via the one-year postgraduate certificate in education (PGCE) route. Very quickly, church colleges diversified, amalgamated or closed.

Diversification was principally into liberal arts degrees, deploying the subject specialisms from teacher education, or parallel professions, especially health related. The extent to which the colleges were consistent in opening up the faith dimension in these other spheres was as variable as had been the degree of zeal with which they had taken seriously the religious education agenda for all their student teachers.

Amalgamations took several forms. Many continued as part of a larger institution which retained explicitly Christian features: St Mary's (CofE) and St Paul's (CofE) into Cheltenham and Gloucester (now University of Gloucester); Ripon (CofE) and St John's, York (CofE) combined as Ripon St John, and now simply York St John College; Christ's (RC), St Katharine's (CofE) and Notre Dame (RC) into the Liverpool Institute of Higher Education (subsequently Hope University College); Whitelands (CofE), Digby Stuart (RC), Froebel (Non-denom) and Southlands (Meth) into the Roehampton Institute; Bishop Otter College (CofE) and Bognor Regis College (LEA) into the West Sussex Institute of Higher Education, now University College Chichester. Three CofE colleges were joined with their local university schools of education: Keswick Hall with the University of East Anglia, St Luke's (CofE) with Exeter University, and St Mary's Bangor with the University College of North Wales. For others, amalgamation was absorption, with little visible remainder: All Saints Tottenham (CofE) within Middlesex Polytechnic; Bishop Lonsdale Derby (CofE), along with Matlock (LEA) within Derby Polytechnic; St Gabriel's (CofE) within Goldsmiths's; St Matthias (CofE) within Bristol Polytechnic.

Outright closure was less common, and perhaps the more painful accordingly. From the CofE, these were: Culham (Abingdon), Hockerill (Bishop Stortford), Sarum St Michael (Salisbury) and St Peter's (Saltley). Of RC colleges, they were De La Salle at Manchester, Mary Ward in Nottinghamshire, Maria Assumpta in Kensington and Coloma in West Wickham. Substantial trust funds have been created from the sale of property and in a variety of ways these continue to promote the cause of Christian education. They, like those amalgamations or absorptions in which connection with church inheritance has but token visibility, were for those involved a twentieth-century equivalent of the Dissolution of the Monasteries – a process viciously engineered, but largely unremarked except by insiders to it.[11]

The years since this massive upheaval have involved retrenchment and heart searching. The surviving institutions have each recognised that their dependence on public funding requires them to prove their effectiveness in terms of the academic and professional marketplace. Thus, in the last 10 years they have had to meet the norms asked of all higher education institutions (HEIs) by the Higher Education Funding Council, and in respect of teacher education as set by the Teacher Training Agency (TTA) and OFSTED. They have also to be successful in recruitment. The government closure of La Sainte Union in 1996, following poor OFSTED inspections (also the fate of Lancaster University's Charlotte Mason College), showed how little can be expected by way of protest from other HEIs. Neither do the Churches' national bodies appear to carry much clout in these respects, unless that varies according to the closeness of association of an individual college with bishops and dioceses, rather than an independent religious order.

The heart searching has included surveys of staff and students about their attitudes and understandings of church 'collegeness', a succession of consultations and reports, and an extended initiative called Engaging the Curriculum. The remaining church colleges have formed a joint Council, but their readiness to act together and speak with one voice is far from proven. They can point to the remarkable achievement of Cheltenham in achieving designation as the University of Gloucester, and of several others being granted degree-awarding powers. One significant test, so far largely dodged, however, is what constitutes 'graduateness' from an institution that claims to give the matter of faith a 'high profile'.

Some recurring themes within the faith traditions

An historical account of faith schools and colleges can be written from several different angles. For instance, it might be argued that the determining logic has been primarily economic: how to provide education at least cost. This argument would refer to the impulse benefactors had to favour charity schools over board schools – it would cost them less than paying on the rates. It would go on to claim that, once the churches had developed schools and training colleges, it became too expensive to buy them out. Though initially suspicious or even hostile to church-sponsored education, many politicians have consistently come round to it as the least costly option and, latterly, even as a vote winner. In fact the public purse has over the years ended up paying the overwhelming proportion of the costs.

It might equally be argued that, notwithstanding the guise of theological argument, the real driver from the churches for school and college provision was institutional self-interest – maximising their 'ownership' and range of contacts. There is no shortage of examples where behaviour can be interpreted in this way. Collectively, there were remarkable scrambles to put down additional territorial markers in the early 1870s, as again in the immediate aftermath of the 1944 Act. There are individual instances of reluctance to amalgamate two small primary schools in the same village – one CofE the other RC – or even two CofE secondary schools;[12] there is also the shameful silence regarding the closure of La Sainte Union.

Without discounting the presence of such factors, the chapter has rather been written with the conviction that particular faith perspectives and theological visions are indeed important in and of themselves, and that in these terms they can make a real difference in driving educational policy towards its proper destination. It is with some of the more telling points of theological difference between the different denominations and faith allegiances that the rest of this chapter is concerned.

Anglican (CofE, Church in Wales)

Something of the tensions within the breadth of the Church is immediately evident in the initial century of contrast between NS and BFSS Anglicans. From the former came a catechising model every bit as single-minded in the focus of its faith as that found in RC schools, designed deliberately as an induction into the church. There is no surprise in this, since its strongest advocates were Anglo-Catholics, sharing the enthusiasms of the Tractarian movement – some of whom, like Newman, subsequently converted to what they saw as the only true Church. From the latter, instead, there was the model of serving the educational needs of the wider community and, like F D Maurice, working with the theological notion of 'kingdom' as much as church.

Mutual abuse and caricature of either party was, and remains, easy: the former exclusive and indoctrinatory, the latter selling out to the world. The sell-out tendency is perceived at its most blatant in church schools designated after 1944 as 'controlled'. It is also attributed to voluntary-aided schools, which, in their determination sensitively to serve the single school community of a village or particular part of town, cease to declare any more Christian, let alone Anglican, distinctiveness as compared with a county school. Just as visible are the characteristics of exclusivity, apparent in denominational admissions tests, catechising and subsequent confirmations.

In fact two different emphases in Anglican theology are apparent in these alternative understandings of what it means to be a church school. The influential *Durham Report: The Fourth R*, which appeared in 1970, identified such schools as giving priority to general education of the whole community and/or to domestic nurture of the church family of faith. The main thrust since 1800 may have included both emphases, but certainly in primary schools, even when voluntary-aided, the second emphasis has been given less, and sometimes only limited, priority. But that has often been because of a theological conviction that what mattered most was to create a community within the school, which could serve as a model for that in the society around it.

In the last 30 years the argument has been more and more strongly advanced that CofE secondary schools (far fewer than the primaries) should take on the more domestic nurturing role of being denominationally Anglican. The argument has powerful advocacy from the likes of Francis, Shepherd and now Lord Dearing. Even within these more selective schools, however, it is unusual for the RE curriculum not to engage with the other faiths and concerns highlighted in the local Agreed Syllabus.

The CofE training colleges were overwhelmingly Anglican in their student admissions, until well into the twentieth century. Since the 1950s the policy became more and more permissive, to the extent that few of them now know anything of the religious allegiance of their students before entry – and often during and after their time in college. Priority may still be given to Anglicans at the level of director/principal, and a chapel and chaplain are provided. But the degree of attention given to RE in the curriculum of all students on initial teacher training (ITT) courses, or to the exploration of religious beliefs and values within other professional and subject-oriented degrees, may be no more than that found in 'secular' higher education institutions. Where this is the case, the wider educational priority of 'faith-fathoming' for life and careers ahead has been lost in the maelstrom of meeting other people's performance indicators (Gates 2002).

The relative autonomy of the governing bodies of Anglican schools and colleges, evident throughout the two centuries, has in part been tempered by reference to dioceses, the National Society and associations of church colleges, but much more so by the National Curriculum, OFSTED and the TTA.

Roman Catholic

Throughout the two centuries the Church's position in relation to both schools and colleges has been consistently that of the 1927 Encyclical *Divini illius magistri*. All education must be controlled by the bishop acting with the authority of Christ as given initially to Peter and thence to the Church. Teachers should come from the Catholic community, as primarily should the pupils, all participating in the process of mutual edification. Religious teaching is intended to instruct in the faith and to initiate into participating membership of the RC Church.

Whereas in most of the rest of the maintained system the conscience clause remains in place to safeguard the rights of pupils and teachers, this is unapologetically not the case in RC schools. The expectation has been that if someone chooses to attend an RC school, that means they are willing to follow all the educational routines of that school. In recent years special negotiations have taken place between the Catholic Education Council and government lawyers to address equality and conscience issues in employment legislation.

There has been no comparable attempt to achieve exemption from the National Curriculum as determined by central government. Theologically, it is reasonable to see this as 'naturally given' and to expect to supplement it with distinctive insights which come from within the community of faith. By contrast, there is no admission of any public RE in the form of reference to an Agreed Syllabus, and for the purposes of public examination in the General Certificate of Secondary Education (GCSE) or Advanced Level (A Level), special syllabuses have been negotiated, even though they are still called 'religious studies'. Without challenging the continuation also of the more catechising model, it is worth asking whether it might not be in the interests of everyone involved for there to be some more open engagement with what is known in other schools as public RE (Rummery 1975). In fact, significant numbers of children who were baptised as Catholics are in non-RC schools and, for the most part, are not withdrawn from RE.

Ambivalence regarding the admission of non-RC pupils and the terms of their presence is illustrated by two reports published: *Where Creed and Colour Matter* from the Catholic Bishops Commission for Racial Justice (Zipfel 1975) and *Learning from Diversity* from a Working Party of the Department of Christian Doctrine (Cosgrove 1984). They actively canvass for the welcoming of minority religious and ethnic groups into RC schools, and appreciative support for them in their parental faiths. There have been and are matching examples in schools. However, special arrangements to recognise and provide for the distinctive theological integrities involved have not been widespread.

Unlike their CofE counterparts, RC training colleges have retained their core recruitment of Catholic students on ITT courses but their overall populations have become increasingly mixed, especially the intakes to diversified degrees. Where it has continued, the self-replicating cycle of RC students from RC schools returning to RC schools has provided a momentum and opportunity for attention to both RE and Catholic school ethos. The challenge from Vatican 2 is to extend the critical theological reflection, which has developed on the schools' front, into the other areas of the higher education curriculum in these same institutions.

Free Church

In general, each of the FC denominations has shown great dispassion in its commitment to the ecumenical cause of building a common national community. Education of the whole society is what matters. If the state has the will to fund it, that is good enough.

There is no need to cling to separate schools. Until well into the 1950s, there were in any case the Sunday Schools to supplement them. Why risk encouraging human divisiveness? There is enough of that around without religion itself providing the excuse for more.

Accordingly, even in the days of very modest public funding, they showed a preference for non-denominational schools. Where separate denominational ones had been developed, many of them became board schools in 1870, and most of those that remained became controlled church schools in 1944. This had also been the stance of French Protestants. It was the consistent position of the Baptists and Unitarians, followed by Congregationalists, New Jerusalemites and, in part at least, more reluctantly by Methodists. Their schools were very largely handed over to be run by the local community and there was no priority to develop more, even when the numbers of those being built by the CofE and RCs rose dramatically. Wesleyan Methodists were the chief exception to this, preferring instead the same line as the CofE.

It may be entirely coincidental that, in the course of the last 150 years, the relative strength of the institutional churches, which have day schools, is visibly stronger than the FCs. This was not the case in 1850. There has been little chance in the FC context for the adage 'And a little child shall lead them' to be acted out. In retrospect, this looks to have been a well-intended gesture which has backfired. The theology of secularity and laicisation has lost the means of delivering its sparkle. In fact, in quotable instances, there is evidence of astute parents deliberately changing denominational allegiance to facilitate entry to a certain Church secondary school. Thus, annual conferences within one or other of these Churches in recent decades have come to reconsider whether even now to re-establish at least a few such schools.

The FC tradition of teacher education and training was once relatively strong, including such institutions as Borough Road, Homerton, Southlands, Westhill and Westminster. But as a result of quite recent changes, the position is now attenuated. Borough Road is visible in the BFSS RE Centre at Brunel. Homerton's Congregationalism is now more historical than current. Westminster (Methodist) is subsumed within Oxford Brookes and Westhill (United Reform) within Birmingham University. Southlands (Methodist) still stands as part of the partnership which is Roehampton Surrey University.

Secularist and Humanist

Differences of belief on the part of those who disassociated themselves from religious belonging were reflected in the preferences for the ascription 'atheist' (as represented by the likes of Holyoake and Bradlaugh) or 'agnostic' (as coined by Huxley). The collective 'nothingarians' was used in a local 1882 Census and, in the most recent one, 'Jedi Knights'. Establishment suspicion of even non-denominational schools in the nineteenth century gave very little prospect for schools founded and managed on atheist principles. However, there were instances of schools providing some moral instruction as an alternative to RE from which pupils had been withdrawn, and the Froebel Institute still professes its humanist approach.

The two most influential stances are represented by the Rationalist Press Association and National Secular Society, on the one hand, and the British Humanist Association (BHA), on the other. Whilst both have consistently expressed principled opposition to denominational schools, it has been the National Secular Society that has been root and branch against any form of RE in publicly funded education. In the 1960s there was a Humanist-led Campaign for Moral Education which sought to replace RE with a rational moral education, at least in county schools. Within the course of a decade, however, curriculum philosophers came to acknowledge that education properly includes an open exploration not only of values, but also of the beliefs that underpin them. This shift may be visible in the relative popularity of Christian–Humanist Dialogue at that time, and in Harold Blackham's association with the Shap Working Party on World Religions in Education, founded in 1969. Most significantly, in 1973, the BHA was one of founding member organisations of the Religious Education Council of England and Wales.

Jews

Throughout the last two centuries there has been diversity in Jewish educational provision and thinking about it. Funding has come both from within the community and from public sources. Significantly, from the time when the first government grant was negotiated, there has been resistance on the part of individual communities to responsibility being borne centrally by the Board of Deputies and Chief Rabbi.

The limited number of maintained Jewish schools (12 in 1902, 33 in 2002) has meant that many children from Jewish families, both Orthodox and Reform, have attended other maintained schools. Most of these have been involved additionally in classes associated with the local synagogue. Others, most especially those from strict Orthodox homes, have attended independently funded day schools, such as those provided by the Lubavitch community in Stamford Hill in London.

Amongst the Jewish maintained schools, such as the Jewish Free School in London and the King David School in Liverpool, there has been a readiness to employ some non-Jewish teachers and to welcome non-Jewish pupils. That principle of openness was true from the inception of public funding in 1853. However, for some other Orthodox schools, it is less acceptable.

Of the Jewish children attending non-Jewish schools, some went to public school with a designated Jewish house, more to local primary and secondary schools, sometimes even church schools. Until recently, there was been an alternative ignominy. Either they behaved 'invisibly' and endured Agreed Syllabus RE and CW, or there was an appeal to the conscience clause and they were publicly withdrawn.

Some, at least partial, readiness to be sensitive to this can be seen in two respects. Biblical RE, which predominated in Agreed Syllabuses until the mid-1960s, could claim to afford some common ground, if parents found that acceptable. Arguably, also, the absence of the word Christian from the specification of CW in the 1944 Act was out of deference to the Jewish community and Jewish schools where the worship was understood to be Jewish.

Much of the education and training of Jewish teachers has been within the community and in the context of the degrees and certification provided by colleges and universities. However, a link was forged between Jews College and Trent Park, then, following its closure, with the London Institute, to provide relevant professional accreditation. Strengthening the flow and training of appropriate teachers is a current issue for the Jewish community (Valins 2001: 150–1).

Hindus, Muslims and Sikhs

In spite of the significant numbers of Hindu, Muslim and Sikh pupils in maintained schools from the mid-1970s onwards, and requests for related voluntary-aided schools, even now the numbers are tiny. Several factors help to explain this. There have been mixed feelings within each community about the relative advantages of having separate schools in a society which has appeared all too ready to keep it divided. There was a financial and administrative challenge involved. This has been partly offset as the percentage asked of the faith community has diminished, and both internal and external wealth of the communities increased. But there was also the appearance of deliberate blocking of the development by politicians and civil servants at every level.

Of course to accept state funding would entail accepting the National Curriculum and, as for some RCs and Jews, that was and is easier for some Hindus, Muslims and Sikhs to accept than others.

Students from each of these religious backgrounds, who are wishing to become teachers in maintained schools, are increasingly found in most colleges and university departments of education. Examples of their experiencing religious and/or racial discrimination during their training or whilst seeking employment are now less frequently recounted.

Inter-faith initiatives

In principle the opportunity is now there for any faith tradition to achieve public funding for its own faith schools. However, their development has been very slow, even though there are large numbers of children from those communities within the present maintained system. In a significant number of instances, these children are attending church schools.

There are now many examples of joint Anglican–Catholic and Anglican–Methodist faith schools. Exceptionally, there has been the proposal for the London 'Four Faiths School'. However, there are many more schools where one or other of the different faiths is now in the majority. At the same time, it has become government policy to promote the development of more faith schools, with readiness to consider easement of transition between county maintained and faith school status, and between voluntary controlled and aided schools. In the interests of greater communal self-understanding and cohesion, the following possibility would be worth consideration. Before any agreement is given for change of status, priority might be given to those schools that seek to go forward in partnership with another faith community. Here, within the Christian framework, would be an affordable opportunity for renewal of the FC inheritance. Moreover, instead of this being confined to Christian interdenominational liaising, it might be either CofE or RC, with Hindus, Muslims or Sikhs.

Concluding quirks

In terms of the expectations with which the chapter began, there are indeed some surprises. The prediction of decline has been partly fulfilled. Nationally in England and Wales there are now proportionally fewer faith schools and pupils in them than at any time since 1800. By contrast, in their local settings, faith schools are enjoying a remarkable degree of popularity and, in contrast to their comparatively low ratings, relative to board schools in the 1880s or 1930s, they are riding high. Perhaps most surprising of all, in the course of this whole period, the growth of the maintained provision for RC schools has been dramatic. These are denominational schools, with denominational RE in denominational control, and they are very substantially on the rates.

The existence of so significant a portion of school-based and higher education associated with a particular faith foundation may also serve to throw into relief an aspect of all other educational provision. Just because it is not grounded in any particular faith does not mean that it depends on no faith. On the contrary, it depends on many assumptions, which are rooted in both reason and faiths. Schools are obliged at least to begin to take this seriously and they do so in RE with different degrees of effectiveness. By contrast colleges and universities generally leave curricular matters in their fallen-apart state – intellectually and emotionally splintered. The faith-based institutions amongst them are missing an opportunity if they fail to demonstrate that the curriculum adventure can be played in more than a post-modernist light.

Notes

1 Lancaster had an earlier society: the Royal Lancastrian Society (RLS), founded in 1808, with King George III as patron. The BFSS was founded to take over the RLS and wrest financial control from Lancaster. Because it predated the NS, and had royal patronage, it was well supported by Anglicans – both evangelicals and broad church.
2 Whatever they 'earned' under the 1862 Revised Code, which remained in force, up to half the total expenditure.
3 That said, not all those projected were actually built. The last grant was not paid until 1881.
4 Nonconformist evidence submitted to the 1888 Cross Commission, which was appointed to review the workings of the 1870 Act following complaints from both RCs and the CofE about the position of church schools. However, it is clear from Nonconformist evidence that the Free Church parents had at least as much to complain about.
5 See the NS *Annual Report* 1934, as cited by Gordon Huelin in Leonard and Yates (1986: 25).
6 The hostility shown by the principals of CofE colleges towards any obligation to admit Free Church students is indicative of both denominational exclusivity and resistance to government control. In all only 168 FC students were involved, yet such devices as the use of an old prospectus indicating that only Churchwomen needed to apply were apparently considered justifiable. Cf. Michael V. Boyd 1984: 10–14.
7 Excerpts from the books of John A.T. Robinson – *Honest to God*, *New Reformation* and *Exploration into God* – were published on the front page of the *Observer*. His brother Edward, himself an accomplished artist and Director of the Religious Experience Research Unit, published *The Original Vision* and *The Language of Mystery*.
8 Cf. Anthony Howard (1987: 127). Variation between dioceses was striking. Blackburn had virtually all voluntary aided schools; Canterbury virtually all voluntary controlled. North-west dioceses overall were strongly voluntary aided, north-east less so. Southern – other than London and Southwark – tended to be voluntary controlled. For current distribution, cf. John D. Gay and Jan Greenough (2000).
9 One RC school became voluntary controlled. Perhaps a form went astray (as Lois Louden has suggested in a personal communication)? Voluntary schools were automatically categorised as voluntary controlled unless they proved to the Ministry, by completing and returning an appropriate form, that they could fund their share of building costs.
10 Since 1980 the proportions of governors changed: voluntary aided schools had a majority of two church appointed governors in primary, three in secondary; voluntary controlled had at least a fifth of the governors must be church representatives. The details have changed again following the 2002 Education Act, but not the balance.
11 The pain and sense of betrayal is conveyed in the Epilogue of Mark Lofthouse's *Church Colleges 1918–39* (1992: 83–94).
12 Cf. Geoffrey Duncan 'Church schools: present and future', in Leonard and Yates (1986: 69).

References

Boyd, M.V. (1984) *The Church of England Colleges, 1890–1944: An Administrative Study*, Leeds: University of Leeds, Museum of History of Education.
Cosgrove, A. (1984) *Learning from Diversity: A Challenge for Catholic Education*, Report of the Working Party on Catholic Education in a Multiracial, Multicultural Society. London: Catholic Media

Office on behalf of the Department for Christian Doctrine and Formation of the Bishops' Conference for England and Wales.

Davie, G. (1994) *Religion in Britain since 1945: Believing without Belonging*, Oxford: Blackwell.

Gates, B.E. (1990) 'Religious Studies in Polytechnics and Colleges of Higher Education', in U. King (ed.) *Turning Points in Religious Studies*, Edinburgh: T&T Clark, pp. 76–88.

—— (2002) 'The credibility of the Anglican model of a Christian university in a secular and multi-faith society', *Prologue: A Journal of Colleges and Universities of the Anglican Communion*, III: 19–45.

Gay, J.D. and Greenough, J. (2000) *The Geographical Distribution of Church Schools in England*, Abingdon: Culham College Institute.

Gibbons, W.J. (ed.) (1963) *Seven Great Encyclicals*, New York: Paulist Press.

Howard, A. (1987) *RAB: The Life of R.A. Butler*, London: Jonathan Cape.

Keiner, J. (1996) 'Opening up Jewish education to inspection: the impact of the OFSTED inspection system in England', *Education Policy Analysis Archives*, 4(5): 1–24.

Leonard, G. and Yates, J. (eds) (1986) *Faith for the Future. Essays on the Church in Education to Mark 175 Years of the National Society* London: National Society and Church House Publishing.

Lofthouse, M. (1992) *The Church Colleges 1918–1939: The Struggle for Survival*, Leicester: Billings.

Louden, L.M.R. (1984) 'Special Agreement Schools in Blackburn Diocese, 1936–70', *Journal of Educational Administration and History*, XVI(1): 57–66.

Maclure, J.S. (1965) *Educational Documents England and Wales 1816–1963*, London: Chapman & Hall.

McGregor, G.P. (1991) *A Church College for the 21st Century? 150 years of Ripon & York St John*, York: William Sessions.

Newsome, D. (1961) *Godliness and Good Learning*, London: J. Murray.

Rummery, R. (1975) *Catechesis and Religious Education in a Pluralist Society*, Sydney: Dwyer.

Valins, O., Kosmin, B. and Goldberg, J. (2001) *The Future of Jewish Schooling in the United Kingdom. A Strategic Assessment of a Faith-Based Provision of Primary and Secondary School Education*, London: Institute for Jewish Policy Research.

Wade, J. (1832) *The Extraordinary Black Book: An Exposition of Abuses in Church and State*, London: Effingham Wilson.

Wilson, H.B. (ed.) (1860) *Essays and Reviews*, London: J.W. Parker and Son.

Zipfel, R. (ed.) (1975) *Where Creed and Colour Matter: A Survey on Black Children and Catholic Schools*, London: Commission for Racial Justice of the Catholic Bishops Conference of England and Wales.

Other sources consulted

Arthur, J. (1995) *The Ebbing Tide Policy and Principles of Catholic Education*, Leominster: Gracewing.

Astley, J. and Day, D. (eds) (1992) *The Contours of Christian Education*, Great Wakering: McCrimmons.

Beales, A.C.F. (1963) *Education Under Penalty*, London: University of London Press.

Beck, R.H. (1965) *A Social History of Education*, Englewood Cliffs, NJ: Prentice-Hall.

Bereday, G.Z.F. and Lauerys, J.A. (eds) (1966) *World Yearbook of Education: Church and State in Education*, London: Evans Bros.

Best, G.F.A. (1980) 'The religious difficulties of national education in England, 1800–70', *Cambridge Historical Journal*, XII: 155–73.

Brighton, T. (ed.) (1990) *150 Years: The Church Colleges in Higher Education*, Brighton: West Sussex Institute of Higher Education.

Burgess, H.J. (1958) *Enterprise in Education: The Story of the Work of the Established Church In The Education Of The People Prior To 1870*, London: National Society and SPCK.

Carey, G., Hope, D. and Hall, J. (1998) *A Christian Voice in Education: Distinctiveness in Church Schools*, London: National Society and Church House Publishing.

Chadwick, O. (1966) *The Victorian Church, Part I, 1829–1859*, London: A & C Black.

—— (1970) *The Victorian Church, Part II, 1860–1901*, London: A & C Black.

Chadwick, P. (1997) *Shifting Alliances: Church and State in English Education*, London: Cassell.

Cruickshank, M. (1963) *Church and State in English Education 1870 to the Present Day*, London: Macmillan.

Cunningham, R. (1971) 'Church and State in Education', in M. Dallet (ed.) *Aspects of Catholic Education*, Belfast: St Joseph's College of Education, pp. 7–13.

34 *Brian Gates*

Curtis, S.J. and Boultwood, M.E.A. (1962) *An Introductory History of English Education Since 1800*, London: University Tutorial Press.

Davies, J. (1994) 'Re-sacralising education and re-criminalising childhood: an agenda for the year 2132', in R. Whelan (ed.) *Teaching Right and Wrong: Have the Churches Failed?* London: IEA Health and Welfare Unit.

Dearing, R. (ed.) (2001) *The Way Ahead. Church of England Schools in the New Millennium*, London: Church House Publishing.

Dent, H.C. (1977) *The Training of Teachers in England and Wales 1800–1975*, London: Hodder and Stoughton.

Department for Education and Skills (2002) *Statistics of Education Schools in England 2002 Edition*, London: The Stationery Office.

Francis, L. and Lankshear, D.W. (eds) (1993) *Christian Perspectives on Church Schools*, Leominster, Gracewing.

Furlong, J. and Smith, R. (eds) (1996) *The Role of Higher Education in Initial Teacher Training*, London: Kogan Page.

Gay, J.D. (1971) *The Geography of Religion in England*, London: Duckworth.

Gay, J.D. (1988) 'The churches and the training of teachers in England and Wales', in V.A. McClelland (ed.) *Christian Education in a Pluralist Society*, London: Routledge, pp. 207–29.

Gedge, P.S. (1981) 'The Church of England Colleges of Education since 1944', *Journal of Educational Administration and History*, 13(2): 33–42.

Gibbs, J. (ed.) (1981) *Understanding Christian Nurture*, London: British Council of Churches.

Halstead, M. (1986) *The Case for the Muslim Voluntary Aided School*, Cambridge: Islamic Academy.

Hencke, D. (1978) *Colleges in Crisis*, Harmondsworth: Penguin.

Holtby, R. (1971) *Partners in Education: The Role of the Diocese*, The Report of the Carlisle Commission, London: National Society and SPCK.

Hornsby-Smith, M. (1978) *Catholic Education: The Unobtrusive Partner*, London: Sheed & Ward.

Hubery, D.S. (1977) *Christian Education in State and Church*, Nutfield: Denholm House Press.

Huelin, G. (1986) 'Innovation: The National Society, 1811–1934', in G. Leonard (ed.) *Faith for the Future*, London: National Society.

Humanist Philosophers' Group (2001) *Religious Schools: The Case Against*, London: British Humanist Association.

Hutton, R. (1996) *The Stations of the Sun. A History of the Ritual Year in Britain*, Oxford: Oxford University Press.

James, W. (ed.) (1994) *An Excellent Enterprise: The Church of England and its Colleges of Higher Education – A Working Party Report*, London: Board of Education of the General Synod of the Church of England.

Jones, D.R. (1988) *The Origins of Civic Universities: Manchester, Leeds and Liverpool*, London: Routledge.

Judge, H. (2002) *Faith-based Schools and the State. Catholics in America, France and England*, Oxford: Symposium Books.

Konstant, D. (ed.) (1981) *Signposts and Homecomings: The Educative Task of the Catholic Community*, Slough: St Paul Publications.

Leonard, G. (ed.) (1985) *Positive Partnership*, London: National Society.

Louden, L. (2003) 'The difficulties in defining the religious affiliation of endowed primary schools: the Lancashire experience', *Journal of Educational Administration and History*, 35(1): 37–49.

—— (2003) *The Conscience Clause in Religious Education and Collective Worship. Conscientious Objection or Curriculum Choice?* Abingdon: Culham Institute.

Marks, J., Burn, J., Pilkington, P. and Thompson, P. (2001) *Faith in Education: The Role of Churches in Education – A Response to the Dearing Report on Church Schools in the Third Millennium*, London: Civitas.

McLaughlin, T., O'Keefe, J. and O'Keeffe, B. (eds) (1996) *The Contemporary Catholic School: Context, Identity and Diversity*, London: Falmer Press.

More, C. (1992) *'A Splendid College'. An Illustrated History of Teacher Training in Cheltenham 1847–1990*, Cheltenham: Cheltenham and Gloucester College.

Murphy, J. (1959) *The Religious Problem in English Education. The Crucial Experiment*, Liverpool: Liverpool University Press.

Murphy, J. (1971) *Church, State and Schools in Britain 1800–1970*, London: Routledge & Kegan Paul.

National Society (1984) *A Future in Partnership: A Green Paper for Discussion*, London: National Society.

Nichols, K. (1994) 'Christian Education and the Maintained School System', in Syed Ali Ashraf and P.H. Hirst (eds) *Religion and Education. Islamic and Christian Approaches*, Cambridge: Islamic Academy.

Niblett, W.R. (ed.) (1978) *Christian Involvement in Higher Education: A Discussion Paper*, London: National Society.

O'Keeffe, B. (1986) *Faith, Culture and the Dual System. A Comparative Study of Church and County Schools*, London: Falmer Press.

Ramsey, I. (1970) *The Fourth R. The Durham Report on Religious Education*, London: SPCK.

Robinson, E. (1971) *The Original Vision: A Study of the Religious Experience of Childhood*, Oxford: Religious Experience Research Unit.

—— (1987) *The Language of Mystery*, London: SCM Press.

Robinson, J.A.T. (1963) *Honest to God*, London: SCM Press.

—— (1965) *New Reformation*, London: SCM Press.

—— (1967) *Exploration into God*, London: SCM Press.

Sacks, B. (1961) *The Religious Issue in the State Schools of England and Wales 1902–1914. A Nation's Quest for Human Dignity*, Albuquerque: University of New Mexico Press.

Salbstein, M.C.N. (1982) *The Emancipation of the Jews in Britain: The Question of the Admission of the Jews to Parliament, 1828–1860*, London: Associated University Presses.

Shepherd, P. (1998) *Values for Church Schools*, London: National Society.

Smith, W.O.L. (ed.) (1954) *The School as a Christian Community*, London: SCM Press.

Voeltzel, R. (1966) 'Religion and the question of rights: philosophic and legal problems in the European tradition', in G.Z.F. Bereday and J.A. Lauerys (eds) *World Yearbook of Education 1966: Church and State in Education*, London: Evans, pp. 217–27.

Wainwright, J.A. (1963) *School and Church. Partners in Christian Education*, Oxford: Oxford University Press.

Williams, B. (1976) *The Making of Manchester Jewry 1740–1875*, Manchester: Manchester University Press.

Wood, K. (ed.) (1999) *The Essence of Education. A Report of the Methodist Conference*, Peterborough: Methodist Publishing House.

3   The legal framework for faith-based schools and the rights of the child

Marie Parker-Jenkins

The Labour government's decision to expand faith-based schools is seen as a victory for parental choice but are they necessarily good for children? Is there not a case for suggesting that, in terms of freedom of conscience, faith-based schools may in fact breach children's rights? This chapter looks at these questions within the legal context of faith-based schools and the developing notion of children's rights. The concept of children's rights vis-à-vis those of the parents is explored together with the potential for 'rights in conflict'. Finally, discussion focuses on the rights of the child with reference to issues of autonomy and self-determination and the ways in which these may appear to be undermined within faith-based schools.

The legal framework

There have been a number of statutes concerning faith-based schools which have provided the legal framework for their establishment and funding. The Education Act (HMSO 1996) has application for all independent schools, which is particularly useful to this discussion because new faith-based schools tend to become independent first and then may apply for funding. This is what has happened in the case of Muslim and Sikh schools, for example, and is likely to be followed by other minority groups (Parker-Jenkins *et al.* 2004).

The 1996 Act defines a school as one in which there are more than five pupils of compulsory school age and, as such, a school can and has been established in a person's sitting room (Hewer 2001). (If there are fewer than five pupils the arrangement is seen as constituting the 'education otherwise' category as stipulated in the Education Act 1944.) An application then has to be made to the Department of Education and Skills to be registered as an independent school and in order to do this the applicant has to comply under a number of headings. These relate to the suitability of the premises, accommodation regarding the age of the pupils and facilities if there are boarding children. 'Suitable and efficient' teaching and learning is also required and the curriculum should be generally broad and balanced. Independent schools do not have to teach the National Curriculum, nor do they have to employ qualified teachers. Their staff must however be 'fit and proper persons'. Interestingly, what constitutes a 'fit and proper person' may be perceived differently within some faith-based schools. Here and abroad there have in the past been incidents when schools have failed to offer employment opportunities to those who are not seen as adhering to the tenets of the faith: for example, in the case of divorcees (Parker-Jenkins, 1985). There is not, however, total licence to employ anyone, for faith-based schools cannot employ anyone on 'List 99': that is, those who have been found to be unfit to teach (Barrell and Partington 1985).

Within six months of registering there is a visit from Her Majesty's Inspectorate (HMI) (the independent sector's equivalent of the Office for Standards in Education [OFSTED]). Under the Children Act and National Care Standards Commission (HMSO 2001) issues of health and safety are also considered which include boarding schools, nurseries and child minders. If the school meets the minimum requirements, HMI may recommend final registration status to the Secretary of State. After that the school is visited every five years. The Education Act 2002 (HMSO 2002) looks to modify the existing arrangement and to have a similar cycle of inspections as maintained schools. Also under the new legislation, those wishing to start a new school require documentation pertaining to the state of the premises before a child may start. Likewise, the Child Protection Act 1999 requires that staff have clearance through the Criminal Records Bureau before commencing teaching duties.

In terms of inspection and accountability, 'voluntary aided' schools are inspected like all state schools except in regard to religious education and the social, cultural, spiritual and moral aspects of the school, which are covered under section 23 of the Act (voluntary aided as opposed to voluntary controlled status allows for a greater level of control by the school community and is an important distinction in terms of such things as staffing policy and choice of curriculum).[1] From September 2003, reports on independent schools have been in the public domain and available on the OFSTED website.[2] Within the new framework these reports will be shorter and very specific with regard to premises, welfare and arrangements for the school having a complaints procedure. An important change is that independent schools are to be charged for their inspection. Small faith-based schools, such as the majority of Muslim ones which presently number 111,[3] may find this difficult. In the consultation paper, it was suggested that the cost may amount to £50 per pupil and on a scale according to the size of the school. This is a significant issue since independent faith-based schools tend to charge low fees and employ staff on lower salaries than in maintained schools. Whilst many faith-based schools welcome inspection, charging fees will be an important issue.

Also relevant to this discussion is the School Standards and Framework Act (HMSO 1998). This provides for the creation of School Organisation Committees consisting of representatives of the local education authority, governing bodies and the Learning and Skills Council. Their role is to decide on proposals to establish, close, alter or change the category of a school. In the absence of an agreement, a decision is taken by an adjudicator appointed by the Secretary of State. A widely based 'Admissions Forum' has been formed to consider school admissions and the policy governing staff recruitment. In considering candidates for the position of head teacher of a voluntary controlled school a governing body may 'have regard to the candidate's ability and fitness to preserve and develop the religious character of the school' (Employment of Teachers in Schools with a Religious Character, Regulation 2003) In voluntary aided schools, however, the governing body may give explicit preference to committed members of the faith-based groups in the appointment of the head teacher and other teachers. Finally, under this legislation a governing body can choose to change from voluntary controlled to voluntary aided status without initial financial penalty. As a result of these changes, faith-based groups are more involved in the decision making at local level, and able to act on collective agreements rather than for any one group.

Currently, there is a wide range of faith schools receiving state funding. They are, as we saw above, designated as voluntary controlled and voluntary aided, but mention should also be made of 'foundation schools': that is, those owned by trustees who may or may not have a religious ethos, for example, city technology colleges.[4] The trust deed determines the basis on which the school should be run, and funding arrangements with the state may cover building works and staff salaries. As of 2003, just under a third of English state-funded schools have a religious foundation accommodating 23 per cent of pupils (12 per cent at Church of England schools, 10 per cent at Catholic schools and 1 per cent at schools of other faiths).[5] Also, in terms of the level of control, the majority of Church of England schools are in the 'voluntary controlled' category, whilst Catholic schools, and those based on Islamic, Sikh and Greek Orthodox traditions, have tended to pursue a policy of voluntary aided status (Parker-Jenkins *et al.* 2004).

The Labour Government's paper *Schools: Building on Success* (HMSO 2001) is supportive of the Church of England's intention to establish 100 new schools, as well as encouraging state funding of faith-based schools in general. To assist in this, it is intended to reduce the financial contribution of the faith group from 15 per cent to 10 per cent for capital items, and to provide for 'faith sponsors' and others taking responsibility for some schools to do so on fixed-term renewable contracts (Archbishops' Council 2001). Overall, there is now the opportunity for expansion in these schools, in keeping with a pattern established in the late nineteenth century, and the further development of a partnership approach between government and various faith-based groups (Francis 2000; Lankshear 1996; O'Keefe 1997; Miller 2001).

Children's rights

Parental choice in schooling has been particularly well-supported by legislative changes since the 1980s: for example, with open enrolment, and more recently with the availability of funding for a variety of schools such as Muslim, Sikh, Greek Orthodox and Seventh Day Adventist (DfES 2003). However, if we look beyond parents' rights to those of the rights of the child, we can see the potential for these separate groups of rights to be in conflict.

The children's rights movement is a feature of the twentieth century with wide international support, but its roots can be traced to earlier times. The Children's Petitions of 1669 were, in a sense, an attempt to single out children as a special need category and to call for the restriction of corporal punishment by teachers (Freeman 1965). Pioneers of the nineteenth-century reforms such as Lord Shaftesbury and writers such as Kingsley and Dickens aimed to awaken the nation's conscience by highlighting the plight of children in Britain and calling for a reduction of hours and improved conditions for young children in factories and mines. Whilst these developments were more in the name of children's best interests rather than their 'rights' *per se*, they laid the foundation of a movement which was to modify the traditional status of children *vis-à-vis* adults.

International recognition of children's rights has been expressed in the form of charters and declarations throughout the twentieth century. Chanlett and Morier (1968: 4) state that 'the concept that a child has rights is of relatively recent vintage', for up until 1914 the focus had been on 'the duties of children to parents and society, but never any question of rights they might be entitled to'. In the aftermath of the First World War, organisations were formed to help with relief, one of which was Eglantyne Jebb's 'Save the Children' dealing with the problems of minors. This was followed by the Save the Children International Union in Geneva 1920 and four years later Jebb presented to that organisation a charter specifically concerned with children's rights. This 'Declaration of the Rights of Geneva' was adopted on 24 September 1924 by the 5th Assembly of the League of Nations. It embodied in the broadest sense the 'basic principles of child welfare, leaving appropriate action to each country, within its needs and resources' (Chanlett and Morier 1968: 4). In

1934 the League of Nations confirmed the principles of the Declaration, one of which pertained specifically to education: 'the child must receive a training which will enable it to earn a livelihood, and must be protected against every form of exploitation' (as cited in Chanlett and Morier 1968: 5).

In the 1970s a variety of documents were written demonstrating the continued desire to recognise and promote children's rights. The Advisory Centre for Education (ACE) published a Draft Charter of Children's Rights in 1971, convinced that 'more than any other group, children need special protection and special facilities' (ACE 1971: 105). (Whether children do in fact need 'protection' or 'rights' is a controversial point, which will be discussed later.) The ACE also argued that 'our society does not readily recognise children's rights' and that greater effort is needed to rectify the situation (ibid.). Accordingly, the proposed draft was intended to serve as a vehicle to provoke discussion of 'the way we treat children and the way we should treat children' (ibid.). In 1972 the National Council for Civil Liberties issued a Bill of Rights for Children which included a range of rights from 'the right to receive parental love' to the right to be recognised 'as a person'. In the United States, Foster and Freed published an American Bill of Rights for Children (1972) with a main concern not to remove from children 'moral and legal obligations but ... to enhance their sense of responsibility' (p. 344). A list of 'legal' as well as 'moral' rights were advocated as a fundamental framework, from the right 'to receive fair treatment from all in authority', to the right of a child 'to earn and keep his own earnings' (p. 347). In Canada, the Berger Commission advocated a Bill of Rights for children in 1975, which would provide enforcement and legal obligations, and the decade culminated in the International Year of the Child in 1979 which is perhaps indicative of the interest in the children's rights movement at that time.

Whilst a number of documents highlight rights and freedoms, they are often only expressing 'principles'. Freeman (1983b) describes these as deliberately vague as to what rights children should have and as to who should bear the correlative duties. In fact, the 1924, 1948 and 1959 Declarations of Children's Rights, he argues, are noteworthy 'by their simplicity of language' and inadequate enforcement (p. 7). Similarly, Bel Geddes (1977: 215) states that:

> ... for the most part ... the principles of the 'United Nations Declaration of the Rights of the Child' have not yet been translated into the constitutions and legal codes of individual nations, with the result that clear affirmation and protection of the child's rights is still lacking in the world today.

As charters of declarations of rights tend not to be legal documents, they rarely have enforcement; the European Convention on Human Rights and Fundamental Freedoms is a notable exception.[6] Instead they provide an ideal situation in which they may say 'too little about means and a lot about ends'. Freeman (1983a) describes many of the documents of children's rights as containing 'blueprints rather than reasoned arguments' (p.19). The drafting of the United Nations Convention on the Rights of the Child started in 1978 and was completed in 1989, containing many principles expressed in earlier documents. The importance of education is recognised in Article 15(1) which calls for: 'the right of the child to education ... with a view to achieving the full realisation of this right on the basis of equal opportunity'. Further, Article 10 of the document provides for: '... the right of the child to freedom of thought, conscience and religion ... [and] ... the liberty of the child and his parents ... to ensure the religious and moral education of the child in conformity with convictions of their choice' (Article 10.3).

Conflict could arise out of this article, however, if the convictions of the child are not compatible with those of the parents; it is also unclear which party's rights in such a dispute should take primacy. It is believed, however, that the United Nations draft goes further than previous documents in that it sets out positive rights for children as individuals (Children's Legal Centre 1986).

In addition to international declarations of 'children's rights', there are now a range of European charters, such as the European Convention on Human Rights, which have particular relevance to minors. The Children's Legal Centre contends that the Convention 'provides unique protection for the fundamental rights and freedoms of children and young people'. This is evidenced by a number of cases but it is noteworthy that invariably the litigation is instigated at the behest of the parent. The European Charter on the Rights of the Child was enacted in 1979 which significantly contained as its first principle: '... children must no longer be considered as parents' property, but must be recognised as individuals with their own rights and needs ...' (p. 4).

Today advocacy of children's rights is no longer unusual, yet there is still some ambivalence about the legality of such claims. International and European documents pertaining to children's rights abound, although enforcement has been far less rigorously defined. Supporters of the children's rights movement can no longer be described as the 'lunatic fringe' (Godfrey *et al.* 1975), particularly in the light of campaigns for 'animal rights'. Furthermore, there has been a shift in terminology from children's 'needs' to 'rights', and a change in focus away from broad educational issues to very specific concerns, such as 'child abuse'.[8] The children's rights movement provides a plethora of issues, each group within it often defining one particular issue. Accordingly, no one policy emerges from the movement; rather it appears as a collection of advocates all deeply committed to the rights and welfare of children.

Parents' rights *vis-à-vis* children's rights

Faith-based schools can be viewed as an important element of the educational system to provide for parental rights, but these institutions may also be seen to conflict with children's rights. Parents' rights are recognised in many national and international documents. For example, the European Convention of Human Rights stipulates: 'in the exercise of any functions which it assumes in relation to education and teaching, the state shall respect the right of parents to ensure such education and teaching is in conformity with their own religious and philosophical convictions' (First Protocol to the European Convention on Human Rights).

It is not the case, however, that all parents can choose schools which reflect their religious or philosophical convictions because of a lack of places, or because small minority groups may not be able to sustain a school. A case in point is that of the development of Muslim schools in Britain, which often open and close at random because of financial difficulties (Parker-Jenkins 2002). However, Muslim organisations in particular have been voicing concerns about issues affecting the moral and spiritual development of children in community schools and they have shown themselves prepared to make substantial sacrifices to ensure their children are educated in Muslim schools. Mukadam (1998) describes the present multi-faith approach to religious education in community schools as inadequate because it does not provide for the spiritual and moral development of children. Conversely, the British Humanist Association (BHA) argues that it is difficult for parents to find 'an ordinary *non-church* maintained primary school' (BHA 2001: 33, emphasis added), nor is it satisfied with the content of the religious education syllabuses, which it sees as compromising their beliefs.

The new Human Rights Act (1998) is useful here in discussion of parents' rights because it states:

> Everyone has the right to freedom of thought, conscience and religion; this right includes freedom to change his [or her] religion or belief, and freedom either alone or in community with others and in public or private, to manifest his [or her] religion or belief, in worship, teaching, practice and observance.
>
> (Article 9.1)

'Freedom of thought, conscience and religion' and 'the manifestation of belief' could provide ample opportunities for use by minority ethnic and religious groups. The clause 'manifestation of belief' is particularly useful for communities whose religious identity is expressed in terms of dress, such as the wearing of turbans, skullcaps and 'hijab' or headscarves (interestingly, this right to manifest belief in the form of religious symbols is presently under threat in French schools because it is perceived to be incompatible with a secular education system (TES 2003b), and has also provoked heated debated in Germany (TES 2002a) and Turkey (TES 2002b)). Alternatively, 'freedom of conscience' could provide for the individual child *not* to wear such clothing. Overall, legal articles contained in this document take a holistic and inclusive approach to child development in that children are expected to develop social and moral responsibility in terms of tolerance and understanding of others, regardless of religion and ethnicity, but also to be reared in accordance with their parents' cultural identity and values. For children who belong to ethnic, religious or linguistic minority groups, therefore, there is an assumption that they have the right to enjoy their own cultural heritage within their community and practise their religion or use their community language(s). At the same time, children should be fully prepared to live an individual life in society, and be brought up in the spirit of the ideals proclaimed in the Charter of the United Nations, and in particular in the spirit of peace, dignity, tolerance, freedom and equality.

Other international documents are also useful on this issue of human rights and the potential for those of parents and children to be in conflict. The United Nations Convention on the Rights of the Child (1989), highlighted earlier, calls for 'the right of the child to education ... with a view to achieving the full realisation of this right on the basis of equal opportunity' (Article 15.1). Further, this document provides for 'the right of the child to freedom of thought, conscience and religion ... [and] the liberty of the child and his [sic] parents to ensure the religious and moral education of the child in conformity with the convictions of their choice' (Article 10.3). This document employs the language of equality but whose rights are being protected here – those of the parent or the child? This lack of clarity serves to perpetuate a certain ambiguity concerning the legal relationship between the parent and child.

The European Charter on the Rights of the Child (1979) is clearer when it states: 'the child must no longer be considered as parents' property, but must be recognised as individuals with their own rights and needs'. This view is also espoused in the Children Act (1989) which requires social services to take into account children's views when making decisions about their futures, although, as Mayall (2002) points out: 'compliance with this requirement is patchy' (p. 174). Whilst there continues to be discussion and debate about the allocation of rights to children, it remains a contentious issue, as Smith (2000) notes also: 'the notion of children having rights tends to be interpreted as being permissive and giving them too much power and control, while at the same time taking power and control away from parents and others in authority over children' (p. 14).

The extent to which children's 'rights' might be exercised if they conflict with those of their parents, whether or not children's voices will be heard, and how this might impact on faith-based schools, requires further examination. There are clearly potential contradictions in this. Legislation makes use of the term 'everyone', which includes children, but the legal 'right' tends to be operationalised by parents. So the clause, 'everyone has the right to freedom of thought, conscience and religion' has clear application to recognition of parent's right to have their children educated in a faith-based school. Further, as parents make decisions about other aspects of life, it could be argued that 'religious parents obviously want to pass on to their own offspring values, doctrines, and practices that they regard as of the first importance' (BHA 2002: 29).

However, the rights of the child can be used as persuasive argument against faith-based schools. Neither the BHA nor the National Secular Society 'accepts education in schools that has a basis in one of the faiths' (Archbishops' Council 2001: 1). Similarly, Gillard (2002) argues: 'religion and education are mutually incompatible. Indeed, religion is the antithesis of education' (p. 22). For him, religion should be a matter of private conscience and choice rather than something supported from public funds, and he advocates that we change to the American model which ensures the separation of church and state. This is unlikely and, rather than disestablishing the Church of England, there are plans to expand Anglican schools.[9]

The BHA (2002) argues that 'a proliferation of religious schools will increase discrimination in favour of Christians'. Also, as the Church of England intends 'to nourish those of the faith, encourage those of other faiths, and challenge those of no faith', this might be seen as breaching the right to 'freedom of thought, conscience and religion', as countenanced in human rights law, and to be discriminatory against non-Christians (p. 32).

Another interesting argument put forward by the BHA is one that derives from the Race Relations (Amendment) Act (HMSO 2000). This legislation states that a public authority: 'shall, in carrying out its functions, have a due regard to the need (a) to eliminate unlawful racial discrimination and (b) to promote equality of opportunity and good relations between persons of different racial groups'. Faith-based schools which have a high number of pupils from the same ethno-religious group cannot, it is argued, assist this process and in fact they divide children along ethnic grounds. The same can also be said, however, of some community schools in Cambridgeshire, for example, which as a result of demographics are also representative of one main group, and could also be described as monocultural.[10] Moreover, the monoculturalist and ethnocentric nature of the National Curriculum does little, according to Gundara (2000), to counterbalance this or encourage a multicultural 'feel'.

Opponents of faith-based schools also maintain that the autonomy of the child is ignored: 'we should not expose children to religious instruction, because to do so would be to take advantage of their vulnerability and to induce in them a belief system to which they are not in a position validly to consent' (Humanist Philosophers Group 2001: 10–11).

Full information is likely to be absent in faith-based schools, it is maintained, because 'the information they impart will be biased towards a particular religion' (ibid.). A further argument is that 'children's adoption of the school's preferred religion may not be truly voluntary, depending on what methods are used' and that a religious identity is being enforced on children (ibid.). As such, '... religious education, teaching children *about* different religions, is acceptable according to the autonomy argument. What is not acceptable is religious instruction or indoctrination which can lead to non-autonomous acquisition and holding of significant beliefs' (ibid.).

As well as these concerns about indoctrination and an absence of self-determination being levelled at faith-based schools, the teachers they employ are also portrayed as 'indoctrinators' rather than educators. Overall, therefore,

> ... parents do have rights to bring up their children. But it should not be thought that parents have these rights in virtue of somehow owning their own children. ... The crucial question is not whether it is best for the parents that their children be given a religious schooling but whether it is best for the children themselves that they are.
>
> (HPG 2001: 30)

Under the Convention of the Rights of the Child (1989) noted earlier, it is stipulated that the child should be protected against all forms of discrimination on the basis of the expressed opinions, or beliefs, of the child's parents, legal guardians or family members (Article 2.2). In addition,

> ... the education of the child shall be directed to the preparation of the child for responsible life in a free society, in the spirit of understanding, peace, tolerance, equality of sexes, and friendship among all peoples, ethnic, national and religious groups.
>
> (Article 29: 1d)

The BHA (2002) maintain that the expansion of faith-based schools result in children receiving a limited type of education which is the preference of parents but not necessarily in the child's interest, and this has been argued in the case of faith-based schools which are seen as segregated from the wider community (Cantle Report 2001). Humanists question whether these schools can really commit and contribute to a 'free society', 'equality of sexes' and 'tolerance' (BHA 2002: 32). In my research into faith-based schools such as those based on a Jewish, Muslim, Sikh and Hindu ethos, this assertion is strongly refuted and indeed counter-claims are made that these schools are often highly representative of different ethnic groups, and as institutions they are very much aware of and part of the wider community (Parker-Jenkins *et al.* 2004; CES 2003).

The Convention of the Rights of the Child also provides that the state shall assure to the child who is capable of forming his or her own views, the right to express those views freely in all matters, and that the views of the child should be given due weight in accordance with age and maturity (Article 12.1). Interestingly the voice of the child is seldom heard, even within the children's rights movement. The HPG (2001) raises the question as to whether local children will be included in consultations on proposed religious schools, or, in fact, whether they are instead being used as 'the means to a group's end' (p. 32).

As it stands, not only are children not consulted on such issues, even the right to withdraw from collective worship and religious education is not permitted for children but rests as a parent's right. There are a number of studies which suggest that children do not, in fact, favour school assemblies, nor cultural segregation (ESRC 1999). Furthermore, in the aftermath of the riots in northern England, there is a strong argument put forward to break down cultural and religious barriers (Ouseley 2001). Finally, the Convention states that 'the child shall have the right to freedom of expression; this right shall include freedom to seek, receive and impart information and ideas of all kinds ...' (Article 13.1).

The BHA argues that this sounds 'educationally uncontroversial' and would be supported by Belief and Values Education which it advocates for all schools. Further,

> ... it is also questionable whether children in all faith-based schools have this freedom. Some doubtless do, but some faith-based schools exist in order to protect children from ideas that are different from those of the parental faith group, or disapproved of by that group.
>
> (BHA 2002: 32)

Despite arguments such as these being raised in opposition to faith-based schools there is little sign of their being abolished. This could only happen by legislative change and the Labour government has signalled its intention to support their expansion, as we noted earlier in this chapter. They are seen as perpetuating the tradition of faith groups instigating education, particularly since the nineteenth century, and in partnership with the government. Indeed, the Labour government sees faith-based schools as exemplars of good practice in terms of diversity and academic success. David Blunkett, the former Secretary of State for Education, has stated the government's desire to 'bottle this success', and apply the ingredients to community schools (*The Guardian* 2001), and support for faith-based schools has also been expressed by Prince Charles (BMMS 2000). What also emerges from this policy is a view that faith-based schools are not only meeting the expectations of parents, but also are ideally placed to act as a moral compass for society as a whole.

So far this discussion has polarised schools in terms of faith-based institutions and community schools, but is there another model which would provide a common school for all children yet be responsive to the issue of religious diversity? One way forward has been the unsuccessful 'four-faith model' proposed by a group of Anglican, Jews, Muslims and Hindus: a visionary and radical move because it marries the issue of religious schooling but also addresses the question of how a faith-based school can be more inclusive.[11] A further alternative model is that proposed by the British Humanist Association (2002) of 'inclusive community schools', which would provide opportunities for all faiths to exist in an environment that acknowledges all religious *and* philosophical views. Such a model, the BHA maintains, would provide reasonable accommodations 'to meet the legitimate wishes of parents and pupils', and as such would do away with the need for separate faith-based schools as we know them and as they have been traditionally established. This model reflects the American Communitarian approach, 'diversity within unity', in which there is a 'neutral common framework' in which all children, whether or not they subscribe to a particular faith, are educated together (BHA 2002: 19). One key aspect of this approach would be the introduction of inclusive assemblies with a re-formed religious education providing more balance and representation than exists now, as it would include the teaching of philosophical viewpoints (BHA 1998, 2002). A number of polls suggest that religion is no longer embraced by a large proportion of our society, the exception being among some minority ethnic groups (Madood *et al.* 1997). Yet, as it presently exists, 'when it states or implies that religion is the sole basis of morality, RE excludes and offends the non-religious' (BHA 2002: 39).

The model proposed by the BHA, therefore, provides a 'third way', moving beyond what could be described as the government's fragmented, diverse approach towards the development of faith-based schooling, to one based on integration and inclusion. Importantly, within this model the complete secularisation of schools is not being proposed, as for example in the French model, but instead, space is to be provided for those pupils who wish to engage in religious study and worship. Further, for those parents who do not wish their children to be educated in isolation of other children, or who wish to have their secular or philosophical convictions recognised, this suggests a possible way forward.

Conclusion

Faith-based schools have existed for many centuries and legislation has been enacted which legally secures their place in the educational landscape, in partnership with the state. They provide for parents who wish to see their children educated according to their own religious convictions, away from what they see as an increasingly secular education system. Whilst national and international documents support this expectation within the context of human rights, the rights of the child have also been invoked, distinct from and at times in conflict with those of the parent. In adjudicating these conflicting rights, those of the parent normally take primacy, and indeed the voice of the child is rarely heard in these matters. There are, however, a number of organisations which challenge the view that faith-based schools are necessarily good for children and on philosophical and legal grounds they question their suitability in terms of autonomy and indoctrination. In the present climate of support for the expansion of this category of school, there is little likelihood of the counter-argument being given equal weight, and only advocacy for children's rights from individuals within faith-based schools and by interested parties outside these communities will keep the issue alive. However, new models have been proposed which suggest that religious and philosophical convictions could be accommodated within an inclusive community school in which both parents' and children's rights might more readily be accommodated.

Notes

1 For more on this theme see Arthur (1995) and Francis (2000).
2 Some Jewish schools have asked for their address to be removed from the Ofsted website, however, due to anti-Semitic activities (TES 2003a).
3 I am indebted here to Idris Sears, of the Association of Muslim Schools, for supplying this statistical information during interview in October 2003.
4 The Vardy Foundation is an interesting case in that it funds CTCs but the religious background of the sponsor impacts on such issues as choice of curriculum (http: www.evangelical-times.org/ETNews/htm).
5 See DfES(2003) website for statistical information at http://www.dfes.gov.uk/gateway/DB/vol/v000417/index.html.
6 For more on this theme see Robertson (1993), Harris *et al.* (1995), Beddard (1993) and Brownlie and Goodwin (2002).
7 An exception to this pattern would be Neilson v. Denmark (App. no. 1092/84, European Commission of Human Rights, Decision as to admissibility, 10 March 1986; *Childright*, July/August 1987, 39: 3).
8 For more on the issue of child abuse, the Children's Legal Centre has produced useful information.
9 See Archbishops' Council (2001).
10 DfES (2003) website on statistical information at http://www.dfes.gov.uk/rsgateway/DB/VOL/v000417/index.shtml.
11 TES (2002d) 'Multi-faith plan is a secularist plot', 2 August: 14.

References

Advisory Centre for Education (1971) 'Draft Charter of Children's Rights', *Where*, 56: 105–8.
Archbishops' Council (2001) *The Way Ahead*, London: Church Publishing House.
Arthur, J. (1995) 'Government education policy and voluntary-aided schools', *Oxford Review of Education*, 21(4): 447–55.
Barrell, G.B. and Partington, J. (1985) *Teachers and the Law*, 6th edn, London: Methuen.

Beddard, R. (1993) *Human Rights and Europe*, Cambridge: Grotius Publications.

Bel Geddes, J. (1977) 'The Rights of Children in World Perspective', in B. Gross and R. Gross (eds) *The Children's Rights Movement: Overcoming the Oppression of Young People*, New York: Anchor Press.

British Humanist Association (BHA) (1998) *Collective Worship and School Assemblies: What is the Law?*, London: BHA.

—— (2002) *A Better Way Forward*, London: BHA.

Brownlie, T. and Goodwin, G.S. (2002) *Basic Documents on Human Rights*, 4th edn, Oxford: Oxford University Press.

British Muslims Monthly Survey (2000) 'Prince Charles visits Islamia', 8(5) (20 June): 1–2.

Cantle Report (2001) *Community Cohesion*, A Report of the Independent Review Team, chaired by Ted Cantle, London: Home Office.

Catholic Education Service (2003) *Ethnicity, Identity and Achievement in Catholic Education*, London: CES.

Chanlett, E. and Morier, G.M. (1968) 'Declaration of the Rights of the Child', *International Child Welfare*, 22: 4–8.

Children's Legal Centre (1986), *Children's Charters*, London: CLC.

DfES (2003) *Aiming High*, London: HMSO.

Economic and Social Research Council (ESRC) (1999), *Children 5–16 Research Briefing: Civil Rights in School:* London: ESRC.

Francis, L.J. (2000) 'The domestic and the general function of Anglican schools in England and Wales', *International Journal of Education and Religion*, 11: 100–21.

Foster, H.H. and Freed, D.J. (1972) 'A Bill of Rights for Children', *Family Law Quarterly*, 6: 343–75.

Freeman, M.D.A. (1965) 'The Children's Petition of 1669 and its sequel', *British Journal of Educational Studies*, 14: 216–23.

—— (1983a) 'Children's Rights – the Literature', *Childright*, November (2): 19–21.

—— (1983b) *The Rights and Wrongs of Children*, London: Frances Pinter.

Gillard, D. (2002), 'The Faith Schools Debate: Glass in their Snowballs', *Forum*, 44(1): 15–22.

Godfrey, G. (1975) *Parental Rights and Duties and Custody Suits*, London: Stevens.

Gundara, J.S. (2000) *Interculturalism, Education and Inclusion*, London: PCP Sage.

The Guardian (2001) 'Blunkett's blunder puts the clock back', 12 December: 18.

Harris, D.J., O'Boyle, M. and Warbrick, C. (1995) *Law of the European Convention on Human Rights*, London: Butterworths.

Hewer, C. (2001) 'Schools for Muslims', *Oxford Review of Education*, 27(4): 515–27.

HMSO (1996) *The Education Act*, London: HMSO.

—— (1998) *Schools Standards and Framework Act*, London: HMSO.

—— (1999) *Child's Protection Act*, London: HMSO.

—— (2000) *Race Relations Act*, London: HMSO.

—— (2001) *Schools: Building on Success*, London: HMSO.

Humanist Philosophers' Group (2001) *Religious Schools: the Case Against*, London: British Humanist Association.

Lankshear, D.W. (1996) *Churches Serving Schools*, London: The National Society.

Madood, T., Berthoud, R., Lakey, J., Nazroo, J., Smith, P., Virdee, S. and Beishon, S. (1997) *Ethnic Minorities in Britain: Diversity and Disadvantage*, London: Policy Institute.

Mayall, B. (2002) *Towards a Sociology for Childhood: Thinking from Children's Lives*, Buckingham: Open University Press.

Miller, A. (20012) 'Inside a Muslim School', *The Tablet*, 9 February: 16.

Mukadam, M.H. (1998) 'Spiritual and moral development of Muslim children in state schools', unpublished PhD, Birmingham: Birmingham University.

Nairn, K. (ed.) *Advocating for Children: International Perspectives on Children's Rights*, Otago: University of Otago Press.

O'Keefe, B. (1997) 'The changing role of Catholic schools in England and Wales: from exclusiveness to engagement', in J. McMahon *et al.* (eds) *Leading the Catholic School*, Victoria NSW: Spectrum Publications.

Ouseley Report (2001) *Community Pride not Prejudice: Making Diversity Work in Bradford*, Bradford: Bradford City Council.

Parker-Jenkins, M. (1985) 'Rights in conflict: the case of Margaret Caldwell', *Canadian Journal of Education*, 10(1) January: 66–7.

—— (2002) 'Equal access to state funding: the case of Muslim schools in Britain', *Race, Ethnicity and Education*, 5(3): 274–89.

Parker-Jenkins, M., Hartas, D. and Irving, B. (2004) *In Good Faith: Schools, Religion and Public Funding*, Aldershot: Ashgate Publishing.

Robertson, A.H. (1993) *Human Rights in Europe: A study of the European Convention on Human Rights*, 3rd edn, Manchester: Manchester University Press.

Smith, A.B. (2000) 'Children's rights: an overview', in A.B. Smith, M. Gollop, K. and *The Sunday Times* (2001) 'Oh me of little faith, 14 April: 11.

TES (2000c) 'The Christian response to help people', 19 April: 9.

—— (2002a) 'Muslim headscarf ban', 19 July: 12.

—— (2002b) 'Police beat girls who defy scarf ban', 22 March: 24.

—— (2002c) 'Charles wants schools to lead faith campaign', 26 April: 1.

—— (2002d) 'Multi-faith plan is a secularist plot', 2 August: 14.

—— (2003a) 'Jewish schools fearful of attacks', 1 August: 3.

—— (2003b) 'Law bans hijab but permits crucifix', 16 January: 20.

Part II

Faith schools

For and against

4 Faith schools

Can they be justified?

Richard Pring

The government has clearly indicated its support for not only maintaining, but indeed also expanding, the number and the diversity of faith schools. The Green Paper (DfES 2001), *Schools: Building on Success*, endorsed the wishes of the Church of England to open 100 new schools. The Green Paper indicated, too, the government's wish to increase the number of state-funded religious schools generally

Several reasons are put forward for this. This chapter will review briefly some of those reasons in turn but argue that they do not address the important issues underlying faith schools. It is those issues which are the basis of increasing concern and opposition to current legislation.

Of course, any discussion of the rights or wrongs of publicly funded faith schools cannot ignore the historical and social context of that discussion. One of the achievements of the 1944 Education Act was to bring church schools (particularly those of the Anglican and Catholic Churches) within the state system of education. That system emphasised partnership rather than control – the provision of an educational system within a national legal and financial framework, locally administered, which would allow for diversity of educational aim and belief.

However, one thing that history teaches is that the context in which agreements are made does not remain the same. There are several events, and anomalies, which have forced people to reconsider the terms of this partnership. First, as much as 33 per cent of the school population goes to church schools – but only 7 per cent (a declining proportion) bothers going to church. The 2001 Census recorded 76.8 per cent as being religious and 15.5 per cent stating they had no religion. The religious and cultural context of Britain has changed enormously since 1944. Second, a link is made in people's minds between religious segregation in education and some of the ethnic and racial problems which society has to face – in Northern Ireland as well as in Oldham and Bradford. Can one have an educational system divided on religious lines that is not thereby also divided ethnically and racially? After the attack on the World Trade Centre on 11 September 2001, the importance of the 'common school' takes on an added significance.

Therefore, this chapter covers the following ground. First, I examine briefly but critically the arguments frequently put forward for the support of faith schools. Second, I focus on and explicate what I see to be the central issue – and the main reason for not supporting faith schools. Third, I look critically at that argument and indicate where the defence of faith schools must lie.

Arguments for faith schools

Academic standards

Evidence is produced (and certainly believed) that faith schools perform better against the normal performance criteria of effective schooling. The then schools minister, Stephen Timms, though admitting that the plans for increasing the number of faith schools was contentious, nonetheless argued that the evidence is clear that faith schools are doing very good jobs, and are doing them in particular in disadvantaged communities (quoted in the *Times Educational Supplement*, 25 June 2002). Hence, if you want to improve performance, then it would seem reasonable to increase the proportion of the population educated in this successful sector.

The empirical evidence would, however, lead one to question this assumption. The National Foundation for Educational Research (NFER) study by the Schagens shows the weakness of the evidence – the relatively small increase in performance scores, which itself might be explained, not by the distinctive ethos of the schools, but by the effects of the hidden selection which takes place (Schagen and Schagen 2001). Put crudely, parents who know how to manipulate the system have a coincidental religious conversion when their children reach the age of 11. Remembering the justification for faith schools in the period before the 1944 Act, one might argue that faith schools, if faithful to their faith, would not be happy with the normal performance criteria of effective schooling; that justification lay in the nurturing of a moral form of life, not simpy in academic attainment.

Choice

It is argued, especially by the Blair government, that the system of education should increase diversity so as to create greater choice for parents. And, indeed, in that respect, the present government has assiduously followed the policy outlined in John Patten's White Paper, *Choice and Diversity* (DES 1993). Faith Schools are but one aspect of that mosaic of school provision which includes beacon schools, grammar schools, comprehensive schools, city academies, training schools and specialist schools of every hue and colour.

But 'choice' is not an end in itself. It can be justified only if it can be shown that such choice, first, achieves desirable educational aims, and, second, does not distort the educational opportunities of those unable to exercise that choice. Indeed, it is that distortion of choice for the often less vocal and less powerful members of society that persuades some to curb the intake into faith schools. Under the proposals of Frank Dobson, the Labour member of parliament for Holborn and St Pancras, faith schools would be obliged to offer 25 per cent of their places to children of parents with other religions or no faith at all. He argued: 'This is an issue of principle. People use public money and exclude children on the grounds of their religion. If someone suggested they were going to do it on race everybody would be outraged' (*The Guardian*, 4 February 2002).

Ethos

Those who point especially to the success of faith schools (ignoring the evidence to the contrary such as that quoted above) argue that the success arises from the distinctive ethos or value system which permeates the whole school – to be contrasted with the lack of ethos or overarching value system in the state system generally.

Such an ethos can no doubt be felt very strongly when one visits certain schools. My own Catholic schooling gives clear evidence of that – the sense of religious purpose even underpinning 'secular' studies, the life of prayer and devotion which was part of the school life, the promotion of certain values and practices, the shared assumptions about the aims and conduct of life. But the espousal of that ethos is conditional upon the acceptance of the values embedded within it – and indeed of the religious beliefs which provide the foundation of the values. A society which questions those values and beliefs, and indeed which might see them as contributing to the divisions within it, might well argue (as indeed does the British Humanist Association (2002)) for the abolition of faith schools. Should public money be given to supporting the ethos of a school system which is seen as divisive – or at least promoting values which are by no means universally accepted?

Equality of treatment

There is no doubt that privileges given to Christian and Jewish schools ought, in fairness, to be extended to other faiths (Muslim, Sikh, etc.). And, indeed, one should in fairness give equal support to those schools which assert an agnostic or an atheist 'faith'. This point was put forcibly by Trevor Phillips, the Deputy Chair of the Greater London Assembly: 'As long as Catholics, Anglicans and Jews have the right to create voluntary-aided schools, it would be a crime to say that Muslims cannot' (quoted in the *Times Educational Supplement*, 25 June 2002). The point is that the very same arguments that supported religious diversity within a national system in 1944 apply equally to the present.

However, seeing the drift of that argument, many would argue, not for the extension of privileges to others, but for the abolition of such privileges for all faith schools – or at least to the extension of voluntary status to any further schools whatever their religious affiliation (see Judge 2001). The reason is that conditions are very different from those of 1944. Division on the grounds of religion now creates division on grounds of race and ethnicity. More faith schools are questionable following the riots in Oldham and Burnley and the events of 11 September 2001. Rather, it is argued, one should follow the example of the United States of America, where 'the common school', inspired by the work of Horace Mann and John Dewey, should be the place where people from different backgrounds, cultures and religions learn to live together and not just come to tolerate or respect diversity, but develop through it. No such common school, with public funding, should profess a distinctive religious viewpoint.

Parents versus the state

The historical context of faith schools (the arrangements for voluntary aided and voluntary controlled under the 1944 Education Act) is that education was regarded as the responsibility of parents and their communities (in most cases, the local church); the state, especially after 1870, provided support for such a system and supplemented it where the churches had not caught up with the growing towns and cities. That subordinate role of the state is reflected in the oral report to me by Dr Marjorie Reeves of her conversation with the Permanent Secretary when, in 1947, she was selected to be a member of the Central Advisory Council for Education. She asked the then Permanent Secretary, Redcliffe Maud, what the main responsibility of the members of the Council was. He replied that they should be prepared to die at the first ditch as soon as politicians got their hands on education. In support of this position, reference might be made to the 1998 Human Rights Act which says:

In the exercise of any functions which it assumes in relation to education, and to teaching, the State shall respect the rights of parents to ensure such education and teaching in conformity with their own religious and philosophical convictions.

None of these arguments, except the final one, stands on its own, even though they are often employed in the defence and promotion of faith schools. They invoke some of the desirable effects of faith schools – academic standards, ethos, parental rights, choice and diversity – although the *desirability* of those effects depends to some extent upon the acceptance of some of the assumptions in the faith itself. But they do not justify the distinctive *faith aspect* of those schools – and hence, they are vulnerable to those arguments that are pitched at the very idea of promoting a particular faith through publicly funded schooling.

The central criticism of state support for faith schools

There are three ways in which the opposition to faith schools (that is, schools whose mission is to nurture a particular set of religious beliefs and attitudes) manifests itself.

The first is that there should not be faith schools of a particular kind or in certain places. Schools of certain faiths are seen to teach, by reason of that faith, doctrines which are inimical to the state, either undermining some of the foundation principles and laws of the state or dividing certain communities from each other, thereby giving rise (as in Northern Ireland) to hostilities, deep-seated prejudices and discrimination. Or such schools are seen to support doctrinal teaching (for example, on evolution) which is regarded as unacceptable within the science community.

However, the divisive nature of faith schools in some areas is not an argument against faith schools *in general* – and indeed one can see how those who normally support faith schools would seek a more integrated school system in certain circumstances. The 'integrated school' movement in Northern Ireland was born, not of a general distrust of faith schools, but of the way in which different Christian denominations reinforced, through a divided schooling, the wider and destructive divisions and prejudices within society. But the seriousness of the divisiveness was outlined by Lord Ouseley, once head of the Commission for Racial Equality, in his damning condemnation of segregated schools as a prime cause of racial hatred. He said, 'There are signs that communities are fragmenting along racial, cultural and faith lines' (Ouseley Report, 2002).

Nonetheless, beneath the opposition to faith schools of this kind – namely, the way in which faith so easily underpins social divisiveness or doctrinal absurdities – lies a deeper source of disquiet about the role of schools in nurturing faith itself.

The second way in which opposition to faith schools manifests itself is in the pressure to make publicly funded faith schools give access to children of other faiths or of no faith at all. There are often practical as well as moral reasons for so arguing. The practical reasons are that children, excluded on grounds of belief, are thereby prevented from attending their neighbourhood school, which happens to be a faith school, and then bussed to a distant and unfamiliar part of the city. There are instances where Muslims, in particular, are excluded from their neighbourhood but highly popular (and hence selective) faith school, thereby reinforcing divisions in the community, causing real difficulties to an often deprived section of that community and denying to them access to a good school to which they seek entry. As Keith Porteous Wood of the National Secular Society argued:

Faith Schools amount to a third of all schools and in some counties there are more faith schools than community schools. In such circumstances it is completely unacceptable for places to be allocated based on the parents' belief.

Hence, for such critics, the distinctive character of a faith school – namely, the nurturing of a particular faith tradition – is discounted as a valid reason for excluding non-believers.

The third kind of opposition, which makes explicit what is so often implicit in the previous reasons, is that the *nurturing of faith* is not an *educational* task, and therefore should not be the aim of a school – and *a fortiori* not the job of publicly funded schools in a society which includes people of many faiths and of no faith at all.

That argument is along the following lines: Faith schools aim to bring about particular religious beliefs and convictions – to nurture a faith-based view of the world. This is clearly shown in the recommendation of the Church of England *Consultation Report* (2000), which was partly the basis for the recommendations referred to in *Schools: Building on Success*. They endorse the view that publicly funded church schools are places

> ... where the faith is proclaimed and lived, and which therefore offer opportunities to pupils and their families to explore the truths of Christian faith, to develop spiritually and morally, and to have a basis for *choice* about Christian commitment.
>
> (para. 3.4)

and

> ... pupils will experience what it is like to live in a community that celebrates the Christian faith; to work within a framework of discipline and yet to be confident of forgiveness; to begin to share the Christian's hope and the Christian experience.
>
> (para. 3.22)

However, such a nurturing of a particular faith (and with it a particular set of beliefs, a particular moral outlook, a particular spiritual tradition) cannot, so the critics argue, be educationally justified. The reason is that education is concerned with the development of the mind and thus the rational life and individual autonomy. To intend to nurture a particular faith – a set of beliefs and attitudes and the strong emotional and devotional attachment to those beliefs – is to deny this. It is to put forward a set of beliefs as true, the truth of which cannot be ascertained; it is, in nurturing a strong emotional commitment to those beliefs, undermining the autonomy of the individual learner; it is, therefore, a form of indoctrination. And in reply to those who invoke the rights of parents, the critics of faith schools will point to the rights of children – the right not to be indoctrinated but to be given the intellectual tools to make up their own minds when the time is appropriate.

Put in a slightly different way, children have a right to be kept free of any ideological position which jeopardises the development of their autonomy (children's rights supersede parents' rights as these are reflected in the Human Rights Act quoted above). Religions are ideological. By that it is meant that they are a system of beliefs, whose ultimate foundations are themselves not open to rational justification but which are maintained through strong emotional attachment. There are no objective grounds for supporting one religious set of beliefs rather than any other – these are beyond the arena of rational argument and evidence-based thinking. To treat religious doctrines as if they were true (and to support them with the emotional force which frequently accompanies those beliefs) is to indoctrinate, and indoctrination is the very antithesis of what education is about.

This argument summarises a philosophical position about liberal education which both reflects the non-philosophical position of many critics and the influential philosophical position of the long tradition of liberal individualism. And it has been admirably developed over several years by John White (1982, and subsequent writings).

Roughly, White's argument is as follows: The aim of education is to develop in young people those capacities to lead the good life. In particular those capacities must include the abilities to engage in rational discourse – to be able to make rational choices about what constitutes the good life. A distinction is to be made between those 'philosophies' of education that purport to show what is the proper purpose of mankind (the end to which they are naturally or supernaturally destined), and thus feel able to direct children to that end, and those 'philosophies' that see there to be no rational basis for such a teleological position. And if there is no such foundation, then any educational goals that assume that there is cannot be justified. Hence, education aims to provide the intellectual tools for students to engage rationally in the public world of knowledge and understanding and, in the light of such rational engagement, to make up their own minds about the ends to be served and what is to count as the good life for them. To do otherwise is to undermine the growing autonomy of the individual rational agent and to indoctrinate children with a particular set of beliefs that have no rational foundation.

The debate, therefore, about faith schools – whether or not they should be publicly funded – hinges ultimately, not upon their academic achievement, the rights of parents, freedom of choice or a distinctive ethos, but upon the aims of education, the rationality of nurturing a particular set of faith-based beliefs, the value of individual autonomy and the extent to which indoctrination should at all costs be avoided. Those who wish to retain faith schools, or indeed to extend them to other religious groups, will need to address the disagreements over liberal education – its aims, its underlying notion of rationality, the significance attached to autonomy and the concern over indoctrination.

Response to the criticism: the defence of faith schools

Educational aims

'Education' is, generally speaking, an evaluative word. It refers to those activities that promote the kind of learning that is picked out by society as worthwhile. What is regarded as worthwhile learning will depend on many different factors – the background of moral beliefs, the economic context, the social structure. An educated person in ancient Greece would be a different sort of person from someone deemed to be educated in twenty-first-century Britain. Circumstances have changed and so, therefore, has our idea of worthwhile learning. Furthermore, just as there is disagreement in society about what is worthwhile, so there will be disagreement over what is to count as an educational activity or an educated person.

In exploring what is to be judged educationally worthwhile, one needs to consider what it means to be a person, and indeed to be a person more fully. Education presupposes that we have some view of personal development and human flourishing. Part of that, but not necessarily the whole of that, will be the development of the capacity to think and thus to be inducted into different forms of knowledge and understanding. Such a development requires an initiation into the different forms of thought through which we have come to see, explain, appreciate and value the world. It requires access to what Oakeshott (1972) referred to, namely, a world of ideas which has evolved through that 'conversation between the generations of mankind' in which one comes to appreciate 'the voices' of history, of science, of philosophy. That world of ideas and of values is one's inheritance. One cannot step outside it to obtain a more objective view, for such a view must itself be from within that world of values and ideas which one has inherited.

The voice of religion and of faith is as much part of that 'conversation between the generations' as any other – as, for example, the neo-liberal tradition of individualism in which many of the critics of faith schools are rooted. These different 'voices' have shaped our view of what it means to be and to become a person more fully. Of course, in so far as they vie for recognition within that conversation with other ideas of personhood (and thus of what it means to be an educated person), those different voices (including that of faith) must partake in a tradition of criticism, which is the mark of a liberal education. But so to partake in a tradition of critical thinking requires an initiation into the ideas and beliefs which have shaped those distinctive modes of religious thinking. Religious traditions have not remained static, nor have their own development remained aloof from the under-standings that are embodied within other forms of knowledge (history or science, for example), or from the more philosophical arguments about the nature and validity of religious thinking.

This idea of a tradition of thought that provides insight into personhood, that shapes our understanding of what is worthwhile and that needs to be protected and enhanced through education is captured in this passage from Jacob Neusmer's book *Conservative, American and Jewish* (1993, quoted in Sacks 1997), which expresses admirably the essential nature of those moral traditions and the custodial role of educators in relation to them.

> Civilization hangs suspended, from generation to generation, by the gossamer strand of memory. If only one cohort of mothers and fathers fails to convey to its children what *it* has learned from its parents, then the great chain of learning and wisdom snaps. If the guardians of human knowledge stumble only one time, in their fall collapses the whole edifice of knowledge and understanding.
>
> (Sacks 1997: 173)

Integral to the acquaintance with these different voices (including that of religion) through which we make sense of the world would be to understand the kind of argument and the kind of belief which they manifest. Thus, to understand science would be to understand the limitations of scientific claims – the kinds of truth which it proclaims, the mode through which those truths are verified and the distinctive modes of scientific enquiry. To understand religion would be similarly to appreciate the nature and the limitations of religious discourse, in particular the relation of belief to evidence.

Moreover, such an aim of education must be embodied within the very processes through which those understandings are achieved, namely, the processes which embrace criticism of received assumptions, openness to evidence and argument wherever it might lead, respect for the different sides to an argument, control of the passions and emotions which distort judgement. Personal autonomy is certainly a central educational aim – the capacity to think for oneself on the basis of appropriate evidence, to be acquainted with the different forms of understanding, to appreciate the limitations of different kinds of truth claim. But to achieve that autonomy, there has to be a careful and delicate initiation into the different forms of understanding so that one might understand them and appreciate them 'from the inside'. Faith and religious understanding are manifest not so much in propositions but in forms of practice and relationships. Indeed, theology might be said to be an attempt to articulate the understandings which are embodied in religious practice. Acquaintance only with the sociology of religion is not to see things from the religious point of view.

But to accept the voice of religion and faith as a genuine voice, and to see an educational institution as embodying it, requires the following. First, it needs to be shown that the distinctive form of education is based upon a deeper philosophical tradition which, over time, has both withstood the critical scrutiny of others but at the same time has evolved as a result of that criticism. Second, it must contain within the educational experience that openness to alternative understandings and attempts to make sense of what it means to be a person and to be so more fully. Jonathan Sacks' recent publication, *The Dignity of Difference* (Sacks 2002), forcefully argues for the recognition of (not just the respect for or tolerance of) other religious and secular traditions through which people have tried to make sense of the world and of their lives.

Indoctrination

It would be contrary to the aim of education to teach so as to close the mind, to curb or atrophy the individual's growing autonomy, or to teach as certain what was essentially controversial. And it is equally claimed that it would be wrong to promote a particular form of life as though, despite the plurality of views, one particular way of life was the correct one. That would be to indoctrinate – the very antithesis of education. Hence, the argument against faith schools.

It is, however, easier to make the accusation of indoctrination than to say precisely what that accusation means. Rarely is the mathematics teacher accused of indoctrination when introducing the learner to the truths of geometry. But that is because there is some consensus over what those truths are. Hence, indoctrination would seem to apply when the *doctrines* or the *content* of what one is teaching are controversial – when there is no public agreement over what is true or false, valid or invalid. Thus, religious truths, in this respect, are rather like political or moral or aesthetic truths. The same arguments against nurturing religious beliefs and attitudes would be similar to those which would be levelled against teaching a particular moral code or attitude, or teaching people how to appreciate literature, or what sort of political stance one should adopt, or a particular interpretation in history of past events. But that indeed would be drastic. Not to nurture beliefs which are in any way controversial would leave the schools bereft of almost anything but mathematics and science.

Therefore, those who make accusations of indoctrination retreat from an emphasis upon the *content* of teaching to the *method* of teaching – of teaching so as to demonstrate the truth of what is taught, not tolerating deviation from the accepted view. Criticism would be discouraged, contrary evidence not revealed, alternative opinions muted.

Even here, however, there are difficulties. The mathematics teacher would not see herself to be indoctrinating if she refused to tolerate a wrong answer – although she might well praise the creative, albeit erroneous, attempt to solve a puzzle. And the history teacher might well justify his attempt to get the pupil 'on the inside' of a particular version of history, even though he knows it is controversial amongst historians (for example, a particular understanding of the Reformation). The keen teacher of literature will not remain indifferent to the beauty of a particular poem or to the significance of a chosen novelist – even though there will be different schools of thought on these matters. Indeed, it is difficult to appreciate a form of education which remains rigidly neutral and dispassionate on those matters – almost always controversial – that interpret human experience at its deepest level. Can the voice of faith really be understood and appreciated unless it is taught in the context of practices that embody the sentiments and beliefs of significant traditions?

Indoctrination, therefore, comes to be associated, not with the teaching ⟨ *content*, nor with the teaching through a particular *method*, but with the *inte* with the appropriate practices and methods) of teaching so as to prevent at a lau. critical reflection upon the truth of what has been taught. Indoctrination lies in closing ⟨ mind, to blocking out, often through strong sentiments or feeling, the possibility of contemplating an alternative point of view. It lies in the removal of the system of belief from the critical tradition through which those very beliefs have evolved. But such a closing of the mind can come in many different ways – the sneering at alternatives, the assumption of self-evidence of what is current, the constant portrayal without insight of what people within a particular tradition believe in. Indoctrination arises as much from the secular assumptions of the media and the cold indifference to religion of the humanist as it does from the closed institutions of religion which create an emotional grip (possibly through the guilt engendered about disbelief) over the maintenance of certain beliefs.

Autonomy

The importance of autonomy as an aim of education (and its apparent incompatibility with the promotion of a distinctive religious outlook) is a self-evident truth of a liberal view of education. 'Autonomy' sums up what is distinctive about the educated person – someone who is free *from* the mental constraints to thinking for oneself and who is free (empowered) *to* make up his or her own mind. Truly autonomous persons are those who can think for themselves. Education is, therefore, concerned with laying the foundation for a truly rational individual – rational in terms not only of intellectual capacity but also of emotional control. The aim of education is not to instil particular beliefs, but to enable individuals to acquire beliefs on the basis of evidence, reason and criticism.

'Autonomy', however, in this sense, is not a straightforward concept. In what way can one be said to be thinking for oneself or thinking independently? To think requires the acquisition of concepts and those concepts, embedded within language, are part of the public form of life which one has inherited. The language, and the concepts which it embraces, shape *what* and *how* to think. At more sophisticated levels, the moral and political perspectives which one adopts are acquired through participation in the ideas, arguments and assumptions which underpin society in general and particular discourses within society. The defenders of autonomy are themselves both empowered and constrained by the philosophical traditions they belong to. And, indeed, it could well be argued that, in the pursuit of autonomy, the teacher, by not giving insight into distinctive faith traditions (not to be equated with the rather superficial knowledge about religious customs and practices), is in fact diminishing the autonomy of the learners. They are prevented from seeing the possibilities in a particular faith tradition.

Conclusion

This very brief examination of the aims of education, reflected in notions of indoctrination and autonomy, does no more than indicate where the defenders of faith schools must find a defence against an articulate and increasingly accepted criticism from a particular liberal perspective. The justification of faith schools, by concentrating upon parental rights, ethos or academic results, has neglected the more important but exceedingly difficult philosophical issues which need to be addressed. That justification must lie, first, in a deeper exploration of the meaning and aims of education; second, in the argument for the importance of certain traditions in our attempt to understand what it means to be human and to be so more fully; third, in the articulation of a defensible ideal of autonomy compatible with participation in those traditions.

In so doing, the defenders of faith schools must reach deeper into philosophical traditions that enable them to combat that kind of liberalism that ultimately undermines their precarious hold on public support. Dubious appeal to academic superiority, especially when accompanied by hidden selection, which contradicts the moral teaching of the faiths themselves, is but a superficial and temporary expedient. Of course, there have in the past been such attempts to reach into deeper philosophical perspectives (for example, the thomistic defence by Maritain 1941 and 1944, reflected more recently in Groome (1998), and briefly brought to light by Carr *et al.* 1995). But these are rare, and therefore the case for faith schools is in danger of going by default.

References

British Humanist Association (2002) *A Better Way Forward: BHA Policy on Religion and Schools*, London: BHA.

Carr, D., Haldane, J., McLaughlin, T. and Pring, R. (1995) 'Return to the crossroads: Maritain fifty years on', *British Journal of Educational Studies*, 43(2): 162–78.

Church Schools Review Group (2000) *Consultation Report*, London: Church House Publishing.

DES (1993) *Choice and Diversity*, London: HMSO

DfES (2001) *Schools: Building on Success*, London: DfES

Groome, T. (1998) *Educating for Life*, Allen, TX: Thomas More Press.

Judge, H. (2001) 'Faith-based schools and state funding: a partial argument', *Oxford Review of Education*, 27(4): 463–74.

Maritain, J. (1941) *The Person and the Common Good*, New York: Scribner.

Maritain, J. (1944) *Education at the Crossroads*, New Haven, CT: Yale University Press.

Nuesmer, J. (1993) *Conservative, American and Jewish*, Lafayette, LA: Huntingdon House.

Oakeshott, M. (1972) 'Education: Its engagement and its frustrations', in T. Fuller (ed.) *Michael Oakeshott and Education*, New Haven, CT: Yale University Press.

Ouseley Report (2002) *Community Pride not Prejudice: Making Diversity Work in Bradford*, Bradford: Bradford City Council.

Sacks, J. (1997) *The Politics of Hope*, London: Jonathan Cape.

Sacks, J. (2002) *The Dignity of Difference*, London: Continuum.

Schagen, S. and Schagen, I. (2001) 'Faith schools and specialist schools', *Education Journal*, 62: 30–1.

White, J. (1982) *The Aims of Education Restated*, London: Routledge and Kegan Paul.

5 Are faith schools divisive?

J. Mark Halstead and Terence McLaughlin

One of the most significant criticisms voiced against faith schools in current debate is the claim that they are 'divisive'. Examples of this claim can be readily pointed to. Richard Dawkins, for instance, has argued that faith schools are 'lethally divisive' (Dawkins 2001) and Polly Toynbee claims that such schools 'foil attempts at future integration', 'cause apartheid' and (in the case of Catholic schools) leave some 10 per cent of their places empty rather than admit 'unwashed heathen' (Toynbee 2001). Harry Judge is not alone in questioning the wisdom of expanding the number of faith schools 'in a contemporary British society already threatened by divisive strains' (Judge 2001a: 470). These are but three examples of a wide range of expressions of concern about the divisiveness of faith schools from many quarters. The charge of divisiveness is particularly damaging to faith schools because it alleges a tangible evil which affects society as a whole. The charge therefore constitutes a potential 'trump' over familiar arguments about the rights of religious communities and parents to not only establish and send their children to faith schools but also to enjoy the support of public funding in respect of these rights. The well being of society as a whole, it can be claimed, 'trumps' the well being of any particular section of it.

In this chapter, we explore the nature of the claim that faith schools are divisive and the extent to which this claim is well founded. Our approach is broadly philosophical and many important empirical matters relevant to a full evaluation of the questions at stake are not addressed here. We shall argue that the claim that faith schools are divisive is less clear and well grounded than is often supposed and that the claim as it is usually developed is unjustifiable when stated in a general way. We concede, however, that particular faith schools in particular contexts may be divisive in some sense of the term but that is something which is true of schools in general and may well also be true of the common school.

The chapter has four sections. The first section is introductory. In the second section, we analyse the concept of 'divisiveness' and explore a number of different senses in which the term can be used and a number of different kinds of claim involved in accusations that faith schools are divisive. In the third section, we bring the notion of a 'faith school' into focus and draw attention to a number of differences between kinds of faith school which are relevant to the present discussion and which arise from considerations of both principle and practice. In the final section, we offer an evaluation of claims that faith schools are indeed divisive in any of the senses of the term which we have distinguished.

Introduction: context and complexity

The range of considerations relevant to an understanding of the recent emergence of faith schools into the spotlight of educational debate in England and Wales are well known and need no detailed rehearsal here. They include the popularity of such schools among parents, a renewed interest on the part of the Church of England in developing and extending its schools within the maintained sector (Church Schools Review Group 2001), continuing calls for faith schools within this sector from other religious communities (especially the Muslim community) (Halstead 1986, 1988; Mabud 2002), the increasing prominence of research and scholarship in relation to faith schools (Grace 2002: ch. 4; Jackson, 2003a; Judge, 2001b; Walford, 1995), and (perhaps above all) government policy which provides for an expansion of the number of these schools within the maintained system. The range of objections and issues of concern which have been raised in relation to faith schools are equally well known and relate *inter alia* to such matters as the extent to which such schools can provide adequately for the development of the autonomy of their students, particularly with respect to religious faith, and for the demands of education for citizenship (cf. Pring in this volume).

The specific charge of divisiveness made against faith schools is not new. A concern with divisiveness is prominent in the discussion of separate schools in the Swann Report (Great Britain, Parliament, House of Commons 1985: ch. 8, II) and a similar concern has long been manifest in discussions critical of denominational schooling from various perspectives (see, for example, Socialist Educational Association, 1986). The charge of divisiveness has been given particular prominence in recent years, however, because of attempts to implicate faith schools in the causes of a number of serious disturbances in parts of the north of England during the summer of 2001. A share of the blame for these disturbances has been laid at the door of faith schools both by journalists and, at least indirectly, by official commissions of inquiry. With regard to the latter, for example, both the Ouseley and the Cantle reports express concern about the possibility that some faith schools may be monocultural and self-segregated and may thus make little contribution to social and racial integration (Bradford District Race Review Team 2001; Community Cohesion Review Team 2001). These developments have led in the policy arena to much discussion about appropriate forms of response, ranging from calls to reconsider the fundamental acceptability of faith schools (especially within the maintained sector) to proposals (particularly relating to policies and criteria governing admissions to faith schools) designed to alleviate the perceived difficulty (see, for example, Community Cohesion Review Team 2001: 34). The claim of 'divisiveness' in relation to faith schools, therefore, enjoys a particular salience and importance at present. Robert Jackson, for example, in judging that this claim constitutes the most convincing argument against faith schools (Jackson 2003b), represents a widely held view.

Before proceeding to discuss the claim in more detail, it is appropriate to note that any discussion of faith schools involves matters of considerable complexity. There are, for example, a range of grounds on which faith schools might be criticised and defended and many of these grounds and the underlying issues of conceptualisation and justification to which they give rise (relating, for example, to such matters as the autonomy of the child and the nature of religious understanding) are far from straightforward. For the purposes of the present discussion, however, the following aspect of complexity is particularly worthy of attention.

Discussions about faith schools involve an intricate mixture of considerations of principle and of practice. Neither the question of how we should interpret 'divisiveness', nor the way we should understand the term 'faith school', nor the overall judgement about whether faith schools are indeed divisive in any sense can be coherently answered on grounds of either principle or practice alone. Considerations of principle are involved in arguments relating to such matters as the educational rights of parents and the duties of the state with respect to the education of its citizens. Considerations of practice arise in relation to questions about the actual operation of particular schools in particular contexts (cf. Brighouse in this volume), including the influence which is actually exerted by the school upon students and upon society as a whole. It is not easy, however, to achieve an appropriate mixture of considerations of principle and practice in any argument and judgement, especially when the distinction between the two kinds of consideration is itself complex.

Claims about divisiveness

The claim that faith schools are 'divisive' can be understood in a number of different ways and it is necessary to bring the different interpretations of the claim carefully into focus. A number of different interpretations are distinguished here, although the distinctions we make are somewhat artificial: different senses of 'divisive' are often combined by critics of the alleged 'divisiveness' of faith schools.

Prior to considering the notion of 'divisiveness' in more detail it is useful at this point to outline briefly two basic related characteristics of faith schools which distinguish them from schools of other kinds, and with which claims of divisiveness are particularly related. These two features of faith schools can be described as involving, first, *distinctive non-common educational aims* and, second, *restricted non-common educational environments*. Putting matters roughly, faith schools can be said to have *distinctive non-common educational aims* in that they typically aspire as part of a particular holistic vision of education to present a particular religion as if it is true and good, together with a range of other beliefs, values and attitudes (particularly of a moral kind) which follow from this. These aims are distinctive and non-common in that, in pluralistic democracies, they are not shared by society as a whole. The extent to which these distinctive non-common aims are compatible with, or to some degree in conflict with, wider society is a matter to which we will return. Faith schools involve restricted *non-common educational environments* because the very nature of the school involves the separation of a group of children and young people for schooling from the rest of society: a Catholic, Jewish or Muslim school, for example, is intended primarily for children and young people of that faith, despite the fact that, for various reasons, admissions to the school may extend beyond these boundaries. The educational environment of a faith school is 'restricted' and 'non-common' in that it is precisely intended for a particular group within society and not for society as a whole. The extent of restriction involved in any given educational environment in a faith school is another matter to which we shall return shortly.

This preliminary delineation of the basic features of a faith school encounters the immediate objection that not all faith schools share these features. Most notably, some Church of England schools espouse a broader 'service' model to the community which involves a rejection of both of these features (Church Schools Review Group 2001). For example, such schools do not necessarily seek to form the religious beliefs of their students, as distinct from providing a particular ethos within which predominantly common educational aims can be pursued. It is schools of this kind which the Humanist Philosophers' Group have in mind in their observation that not all faith schools satisfy their definition of a religious school as one which '... intentionally encourages its pupils to have particular religious beliefs and ... regards such encouragement as a significant part of its mission' (Humanist Philosophers' Group 2001: 8). Geoffrey Short does not include such schools in his consideration of the divisiveness or otherwise of faith schools (Short 2002: 570, footnote 1). Whilst such schools do not fall within the scope of our immediate concern we do consider that they give rise to some questions of alleged divisiveness and we will touch on these questions at a later point. At this stage of the discussion, however, we will focus discussion on faith schools which possess and embrace in a more straightforward way the two basic features we have identified.

Both of these basic features of a faith school, distinctive non-common educational aims and restricted non-common educational environments, can be seen as potentially generative of 'divisiveness' in some sense of the term. The notion of 'divisiveness' can be clarified by distinguishing three broad categories of 'divisiveness' discernible in contemporary discussion.

The first sense of 'divisiveness' involves nothing more than a truism: that, of their very nature, faith schools provide a distinctive education designed specifically for a distinctive sub-group of society. Here, 'divide' may mean little more than 'categorise' and 'separate'. It is true that faith schools of their nature 'categorise' and 'separate' students, but a description of such processes as 'divisive' in any sense which implies criticism requires attention to specific intentions and consequences judged as negative or harmful.

The second sense of 'divisiveness' points to a range of consequences of faith schools that relate to evident negative and harmful social phenomena, including the encapsulation of students in particular cultural traditions, the creation and reinforcement of social divisions, damage to social integration and harmony by a failure to bring students from different faith and cultural backgrounds together at a formative stage of their development, and a tendency for faith schools to serve sectional interests. Claims about the 'divisive' effects of faith schools in these respects can be readily illustrated. Faith schools have been accused of fragmenting society by segregating communities in a kind of 'educational apartheid' (Herbert 2001), encouraging insularity, a sense of 'self-identity' forged in opposition to the broader society and the leading of 'parallel lives'. In these and other ways faith schools stand accused of bringing about and perpetuating forms of ghettoisation, where loyalties to a particular faith community predominate over loyalties of a wider kind. Evils of these kinds, it is argued, lead to strife between communities and affect the social and political stability of the broader society, producing or perpetuating the sort of strife seen in Northern Ireland (brought into particular focus in recent years by the dispute involving the Holy Cross Primary School in Belfast) and in the riots in the north of England in 2001. Faith schools have been seen as a possible contributory factor in both contexts of strife (on the role of segregated schooling in Northern Ireland, see Cairns, Dunn and Giles 1993, and for the attitude of the Ouseley Report towards faith schools in the context of race relations, see Bradford District Race Review Team 2001). Faith schools have even been accused of being potential breeding grounds for terrorism (cf. the comments by Peter Smith in a speech to the annual conference of the Association of Teachers and Lecturers – see Sellgren 2002). The claim that faith schools serve only sectional interests can be seen in accusations that (for instance) Seventh Day Adventist, Muslim and Sikh schools serve the interests of the adherents of these faiths at the expense of broader interests. A prominent source of concern in relation to these alleged negative and harmful social consequences of faith schools is the involvement of ethnic minorities in many of the phenomena. Here faith schools can be seen as exacerbating the prejudice, exclusion and alienation which many members of such groups experience. Another source of concern is ambiguity about the role of specifically religious motivation on the part of families in choosing faith schools. In many cases, other motives and factors with implications for social divisiveness (such as those relating to racial prejudice, social class and academic ambition) may be operating.

A third (and clearly related) sense of 'divisiveness' involves the beliefs and attitudes which faith schools develop in their students about a range of matters. Some beliefs and attitudes may be seen as related in a very close way to the negative and harmful social phenomena, such as cultural encapsulation, which feature in the second interpretation of 'divisiveness'. It is useful, however, to separate allegedly divisive beliefs and attitudes from negative and harmful social phenomena, for at least two reasons. The first reason is that the link between any given set of beliefs and attitudes and the social phenomena in question cannot be merely assumed but is an important matter for investigation. The second reason is that attention is needed to the detailed beliefs and attitudes which faith schools are in fact seeking to develop in their students as part of the non-common educational influence which they exert. Some lines of criticism imply that certain beliefs and attitudes are themselves 'divisive', whether or not they lead to the kinds of social consequences described earlier. The beliefs and attitudes in question here include claims that (for example) a certain religion and its associated values and perspectives are true and that others are false or at best suboptimal, that certain lifestyles and moral choices within the law are in fact morally unacceptable from the point of view of that religion, and so forth. Such beliefs and attitudes can be seen as undermining the 'respect' which is due to others with whom we disagree, and are therefore in conflict with the demands of a liberal democratic society even if they do not lead to overt social expression. The demands of a liberal democratic society, it is implied, must ensure that attitudes to difference must be located firmly within forms of respect inconsistent with the sorts of beliefs and attitudes which have been described. Faith schools may therefore be accused of failing to develop, model and institutionalise attitudes necessary for the well-being and development of a liberal democratic society, sometimes in quite subtle ways.

The forms of alleged divisiveness which have been distinguished underpin calls for the 'common school' to be seen as the preferable environment in which students in a liberal democratic society can be appropriately educated.

Before examining these claims of alleged divisiveness in more detail it is appropriate to examine the notion of a faith school more closely.

Faith schools: nature and variety

We have identified two basic related characteristics of faith schools as involving *distinctive non-common educational aims* and *restricted non-common educational environments*. We have also acknowledged that not all faith schools can be seen as exhibiting these characteristics unproblematically, most notably Church of England schools pursuing a 'service to the community' conception of their task.

Faith schools differ from each other in a number of different and familiar ways. Some of these differences are shared with schools in general, such as social and geographical location (with its wide-ranging educational implications of various kinds), the age range of the students admitted, the specific circumstances of the history and situation of the school, whether the school is part of the publicly funded educational system (and, if so, in what category) and so forth. A number of differences are, however, specific to faith schools. These differences relate *inter alia* to the particular 'sponsoring' religious body with which the faith school is associated together with the specific educational aims, principles and values derived from the beliefs and tradition of the religion in question.

One major difference between faith schools which is pertinent to the question of their divisiveness is often expressed roughly in terms of the extent to which a given faith school is 'liberal'. In this connection, the distinction between 'old' and 'new' religious schools is particularly significant (Halstead 2002). Whilst the description of this aspect of difference in terms of the extent to which faith schools are 'liberal' is inadequate as it stands, it can serve for the moment as a very broad way of referring to a range of matters often considered significant for the present discussion. These matters involve concerns about the extent to which, whilst faith schools are inevitably engaged in 'education in religion from the inside' (Alexander and McLaughlin 2003: 369–72), their engagement embodies a concern with the development of forms of rational autonomy (including critical understanding) and democratic citizenship (including civic virtue). Such concerns are reflected in questions about the extent to which faith schools are 'indoctrinatory' and inattentive to the demands of a liberal democratic society. Any attempt to distinguish between faith schools on these kinds of grounds is, however, fraught with the sorts of complexity and difficulty alluded to earlier.

This complexity and difficulty can be seen in connection with matters of both principle and practice together with the relationship between the two. It might be thought that one way of identifying faith schools which are more rather than less concerned with matters such as rational autonomy and democratic citizenship would be to look at issues of principle relating to the religious faith in question and its educational vision (for a categorisation of different kinds of religious faiths relevant to this question see Spinner-Halev 2000: ch. 1). At least two problems at the level of principle arise immediately. First, the nature, demands and justification of the notions of 'rational autonomy' and 'democratic citizenship' are themselves complex and contestable. With regard to rational autonomy and critical reason, for example, some forms of these notions and ideals are part of any coherent and flourishing religious tradition. It is difficult, however, to specify the precise ways in which a given religion might fall short in respect of its conceptualisation and valuing of such matters viewed from a liberal educational perspective. The same general point can be made about 'democratic citizenship' and 'civic virtue'. The need for careful and nuanced interpretation of these matters in relation to any religious tradition is intensified when diversity *within* religious traditions is acknowledged.

A second difficulty at the level of principle is that the educational vision of faith schools is rarely articulated in precise terms, including matters such as those which are of present concern. Mission statements of faith schools, for example, are often laced with imprecise and platitudinous rhetoric or 'edubabble' which requires a good deal of clarification and interpretation, much of it in the context of complex forms of pedagogic judgement exhibited in practice by teachers and educational leaders (McLaughlin 1999).

At the level of practice, two problems can be identified. First, the complexity of the task of judging the extent to which any school is failing with respect to the development of rational autonomy and democratic citizenship is clear. The difficulties here arise in part from the need to arrive at a clear and defensible interpretation of these notions and in part from the sheer practical difficulty of making confident empirical judgements about what is happening in the school with respect to them. A second difficulty at the level of practice is that, even within the faith schools of a particular religion, there is a diversity of inter-pretation about what some of these notions imply. Further difficulties arise in relation to the interface of the domains of principle and practice. One of the difficulties here lies in assessing the extent to which any practical state of affairs in a faith school is genuinely reflective of principle or expressive merely of the need to achieve a *de facto* compromise. It is often difficult, for example, to assess the extent to which the admission by a faith school of numbers of students who are not adherents of the faith in question is based on grounds of principle or pragmatic adjustment.

Some of the issues discussed in this section will come more clearly into focus as our discussion proceeds.

Exploring faith schools and divisiveness

Having attempted to bring both the notion of 'divisiveness' and the notion of a 'faith school' into clearer focus, we turn to an examination of our main question, 'Are faith schools divisive?'

In the first sense of 'divisive', where 'divisive' means nothing more than 'categorised' and 'separate', it must be conceded that, of their very nature, faith schools are 'divisive' in this sense. Since, however, this sense of 'divisive' does not, without further argument, necessarily imply any criticism, it will not be pursued here.

In the second sense of 'divisive', which points to a range of consequences of faith schools relating to negative and harmful social phenomena of various kinds, a number of important points can be made. Two points will be concentrated upon here.

The first point is that the relationship between faith schools and any given social phenomenon is a matter for detailed and sensitive empirical investigation. A number of alternative perspectives on the relationship between faith schools and negative and harmful social phenomena of various kinds are not only possible but plausible. For example, it can be argued that faith schools do not create *de facto* segregated ghetto-like social environments, but that these schools are themselves created by these environments (this is a particularly plausible claim in the case of the Muslim minority community, in that the concentration of Muslim children in inner-city common schools generally predates any attempts to establish Muslim schools). Similarly, it can be argued that separate schools in Northern Ireland are not the cause of community conflict, but one of the results of it. Further, it can be argued that the disturbances in the north of England in 2001, and the 'parallel lives' of which the Cantle Report speaks (Community Cohesion Review Team 2001: 9), are caused by economic disadvantage, unfair treatment, discrimination, exclusion and social despair, not by disagreements about faith. There is something ironic about criticising the victims of divisive socioeconomic policies (the disadvantaged ethnic minorities) for favouring divisive educational policies. There is currently no evidence available to link Muslim or other faith schools to political extremism or civil unrest; the hypothetical possibility remains that this might happen in the future, but it is unlikely because children who have a strong self-identity and who are treated fairly and justly by the broader society are much more likely to grow up into tolerant, balanced and responsible citizens. There is no evidence that faith schools are the cause of enmity between religious groups in general. In sum, any confident or wide-ranging claims about the relationship between faith schools and social phenomena of a negative and harmful kind are misplaced. This is not to suggest that equally confident and wide ranging claims about the non-involvement of faith schools in such phenomena can necessarily be made. Our point is rather that careful and sensitive empirical investigation is needed about these matters, which is attentive to some of the aspects of complexity which we have identified.

The second point is that it is important to take into account in the overall evaluation of matters the contribution of faith schools to positive and beneficial social phenomena (Short 2003). There is much research which demonstrates the positive relationship between attendance at Catholic schools and positive social outcomes of various kinds. The sociological research of Greeley and Rossi (1966), for example, concludes that Catholics educated in Catholic schools are just as likely as Catholics educated in public schools to be interested in community affairs and to have non-Catholic visitors, friends, neighbours and co-workers, and that there are no differences in tolerance or divisive attitudes between the two. The more recent research by Bryk *et al.* concludes that, compared to public schools, Catholic schools in the United States of America have not only a more positive effect upon the achievement of students (particularly those from minority and disadvantaged backgrounds) but also that these schools are contributing more successfully to the development of citizens and to the common good in a pluralist democratic society (Bryk *et al.* 1993). There are many faith schools, both Christian and Muslim, that serve the most deprived inner-city communities, and some (e.g. Church of England schools) that serve communities other than their own (either Muslim or mixed faith) and thus contribute directly to the multicultural society. Other faith schools (e.g. Muslim ones) are designed to serve children from their own communities, but as they become more accepted and established may come to serve other communities as well (as do the Muslim schools in Hong Kong, for example). There is a growing number of joint faith schools that offer children many opportunities to learn respect and understanding for those of other faith traditions than their own. The experience of integrated schools in Northern Ireland and joint Roman Catholic-Anglican schools on mainland Britain has generally been positive (Chadwick 1994; Smith 2001), and in 2002 plans were put forward by a committee made up of Christian, Jewish, Muslim, Hindu and Sikh representatives for a multifaith secondary school in Westminster (Wittenberg 2002).

The third sense of 'divisive' points to the beliefs and attitudes which faith schools develop in their students about a range of matters which may be seen as 'divisive' not because they lead in to clearly negative and harmful social phenomena, but because they are 'divisive' in a deeper sense. Thus it might be claimed that if a faith school teaches that its faith is true, and that (for example) certain sexual practices within the law such as premarital and homosexual sex are from its perspective gravely wrong, then it is failing to show toleration and respect to adherents of other faiths and of no faith, to unmarried couples engaged in a sexual relationship and to sexually active homosexual persons. In order to evaluate this claim, it is necessary to bring into focus a proper understanding of notions such as 'diversity' and 'pluralism' within the context of a pluralist liberal democratic society. 'Diversity' and 'pluralism' involve a complex balance between unifying and diversifying values, forces and imperatives. The unifying elements involve a framework of commonly accepted values, practices and procedures within which the diversifying elements (particular conceptions of the good held by, say, religious citizens) are situated. Unifying elements in pluralist liberal democratic societies are essential. In such societies the specific teachings of particular religions cannot be definitive in the 'public' domain because religious concepts, assumptions and interpretations are significantly controversial, and they lack the capacity to secure the free assent of all citizens on grounds which all can regard as reasonable. A concern to prevent conflict arising from controversial religious beliefs in relation to 'public' matters in such societies has long been a central feature of the liberal project in its various forms. However, this project has also been concerned to secure as much religious freedom as is compatible with fundamental liberal democratic values and to this end has postulated and insisted upon the important distinction between 'public' and 'non-public' domains (Rawls 1993).

However, attention has recently been focused by a number of thinkers on the need to recognise in a more sensitive way the significance and demands of normative diversity and the 'non-public' domain and the respects in which the unifying elements in such societies can exert an illicitly homogenising effect upon them (Spinner-Halev 2000; Tomasi 2001). One of these homogenising forces is an interpretation of notions such as 'toleration' and 'respect' in an inflated way which blurs the distinction between 'public' and 'non-public' domains and modes of evaluation and which suggests that any espousal and advocacy of a religiously based evaluation of a controversial matter is *ipso facto* expressive of intolerance or lack of respect (White 2003: 155–7). However, this view neglects the important point that whilst citizens must grasp the importance of public values for political purposes, they should also come to appreciate the limitations of these values with respect to overall moral evaluation and to life considered more broadly. The language of public evaluation is a kind of 'moral pidgin' (Strike 1994: 19) and a form of 'moral economising' (Gutmann and Thompson 1996: 85–91) which is self-consciously circumscribed and limited. 'Civic' respect does not constitute the only form of respect and what is worthy of 'civic' respect is not necessarily worthy of respect considered from all points of view. The shortcomings of liberal public reason in relation to our thinking about human good in an overall sense needs to be acknowledged (Callan 2002, especially pp. 131–2). 'Respect' therefore cannot be interpreted as requiring the ✓ necessary approval of choices which people make within the limits of their civic rights. John Tomasi argues that greater attention is needed to the non-public virtues and personality traits which should characterise citizens in a pluralist liberal democratic society and which are not related solely to 'public' questions of justice and legitimacy. Such a society must, in his view, be as welcoming as possible to '… the aims and self-understandings of all politically reasonable citizens' (Tomasi 2001: 74). For Tomasi, citizenship requires the skilful exercise of non-public reason by 'diverse good souls' as part of their making a success of their lives '… lived on the interface of public and personal identity components' (*ibid.*: 75) and involving their search for personal meaning across this interface in the discovery of what their political autonomy means for them in the light of their fuller conception of the good and the guidance it offers to them regarding the way in which they should live their lives and exercise their rights. Religious citizens, for example, need to be able to understand the *fit* between the demands of public reason and the demands of their own religious faith. In presenting to students the distinctive moral perspectives of their particular faith, faith schools are contributing to the formation of citizens who can achieve the sort of equipoise between their political standing and their fuller view of life as a whole which Tomasi sees as an important feature of liberal citizenship, properly understood.

Common schools often fail to deal adequately with matters of moral texture and complexity, and their influence can often be biased towards 'public' considerations and modes of evaluation, sometimes in a subtle way (McLaughlin 2003). The faith school is well placed to counteract this tendency. Much depends, of course, on the extent to which faith schools undertake this task in a way which respects legitimate 'public' and unifying values, forces and imperatives. The task of faith schools – and, for that matter, common schools – in relation to the proper educational handling of 'respect' is very complex. Spinner-Halev identifies a central problem here in his question: 'How do we teach mutual respect and appreciation for others while avoiding teaching that each way of life is equally acceptable to the others?' (Spinner-Halev 2000: 133). However, the claim that the sort of influence of faith schools in relation to the kind of distinctive moral perspectives which we have identified is in principle inherently divisive is unjustified. Such influence can contribute to the development of liberal citizenship properly understood and it should be remembered that illicit homogenisation based on 'public' values is itself divisive.

With these considerations in mind, we can now turn to what Greeley and Rossi call 'the central assumption of the divisiveness theory' (1966: 117), namely that 'if young people are put into a school with members of other religious denominations, the probability of their associating on a fairly intimate basis with these members of other faiths are [sic] increased' (ibid.). It is assumed that the core civic virtues needed in contemporary multicultural societies (such as tolerance, respect and goodwill towards others) will thus be more easily developed in the common school. However, the deceptively simple form in which this 'contact hypothesis' is presented masks a number of further complexities, which once again combine issues of principle and practice.

First, it is clear that where the common school serves different cultural and religious communities it has to adopt a form of neutrality with respect to significantly controversial matters, either by attempting to illuminate different perspectives for discussion or by remaining silent about, or underplaying, points of controversy. This stance can help to reinforce a number of core liberal values, including the need for fairness, equality and impartiality in the public domain and the need to avoid privileging one particular faith or worldview in that domain. The problem is that it may also encourage a strong form of relativism. Children may learn not only that different religions must be treated this way in a pluralist society, but also that all religions are as good as each other and that they themselves should be equally accepting of each in an unequivocal as well as in a civic way. This will tend to undermine the distinctiveness and integrity of any particular faith and the significance of that faith in the development of individual children. One important aim of faith schools is to counter the dominant ethos of secularity and cultural relativism in common schools and to provide a context in which children can explore and develop their own distinctive religious beliefs and identity. This aim is far removed from making pupils intolerant and disrespectful of others. Whether it is 'culturally encapsulating' – like indoc- trination, an emotive term – may depend on one's perspective. Our view is that it is not necessarily so, and from the perspective of the believer it might actually liberate children from the dominance of religious and cultural relativism.

Second, we have already referred to one of the key findings of the socio-psychological research of Greeley and Rossi (1996): that there were no differences in tolerance or divisive attitudes between Catholics educated in common schools and those educated in Catholic schools. But there is nothing in principle that should surprise us about this. Faith schools can make a strong contribution to preparing their students for citizenship and life in a liberal democratic multicultural society. Many faith schools emphasise attitudes such as tolerance and respect and are attempting to be more responsive to issues of citizenship and multicultural understanding (Jackson 2003b; Short 2002, 2003; Sasano 2003). The distinctive contribution which faith schools can make to citizenship and life in a liberal democratic society includes the nuanced understandings which it can provide for students of concepts such as 'respect' and 'tolerance', which are necessary if religious believers are to be protected against illicitly assimilative pressures of the sort alluded to earlier. If we interpret 'toleration' as referring to the disposition to accept or put up with something of which one disapproves, then this implies that the tolerant person possesses a framework of distinctive values which provides the basis both for the initial and continuing disapproval and for the conscious decision for various reasons not to interfere with others and to accord them 'civic respect'. There is a sense, then, in which toleration presupposes being confident in one's own beliefs and values and having a clear self-identity. Perhaps this is just as important as actually being educated alongside children from different faiths and worldviews, and this is something that faith schools are well placed to provide. It should also be remembered that religious faiths provide much evaluative 'capital' which supports the 'unifying' aspects of a society, including love of others and a contra-individualistic concern for the common good.

In sum, it has been suggested that, as far as children brought up in a religious tradition are concerned, faith schools may help them to explore their own distinctive faith and culture in greater depth. Further, they may provide a stable, secure context in which they can develop a confident sense of identity and self-image and a basis on which they can locate themselves as citizens of a liberal democratic society in a way that helps them to resist assimilative pressures whilst providing them with deep resources for motivations of a contra-individualistic kind, which are strongly resonant with the 'unifying' needs of a liberal multicultural democratic society.

Conclusion

To return to the point made at the beginning of this chapter, we have argued that a close examination of the charge of divisiveness against faith schools suggests that it carries insufficient *prima facie* general weight to 'trump' the right of religious parents and communities to send their children to these schools with the support of public funding, not least because common schools can themselves be divisive in various ways. The divisiveness or otherwise of faith schools can only be properly judged in the light of an assessment of the adequacy with respect to divisiveness of the alternatives. We have suggested that sectional interests sometimes need special attention, to avoid domination by the cultural majority, and that for a society to be truly plural it needs the recognition of group rights and a plurality of structures. It may also be divisive to make some parents but not others pay twice for an education which is in line with their own cultural values and philosophy (cf. De Jong and Snik 2002). It needs also to be borne in mind that if faith schools are divisive only in the sense that they provide a distinctive education for a distinctive sub-group of society, this does not in itself generate more serious consequences than those schools which divide children by age, sex, ability, language, subject specialism or the ability of their family to pay fees.

We have conceded that divisiveness in some significant sense may be a matter for concern in relation to some faith schools in some contexts. Some Church of England 'service' model faith schools, and others, may be implicated in attempts by some parents to avoid their children mixing with members of ethnic minority groups (Harris 2002: 34). It may be true that some middle-class parents will try to search out whatever they consider to be the best education for their children, whether in terms of academic results, ethnic composition or caring ethos (cf. Schagen *et al.* 2002: 47), and if church schools are perceived to provide these, then they will do all they can to get their children accepted by such schools, even to the extent of being economical with the truth about their religious beliefs and practice. However, we would argue that the divisiveness in this case is incidental rather than intrinsic to the mission of these schools (cf. Hinsliff 2001), and is best dealt with as any examples of unfair privilege would be dealt with, by equalising provision and resources, rather than by getting rid of the whole category of faith schools. A further difficulty is that forms of regulation may be needed to ensure that faith schools are indeed satisfying defensible civic imperatives in their teaching (cf. Community Cohesion Review Team 2001; Halstead 2003), and these forms of regulation may be difficult to specify.

Overall, however, we conclude that an important step forward in assessing the divisiveness or otherwise of faith schools is to acknowledge that questions about the divisiveness or otherwise of these schools do not involve merely complex empirical judgements. Deeper issues are at stake, including related philosophical, religious, political and cultural considerations, which touch *inter alia* upon what is thought to constitute divisiveness and its corresponding virtues.

References

Alexander, H. and McLaughlin, T.H. (2003) 'Education in Religion and Spirituality', in Blake N., Smeyers P., Smith R. and Standish P. (eds) *The Blackwell Guide to the Philosophy of Education* (Oxford: Blackwell).

Bradford District Race Review Team (2001) *Community Pride not Prejudice: Making Diversity Work in Bradford (the Ouseley Report)* (Bradford: Bradford Vision).

Bryk, A.S., Lee, V.E. and Holland, P.B. (1993) *Catholic Schools and the Common Good* (Cambridge, MA: Harvard University Press).

Cairns, E., Dunn, S. and Giles, M. (1993) 'Surveys of integrated education in Northern Ireland: a review', in Osborne, R., Cormack, R. and Gallagher, A. (eds) *After the Reforms: Education and Policy in Northern Ireland* (Aldershot: Avebury).

Callan, E. (2002) 'Autonomy, child-rearing and good lives', in Archard, D. and Macleod, C.M. (eds) *The Moral and Political Status of Children* (Oxford: Oxford University Press).

Chadwick, P. (1994) *Schools of Reconciliation: Issues in Joint Roman Catholic–Anglican Education* (London: Cassell).

Church Schools Review Group (2001) *The Way Ahead: Church of England Schools in the New Millennium* (London: Church House Publishing).

Community Cohesion Review Team (2001) *Community Cohesion: Report of the Independent Review Team Chaired by Ted Cantle* (London: Home Office).

Dawkins, R. (2001) 'No faith in the absurd', *Times Educational Supplement*, 23 February: 17.

De Jong, J. and Snik, G. (2002) 'Why Should States Fund Denominational Schools?' *Journal of Philosophy of Education*, 36(4): 573–87.

Grace, G. (2002) *Catholic Schools: mission, markets and morality* (London, RoutledgeFalmer).

Great Britain, Parliament, House of Commons (1985) *Education for All*. The Report of the Committee of Inquiry into the Education of Children from Ethnic Minority Groups (Swann Report) cmnd 9453 (London: HMSO).

Greeley, A.M. and Rossi, P.H. (1996) *The Education of Catholic Americans* (Chicago: Aldine).

Gutmann, A. and Thompson, D. (1996) *Democracy and Disagreement: Why Moral Conflict Cannot be Avoided in Politics and What Should be Done About it* (Cambridge: Cambridge University Press).

Halstead, J.M. (1986) *The Case for Muslim Voluntary-aided Schools: Some Philosophical Reflections* (Cambridge: Islamic Academy).

Halstead, J.M. (1988) *Education, Justice and Cultural Diversity: An Examination of the Honeyford Affair 1984–85* (London, Falmer Press).

Halstead, J.M. (2002) 'Faith and diversity in religious school provision', in Gearon, L. (ed.) *Education in the United Kingdom: Structures and Organisation* (London: David Fulton).

Halstead, J.M. (2003) 'Schooling and cultural maintenance for religious minorities in the liberal state', in McDonough, K. and Feinberg, W. (eds) *Citizenship and Education in Liberal Democratic Societies: Teaching for Cosmopolitan Values and Collective Identities* (Oxford: Oxford University Press).

Harris, F. (2002) 'Do We Really Want More Faith Schools?' *Education Review*, 15(1): 32–6.

Herbert, I. (2001) '"Apartheid" fears over first Muslim secondary school in state sector', *The Independent*, 2 April: 11.

Hinsliff, G. (2001) 'Single-faith schools target well-off', *The Observer*, 18 November.

Humanist Philosophers' Group (2001) *Religious Schools: The Case Against* (London: British Humanist Association).

Jackson, R. (ed.) (2003a) Special issue, 'The faith-based schools debate', *British Journal of Religious Education*, 25(2).

Jackson, R. (2003b) 'Should the state fund faith-based schools? A review of the arguments', *British Journal of Religious Education*, 25(2): 89–102.

Judge, H. (2001a) 'Faith-based Schools and State Funding: a partial argument', *Oxford Review of Education*, 27(4): 463–74.

Judge, H. (ed.) (2001b) Special issue, 'The state, schools and religion', *Oxford Review of Education* 27(4).

Mabud, S.A. (2002) Editorial, 'Can Muslim faith schools be divisive?', *Muslim Education Quarterly*, 19(2): 1–3.

McLaughlin, T.H. (1999) 'Distinctiveness and the Catholic School: balanced judgement and the temptations of commonality', in Conroy, J.C. (ed.) *Catholic Education: Inside-out/Outside-in* (Dublin: Veritas).

McLaughlin, T.H. (2003) 'The Burdens and Dilemmas of Common Schooling', in McDonough, K. and Feinberg, W. (eds) *Citizenship and Education in Liberal Democratic Societies: Teaching for Cosmopolitan Values and Collective Identities* (Oxford: Oxford University Press).

Rawls, J. (1993) *Political Liberalism* (New York: Columbia University Press).

Sasano, Y. (2003) 'The creation of British Muslim identity in the Islamic schools of London'. Unpublished MPhil thesis, Hitotsubashi University, Japan.

Schagen, S., Davies, D., Rudd, P. and Schagen, I. (2002) *The Impact of Specialist and Faith Schools on Performance* (Slough: National Foundation for Educational Research).

Sellgren, K. (2002) 'Warning about "Bin Laden schools"', *BBC News Online*, available online at http://www.news.bbc.co.uk/hi/english/education/vewsid_1893000/1893911.stm.

Short, G. (2002) 'Faith-based schools: a threat to social cohesion?', *Journal of Philosophy of Education*, 36(4): 559–72.

Short, G. (2003) 'Faith schools and social cohesion: opening up the debate', *British Journal of Religious Education*, 25(2): 129–41.

Smith, A. (2001) 'Religious segregation and the emergence of integrated schools in Northern Ireland', *Oxford Review of Education*, 27(4): 559–75.

Socialist Educational Association (1986) *All Faiths in All Schools* (London: SEA).

Spinner-Halev, J. (2000) *Surviving Diversity: Religion and Democratic Citizenship* (Baltimore and London: The Johns Hopkins University Press).

Strike, K.A. (1994) 'On the construction of public speech: pluralism and public reason', *Educational Theory*, 44(1): 1–26.

Tomasi, J. (2001) *Liberalism Beyond Justice: Citizens, Society, and the Boundaries of Political Theory* (Princeton and Oxford: Princeton University Press).

Toynbee, P. (2001) 'Keep God out of class', *The Guardian*, 9 November.

Walford, G. (1995) *Educational Politics, Pressure Groups and Faith-based Schools* (Aldershot: Avebury).

Wittenberg, J. (2002) *A Faith-based School for Many Faiths* (London: Multifaith Secondary School Trust).

White, J. (2003) 'Five critical stances towards liberal philosophy of education in Britain', *Journal of Philosophy of Education*, 37(1): 147–84.

6 Religion and schools – a fresh way forward?[1]

A rights-based approach to diversity in schools

Marilyn Mason

This chapter is based on the British Humanist Association's ongoing work on education policy and is in part a response to the Church of England's proposals in The Way Ahead (Archbishops' Council, 2001) to expand the number of church schools. Responses to the initial proposals made by the British Humanist Association (BHA) were analysed and assimilated, and this evolved into a policy paper A Better Way Forward, now published in full on BHA's website (BHA 2002).

Contemporary thinking and legislation on human rights and discrimination have implications for religion in schools and religious schools, and this chapter focuses on arguments against the existence and expansion of religious schools based on considerations of human rights (particularly children's rights). It is also based on a positive and inclusive alternative located in reforms and accommodations within the community school system – a 'way forward' from the incoherent and problematical status quo. It also asks whether the necessary changes would be possible within religious schools.

Humanists and faith-based schools

Humanists have long opposed religious schools as discriminatory, unnecessary and potentially very divisive. Our policies arose out of humanist principles and concern for the common good and commitment to human rights. Humanists think that religious belief should be a private matter, that there should be no state religion, and that the public arena, including schools, should be strictly neutral on matters of religion and belief; schools should promote social cohesion, based on shared human values and mutual respect.

Humanists believe that inclusive pluralist community schools, and even inclusive pluralist religious schools if they were feasible, could meet the requirements of both the religious and the non-religious without compromising the human rights and educational entitlements of all pupils, and that this is vastly preferable to fragmenting the education system along religious lines. This does not entail the exclusion of religion from schools. Humanists respect the right to hold and practise religious beliefs and are not advocating a completely secular system: religious education (RE), as long as it is genuinely educational, has a place in schools, and there should be room for religious observance, as long as it is voluntary.

The history of these proposals

A policy on religion and schools, A Fresh Way Forward, was drafted and presented to Government by the British Humanist Association in late 2001. The policy was refined during a period of discussion and consultation in 2001 and 2002. This included public presentations, debates, seminars (including a very useful one in March 2002 hosted by the Institute for Public Policy Research), correspondence with the Minister for Schools, and a consultation document circulated to faith communities and other interested parties in March–May 2002. Written responses were received to that consultation, as well as e-mails and letters, and many useful and relevant meetings and conversations took place with people of all faiths and none. Reminders along the way that humanists share some of the desires and complaints of religious minorities included: participation in an inter-faith working party brought together by the Sex Education Forum; reading the contribution of Professor Marie Parker-Jenkins to a Home Office research study on religious discrimination (Weller et al., 2001); and talking to a young Jewish father who had been so unhappy as the sole Jewish pupil at his comprehensive school, 'excluded' (his word) from assemblies, that he was determined to protect his children from similar experiences by sending them to a Jewish school. This process, though far from scientific and largely unquantifiable, influenced the development of our policies.

Human rights and other relevant legislation

Humanists note with approval that legislation on human rights and discrimination now normally includes us by using the terms 'religion or belief' or 'religious and philosophical convictions'.

However, discrimination on grounds of religion or belief remains widespread in the educational system, and demand for religious schools is partly fuelled by that discrimination. Professor Parker-Jenkins' research on religious discrimination found that schools and teachers were among the worst perpetrators of discrimination, the victims of which included Hindus, Bahá'is, Pagans, Jehovah's Witnesses, Muslims, Sikhs and black Christian groups. Examples of discrimination included the institutional (admissions policies, aspects of the National Curriculum, collective worship, inflexibility over dress, holidays and examination time-tables, school outings and marginalisation) and the personal (insensitive remarks). One example was of a teacher exclaiming to a Bahá'i child that he'd never heard of Bahá'i and that the child must be making it up.

Humanists can provide their own examples of discrimination, exclusion and marginalisation, caused by the admissions policies of church schools, by the legal 'default Christian' position of community schools, and by human failings, such as the incident reported by a humanist parent whose son, when he admitted not believing in God in a junior school music lesson, was told by the teacher, 'Well, you will when you grow up.'

It may seem paradoxical to use human rights to argue against religious schools, but less so if one begins with children's rights as expressed in the Convention on the Rights of the Child (CRC), adopted by the United Nations in 1989 (United Nations 1989), and ratified by the British government in 1991.

> States Parties shall take all appropriate measures to ensure that the child is protected against all forms of discrimination or punishment on the basis of the status, activities, expressed opinions, or beliefs of the child's parents, legal guardians, or family members.
> (CRC, Article 2, 2)

The exclusion of children from religious schools on the grounds of parental belief must be contrary to the intentions of the CRC, and a proliferation of religious schools will increase discrimination on the grounds of family belief. For example, the admissions procedures of many church schools discriminate in favour of Christians, as does an Anglican ethos that claims to 'nourish those of the faith, encourage those of other faiths, and challenge those of no faith' (Archbishops' Council 2001).

> In all actions concerning children ... the best interests of the child shall be a primary consideration.
>
> (CRC, Article 3, 1)

> ... the education of the child shall be directed to ... the preparation of the child for responsible life in a free society, in the spirit of understanding, peace, tolerance, equality of sexes, and friendship among all peoples, ethnic, national and religious groups ...
>
> (CRC, Article 29, 1d)

The expansion of religious schools could result in more children getting a limited type of education, chosen by their parents but not necessarily in their best interests. In practice, by dividing children by religion and narrowing their experience, some religious schools will prepare their pupils for segregated lives with restricted future options. Humanists question whether all religious schools can really commit and contribute to a 'free society', 'equality of sexes' and 'tolerance'.

> States Parties shall assure to the child who is capable of forming his or her own views the right to express those views freely in all matters affecting the child, the views of the child being given due weight in accordance with the age and maturity of the child.
>
> (CRC, Article 12, 1)

How much are children's opinions being taken into account? One wonders if local children are included in consultations on proposed religious schools, or if parents will consider their children's views about attending such schools. Young people, including those from ethnic minorities, generally favour integration, as shown, for example, in two recent reports:

> We have been particularly struck by the views of younger people, who, in strong terms, emphasised the need to break down barriers by promoting knowledge and understanding of different cultures.
>   ... Many of those we spoke to preferred integration on many levels and those who had experienced schools with a mixture of faiths, races and cultures were very positive about that environment ...
>
> (Cantle 2001: 5.7.1)

> What was most inspiring was the great desire among young people for better education, more social and cultural interaction ... Some young people have pleaded desperately for this to overcome the negativity that they feel is blighting their lives and leaves them ignorant of other cultures and lifestyles ...
>
> (Ouseley 2001: 5.7.2)

> The child shall have the right to freedom of expression; this right shall include freedom to seek, receive and impart information and ideas of all kinds ...
>
> (CRC, Article 13, 1)

This sounds admirable, and would be furthered by the inclusive policies advocated by the BHA. It is less evident that current school practices conform to the spirit of these statements. It is also questionable whether children in all faith-based schools have this freedom. Some doubtless do but some faith-based schools exist in order to protect children from ideas that are different from those of the parental faith group, or disapproved of by that group. Religious schools are not obliged, as community schools are, to teach religious education covering the principal religions of this country (though even that is woefully narrow when one considers the diversity of beliefs that children could and should learn about in a plural society). The Humanist Philosophers' Group suggests that '… in a free and open society, beliefs about fundamental religious and value commitments should be adopted autonomously and voluntarily' (Humanist Philosophers' Group 2001: 36) but some religious schools are unlikely to accept that.

Up to now, parents' rights (and choices) have tended to take precedence in the debate about religious schools, though it is questionable whether they should always trump other good ends such as children's rights or the cohesion of society, or even whether proposals to increase diversity of school provision will be effective in securing parental rights.

> … In the exercise of any functions which it assumes in relation to education and teaching, the state shall respect the right of parents to ensure such education and teaching in conformity with their own religious and philosophical convictions.
>
> (Human Rights Act 1998 (HRA), First Protocol, Article 2)

Although this clause has been used to argue for diversity of provision and parental choice, it could in fact be better used to argue for common schools that respect many beliefs and offer facilities and opportunities for observance and teaching in conformity with them. Religious schools are unlikely to secure real choice. It is often the school that chooses the children rather than the parent choosing the school, so parents may not get the education they want for their child even where there is, supposedly, choice. Choice tends to favour large well-organised groups, and there will always remain many places where religious minorities are too small to demand or sustain their own schools. And choice or rights for one group often limit the choice or rights of everyone else; for example, there are parts of the country where it is already difficult to find an ordinary (non-church) maintained primary school.

Amnesty International UK has said of this Article that it

> … guarantees people the right to access to existing educational institutions; it does not require the government to establish or fund a particular type of education. The requirement to respect parents' convictions is intended to prevent indoctrination by the state. However, schools can teach about religion and philosophy if they do so in an objective, critical, and pluralistic manner.
>
> (Amnesty International 2000: 22)

The Humanist Philosophers' Group suggests that 'neither parents nor faith communities have a right to call upon the state to help them inculcate their particular religious beliefs in their children …' (2001: 36).

> Everyone has the right to freedom of thought, conscience and religion; this right includes freedom to change his religion or belief, and freedom, either alone or in

community with others and in public or in private, to manifest his religion or belief, in worship, teaching, practice and observance.

(HRA, Article 9, 1)

Presumably 'everyone' includes children but it is unclear how these rights can be adequately respected in religious schools, many of which exist to support and perpetuate one faith rather than to permit the observance of other religions, freedom of thought or changes of belief. Certainly religious schools will be better at permitting the practice of their own religion and at affirming that religion than community schools are, though that raises questions about whether this is rightly the business of the state.

Some vigorous opposition to religious schools has come from women of Asian back-grounds who complain that religious schools stem from an undemocratic multiculturalist model that would deny them the right to change, or to integrate or assimilate, if they want to:

For girls, single-faith schools can become yet another agency that polices their behaviour. Who defines these so-called values and culture? The British state is once again identifying Asian tradition and values with those of the patriarchal forces within the community and excluding other voices that challenge those stereotypes ...

(South Asia Solidarity Group and Asian Women Unite! 2002: 10)

It is not, of course, only religious schools that infringe the right to 'freedom of thought, conscience and religion'. Much appears to depend on the religious beliefs of the head teacher or, in the case of City Technology Colleges, of the sponsors. Most community schools give pupils little or no opportunity to practise any religion other than Christianity, and children do not have the right to excuse themselves from religious observance on grounds of belief or conscience.

The Race Relations (Amendment) Act 2000 places a duty on public authorities, including Whitehall departments and local councils, that they 'shall, in carrying out its functions, have a due regard to the need (a) to eliminate unlawful racial discrimination and (b) to promote equality of opportunity and good relations between persons of different racial groups.'

(Section 71)

It is difficult to see how religious schools can assist this process, when some of them, because of the existence of ethno-religious groups, divide children racially. The government's rather belated recognition of this problem has led to its demand for inclusive policies and for partnerships between schools. But if inclusion and partnerships are genuine and thorough, the raisons d'être of many religious schools will be undermined, as some religious groups have already realised. If they are not, some religious schools will not be able to meet their legal obligations to avoid discrimination and promote good race relations.

Inclusive pluralist schools

In the BHA consultation document responses were asked to the proposals below (which are explained and argued more fully elsewhere [BHA, 2002]). The underlying principles are that common core activities in schools should recognise the rights of all and be acceptable to people of all beliefs and none, and that schools should make 'reasonable accommodations' to meet the legitimate wishes of religious pupils and parents. Support came from a range of respondents, as did opposition: some opposed the proposals for being 'assimilationist' and not sufficiently recognising the importance of religious faith, while others thought them far too accommodating of religious requirements. Though we include some figures in the section below, these should be treated cautiously as respondents were self-selected and selective in their responses.

'*Inclusive school assemblies should replace 'collective worship' with 'quiet rooms' and separate optional prayers and worship for those that require them.*' There was considerable support for the first proposal, including comments to the effect that this was already the position in many schools. Seventy-eight per cent of written responses agreed with it, and with the proposal for 'quiet rooms'. Seventy-two per cent thought that religious schools could also accept these proposals. But respondents pointed out practical difficulties, including problems in ensuring genuinely voluntary participation and distinguishing the wishes and rights of parents from those of children. Comments included: 'Who would decide whether children attended optional prayers – parents or the child?'; 'Would schools become vulnerable to extreme religious groups?'; 'Quiet room ... excellent in theory, but many schools currently lack appropriate space or staff. In schools where there are many faiths, time-tabling such a room might be difficult.'; 'Until the law is changed, we support making it much easier for those who do not wish to take part in worship to avoid doing so, perhaps by scheduling it at the end of the school day.'

'*Religious Education should be impartial, fair and balanced, and schools should offer optional faith-based Religious Instruction classes.*' Most respondents agreed with both proposals (86 per cent with the first and 77 per cent with the second) but many pointed out the practical difficulties of voluntary confessional instruction, including, again, problems in ensuring genuinely voluntary participation and distinguishing the wishes and rights of parents from those of children. Instances of child abuse and over-long hours at some supplementary religious schools were cited by some respondents as good reasons to invite such schools into the mainstream education system or, at the very least, to improve links between them and mainstream education.

Seventy-three per cent thought that religious schools could also offer this religious education plus religious instruction model but there was a high abstention rate on this question (34 per cent). Curricular, management and funding problems were pointed out: 'There is already too much content and not enough reflection, discussion, analysis ...'; 'Minimum educational standards imply adequate resources ... which some faith communities may be unable to provide without assistance'; 'There should be safeguards to ensure that children are not indoctrinated on school premises'; 'Great in theory, but who is responsible for what happens? If it is the school ... does this become subject to Ofsted [the Office for Standards in Education]? If it is the faith community, who decides what is taught and by whom?'

'*More religious holidays should be recognised as public holidays.*' Forty-four per cent of respondents agreed with this proposal in principle but many foresaw difficulties in selecting which holidays to recognise. Few offered suggestions, though some simply suggested more holidays, unrelated to any particular religion. Most agreed that examination boards should pay attention to religious holidays (77 per cent) while acknowledging the difficulties: 'In 2002, Shap lists 11 [religious holidays] in the exam period.' Comments included: 'Why six new holidays? Why not 60?'; 'Religious holidays that follow the moon are very disruptive.'; 'Would Muslims want to celebrate Yom Kippur?' One organisation suggested more flexibility for local education authorities and schools, together with national guidance.

'*Other cultural requirements should be respected.*' The BHA proposes that other cultural requirements should be respected as far as practicable without infringing the entitlements of others. This would include: school uniforms flexible enough to permit religious and cultural differences; schools providing food suited to all religious requirements and space(s) for children to eat food provided from home and for those undertaking fasts; sex and relationships education (SRE) in single-sex classes if required, and taught in a values framework including faith perspectives as well as secular ones. These proposals, many of which are already implemented in some schools, particularly in multicultural areas, proved the least controversial, and were largely supported. Schools are already being advised by the Department for Education and Skills to move in this direction. 'Schools could try harder,' was one response, though some pointed out the difficulties of respecting the strictest dietary requirements, and that schools might require time and support to adapt. The most dissent was over the matter of single-sex SRE which a few respondents thought a form of sex discrimination, though preferable to mass opting out. And some respondents pointed out the importance of such accommodations being 'reasonable' and respecting the 'rights and best interests of the children, as opposed to parents' demands'.

'*The training and professionalism of teachers should be improved.*' With very few exceptions the proposals for improving initial and in-service training and for strengthening the teachers' code of practice were supported (by 86 per cent): 'A strong case can be made for this. Many of the deeper prejudices of our society are reinforced by teachers.'; 'Anecdotal evidence from members [of an interfaith group] suggests that instances of insensitivity to issues of faith and belief currently occur in both mainstream and religious schools.'; 'I agree with this [but] there is the problem of accurate teaching of the teachers.'

'*There should be better procedures for dealing with complaints and suggestions.*' Ninety-five per cent of respondents agreed.

'*Good practice should be shared.*' Seventy-five per cent of respondents agreed, though some objected to the 'divisive' concept of beacon schools as a means of achieving this. Many thought that all schools, whatever their foundation, should implement good practice as quickly as possible and that it should be widely shared in a variety of ways.

'*Local people should be consulted.*' Seventy-three per cent agreed that local religious groups should be consulted about the exact nature of these accommodations, possibly on the model of local Standing Advisory Councils for RE, but there were reservations about how representative such groups would be, and about the difficulty of getting local communities involved. Some respondents preferred national arrangements.

'*Some aspects of the law should be reformed, coupled with clear and firm guidance for schools.*' Though it was accepted by an overwhelming majority of respondents to the consultation that guidance would be useful, indeed was badly needed by governors and teachers, it was also pointed out that guidance could always be ignored and that statutes would always take precedence – and there was general pessimism about the possibility of the necessary changes in the law. There were also pleas not to increase the burden of bureaucracy on teachers.

'*Religious schools should be phased out by absorption into a reformed community school system, or become independent.*' Although many outside the formal consultation agree that religious schools should be phased out, only 50 per cent of written respondents supported this view. Some opposed expansion, but were pessimistic about the likelihood of phasing out existing religious schools. Some minority religious groups continue to want their own state-funded schools, largely for reasons of equity, but sometimes because they believe that only religious schools can sufficiently affirm their religious beliefs; some support them on the grounds of parental choice or human rights; some are content with the overwhelmingly Christian status quo. Some who would like religious schools to be phased out would object to their becoming independent: 'We agree, but with a major reservation. We would be concerned if most religious schools became independent instead of joining a reformed mainstream. The independent sector in education does not do anything for the cohesiveness of society and detracts from the inclusiveness of mainstream community schools.'

Common responses to questions on whether religious schools could implement inclusive and accommodating policies were: 'Yes, if they wanted to,' and: 'Some could (and do) and some could not (and would not),' and some respondents gave examples of schools which were, in some respects, inclusive. Some drew attention to the huge variety in ethos and practice within the religious schools sector, and others to the trust deeds of religious schools which constrain them in various ways. Comments included: 'Changes in the law would be needed to require them to do this.'; 'In a society where people of different beliefs live in close proximity, it is vital that children learn about the beliefs of their neighbours as well as their own ... It is very hard to see how [religious schools] can be true to their own faith and also operate an inclusive approach.'; 'All children should have the freedom of choice and opportunity to independently assess religious activities in a pluralist environment away from parental pressure and close cultural influences. The freedom of choice of the child, not the parents, needs to be given the foremost consideration.' There was considerable support for the idea that all schools, regardless of status, should be accommodating, tolerant and inclusive.

Conclusion

Despite varied responses to these proposals, the BHA continues to believe that implementing them would end a great deal of discrimination in schools on grounds of religion or belief, and significantly decrease demand for separate religious schools. Many of the problems highlighted are practical ones which could be overcome. There is much support for our opposition to schools that discriminate in favour of particular faiths through their practices and admissions policies, but if religious schools became genuinely inclusive, existing only as charitable institutions serving the whole community on the model suggested above, most of the objections to them would no longer apply.

Note

1   An article based on this paper was published in the *British Journal of Religious Education*, Spring 2003, 25(2).

References

Amnesty International (2000) 'Our Rights Start Here', *Amnesty*, September–October.
Archbishops' Council (2001) *The Way Ahead: Church of England Schools in the New Millennium*, London: Church House Publishing.
BHA (2002) *A Better Way Forward: BHA Policy on Religion and Schools*, September. Available online at http://www.humanism.org.uk.
Cantle, T. (2001) *Community Cohesion*, London: Home Office. Available online at http://www.homeoffice. gov.uk/comrace/cohesion/index.html.
Human Rights Act (1998) available online at http://www.legislation.hmso.gov.uk/acts/acts1998/ 19980042.htm.
Humanist Philosophers' Group (2001) *Religious Schools: The Case Against*, London: BHA.
Ouseley, H. (2001) *Community Pride not Prejudice*, Bradford: Vision.

Race Relations (Amendment) Act (2000) available online at http://www.legislation.hmso.gov.uk/acts/acts2000/20000034.htm.

South Asia Solidarity Group and Asian Women Unite! (2002) *Undermining Education: New Labour and Single Faith Schools*, London: Londec.

United Nations (1989) Convention on the Rights of the Child. Available online at http://www.unicef.org/crc/crc.htm.

Weller, P., Feldman, A. and Purdam, K. (2001) *Religious Discrimination in England and Wales*, Home Office Research Study 220, London: Home Office.

7 Faith-based schools in the United Kingdom

An unenthusiastic defence of a slightly reformed status quo

Harry Brighouse

I shall approach the question of whether the government should support single-faith schools through the prism of a liberal theory of educational justice. This theory requires, among other things, that children have a substantive opportunity to become autonomous adults; on the liberal view this principle has very high priority in evaluating education policy, outweighing, for example, any parental interest in having a child educated at a school which promotes the parent's religion. So when addressing state support for faith schools we ask whether they contribute to a child's right to become autonomous. Many liberals think that they do not. If a child is subject to the same religious influences in the home and in the school, s/he is less likely to gain the necessary resources to reflect critically on what s/he is learning. Especially telling is the complaint that, because children learn a great deal from their peers, a child attending a school in which her peers have the same religious commitments as those of her family and school is profoundly disadvantaged with respect to the ability to become autonomous.

Separationism, secularisation, and autonomy[1]

Accordingly, some liberal commentators take it as obvious that the state should not support faith schools. A.C. Grayling (2001) wrote in the *Observer*: 'Society should be blind to religion both in the sense that it lets people believe and behave as they wish provided they do no harm to others, and in the sense that it acts as if religions do not exist, with public affairs being secular in character. The United States (US) constitution provides this, though the religious lobby is always trying to breach it – while George W. Bush's policy of granting public funds for "faith-based initiatives" actually does breach it. To secularise society in Britain would mean that government funding for church schools and "faith-based" organisations and activities would cease, as would religious programming in public broadcasting.'

But notice that Grayling's recommendation makes no appeal to the interest of children in becoming autonomous. He wants to 'secularise society', which involves disentangling the state from religious institutions: depriving them of any funding or privileges. He identifies secularisation with a particularly strong form of separationism: that the state should have nothing to do with religious institutions.

In this Grayling accepts the mainstream of American liberal thinking about separationism. In the US all government schools are secular, so that not only do religious organisations have no role in running schools, but the schools provide no religious education and make little reference to religious symbols and ceremonies. The Christmas holidays are called 'the holiday season', and Easter is conceded to with a (unreasonably brief) 'spring break'. Religious commitment has no place in defining the curriculum or ethos of the school.

It is worth noticing a consequence of Grayling's identification of secularisation with separationism. Defenders of strictly secular public schooling in America typically argue for very extensive freedom for the running of private schools by religious foundations, and the law in most American states allows private schools to practise straightforward indoctrination of children. For example, 300,000 children attend Accelerated Christian Academy schools where unqualified teachers (some of whom have not graduated high school) instruct them from workbooks designed to reflect the values for and literal truths in the Bible. Sandra Feldman, leader of the American Federation of Teachers, and *bête noire* of the voucher movement,[2] is very clear where she stands on the issue of children's prospects for personal autonomy:

> For religious schools, public scrutiny and accountability raise issues of religious freedom; the deep infusion of religion throughout their curriculum and lessons is essential to them, as is their freedom to require children to attend religious services. They don't want state interference in any of that. Yet, accountability to the broader public must go along with public funding.
>
> (Feldman 1999)

In other words, separationism is so important that if some children cannot become autonomous because their parents send them to private, 'free' religious schools, that's a sacrifice worth making.

Secularisation of society is, indeed, an aim of liberals. But secularisation should not be identified with separationism, still less with the odd interpretation it is given by American liberals. A society is secularised when the religious cleavages that characterise it are not pertinent to public political debate, and when the barriers between religious and ethnic subcultures are porous. Before examining why liberals seek secularisation in this sense, let me deflect the objection that it is because they trivialise religion, thinking of it as a purely private matter of preference. Liberals take religion seriously. They endorse freedom of religion as a matter of deep principle, because they believe that there is a great deal of mystery in human experience that pure reason cannot settle. They consider that religious belief helps many people explain some of these aspects of human experience, and that, from the perspective of pure reason, religious explanations are as good as any others. But they also think that in order to contribute fully to the well-being of the individual religious commitment must be authentic. That is, it must reflect the freely exercised reason of that individual. For our life to be truly ours, and to contribute to our well-being, it is we who must endorse it.

This is why liberals place such weight on individual autonomy. People need to be autonomous so that they can live lives that *they* have judged to be of value. And for this they do not just need autonomy-facilitating schools, but an autonomy-facilitating general culture. If the public culture allows different ethnic or religious groups to feel embattled and underconfident, they are liable to look in on themselves, and devote energies to building strong boundaries between themselves and other cultures. This, I believe, is what has happened to the more fundamentalist sects of Christianity in the US since the 1960s. Despite the energy with which certain entrepreneurs have mobilised them politically, they have essentially seceded from the public culture. But strong boundaries between ways of life undermine autonomy, because they make it harder for children (and adults) who grow up within one way of life to come to know and understand the values of alternatives, and to see them as realistic options.

The second reason liberals seek to undermine the barriers between religious faiths is because they accept a principle of legitimacy that says that it is a prima facie wrong to use the coercive power of the state against people on justificatory grounds that they could not reasonably be expected to endorse. This means that when we vote for the state to act coercively we should base our vote on sincere reasons that reasonable people could come to endorse. Purely religious reasons fail this test, because religion is a matter on which free reason is not decisive. This does not mean that religious voters cannot be motivated by their sincere moral commitments, because often those are commitments that they have reason to believe could be accepted by reasonable people: for example, the idea that killing is usually wrong, or that the elimination of human suffering is a high moral priority. Nor does it mean that the state should directly police the reasoning of voters: it cannot and should not, for numerous reasons. But it does allow that the state should favour institutional structures – as long as they are consistent with maintaining basic liberties and distributive justice – that support public, rather than private, reasoning in the justification of state power.

Autonomy and faith schools

So we now have two liberal aims: ensuring that every child has a real opportunity to become an autonomous adult, and minimising the extent to which religious cleavages have pertinence in public political debate. Let's take the first consideration. We want to establish the system of public schooling that maximises the probability that each child will have a reasonable opportunity to become autonomous. We have to ask whether the kinds of secular schools we can reasonably expect in a strictly secular public system will promote autonomy better than the religious schools that would otherwise be incorporated, and also whether the involvement of the state in funding and regulating religious schools makes them more autonomy-facilitating than if the state refrains from provision but allows private religious schools. The best control we have is the US, whose model Grayling advocates.

The typical American urban or suburban public high school has little in common with the liberal ideal of the autonomy-fostering common schools. It is a 2000-plus student institution, in which no individual knows every other individual, in which many children never have any teacher for more than one year of instruction, in which the prevailing values include pep-rallies for school sports and a slavishly conformist loyalty to the school and neighbourhood. These schools maintain a deafening silence about spiritual or anti-materialist values, take sides in the Cola wars, and accept as given the prevalence of brand names and teen marketing. Religious parents often, with justice, believe that their own beliefs are at best ignored, at worst actively worked against, by the schools. Since 11 September 2001 countless school districts have enforced a morning recitation of the pledge of allegiance, a ritualistic affirmation of patriotism as a quasi-religious commitment. The reasonable liberal parent shrinks in horror at the thought of any children, let alone their own, attending these places. There are, of course, some better alternatives in the public sector, but few school districts or school leaders show signs of being inclined or able to foster the ethos needed to facilitate autonomy for all students.

Similarly, while many private religious schools are indeed deeply sectarian, many are not. You cannot judge how well a school facilitates autonomy simply by looking at its mission and how it carries it out. A Christian school with a religiously diverse student body may facilitate autonomy just because children learn about the articulation of other ways of life primarily by seeing it articulated in the lives of their peers. The key issue of liberal principle is not whether schools in *the state system* serve autonomy, but *what system of regulating all schools, state and private, will do so.* The distinction between public and private schools in this context is artificial. The state is the guarantor of liberal justice, and it is as responsible, in the *political* sense, for the operation of private schools as it is for that of state schools. I would conjecture that in the United Kingdom (UK) religious schools that cooperate with the state in running a school will, over time, come to be better at facilitating autonomy than religious schools that do not, other things being equal. I would conjecture, with more confidence, the same thing in the US, partly because I am confident that political coalitions that succeed in getting funding for religious schools will have to concede a good degree of public regulation (just as Sandra Feldman suggests). Proponents of the US model often talk as if the alternative to state-funded religious schools is state-funded secular schools. But for many students it is not – the alternative is a private religious school, which is less likely to promote their autonomy than state-run schools (whether religious or secular), other things being equal.

I suspect that in the US many parents are drawn to private religious schools not by any interest in having their children indoctrinated, but by their horror at the experience of the shopping-mall high school, and, in fact, an unarticulated sense that the values of the peer group, tolerated by the school, threaten, rather than serve, their children's prospective autonomy. If they do, I feel considerable sympathy. Fundamentalist Christians have managed to foster a counterculture in the US which includes a whole parallel world of rock music, kids' videos, and teen magazines. Margaret Talbot (2000: 40) describes the magazines available for teenagers: '[Fundamentalist Christianity] has its own magazines for every demographic niche, including *Hopscotch* and *Boy's Quest* for kids 6–13, which promise anodyne themes, no boyfriends, girlfriends, makeup, fashion or violence and NO ADVERTISING.' Religious parents fear that schools which do not incorporate strong moral values, and which treat spirituality as just another lifestyle option, one which may not even be presented to children by sincere believers, endanger their children's prospects for a balanced and satisfying life.

Advocates of the American model should bear this in mind. Once we understand that the principle of promoting the prospective autonomy of all children trumps the merely institutional measure of separationism, we have to make a hard-headed comparison between how well a strict secular model and something like the current English model serve autonomy. I certainly believe that autonomy would be better served in the US if policymakers adopted something closer to the UK model. I doubt the UK has much to gain from adopting the US model.

Of course, the live issue in the UK is that the government has begun to grant voluntary status to Hindu, Sikh, and, most controversially, Muslim schools. A great deal of fire is directed against Muslim schools because Islam is a religion which supposedly degrades women, so that the schools can be expected to diminish the opportunities of female pupils. Let's assume that Islam is indeed more misogynistic than Christianity and than the mainstream secular culture. Does it follow that Muslim girls will get a worse education if the state gives voluntary status to some Muslim schools than if it does not? No. It depends on which schools the girls would have attended if the state had not granted Muslim schools voluntary status, and on how the schools respond to being granted voluntary status. If the girls would otherwise attend private Muslim schools which have no reason to negotiate with the mainstream culture and its educational expectations, they are no worse off in voluntary status Muslim schools. And the state has equal responsibility for their well-being regardless of where they are going to school.[3] It, and its taxpayers, cannot say 'We are implicated if we fund the schools but we're off the hook if we merely permit them.'[4] The state does no less wrong when it neglects children than when it pays attention to them.

Secularisation and separationism

Why is the issue of government involvement in faith schools relevant to secularisation? Here is a conjecture about the overall effects of excluding religion from public schooling in the US. I think this conjecture is true, although I cannot prove it, and would not know how to start. If it is true, though, it suggests that the strictly secular schooling model of the US will not be a promising model to copy, if we take seriously the aim of secularisation.

In the US parents must choose between secular public schools and religious private schools. The state exercises minimal control over private schools, and private religious schools have two markets: the religious sectarians who would send their children there even if there were public faith schools available, and the religious moderates who would choose public faith schools if they were available. So religious moderates send their children to schools influenced by sectarians rather than by secularists.

Because the public schools do not accommodate religious parents, they are inclined to defect to sectarian schools. A striking example is the well-known Tennessee case of *Mozert vs Hawkins*. The Mozert parents objected to a primary-level civic education programme using readers in which boys were seen making toast for girls, in violation of what the parents regarded as God-given sex roles; which quoted Anne Frank's speculation (false, according to the parents) that unorthodox religious belief was better than no belief at all; and in which mention was made of witches and magic. The School District refused the parents' request to exempt their children from the readers, and ultimately the courts found for the School District. The consequences: the publishers of the textbook removed the offending passages from subsequent editions, in order to maintain their market, and the parents removed their children from the district to a self-run school which taught fundamentalist values and which only children of fundamentalists attended. In other words, the rules give artificial market power to the extremists in the marketplace of ideas. I suspect that if the state acted as it does in Britain, cooperating with, but heavily influencing, religious authorities in providing schools, the market for sectarian schooling would collapse, and sectarians, rather than being able to influence the children of moderates, would have their children subject to influence by the mainstream and the moderates.

On top of that, sectarian religious entrepreneurs are able to present the state as an enemy of religion. Stories abound in the fundamentalist Christian world of Bibles being banned from the classroom, of prayer groups being harassed by school authorities, of ministers and religious parents being excluded from school parent and teacher organisation activities. In every case I know of where these stories contain a grain of truth the courts have finally found in favour of religious freedom as properly understood – that is, against the school authorities. But the grain of truth is enough for sectarian entrepreneurs, and independent information is hard to come by and not scrupulously sought by the fundamentalist community. The strict understanding some people have of the implications of state–church separation contributes to the alienation of religious communities from the mainstream public culture, and hence to the pertinence of religious cleavage to public disagreement.

My conjecture is that a system in which the state collaborates with faith organisations in the provision of schooling is more likely to produce autonomy-facilitating schools and an autonomy-facilitating culture, other things being equal, than a system in which the state refuses to collaborate with faith organisations, but allows them to run their own schools independently. This is only a conjecture, and, as I have indicated, I do not know how to prove or disprove it (especially because I have a preference for quantitative methods of proof). But I think opponents of funding faith schools should take it more seriously than they do. At the very least they should consider far more elements of the US situation as a whole than they sometimes seem to.

Reforming faith schools

How should the status quo be reformed? I have not argued that any particular faith school facilitates autonomy better than any particular secular school, but that a system in which the state collaborates with faith organisations in providing some schools will have a better effect than adopting a strictly secular system would. I want to advocate a reform that would help both secular and religious schools facilitate personal autonomy for their pupils: prohibiting them from selecting students on any basis whatever.

How would this help with autonomy? If religiously based schools could not select on the basis of the family religion of the child, such schools would have a more diverse student population. And since the main way that children can be expected to learn about the articulation of the ways of life recommended by other religions is by observing the lives of their peers, this will make for more of an opportunity for children in faith schools to become autonomous. But a second reason is that it will also make for more of an opportunity for children outside faith schools to become autonomous. Contrary to the much-expressed fear that faith schools undermine the opportunities for autonomy of those children who attend them, I fear that they undermine the opportunity for autonomy of those who do not. Children from secular homes cannot become autonomous without an appreciation of what the religious life involves, and this is something that, I am only too aware, their parents cannot give them. They need children from religious backgrounds to be in their schools and their classes, which is more likely if those children are not hived off into faith schools. If faith schools are not allowed to select on grounds of family faith, and some children from atheist families apply, more religious students will attend secular schools.

Does this measure violate the right of parents to send children to schools that reflect their religious commitments? Sure, if they had such a right. But they do not. I understand that Catholic parents may feel that Roman Catholic schools are 'theirs' in the sense that I might feel that a socialist school was 'ours'. But in fact it is a public resource, the purpose of which is to contribute to a just system of public education. Suppose an atheist parent chooses to send her child to a Roman Catholic school so that the child will have a proper understanding of one of the world's central religions, and an enhanced opportunity to become autonomous. It is hard to see what reason the state could have to allow a child whose parents simply want her to be a good Catholic to be preferred over that child.

Conclusion

Many secular American visitors to the UK are struck by two features of the public culture. First is the open discussion and debate about religious matters. Some politicians are openly atheist, others appear to be genuine believers; few make ritualistic and insincere invocations of God and the Bible. Openly atheistic and avowedly religious public figures discuss religious matters as if they were matters of real significance. The second is the fact that on any given public issue a diversity of religious and non-religious perspectives is found on all sides. The public reasonableness of religious believers is particularly striking. Religion in the US is treated by the public culture as a purely private matter, the boundaries between religious and mainstream culture are sharply drawn, to the detriment of the inhabitants of both, and religious cleavages are far more politically pertinent than in the UK. Introducing the American model of separationism would jeopardise the level of secularisation British society has achieved. British liberals should proceed cautiously.

Notes

1 Separationism is the practice of not having an established church or religion.
2 The voucher movement in the United States consists of a coalition of urban black liberals, socially liberal religious (mainly Catholic) schools, and conservative foundations, academics and political activists. The movement promotes policies in which states fund children to attend private schools; it has had notable successes in Cleveland (Ohio), Milwaukee (Wisconsin) and Florida.
3 I am ignoring, for the purpose of this discussion, the problem that the British state has systematically discriminated against non-Christian religions, which gives it an urgent responsibility to treat Islam (and other non-Christian religions) fairly.
4 Grayling is quoted as saying, 'Given the great harm that religions do ... in the way of conflict, war, persecution and oppression and preventing the growth of science and freedom of thought, I object profoundly to my taxes being used to this end', in Clare Dean, 'Backlash against Church Schools', *Times Education Supplement*, 23 February 2001.

References

Grayling, A.C. (2001) 'Keeping God out of public affairs', *Observer*, 12 August 2001: 26.
Feldman, S. (1999) 'Education: a commentary on public and other critical issues – first choice', *New York Times*, 3 October 1999: 12 (Midwest edn). Also available online at http://www.aft.org/presscenter/speeches-columns/wws/1999/1099/htm.
Talbot, M. (2000) 'A mighty fortress', *New York Times*, 27 February 2000.

8 Keeping the faith with social capital

From Coleman to New Labour on social justice, religion and education

Eva Gamarnikow and Anthony Green

The context of our interest in faith schools is an ongoing concern with school differentiation and specialisation in recent United Kingdom (UK) government education policy. The issue we are addressing is not whether education policy should promote faith schools; our focus is the articulation of policy discourses and its relations with social and educational differentiation. Our aim in this chapter is to locate and discuss the place of faith schools within overall policies on standards, specialisation, excellence and parental choice. Our argument is that, in the context of a broadly neo-liberal agenda with enormous emphasis on generating assent to the system of state schooling by elaborating and maximising the possibilities of parental choice, there are clear policy tensions between the current New Labour *equity* agenda, expressed in terms of 'zero tolerance' for low standards overall, and the differentiating excellence *market* agenda. The outcomes of such ambiguous policy aims are likely to draw faith schools into the overall educational machinery of class formation. Our particular focus is that themes, concepts and perspectives drawing on *social capital theory* are deeply embedded in policy thinking and the accompanying legitimating rationales, for promoting both educational diversification and the benefits of faith schools. As a contribution to the 'faith schools debate' we do not claim to have produced an exhaustive analysis of the issues. At best our argument and our secondary analysis of some recently published information can only stand as indicative of the need for a more fully grounded investigation, especially around comparing the equity effects of education within and between faith and non-faith communities.

We begin by reviewing the legacy of James Coleman, with respect to social justice and social capital, in the context of his work on Catholic schools in the United States of America (USA). This leads us to a more in-depth theoretical exploration of social justice and social capital. Having developed the argument about the crucial significance of social capital in New Labour's social policy thinking in general, we discuss current education policy developments, specifically focusing on faith schools under the umbrella of *diversification*. Returning to the Coleman legacy, we report our partial re-analysis of data recently published by Gerald Grace[1] (2002) and exposition of its implications for the role of Catholic schools in promoting equity.

The Coleman legacy: social justice and social capital

Two key issues in the Coleman legacy are relevant for our present purposes, namely, his educational research concerned with social justice and his theorisation of the link between education and social capital. Turning to the former, the Coleman Report *Equality of Educational Opportunity* (Coleman *et al.* 1966) and subsequent work on ethnic minority educational achievement in public (state) and private schools (Coleman 1968, 1990; Coleman and Hoffer, 1987; Coleman *et al.* 1982) had social justice as its central theme. Coleman drew specifically on Rawls's (1973) theory of distributive justice, which is concerned with establishing the parameters of social justice in unequal societies. The classical Rawlsian argument is that social inequalities can be justified if they benefit the worst off. In terms of inequalities of educational achievement, a socially just system of educational opportunities would be represented by convergence, over time, of trajectories of originally differential educational outcomes of the dominant in relation to disadvantaged social groups.

It was this equal opportunities research which led to Coleman's theorisation of the relationship between social capital and educational outcomes. Put very simply, he seems to have discovered social capital *ex post facto to his empirical study* as the way to make sense of his data, which indicated that disadvantaged children achieved better educational outcomes than their similarly disadvantaged peers if they attended a Catholic school. Specifically, he argued, initially in an appendix (Coleman *et al.* 1982), and later in his iconic 'Social capital in the creation of human capital' (Coleman 1988), that the success of Catholic schools lay in the coherence of norms and values between the family, the faith-based neighbourhood community and the faith school, and the articulation and closure of social networks between them.

This research on public, Catholic and other private schools in the US is an essential resource for people engaging in faith schools debates because of the richness of his conceptualisation and seriousness with which his empirical studies are taken. However, acknowledging the influence of Coleman does not detract from our reservations about the ways in which his research findings are used, both explicitly and implicitly, to make general arguments in the current policy moment, about the significance of faith schools in supporting equity. First, his research is concerned with US education from the 1960s to the early 1980s. There always were questions about Coleman's results, namely, whether there was a social class effect in parental choice of, and the selection of black and Hispanic students into, fee-paying Catholic schools. More recent research (Bryk *et al.* 1993) seems to suggest that there are unresolved questions about the role of Catholic schools in continuing to enhance social equity. These issues continue to resurface, for instance, in the context of the fall in recruitment to religious orders, closures of inner-city parochial schools, and the growing concentration of private Catholic schools in more affluent suburbs. Second, Coleman's findings concerning the high achievement and low drop-out rates of students in Catholic schools are very specific: Catholic schools produce higher educational achievement and lower drop-out rates than public schools serving the same disadvantaged communities – African-American and Hispanic students. Given the very low achievement of these students in the public school system, the baseline for a comparative equal opportunity argument is not very high. If there is a social justice convergence effect it is likely to be very small, and perhaps even negligible in socio-economic terms. However, this is certainly not so in ideological terms. Third, our reservations about Coleman's argument concerning the significance of social capital in educational achievement are linked to our critique of social capital theory more generally, namely its role in obscuring social class inequalities in current education policy. We will now turn to exploring social justice and social capital in greater depth, to lay the foundations for the subsequent argument about current faith schools policy.

Social justice

We would argue that Rawlsian considerations, as developed by Coleman, continue to be relevant in education policy. In fact, the bottom line of policy agreement is that equality of opportunity is a social good to be aspired to and that any policy development should be assessed against this, whether policy is coming from old-style social democracy, neo-liberalism or Third Way formulations. The issue, however, is not whether this ideal is constructed as a distant target, but the policies, processes and procedures promulgated to move in the direction of its realisation. Thus our first consideration is about feasible policy under any model of progressive capitalism that can be assessed as moving in the direction of equalising opportunities. That is to say, over time, a socially just policy in these terms would be presentable in a graphic model (following Coleman 1968), in which, while everyone in the system is showing signs of improving, no matter from which position they start, those best placed are improving at slower rates than those who start from a lower position in the system of opportunities. Thus their respective graphs of attainment of social goods over time, in this case significant educational credentials which are exchangeable in the market for life chances, tend to converge, as the downsiders improve more rapidly than the upsiders. Thus *everyone is winning*, an oxymoronic proposition left as such, but rendered reasonable if the disadvantaged are indeed doing relatively better than the well off. The issue then becomes about whether we can be confident that this is systematically happening, or likely to happen, in relation to contemporary diversification and specialisation trends in education policy, especially in relation to promoting faith schools. We argue that it is unlikely.

The second consideration picks this issue up as a matter of distributive justice and focuses on how current policy fares in relation to Rawls's basic model as it might apply to the circumstances of current English state education. In recognition of the argument that opportunities are systematically and unequally distributed, the problem shifts to whether the continuing systematic inequality can be rationalised in Rawlsian terms. Thus, so far as educational outcomes are concerned, every student should have an equal opportunity to attend a school that has parity of esteem with every other school in the system of the available differentiated and specialised schools. Similarly, within each school parity of opportunities to achieve should prevail. This implies horizontal differentiation of school types with vertical equality of student outcomes, or different but equal – a highly contestable, perhaps essentially contradictory, policy aspiration. However, in Rawls's terms, where hierarchy does manifest itself in the educational system, giving rise to patterns of differentially credentialled outcomes, to be socially just it must operate in the name of fostering the best interests of the least well placed. We argue that current policy does not measure up well in these terms, indeed it obfuscates the issues, constructing hierarchical distinction as egalitarian difference. This takes us to our third main consideration, namely, that social capital theory is importantly, though not solely, implicated in these policy obfuscation processes. Thus the modes and mechanisms of social capitalism are implicated as ideology so far as the state's role in the formation of educational outcomes is concerned.

Social capital

There are several different variants of social capital theory (Coleman 1988; Putnam 1993, 2000; Fukuyama 1995; Bourdieu 1983) each of which we have discussed elsewhere (Gamarnikow and Green 1999a, 1999b). Although the specificities of focus and emphasis vary between them, in particular between Coleman, Putnam and Fukuyama on the one hand and Bourdieu on the other, all agree about the traditionally recognised ingredients: norms of trust and reciprocity, networks and civic engagement. Social capital theory is fundamentally concerned with two aspects of the social. Firstly, benefits accrue to individuals from being located in social networks. In this context, social capital theory positions social structures and social relations as tactical and strategic resources at the personal level. The second aspect flows from the first and is concerned with the collective benefits which derive from social networks. Social capital theorists argue that generalising the trust and reciprocity embedded in social networks can lead to increased economic productivity (Fukuyama 1995), greater participation by citizens (Putnam 1993, 2000), or, for our purpose, more educogenic parenting and higher educational achievement (Coleman 1988). In simple terms, social capital theory claims that a society with high levels of social capital is a cohesive, well-functioning society, with improving socially desirable outcomes, such as high educational achievement, and fewer negative ones, such as crime and social exclusion.

As far as social policy is concerned, social capital ideas are highly favoured, and in post-socialist, post-welfarist, late modern societies they have become a standard policy instrument (Office of National Statistics 2001), though only rarely named as such. The take-up of these ideas is global (Giddens 1998, 2001): the World Bank, for instance, has a dedicated social capital website (www.worldbank.org/poverty/scapital) and promotes anti-poverty and development strategies which focus on social capital building (Fine 1999; World Bank 2000). In the UK context, social capital is a named policy *desideratum* in public health (Department of Health 1999) and in the regeneration agenda (Social Exclusion Unit 1998, 2000); in education, as we will discuss below, it operates under a variety of pseudonyms.

From the perspective of critical policy analysis, social capital theory is interesting in that it draws attention to the social as both a *topic* for policy development and a *resource* in policy implementation. Sociologists (for example, Baron *et al.* 2000: Morrow 2001) have argued that social capital theory has useful heuristic properties in drawing attention to social networking, informal structures, communities, etc. In this sense, social capital is neither intrinsically good nor bad; it is simply a way of conceptualising aspects of the social. Difficulties arise, however, if, as we argue below, social policy draws upon social capital mechanisms when these have the *ideological* effect of both obscuring and reinforcing structures of inequality and social injustice. This tendency to ignore or mis-recognise structures of inequality can arise from particular forms of social capital theory itself, most notably theories drawing on Putnam's (1993, 2000) functionalist model of a plurality of equivalent networks which are said to secure democratic participation. However, ignoring or mis-recognising structures of inequality can also be related to the socially constitutive processes of governmentality which emerge in, amongst other places, proposals for creating social integration. Our particular concern is focused on the links between social justice and social capital as resources which can be found in contexts where the role of social networks is to produce and reproduce differential advantages in social and cultural formations. In particular, we draw attention to discourses where problems produced by social exclusion and deficits of social capital are framed as problems of the social, not problems of the economic.

Bourdieu's (1983) approach, by contrast with these other approaches, regards the social capital of networks as linked to other unequally distributed capitals: cultural, symbolic and, of course, economic. We are relatively sympathetic to his approach and will draw on the logic of his arguments in the rest of the chapter.

New Labour social policy and social capital

New Labour relies heavily on social capital ideas as solutions. Here the idea is to encourage professional networks by rewarding those who achieve better results. Thus social capital policies tend to focus on networks and partnerships of providers, with policy claiming that the synergy produced by this type of joined-up working produces better results for clients. Here the social capital generated within networks of providers operates, in part, to make up for social capital deficits in the community served and, in part, as a redemptive force, developing social cohesion through the positive effects on social trust of services improved by networked professionals (Gamarnikow and Green 1999a; Glendinning *et al.* 2002).

There is also a second dimension to policies based on social capital ideas – a focus on encouraging the development of values inspired by the post-socialist, post-welfarist communitarian agenda (Arthur 2003; Arthur with Bailey 2000; Gamarnikow and Green 2000). Here the emphasis is on duties and responsibilities, and promoting community values which embrace responsible parenting, appreciation of the value of education, commitment to self-reliance through labour market participation and so on. In this context the role of government social policy is to create institutional forms which embody, support and develop this constellation of community values.

This 'values education' through social policy is linked, as we have argued elsewhere (Gamarnikow and Green 1999a, 1999b, 2000), to the notion of the Third Way state. This is the nation state located in a globalised 'turbo-capitalist' economy in which traditional national economic policies are regarded as ineffective (Giddens 1998, 2001). Traditional economic policy thus metamorphoses into two moments of education policy: human capital creation, to enable the population to face the challenges of globalised labour markets in the 'knowledge economy', and the creation of moral, democratic citizens, who take advantage of all the opportunities offered by the state to form themselves into responsible students, workers and parents. The specifically New Labour element in this lies in the recognition of poverty and social exclusion as effects of globalisation which the hidden hand of the market alone will not cure and which, therefore, require additional, compensatory social inclusion work (Secretary of State for Social Security 1999).

New Labour's education policy

Very broadly, New Labour's education policy oscillates between forms of (egalitarian) compensatory education (Education Action Zones (EAZs), Excellence in Cities) and a (hierarchical) excellence agenda (specialist/beacon schools). The reason for this contra-dictory educational policy agenda lies in the attempt to extend the neoliberal policy of marketisation and parental choice while combining it with the New Labour focus on equity, to increase educational achievement for the disadvantaged. Thus the standards agenda has to produce both hierarchy, in the form of high-achieving schools which reduce the likelihood of middle-class flight, and social justice, by improving educational achievement for disadvantaged children. However, research continues to demonstrate the tensions between parental choice of schools and equalisation of standards (Gewirtz *et al.* 1995; Whitty *et al.* 1998; Power *et al.* 2002; Ball, 2003; Power *et al.* 2003). This is increasingly recognised by the government, and fairly traditional compensatory strategies (e.g. EAZs, Excellence in Cities) are used to try to intervene to increase equity.

In more detail, New Labour's current education policy perspectives are shifting away radically from the initial (Blunkett) era when the focus was on 'standards not structures'

(Department for Education and Employment [DfEE] 1997). In 2003, policy aims have continued with the emphasis on improving the quality of all institutions, but particularly of those falling below minimum standards. The new element is to refocus on structures, on the system of educational provision. Current secondary education policy (DfEE 2001; Department for Education and Skills [DfES] 2001, 2002, 2003) emphasises this change, and does so by identifying diversification, or 'specialisation', of educational institutions as the mechanism for achieving higher-quality education. At the heart of this lies the rhetorical move from Old to New Labour on education, symbolised in the critique of 'one-size- fits-all' comprehensives (Blair 2002; DfES 2002; Morris 2002), and immortalised in recent education history's new discourse of derision as the 'bog standard' or 'bargepole' comprehensive, which carries with it the concomitant push for further diversification of secondary provision. According to the policy rationale, this is intended to support individual students' different abilities and talents, satisfy parental demands for quality education, and institutionalise and celebrate diversity of educational provision. Faith schools are one element in this overall shift.

The faith schools debate in England

There seem to be three main justifications for the current faith schools policy: equal cultural rights for all faith identities; the positive, socially cohesive effects of a developed and articulated school ethos, in particular a non-secular one; and democratising access to faith schools. There are obvious tensions in this collection of justifications for faith schools. Most notably, the first seems to imply reproducing faith identities through separation from other faith and non-faith social groups, whereas the third suggests that the benefits of faith schools should be shared among all cultural communities.

While we recognise that these issues are important as well as highly controversial in the context of delicate issues of faith and identity in late modernity, we are not intending to focus on the first of these rationales, namely, equal cultural rights in the current policy context. In other words, we are not entering into any form of particularistic advocacy. Thus, we accept the argument that if some faiths have the right to state-funded schools, then all faiths should have the same right. Equally, we accept the logic of the Dearing proposals (2001) to increase the number of Anglican schools to equalise spatial coverage. We are also not entering into the human rights debate (British Humanist Association 2002: Humanist Philosophers' Group 2001) concerning equality of representation, in a multicultural curriculum, for all and no faiths in every state-funded school. Instead our focus is on the other two rationales – ethos and access – individually and in relation to each other, in the context of an education policy embedded in social capital thinking.

Turning first to the second justification for faith schools, namely, ethos, current education policy advocates as a distinct act of policy implementation that each school, whether faith-based or non-denominational in character, should have its own distinct identity expressed through a statement of its *ethos*.

> At the heart of our vision for transforming secondary education is the ambition for every school to create or develop its *distinct mission and ethos*, including a mission to raise standards and enlarge opportunities for all its pupils ... Schools with a *distinct identity* perform best.
>
> (DfES 2001: 38, our emphasis)

> We know that not all schools are the same. They have different strengths and serve
> different communities. We must encourage and celebrate this diversity. All schools
> needs to: develop their own *ethos and sense of mission.*
>
> (DfES 2002: 13, our emphasis)

While such ideas are part of a long-standing common sense in terms of the integrity of all
kinds of human association, these themes also occupy a particular place in social capital
theory, specifically those variants which focus on norms and values as the key constitutive
element of distinct communities. As discussed previously, this connects directly to more
communitarian versions of social capital theory, where the focus is on the collective benefits
of value consensus, whether as an integrative principle or as a disciplinary mechanism.

In the context of faith schools policy, ethos occupies an ambiguous position in relation
to the boundaries between the sacred and the profane. The ethos of faith schools is
concerned with both religious identity (the sacred) and educational achievement (the
profane): '[faith schools] have a good record of delivering high-quality education to their
pupils and many parents welcome the clear ethos of these schools' (DfEE 2001: 48).

There is a great deal of slippage in policy between ethos as mission and ethos as
pragmatic instrument or unique selling point in education markets. Here, access to ethos
as proxy for access to education as a *positional good* (Hirsch 1978) slips into being.

There is a congruence here between reforming and improving secondary education in
general on the basis of ethos and the emphasis on 'ethos' and the 'values base' of faith
schools as the key to their success. At this level of policy thinking there is a curious sleight
of hand which turns the faith ethos of faith schools, their sacred distinctiveness, into a
marker of profane, market-orientated educational desirability, rather than a marker of an
altruistic religious mission. This, as Grace (2002) has pointed out, creates tensions for
Catholic schools – should they be concerned with the 'option for the poor', educating
youngsters from disadvantaged communities, or with marketing high achievement, thus
recruiting from and reconstituting those pursuing educational distinction through excellence,
namely the middle class?

This leads us to consider the third policy argument for faith schools, namely, universalising the benefits of the specifically Anglican religious ethos and its educational effects.
There is a fundamental difference in the policy discourse in how Church of England
schools and other faith schools are positioned. Only Church of England schools are expected
to be faith inclusive. The official Anglican line on admissions, 'Christian ethos but inclusive
admissions policies', coincides with the government's view that 'We want these [Anglican]
schools to be inclusive' (DfES 2002: 45). This seems to reposition family religious beliefs in
relation to recruitment to Church of England schools in order to weaken the schools'
Anglican faith exclusivity. The question which arises in this context is whether this constitutes
an extension of faith schooling, as recommended in the Dearing (2001) review of Anglican
schooling, or an increase in the opportunities for educational choices *of distinction* for those
who are likely to be the more sophisticated educational choosers. Our view is that this is
one of the ways in which the *positional currency* of faith schooling being underwritten.

From equity to ethos

Whereas Coleman is concerned with distributive justice, and his argument about faith
schools focuses almost exclusively on their contribution to enhanced educational equity,
current UK policy discourse does not talk about equity as redistribution of access to

positional goods, but as the right to distinctiveness. In Coleman's original formulation, convergence of socially unequal educational outcomes is an essential part of the agenda. In New Labour thinking, serious commitment to convergence is replaced by faith ethos, itself simply one among a collection of possible school identities in the era of diversification of secondary education (Gamarnikow and Green, forthcoming). We would argue that the relative positioning of differentially 'ethosed' schools is more concerned with product identity in the educational market place than with the redistribution of access to the structure of educational opportunities.

Taking Catholic schools as a case in point, there are, for instance, many questions and issues of concern arising from Grace's research (2002). By way of illustration of this, our aim in the next part of this discussion is to draw out some of the equity/ethos issues from the information he provides on educational outcomes, gender composition and free school meals (FSM). Our reasons for concentrating on Grace's data are two-fold: first, the range of information he provides, and second, the social justice focus of both his research and the schools investigated. With regard to the first, there are no equivalent studies of other systems of faith schools. For example, the Dearing report (2001: 87–8) provides only minimal (mean and median) overall figures for achievement and English as an additional language (EAL) and special educational needs, and the overall FSM average. There also seems to be a certain official coyness about providing this information. In a recent *Times Educational Supplement* survey (Gold 2003) on poverty and achievement the researchers complained that access to collated school-based FSM and achievement data was refused by both the Office for Standards in Education (OFSTED) and the DfES. Turning to the second reason, one of the issues Grace explores is whether Catholic schools embrace the post-Vatican II 'preferential option for the poor': whether, that is, they are doing the educational work of social justice which should resonate with Coleman's findings. In this strand there is a strong focus on the reproduction of an ethos of social progressivism as a collective belief system – commitment to service to the poor. The difficult question in the English context is how this can be translated into real practices which are about redistribution and convergence in the widest sense, i.e. class struggle over access to *quality* education. If Catholic schools are able to develop such practices, the question arises concerning whether there are strategies for insulating the Catholic school system from the structuring mechanisms of the unintended consequences of choices in the market, from themselves being class structured? A reworking of Grace's data seems to suggest that Catholic schools are not immune from the sadly familiar educational outcome effects of social class and gender structuration, and strengthens his argument that 'mission' or ethos alone cannot overcome inequity.

A number of relevant themes emerge from Table 8.1. We will look initially at social class and gender issues. There is, first, a great diversity in average educational outcomes at the school level. While we are not certain of the precise year of comparison (between 1997 and 2000) (Grace 2002: 115), Grace's data come from the time when the national average in the A–C economy (Gillborn and Youdell 2000) was just below 50 per cent (45.1 per cent in 1997; 46.3 per cent in 1998; 47.9 per cent in 1999; 49.2 per cent in 2000). Thus the high-achieving Catholic schools are clearly above the national average, with the other two categories of schools ('above average visible success' and 'below average visible success' with respect to the local education authority [LEA]) achieving below that. A more appropriate and relevant comparison between these two categories of lower-achieving schools and the overall LEA achievement is not possible because we do not have the data for all schools in each of these inner-city LEAs in London, Birmingham and Liverpool. Second, in relation to social class, identified by proxy as 'deprivation' (Power *et al.* 2002) in the FSM column, achievement in the A–C economy would appear to reproduce the

Table 8.1 Catholic schools: educational achievement, social class, gender and faith exclusivity

Achievement	A*–C (%)	FSM (%)	Gender (%)			Catholic students
			G	B	M	(%)
High visible success (n = 9)	65.55	19.40	55.50	33.3	11.20	95.50
Above average visible success (for LEA) (n = 24)	39.44	37.08	41.66	16.6	41.66	85.83
Below average visible success (for LEA) (n = 25)	20.76	50.16	4	32	64	81.52

Source: Grace (2002), table 7.1, p. 158; table 7.2, p. 159; table 7.3, p. 161.

Key: LEA, local education authority; FSM, free school meals; G, girls; B, boys; M, mixed.

traditional pattern of an inverse relationship between educational outcomes and FSM. This suggests that Catholic schools are not immune from familiar social class effects. This is significant in that the percentage of FSM in Catholic secondary schools (16.5 per cent), unlike that in Anglican (11.8 per cent) and other faith schools (7.1 per cent), tends to hover at the national average in non-faith schools (16.8 per cent) (Humanist Philosophers' Group 2001). Thus Catholic schools would appear to be recruiting students from social class backgrounds which are, on average, the same as those of students in non-denominational schools. This seems to indicate no distinctive commitment to a mission for the education of the poor. They seem, also, to be producing stratified national achievement patterns. Thirdly, the gender pattern presents a similarly familiar picture – girls overall are performing better than boys. Fourth, the social class/gender interface is likewise interesting. Single-sex schools, in general, tend to recruit students from higher social class backgrounds than mixed schools (Arnot 2002). In Grace's data this would also seem to be the case. It is the schools with the higher proportion of FSM which are clearly overrepresented as mixed schools. It is also these schools which are at the lower end of visible achievement. Single-sex schools are more predominant at the upper end of the A–C economy and lower end of FSM for Grace's Catholic schools. We would conclude that there is *prima facie* evidence in Grace's data that Catholic schools in England are not immune from the social reproductive effects characteristic of English education in general. Even schools in what we term the 'Coleman row' (above average success for low-achieving LEAs) have not been able to produce results close to the national average in the A–C economy: 39.44 per cent as against just under 50 per cent. This relates to our earlier argument about the care that must be exercised in developing social justice arguments when focusing on intra-group differences in achievement where educational outcomes of faith-school downsiders are compared with very low achievement among non-denominational downsiders.

Returning to Coleman's notion of social capital built around faith exclusivity and links to higher achievement, our interpretation of Grace's data indicates that this does hold, but with an important social class proviso. There is a tendency towards greater faith exclusivity amongst schools with lower FSM rates which also tend to be those schools at the higher end of the A–C economy. Conversely, lower faith exclusivity lies at the lower end of the social class spectrum of recruitment (higher rates of FSM) and achievement. Faith-based social capital networks thus appear to be more productive of beneficial outcomes at the higher end of the social class system, where they are also less inclusive. This is interesting to note in relation to the links between social capital, in the form of norms and values of social networks, and the social distribution of educational achievement. Closure of school–community faith networks appears, in the English context, to support Bourdieu's, rather than Coleman's, take on the consequences of social capital on social class formation. In other words, faith-based social capital networks, organised around a school faith ethos, may result in marginally higher achievement among some downsiders, but they clearly also contribute to high achievement among the upsiders. Thus the contribution of faith ethos to equity remains an open question, particularly in contexts where access to the *relatively more effective* social capital of social networks of the 'faithful' remains class-based.

Conclusion

In this chapter we have pointed to questions about the social justice implications of the social effects of faith schools. Our general argument is that the significance of faith schooling for equity resides in its emergent social scarcity value in the school system as a whole. In this case, and in the broader context of educational markets and parental choice, faith schooling remains a positional good. The preoccupation with a faith ethos, which we connect to the social capital arguments of Coleman, is masking the structural equity issues of a market-based system for distributing educational opportunities. Coleman identified relatively successful schools; that is to say, amongst schools serving the poor, Catholic schools seemed to make a positive contribution to their educational achievement amongst the poor. Current education policy appears to attach a great deal of significance to the supposed influence of faith ethos and its social capitalisation for remediating the effects of the education market. Ethos becomes the mechanism for universalising these beneficial effects across the system as a whole. We remain sceptical about the progressive social justice possibilities of successful universalisation of access to faith schooling, to what is, in effect, a market-based positional good.

Note

1   We are very grateful to Professor Gerald Grace for his helpful comments on an earlier draft of this paper.

References

Arnot, M. (2002) *Reproducing Gender? Essays on Educational Theory and Feminist Politics*, London: Routledge Falmer.

Arthur, J. (2003) *Education with Character: The Moral Economy of Schooling*, London: RoutledgeFalmer.

Arthur, J. with Bailey, R. (2000) *Schools and Community: The Communitarian Agenda in Education*, London: Falmer Press.

Ball, S.J. (2003) *Class Strategies and the Education Market: The Middle Classes and Social Advantage*, London: RoutledgeFalmer.

Baron, S., Field, J. and Schuller, T. (eds) (2000) *Social Capital: Critical Perspectives*, Oxford: Oxford University Press.

Blair, T. (2002) 'Speech to Labour Party Conference', *Guardian*, Tuesday, 1 October.

Bourdieu, P. (1983) 'The forms of capital', in A.H. Halsey, H. Lauder, P. Brown and A.S. Wells (eds) (1997) *Education: Culture, Economy and Society*, Oxford: Oxford University Press.

BHA (2002) *A Better Way Forward: BHA Policy on Religion and Schools*, London: BHA.

Bryk, A., Lee, V. and Holland, P. (1993) *Catholic Schools and the Common Good*, Cambridge, MA: Harvard University Press.

Coleman, J.S. (1968) 'The concept of equality of educational opportunity' *Harvard Educational Review*, special issue, vol. 38, no. 1, winter, pp. 7–22.

Coleman, J.S. (1988) 'Social capital in the creation of human capital', in A.H. Halsey, H. Lauder, P. Brown and A.S. Wells (eds) (1997) *Education: Culture, Economy and Society*, Oxford: Oxford University Press.

Coleman, J.S. (1990) *Equality and Achievement in Education*, Boulder, CO: Westview Press.

Coleman, J.S. and Hoffer, T. (1987) *Public and Private High Schools: The Impact of Communities*, New York: Basic Books.

Coleman, J.S., Campbell, E.Q., Hobson, C.J., McPartland, J., Mood, A.M., Weinfeld, F.D. and York, R.L. (1966) *Equality of Educational Opportunity*, Washington, DC: US Government Printing Office.

Coleman, J.S., Hoffer, T. and Kilgore, S. (1982) *High school achievement*, New York: Basic Books.

Dearing, R. (2001) *The Way Ahead: Church of England Schools in the New Millennium*, Report of the Church Schools Review Group, London: Church House Publishing.

DfEE (1997) *Excellence in Schools*, London: Stationery Office.

DfEE (2001) *Schools: Building on Success*, Cm 5050, London: Stationery Office.

DfES (2001) *Schools: Achieving Success*, Cm 5230, London: Stationery Office.

DfES (2002) *Investment for Reform: Comprehensive Spending Review 2002*, London: Stationery Office.

DfES (2003) *A New Specialist System: Transforming Secondary Education*, London: DfES, available online at http://www.teachernet.gov.uk/makingadiff/.

Department of Health (1999) *Saving Lives: Our Healthier Nation*, London: Stationery Office.

Fine, B. (1999) 'The developmental state is dead – long live social capital?' *Development and Change*, 30: 1–19.

Fukuyama, F. (1995) *Trust: The Social Virtues and the Creation of Prosperity*, London: Hamish Hamilton.

Gamarnikow, E. and Green, A. (1999a) 'Developing social capital: dilemmas, possibilities and limitations in education', in A. Hayton (ed.) *Tackling disaffection and social exclusion: education perspectives and policies*, London: Kogan Page.

Gamarnikow, E. and Green, A. (1999b) 'The Third Way and social capital: Education Action Zones and a new agenda for education, parents and community', *International Studies in Sociology of Education*, 9(1): 3–22.

Gamarnikow, E. and Green, A. (2000) 'Citizenship, education and social capital', in D. Lawton, J. Cairns and R. Gardner (eds) *Education for Citizenship*, London: Continuum.

Gamarnikow, E. and Green, A. (forthcoming) 'Social justice, identity formation and social capital: school diversification policy under New Labour', in C. Vincent (ed.) *Social Justice, Identity and Education*, London: Routledge.

Gewirtz, S., Ball, S.J. and Bowe, R. (1995) *Markets, Choice and Equity in Education*, Buckingham: Open University Press.

Giddens, A. (1998) *The Third Way: The Renewal of Social Democracy*, Oxford: Polity Press.

Giddens, A. (ed.) (2001) *The Global Third Way Debate*, Oxford: Polity Press.

Gillborn, D. and Youdell, D. (2000) *Rationing Education: Policy Reform and School Inequality*, Buckingham: Open University Press.

Glendinning, C., Powell, M. and Rummery, K. (eds) (2002) *Partnerships, New Labour and the Governance of Welfare*, Bristol: Policy Press.

Gold, K. (2003) 'Poverty *is* an excuse', *Times Educational Supplement*, 7 March.

Grace, G. (2002) *Catholic Schools: Mission, Markets and Morality*, London: RoutledgeFalmer.

Hirsch, F. (1978) *The Social Limits to Growth*, London: Routledge and Kegan Paul.

Humanist Philosophers' Group (2001) *Religious Schools: The Case Against*, London: British Humanist Association.

Morris, E. (2002) *Reform of the Comprehensive System*, speech given to the Social Market Foundation, London, 24 June, available online at http://www.smf.co.uk/Morris_24_06.html.

Morrow, V. (2001) *Networks and Neighbourhoods: Children's and Young People's Perspectives*, London: Health Development Agency.

Office of National Statistics (2001) *Social Capital: A Literature Review*, available online at http://www.statistics.gov.uk/socialcapital.

Power, S., Warren, S., Gillborn, D., Clark, A., Thomas, S. and Coate, K. (2002) *Education in Deprived Areas: Outcomes, Inputs and Processes*, Perspectives in Policy, London: Institute of Education.

Power, S., Edwards, T., Whitty, G., Wigfall, V. (2003) *Education and the Middle Class*, Buckingham: Open University Press.

Putnam, R.D. with Leonardi, R. and Nanetti, R.Y. (1993) *Making Democracy Work: Civic Traditions in Modern Italy*, Princeton, NJ: Princeton University Press.

Putnam, R.D. (2000) *Bowling Alone: The Collapse and Revival of American Community*, New York: Simon and Shuster.

Rawls, J. (1973) *A Theory of Justice*, Oxford: Oxford University Press.

Secretary of State for Social Security (1999) *Tackling Poverty and Social Exclusion: Providing Opportunities for All*, Cm 4445, London: Stationery Office.

Social Exclusion Unit (1998) *Bringing Britain Together: A National Strategy for Neighbourhood Renewal*, Cm 4045, London: Stationery Office.

Social Exclusion Unit (2000) *National Strategy for Neighbourhood Renewal: A Framework for Consultation*, London: Social Exclusion Unit.

Whitty, G., Power, S. and Halpin, D. (1998) *Devolution and Choice in Education: The School, the State and the Market*, Buckingham: Open University Press.

World Bank (2000) *Attacking Poverty*, World Bank Development Report 2000/01, Oxford: Oxford University Press/World Bank.

Part III

Faith schools

In practice

9 Perceptions and practices of Christian schools

Bart McGettrick

In many countries, 'faith-based schools' are currently under scrutiny and consideration. In societies which seek social inclusion and which strive towards peaceful co-existence among all pupils, questions are often raised about the value of faith-based schools.

It would be very easy to assume that faith-based schools are to be considered only in societies where there is peaceful co-existence. The current experiences in the Middle East highlight the serious concerns of faith-based schools in a region of conflict – especially religious and political conflict. The faith-based schools there raise questions about whether peace is an ultimate objective of social transformation. Peace may not be an end in itself but a means of expressing harmony between our fellow human beings. It is a way of being which dignifies each person and which promotes a life of care and celebration of the goodness of God.

It might be noted in passing that war is undertaken so that peace may flourish. Peace does not, however, exist so that war might follow but to allow the celebration of human dignity among all peoples. It is worth considering whether this is the aim of a faith-based education, that people of all faiths might celebrate the goodness of humanity freely, and with the dignity of the person at its heart.

This debate and dialogue about the purposes of education and how these are to be seen in the light of faith is an ancient debate. Neither the antiquity of the questions nor the continuing discourse leads to a final conclusion since all human development has to be interpreted within a culture, place and time. Christians, Jewish and Muslim educators in the Middle East each seek a land of peace, so that they might know God more fully and serve Him by the fulfilment of their humanity through using their gifts to the full. The faith-based schools promote that thinking and those aspirations.

For Christian educators there is a major question about students living in a society where they witness and are even involved in human atrocities. The issues that arise internally in such environments are difficult to analyse and are profound in their significance. They include matters which certainly affect interpersonal and inter-faith tensions, as well as raising institutional questions on matters such as curricular decisions which are affected by the multi-faith dimension of communities. Sometimes these extreme circumstances highlight the key issues of what it is to be human; what it is to be educated; and the role of Christian education in a wider community.

Perhaps we know that we are succeeding in education when each person treats his neighbour as if he was his brother. It sounds a simple aspiration, but this is far from prevalent attitudes.

There is no doubt that the social and political contexts in which faith-based education is being conducted significantly affects the nature of that education, and the perceptions and practices of these are given brief reflection in the issues raised below.

The future pattern of educational provision

The future of policy development in education currently is not clear. There are different ways of seeing what is likely to be the optimum arrangement which will allow faith-based schools to flourish.

We may wish to reflect on whether it is likely that there will be political involvement, possibly with government ministers expressing views about national priorities, and government officials and departments prescribing the ways by which we are to achieve these outcomes or targets. In such a system the role of professional teachers is largely concerned with the 'delivery' of priorities set in communities external to the faith community. There is a tendency for external agendas to be set in relation to matters such as targets, outcomes, standards and competencies, etc. Governments and civic authorities are much more inclined to be interventionist in these matters. They are however rarely interventionist in relation to matters of faith and personal conviction. They have a reluctance to become involved in issues of faith, values and ethics, other than to speak of pluralism and the celebration of diversity.

An alternative way of thinking of this is to consider a model which highlights the significance of communities setting their own vision and related agendas for education. At its best this involves the formation of a community of learning establishing its own mission, articulating that mission, proclaiming it, defending it and evaluating it. In a faith-based school faith is a critical dimension of that learning. The role of leadership in a faith-based school is to be able to define, articulate, defend and evaluate the agenda for the school which is based on principles established by the community which the school is there to serve. This includes those ideals, values and attitudes deriving from a particular faith. One of the major requirements for the teaching community in such schools is to have the professional ethical courage to ensure that education is not just to be found in the market place.

These different conceptualisations of the school systems would lead us to select either a 'systems-driven' approach or a 'values-based' approach to education. To some extent the question is whether we are focussed on the education system or the individual school. In a sense it is the education system which has the greater significance since it is there to serve 'the common good'. Of course it would be perverse to believe that the common good could be served if individual schools or elements in the system were a source of division or conflict.

In practice it would seem, in a participative democracy, that both approaches to education are likely. The role of leadership is to integrate these and not see them as alternatives. There can be little doubt that faith-based schools are more likely to thrive under the system which gives precedence to the values and aspirations of the community, and the state is a servant of that community.

The purposes of faith-based schools are likely not to be different from other schools but they will be distinctive. They will be concerned to form young people characterised by:

- Love, care and compassion
- An appreciation of beauty
- Service to others.

The nature of faith-based education

Schools might be defined as communities of learning. A faith-based school has to put faith as a significant dimension of the learning which takes place in that school. The community of such a school is also a faith community – inspired by the values and ideals of that faith. Often the distinctive approach to the faith arises from a distinctive charism or approach to the faith. For example, in the Christian tradition there are Catholic schools, and some of these can be variously described as Jesuit schools, Dominican schools, Lasallian schools, Franciscan schools, etc., each reflecting the charism of the founder of the religious Order which began the school.

It is the expectation of lawful societies that the education systems will be concerned with equity, justice and peace. It is therefore necessarily the case that the existence of faith-based schools should be understood in the fuller context of a society which seeks justice, harmony and peace. Faith-based schools therefore have a responsibility to ensure that both their external relationships, and their internal practices, are consistent with these broader objectives of society. They are communities which are hostile to the abuse of human rights, the degradation of the environment and the abuses of justice and peace in the world. They represent certain values and are prepared to stand for these values. These are the values which derive from the faith of the community in whose interests the school is run.

In certain countries, such as in the countries of the United Kingdom, they are not alternatives to state provision but are a part of that provision. They have a duty to teach through an education which is unequivocally 'in the common good'. These faith-based schools have a duty to work within a framework which is genuinely educative in the widest sense for the society of which they are part.

The purpose of faith-based schools will differ according to different societies. In the United Kingdom, for example, a Christian school is part of the state provision and is normally a place for educating Christians. On a world scale this is in fact a rather narrow purpose for a Christian school. In Jordan, Palestine and Israel, for example, a Christian school is a school which is founded on the values of Christianity and its practices are orientated towards that value system. In many of these schools the majority of students are Muslim and in some cases less than 40 per cent of the students are Christian. In such schools the purpose of teaching religion to Muslim children is to 'form them as better Muslims'. This is an interpretation of the Christian injunction 'to love your neighbour'. To love one's neighbour is to support them in being better and more devout members of their own particular faith. It is certainly not a role for a school to be engaged in proselytising among the students. To do so would be to abuse the professional privilege of education, and to deny the professional love which the teachers have for their students.

Characteristics of faith-based schools

There are a number of characteristics of faith-based schools, although these characteristics are rather dependent on society and the community in which the school is set. In general the characteristics would normally include:

- A concern for religious education taught through a particular religious tradition;
- An interest in the way teaching and learning in other areas of the curriculum are being set in the context of a particular faith (e.g. the place of biology, social studies, physical education);

- Building a special ethos of the school characterised by the nature of the relationships which arise from a particular faith tradition;
- Paying attention to the spirituality of the school which emerges from its faith base;
- Monitoring the admission of students who will be able to benefit from this form of education;
- Giving attention to the appointment of staff who are supportive of the particular faith of the faith-based school.

The particular faith tradition has an effect on the ethos and spirituality of the community of learners that forms the school. Of course it would be inappropriate to think of these as quality indicators which, if they were given due attention, would be sufficient to describe the faith-based school. At its heart it is the spirit of the school which matters. It is the life that flows through the organisation which brings meaning and wholeness to the school – and not merely the presence or otherwise of indicators.

The question of what the 'faith basis' of a school is therefore merits some attention. Faith has several aspects: first, it consists of a body of knowledge or dogmas; second, it involves certain practices and celebrations (including feasts and festivals); and third, it has a characteristic spirituality. All of these elements are consistent and reinforce each other in the development of a faith community.

In the modern world the faith-based school has to be fully and unequivocally part of the wider educational system. This raises some issues which need to be explored.

For example:

- Is there any distinctiveness about the faith-based school?
- Are there ways in which it stands apart from other provision?

The answer has to be that it is distinctive in certain ways. It must have a vision and a set of values which are distinctive to that faith.

One of the difficulties encountered in this regard is that the state has developed a strong discourse of professional accountability based on systems thinking. Many faiths have not developed a similar code of discussion, and consequently find it increasingly difficult to engage in the discourse on the same terms as the state. Faith-based organisations have maintained their interest in the personal and pastoral interests of students, and have failed to make an impact at the level of systems, where so much effort is placed in terms of policies and accountability. This can lead to a distinction between professional interests in faith-based schools and other schools.

In an effective system of education there would be opportunities for faith-based schools and other schools to engage in the same discourse and dialogue about what each has to offer because both have something to share. A mission without targets can be hazy and ill-defined; a system which pays no attention to the values underlying it can be superficial, poorly guided and uninspired. This is not to suggest all depth, guidance and inspiration comes from faith alone. The dialogue is, however, essential.

The curriculum

Current issues in education are often based around the curriculum. This has to be set in context. There is a very rapid change taking place in education such that the knowledge, facts and even ideas which we have will be transformed within the foreseeable future.

These are not static and certainly do not last a lifetime. So there is a need to review the place of 'content' in what we teach. Many educational systems are looking more at learning how to learn, and learning 'how to be' as part of the curriculum in schools, as well as part of the extra-curricular provision.

One of the developing or emerging aspects of faith-based schools is an understanding of the pervasive and underpinning spirituality in the community of the school. Increasingly it is being understood that there is a unity in the person, the subject content, the processes of learning and the community of which we are part. In faith-based schools these are conceptualised as a unity and practised in an integrated way. It is therefore likely that there is coherence between what is taught and a philosophy of life. This unity is based on a spirituality of education which places faith and learning together, bonded by mutual inspiration and emotions, to form the inner self.

This is not a claim for uniqueness, but a striving towards an understanding of the unity of person, scholarship and community.

Parents and others in the Middle East have raised interesting questions about the curriculum in faith-based schools. There are examples of how the faith base of a state such as in the Hashemite Kingdom of Jordan and the current Palestinian Education Authority has led Christian schools to look at the implementation of General Certificate in Secondary Education (GCSE) frameworks for the curriculum with great interest. This is in the interests of freeing certain faith-based schools from the influences of national requirements in a particular faith. (For example, Christian schools who currently have to teach Islam may seek ways of having the freedom to teach Christianity alone.)

This is not just a matter for schools such as those in the Middle East; in Scotland, for example, there is a requirement in the curriculum for children aged 5–14 years to study three world religions, one of which must be Christianity.

The relationship of church and state

The relationship between church and state is a very important area for consideration. It is also an area which is slippery. It moves from place to place and from time to time. De Toqueville's hypothesis is that the harmonious separation of church and state is the optimum condition for both to thrive. This is a hypothesis which is worth considering at some length. The implied separation of church and state is important in certain political and social settings. It is seen clearly in countries such as the United States and Italy.

The harmonious integration of church and state may be a more desirable arrangement which is to the advantage to both. This is clear in countries such as Scotland where the Catholic schools are state schools, fully funded and integrated into the state system.

In many countries there are variations on this theme which derive from the history, politics, and interests of both church and state. There is undoubtedly a trend towards a plurality of knowledge and understanding, although questions arise about inclusiveness in relation to celebration. There are also trends towards greater unity of spiritualities and shared feelings among different faith groups. The extent to which this leads to unity or to pluralism varies from country to country and faith to faith.

Associated with this are ecumenical and multi-faith perspectives which are growing in significance and importance, although in many countries and schools practices are not yet advanced in terms of faith inclusivity. There is an undoubted nervousness in faith-based schools to explore common themes, common issues, common practices and common beliefs. There is, however, a concern for spirituality which is growing in schools. Much of this derives from an interest in what faiths offer in common. Not all spirituality derives directly from a religious source. It can be seen in faith-based schools and is emerging from the concern that young people have with matters of deep human interest.

The trend towards secularisation

There is a global tendency towards secularisation and the increased marginalisation of the churches in relation to educational tradition. Secularisation is, however, as much a feature of society and of faith as is 'holiness'. Secularisation is not entirely a negative and insidious influence but is a dimension of the dominance of the market place in a systems-driven education system.

The faith-based school has a duty to offer a different perspective from this, and to proclaim the values of that faith as integral to education. The values of an education system which supports and promotes faith-based schools are influenced by secularisation but may still survive, and even thrive, in particular educational settings.

The effects of secularisation in schools is to introduce a different value system into the faith-based system. This is a form of values pluralism and is a characteristic of contemporary society.

Fundamentalism and globalisation

One of the universal trends in society is the emergence of fundamentalism of all kinds. The tendency towards fundamentalism often derives from flash points and areas of conflict. In recent months and years the issues that surround the events of 11 September 2001, the Lockerbie bombing and other flash points can be seen to be stimuli for fundamentalist tendencies.

Since public education has to operate in the common good, the question arises as to whether fundamentalist approaches to religion have a generally adverse effect on the common good and how this might impact on faith-based schools. This intense concern often for narrow aspects of religious practice can be detrimental to matters such as harmony, peace and equity in social systems. Where views are held with conviction and passion, these need not be contrary to some of the broader views of the purposes of education. In such circumstances, this is not detrimental to an effective educational system. Where, however, there are ideas, beliefs and practices which are contrary to the common good, these become hostile to education and the purposes of faith-based education.

One of the important areas for consideration is the extent to which being more educated leads to greater tolerance. It is true in most cases that being more educated (regardless of subject) leads to less tolerance of intolerance particularly in matters of politics and religion. That is, the more educated person is a more tolerant one except in relation to extremism and fundamentalism in religion and politics.

Generally speaking the trend towards fundamentalist thinking and practices is narrowing in its outlook and therefore detrimental to taking a broad view of educational thinking. It tends not to be liberating or providing a balance in thought and a width of reflection. The faith-based school should ensure that teachers understand how these values operate among the pupils. Only through a deep understanding of matters such as this can we hope to promote direct action which will promote and sustain educational advancement.

The prevailing culture of faith schools

Faith schools are generally concerned about their climate and ethos. Normally in a faith school the climate derives from a particular faith perspective. In a Christian school the faith base is normally one concerned with relationships and care and it is these relationships which carry the values of the school and of society more generally.

These relationships are among the strongest forces in carrying the values which will be influential with the students. To some extent, of course, the values are carried through by the staff of the school, because the staff are the permanent infrastructure for creating relationships and offering continuity – two very important attributes for forming and supporting values.

This prevailing ethos is often the underlying cause of the effectiveness of the particular school. This would be true of all faith-based schools. It raises a question about whether all faiths are concerned with relationships, and it seems pragmatic to conclude that they are.

Admission of students

Faith-based schools can have criteria for admitting students based on the practice of their faith. This is by no means a universal criterion. It is, however, normal for the school to require a student to be committed to support the general tenets and implications of the faith, even if they themselves are not practising members of that faith community. This can be an area which is hotly disputed, and it is very much part of the wider concerns for inclusion in society. It cannot be considered without that broader context.

Staff

Similarly there are issues surrounding the employment of teachers in faith-based schools. In many schools which are faith-based there are significant numbers of staff members who are not of that faith. Again there is an expectation that teachers will support the practices and values of the particular faith. This is an essential feature of schools since it is the teachers who form the most stable and lasting element in the school community. In effect they set the values of the school, and create its culture and ethos.

A question which arises from this is whether it is possible to have a faith-based school in which the majority of teachers are not of that faith. It would seem possible to have a faith-based school where the majority of teachers, or the majority of students, are not of that faith. The criterion for the school being faith-based is its leadership, mission and values, and how these are reflected in the culture of the school. It is not dependent on the particular practices of individual people in the school and in the hearts and minds of people and the community of which they are part. The leadership of the school must therefore pay attention to the values of the school and how these impact on practices, symbols and attitudes. These are carried in the relationships and management of the school. Much therefore depends on *how* things are taught rather than *what* is taught.

Conclusion

In relation to this range of matters there are several questions which remain. These include:

- Are faith-based schools more concerned with a single religion or a respect for pluralism?
- Are faith-based schools concerned with identifying common issues which relate to more than one faith?
- Is there a danger in a world of secularisation of a loss of direction inspired by faith?
- Is there the capacity to develop a distinctive spirituality in all faith-based schools?

Essentially these perceptions of faith-based schools lead us to a view that if they are genuinely inspired by their faith, and by a love of learning, they will undoubtedly be forces for the common good.

Sources consulted

Bailey, R. (2000) *Teaching Values and Citizenship Across the Curriculum: Educating Children for the World*, London: Kogan Page.
Bell, J. and Harrison, B.T. (eds) (1995) *Vision and Values in Managing Education*, Essex: David Fulton.
Bottery, M. (1987) *Issues in Moral and Values Education*, Hull: University of Hull.
Bottery, M. (1990) *The Morality of the School: The Theory and Practice of Values*, London: Cassell.
Carr, D. and Haldane, J. (1993) *Values and Values Education: An Introduction*, St Andrews: University of St Andrews.
Christie, D., Maitles, H. and Halliday, J. (1998) *Values for Democracy and Citizenship*, Glasgow: University of Strathclyde.
de Tocqueville, A. (1990), *Democracy in America*, Vol. 2, New York: Vintage Books.
Dower, N. and Williams, J. (2002) *Global Citizenship: A Critical Reader*, Edinburgh: Edinburgh University Press.
Downie, R.S. and Fyfe, C., Tannahill, A. (1990) *Health Promotion: Models and Values*, Oxford: Oxford University Press.
Grace, G. (1995) *School Leadership*, London, Falmer.
Hargreaves, A. and Fullan, M. (1995) *What's Worth Fighting for in Education*, Buckingham: Open University Press.
Magnell, T. (1998) *Values and Education*, Amsterdam: Rodopi.
McGettrick, B.J. (1995) *Values and Educating the Whole Person*, Dundee: Scottish Council for Consultation on the Curriculum.
Murphy, P.J. (1991) *Visions and Values in Catholic Higher Education*, Kansas City: Sheed & Ward.
Rodger, A. and Squires, J. (1995) *A Handbook for School Values Development*, Dundee: Northern College.

10 Learning together

The case for 'joint church' schools

Alan J. Murphy

The great majority of 'church schools' or 'faith schools' were originally founded by particular Christian denominations, religious orders or other single-faith communities. A case will be made for consideration of the potential advantages of different Christian denominations or traditions joining together to form 'joint church schools'. The term 'joint church school' will be defined as the type of school formed when two Christian church traditions join together to found and develop a maintained school, admitting primarily, but not necessarily exclusively, members of the founding traditions.

Currently, there are fewer than 10 'joint church' maintained secondary schools in England, and a small number of primary schools. The term 'integrated school' is used in Northern Ireland, 'inter-church' in Cambridge and 'shared school' is the working term for a school under development in Wales.

The advantages of working ecumenically will be put forward, practical points will be raised and hindering factors will be faced. St Edward's School, in Poole, Dorset – a joint Roman Catholic–Church of England comprehensive school for 12–18-year-olds – will be offered as a case study. The author was headteacher from 1985 to 2001 and as he is a Roman Catholic the issues are discussed from this perspective.

Economics or ecumenics?

It is probably true that 'economics' played a greater part in the founding of the majority of the current crop of joint church schools than did 'ecumenics'. During the 1980s and 1990s, schools were required to demonstrate that they were viable units within an educational marketplace. In some areas where the Christian communities were more widely dispersed, it became difficult to justify the maintenance of separate schools for each denomination. If communities were ecumenically minded, then they saw the formation of a joint church school as a positive response to the economical imperative.

This was particularly the case at secondary level. Pupils began to be considered as 'age-weighted pupil units' rather than children and perhaps the 'cash' they brought in became more important than the 'catholicity' they brought with them. A small secondary school was not considered to be viable in financial terms even though many parents were attracted to small secondary schools and many teachers liked working in them. The need to maintain numbers but still maintain a 'Christian ethos' led to the opening up of Catholic schools to the wider Christian community.

It was perfectly understandable that Catholic (and it was mainly Catholic schools that faced this dilemma, Church of England secondaries being a rare species) schools responded to changing times in this way, for they must exist in the real world and budgets must be balanced. A problem was that frequently the other maintained schools serving the same geographical area felt that these expanding Catholic schools were succeeding at their expense. Popular church schools were believed to be taking the pupils who should have been attending their local community comprehensive, which the government required to offer religious education and acts of worship that were 'broadly Christian'.

Another perception was that admissions policies to these church schools favoured children from a more supportive background. The suspicion was that, as well as balancing their budgets, these children were helping the church schools to clamber over their neighbours as they strove to achieve a good position in the local 'league table'. Perhaps now is the time to argue the case for joint church schools from an ecumenical standpoint rather than from a financial or survival perspective.

Serving different communities?

Church of England schools, both primary and secondary, have traditionally served the local community in which they are based. Lord Dearing, in his report *The Way Ahead* (Church Schools Review Group, 2001), reminds us that Church of England schools 'are places where the beliefs and practices of other faiths will be respected' (paragraph 3.12): 'In offering an invitation to children and young people from all backgrounds to participate in a Christian community, Church schools can provide a real experience of God's love for all humanity' (Church Schools Review Group 2001: paragraph 3.23).

Roman Catholic schools, on the other hand, were generally founded to serve the Catholic faith community in which they were based: 'The Catholic school forms part of the saving mission of the Church, especially for education in the faith' (Congregation for Catholic Education 1977: paragraph 9).

The formation of a joint church school would therefore have to reconcile these different approaches to education. However, both churches are committed to meeting the spiritual needs of all those admitted to their schools. The Roman Catholic Bishops of England and Wales in their statement on religious education in Catholic schools (2000) challenged schools to ensure they met the spiritual development of pupils of other faiths. It is no longer considered satisfactory for Catholic schools to offer the same diet to pupils from many backgrounds, traditions and faiths.

Joint church schools will see such a challenge as an opportunity to be welcomed rather than a problem to be faced up to.

Next, the case for joint church schools is set in the context of all Christian churches working hard to achieve the goal of unity among all Christians and the desire to engage in dialogue with those of other faiths or of no faith.

Towards dialogue and commitment

The Sacred Congregation did, however, recognise the realities that needed to be faced when offering Catholic education within a pluralist society. The Church was moving away from a one-size-fits-all prescription: 'Yet the diverse situations and legal systems in which the Catholic school has to function in Christian and non-Christian countries demand that local problems be faced and solved by each Church within its own social-cultural context' (Congregation for Education 1977: paragraph 2).

While this response was related to 'problems' to be faced, in parallel with this, the Catholic church was also working hard to stress its commitment to the search for unity among Christians.

Account has to be taken of new pedagogical insights and collaboration with others, irrespective of religious allegiance, who work honestly for the true development of mankind – first and foremost with schools of other Christians – in the interests, even in this field, of Christian unity but also with State schools.

(ibid. 1977: paragraph 67)

The late Cardinal Basil Hume spoke at a major Christian Unity conference held at Swanwick in 1987. The conference, which included representatives from 37 denominations, laid the foundations for the 'Churches Together' movement. He drew the conference to a close by suggesting that unity, when achieved, would be enriched rather than diminished by the diversity of the traditions that formed the movement, but that all needed to work actively towards the goal of Christian unity. He stated: 'It is important that we move quite deliberately from a situation of co-operation to one of commitment to each other.'

The Catechism of the Catholic Church proclaims that 'The desire to recover the unity of all Christians is a gift of Christ and a call of the Holy Spirit.' It is then explained what must happen for this to come about:

Certain things are required in order to respond adequately to this call: renewal, conversion of the heart, dialogue, prayer in common, ecumenical formation, fraternal knowledge of each other and collaboration among Christians in various areas of service to mankind.

(*Catechism of the Catholic Church* 1994: paragraphs 820–1)

The importance of dialogue between Christians was stressed by Archbishop Pablo Puente, the Pope's representative in Britain, in a homily given during a visit to the school: '… we need reconciliation which grows in dialogue with other Christians and other religions. As the Pope said, this will be one of the characteristics of the new world' (Archbishop Pablo Puente, July 2002).

There is, therefore, a strong case to be made for a school community becoming a focus for this dialogue and for being a practical demonstration of commitment by Christians to work together for the benefit of young people. 'If we don't help Christ to approach youth, we close the door on a bright future for the Church' (ibid.).

Learning together: a case study

The first joint church school in England, St Cuthbert Mayne School in Torquay, was founded in 1969 within the Roman Catholic Diocese of Plymouth. In the same diocese, St Edward's School in Poole, Dorset, was a small Roman Catholic secondary school that had in the late 1960s agreed to help the local education authority cope with a bulge in pupil numbers by welcoming the admission of children from other Christian traditions.

In 1988 the Governors of St Edward's decided that there would be many advantages in following the lead given by St Cuthbert Mayne School. The proposal was given the full support of Christopher, the Bishop of Plymouth, and John Baker, who was the Bishop of Salisbury at that time. They made the following joint statement in the document produced to outline the proposal: 'The proposal to create a joint Roman Catholic–Anglican comprehensive school at St Edward's, Poole, is one that reflects the commitment between Christian communities to work together.'

On the feast of St Edward, King and Martyr, June 1991, Bishop Christopher led a service in St George's, our local Anglican church, to celebrate the achievement of joint church school status. During his homily, he challenged us to become a 'beacon for ecumenism'.

To do nothing apart which we can do together

The local context for every joint church school is different and there is no intention to suggest that this case study provides a template for the development of other joint church schools. Although we were fortunate to have another joint school within our diocese, we still had to learn from our successes and from our mistakes.

The key is to involve all 'stakeholders', particularly diocesan partners, in all major decisions and in all stages of development of the school.

The first stage of this process was to involve both dioceses in the drawing up of a 'covenant', a statement that defined how the school would put into practice its joint church status. After a series of consultations between the school and the two dioceses, the following 'covenant' was agreed:

> *St Edward's school covenant*
> God Our Father
> In the name of Christ
> and in the Power of the Spirit
> we commit ourselves
> to you and to one another
> to Work, Learn and Pray
> as one body in Christ;
> to do nothing apart
> which we can do together
> to serve your purposes
> of Justice, Love and Peace

The final document was signed by Bishops Christopher Budd and John Baker during a liturgy of celebration held at St Mary's Roman Catholic Church, Poole.

Ready, fire, aim!

Those involved with joint church schools usually accept that firing the starting gun for a new integrated school involves adjusting the triplet of orders generally involved in firing a gun: not READY, AIM, FIRE, but READY, FIRE, AIM. Now we had to AIM. To guide our aim, we needed to ensure that all involved at school level – governors, teachers, support staff, parents and students – shared a common vision. This was achieved by drawing up a mission statement. A team representative of all staff was given time to draft and consult on the statement. The group included colleagues from our feeder schools, to ensure that understanding and commitment to ecumenism was shared throughout our family of schools. To ensure this was not a top–down model, the headteachers were not part of the group. In drawing up a mission statement, the process is more important than the final statement. The statement produced by the working group has worked very well in practice. This was recognised during the school's first inspection: 'This is a school which lives up to its Mission Statement' (Office for Standards in Education [OFSTED] 1997).

St Edward's Roman Catholic–Church of England School
MISSION STATEMENT

'Jesus says – Where people come together in my name, I am with them.'

Matthew 18.20

✦ As a Christian learning community, which promotes the value of family life, we support the parents as primary educators of their children.
✦ We challenge every student to strive for the highest standard of personal, social and intellectual development, and aim for excellence in all they do.
✦ We recognise that all children are unique and aim to guide them along their personal Journey of Faith.
✦ During the day to day life of our school and in all aspects of the curriculum we promote Gospel values.
✦ We provide opportunities for every member of our community to experience prayer, worship and reflection.

'My commandment is this – Love one another just as I love you.'

John 15:12

The working ratio

Which pupils should be admitted? Who pays the 'governors' contributions' to building projects? These questions present challenges to the governors and leaders of a joint church school.

At the foundation stage, most joint church schools agree a 'working ratio' which helps guide decisions in these areas. St Edward's had been a Catholic secondary school which became a joint church school. Keeping in mind the principle that Catholic schools are founded to serve the faith community in which they are based, the ratio agreed was 75 to 25 per cent. This ensured that there would always be places for all members of the local Roman Catholic community seeking a comprehensive church school education for their children. Other joint schools, with a different history, may offer the greatest proportion of places to Anglican families, while some have a straightforward 50:50 ratio. This case study will explain what the agreement of a ratio means in practice.

Admissions

The calculation which led to the ratio of 75 per cent 'in favour' of the Catholic community was a 'maximum figure' based on projections from Catholic primary school intake data and Baptismal numbers of places made available to Catholic families. The Roman Catholic diocese that had originally founded the school thus retained its commitment to provide secondary school places to those who wished to take them up. The reality was that not all Catholic families chose to take up these places – the school is situated in a town which has retained a selective system. The issues arising from this situation are beyond the scope of this chapter as the same problems arise for any church comprehensive school co-existing with selective schools. If Catholic families did not take up the places made available for them, then more places were available for Anglican or Free Church Christians who were committed to denominational comprehensive education. The admission policy was phrased to allow this, stating that 75 per cent was the maximum number of Catholic admissions and that 25 per cent was a minimum for the Anglican community. In practice, the numbers of pupils admitted were in the order of 55 per cent Roman Catholic and 45 per cent Anglican and Free Church children.

Was 'admissions' a straightforward process? No, as with any popular and successful school, we were oversubscribed. This meant that sadly the school had to turn away church-going families desperate to secure a place. The perception of 'rejection' ran contrary to the values we proclaimed, but again this is a problem common to all popular church schools.

Foundation governors

The working ratio also informed how the governing body was constituted. Seventy-five per cent of the foundation governors were drawn from the local Catholic community and 25 per cent from the Anglican community. A commitment to working ecumenically was looked for from all appointments to the governing body.

Financial contributions

All voluntary aided schools must make a contribution to the capital costs of maintaining and developing buildings. When a £1m building project was secured, the costs of the 'governors' contribution' of 15 per cent was £150,000. The responsibility was shared according to the 75:25 ratio previously mentioned, with 75 per cent of the costs being found by the Roman Catholic community and 25 per cent by the Anglicans. The parents helped with fund raising by the church communities making contributions to a 'Building Development Fund'.

Religious education

How is religious education (RE) taught in a joint church school? Again, there is no single answer for all schools as the local context is crucial. The key is to involve the diocesan RE advisers in the planning of schemes. Children learn about both traditions and, of course, as in all good religious education programmes, they must learn about other faiths.

Any church school, but particularly a joint church school, must be clear about the contribution it makes to evangelisation and catechesis. Peter Humfrey (2002: 80) explains that '... religious education programmes intend to educate students to be religiously literate, though some may receive this as catechesis, and others as evangelisation.'

The document from the Congregation of the Catholic Church, *The Religious Dimension of Education in the Catholic School* (1988), stresses that the prime responsibility for catechesis lies with the family and the parish and clarifies the role of the school:

> The aim of catechesis, or handing on the Gospel message, is maturity: spiritual, liturgical, sacramental and apostolic; this happens most especially in a local Church community. The aim of the school, however, is knowledge. While it uses the same elements of the Gospel message, it tries to convey a sense of the nature of Christianity, and of how Christians are trying to live their lives. It is evident, of course, that religious instruction cannot help but strengthen the faith of a believing student, just as catechesis cannot help but increase one's knowledge of the Christian message.
>
> (paragraph 69)

Well-planned programmes of religious education, therefore, provide a solid foundation of 'instruction' on which those primarily responsible for catechesis of Roman Catholic, Anglican or Free Church children – the family and the church community – can build.

Praying together

My experience is that Christians of all denominations, when thrown together in an ecumenical community, become quite passionate about working ecumenically. Colleagues who gathered for our weekly staff morning prayer sessions gained greatly from the varied expressions of faith that individual members brought to the shared act of worhip. We realised that we all had a great deal to learn from each other and very much valued the mutual support, particularly when we faced difficulties as a school or when individual colleagues were experiencing problems in their personal lives.

For students, the morning act of worship was held in year group assemblies or in form rooms led by tutors. Support was provided for tutors who were hesitant about leading morning prayer. Each form had its own 'prayer box' filled with resources – laminated prayer cards, prayers composed by students, icons, candles and matches, a Good News Bible and various published collections of prayers. A regular swap shop was held – tutors brought their boxes to the staffroom and exchanged items and refreshed collections.

During major liturgical celebrations the theme would often include the opportunity to celebrate both our unity and our diversity. Our favourite image was the rainbow. Each Christian tradition brought a colour to build the beauty of the rainbow. However, if you mix these same beautiful colours on a palette in the art room, you finish up with a dull muddy brown colour. This reminded us that, as Cardinal Hume had stated, within unity there would be diversity. Christians who worship together at Taize are always advised to return to their own church communities and not form a new church group. If we didn't work hard to celebrate the fact that we belonged to different traditions and instead formed a new 'Church of St Edward's', we would have further fragmented the Christian community and would be making the achievement of unity more difficult to attain.

Kevin Treston suggests that Christian spirituality had been enriched by the 'interchange of insights among various Christian Churches and by an increasing openness to the wisdom of Eastern religions' (1991: 22). As a biology teacher, I had often taught about the phenomenon of 'hybrid vigour'. I believe the school benefited greatly from inspiration brought to the planning of worship by members of many Christian traditions.

Eucharistic celebration

Perhaps the most 'frequently asked question' concerning our development as a joint church school related to how Mass was celebrated or how we involved the whole school community in Eucharistic celebration. I always hesitate to use the phrase 'the Eucharist can be a problem' but that is the reality. Working ecumenically raises expectations and presents dilemmas. In the early days, we always took advice from clergy from both the dioceses who had been involved in the foundation of our school.

Each tradition has its 'disciplines' and we were always clear that these must be followed to the letter. Being 'in communion' with each other would be the principle indication that unity had been achieved. We were simply pilgrims on a journey towards unity, not a symbol that unity had been achieved.

This journey towards unity is a painful one and perhaps the greatest pain is experienced through Eucharistic separation. We want to break bread together but we cannot. The pain manifested itself in a number of ways. When we held an Anglican Eucharistic celebration according to the disciplines of the Anglican church, Roman Catholics were welcome to receive the Eucharist. But the disciplines of the Roman Catholic Church demand that members of the church should not receive the Eucharist from an Anglican minister – except in very specific circumstances, which do not include celebrations within a normal school setting. Similarly, a Catholic priest may not normally give the Eucharist to Anglican brothers and sisters. Both situations were potential causes of pain and on more than one occasion led to tears of frustration and disappointment.

How did we make the best of this situation? On one 'holy day of obligation' for the Roman Catholic Church, the feast of Corpus Christi, the students and staff of the school walked to Mass at our respective local Catholic church or our local Anglican church. At each a Mass was celebrated by the respective Catholic or Anglican chaplain – but we had no final hymn in the churches. Instead we walked back to school, gathered together in the Assembly Hall and together we sang 'Shine Jesus Shine' with great feeling and passion (not always a hallmark of adolescent hymn singing).

Perhaps those of us involved with church schools should ask ourselves the question: should a school be a 'Eucharistic community'? Although Arthur (1995) sees the failure to reserve the Blessed Sacrament in the chapel of a Catholic school as an indication that the 'tide has ebbed', I would argue that a church school's prime responsibility is to always work in partnership with local parish churches as the Eucharistic communities the school is founded to serve. Discussions involving schools and parishes in deanery groups concerning the respective roles of school and parish in instruction, evangelisation and catechesis is surely the way forward. At the very least, it would provide opportunities to dispel the myths that often arise concerning the role of single-tradition schools, never mind those tricky joint church operations.

Distinctive and inclusive?

Being inclusive in terms of offering educational opportunities to children of all abilities in the communities we serve is crucial. St Edward's attracted an above-average percentage of children with special educational needs but still achieved two Department for Education and Skills awards for 'excellence'.

The problem of achieving a rich diverse and fully inclusive community is a practical one. Many church schools are oversubscribed; a top-achieving joint church school will be heavily oversubscribed.

The joint church school cannot be 'all things to all people'. If the doors are opened wide and all are welcomed in, the school may harm the balance in the local community of schools. Many community and foundation schools also meet the needs of local Christian families and are also excellent schools. The reality is that no one school can be fully inclusive. The aim should be to achieve an 'inclusive community of schools' working collaboratively to offer educational excellence to all the children in the local community.

Learning together

There are a small but significant number of joint church schools in England that demonstrate that 'learning together' can be successful. Not all joint church schools have stood the test of time, but in the same year that we experienced the painful loss of an excellent joint school in Oxford, a new joint church school was opened in Barnsley and an exciting new venture is planned in North Wales. The potential gains far outweigh the difficulties; it is a journey worth taking.

References

Arthur, J. (1995) *The Ebbing Tide*, Leominster: Gracewing.

Bishops' Conference of England and Wales (2000) *Bishops' Statement on RE in Catholic Schools*, London: CES.

Church Schools Review Group (2001) *The Way Ahead: Church of England Schools in the New Millennium*, London: Church House Publishing.

Congregation for Catholic Education (1977) *The Catholic School*, London: Catholic Truth Society.

Congregation for Catholic Education (1988) *The Religious Dimension of Education in the Catholic School*, London: Catholic Truth Society.

Congregation for the Doctrine of the Faith (1994) *Catechism of the Catholic Church*, London: Geoffrey Chapman.

Humfrey, P. (2002) 'Worship in Catholic schools' in M. Hayes and L. Gearson (eds) *The Contemporary Catholic School*, Leominster: Gracewing.

OFSTED (1997) *Report on St Edward's RC CE School, Poole LEA*, London: OFSTED.

Puente, P. (2002) 'The church and the future', *Pilgrim Post* (Newsletter of Churches Together in Dorset) Issue 40.

Treston, K. (1991) *Paths and Stories*, Dublin: Veritas.

11 Segregation or cohesion

Church of England schools in Bradford

Rachel Barker and John Anderson[1]

The Bradford context

After the disturbances in the summer of 2001 in Bradford and other northern towns, which much of the media dubbed 'race riots', both the Cantle and Ouseley Reports made specific reference to education (Cantle 2001; Ouseley 2001). This sparked a concerned debate about the value of 'faith schools' and their contribution to the social make-up of the city. Indeed it was even suggested in some quarters that faith schools had contributed to the disturbances. Yet given the nature and scale of faith school provision, this assertion was clearly untenable.

It should be noted that in law there is no such thing as a 'faith school'. There are schools with a religious character, and it may be argued that this is a less emotive and more accurate description, providing for the distinction between faith and denomination. Moreover, where 'faith schools' receive funding from the government, they are known as voluntary aided schools. The Cantle Report focuses on the 'existing and future mono-cultural' nature of such schools and sees them as 'a significant problem', adding to the separation of faith and ethnic communities in Bradford. The link between education and segregation, and the concern that this was a key factor contributing to the disturbances, has led schools in general, and faith schools in particular, to become something of a scape-goat for the city's problems. This is dangerous on at least two counts: it prejudices faith schools without looking at the evidence and it tends to mask underlying problems.

This chapter offers a preliminary view of the situation Bradford faces, looking at: social and economic conditions, the distribution of schools and population, the way in which the Church of England (CofE) voluntary aided schools are trying to respond and the tensions involved in educational provision which affect cohesion. It attempts to offer an initial explanation of what is happening in Bradford from a CofE perspective and therefore only looks at one facet of a very complex issue. It does however also try to make clear the urgent need for much more detailed research about faith schools in multi-faith and multi-ethnic settings, as well as the tensions that arise as education is called to play its part in establishing identity in a divisive context whilst also trying to achieve social cohesion.

Both Christianity and Islam are worldwide faiths and have followers from a wide variety of cultures and ethnic groups. Bradford reflects this situation and needs to examine the role of faith schools and how they can contribute to improving social harmony. The Education Policy Partnership (EPP), the group which links the client city council with the private education provider Education Bradford, asked the Anglican, Catholic and Muslim providers of voluntary aided schools to consider this. The resulting EPP and voluntary provider joint paper opens the way to a continuing review of what is happening. It highlights the common tendency to use the term 'Christian' to mean the Western white, indigenous population, and 'Muslim' to mean the South Asian community. The consequences of this include stereotyped images and viewpoints which tend to give the impression that by having a Christian foundation a school excludes Asians, only promoting Western culture, and that a school with a Muslim foundation may be similarly divisive.

Although Anglican schools in the city have a clear Christian foundation, they attempt to operate inclusive admissions policies. In the words of the former Bishop of Bradford, David Smith, 'Church schools seek to enter into the life of the community rather than to provide an opportunity to opt out into a rarefied group.' The new Bishop, David James, is now reinforcing this view. The number of Muslim parents who recognised this and supported Church schools during Bradford's school reorganisation was notable. The EPP voluntary provider joint paper concludes:

> ... turning the debate about social cohesion into one about the existence of 'faith schools' is, at best, a diversion. They [voluntary aided schools] are here; they have a good track record on which to build; they have an important role to play in the future success of Bradford education. What we do have the right to expect is that each and every 'faith school' in the district recognises that, wherever it is located and whatever the ethnic and religious composition of its community, it has a duty to strengthen the social cohesion of our wider community ...

Social and economic conditions

Like most cities, Bradford Metropolitan District has its more and less prosperous areas. The more prosperous lie towards the outer edges where the suburbs have grown around the villages and small towns: for example, Ilkley. The less prosperous are in the inner city and the poorest housing estates, several of which are very rundown. A key underlying problem for Bradford is the steady loss of industry and employment.

> Bradford lost 80 per cent of the jobs in textiles over the period 1960–90 alone – 60,000 jobs in a population of 295,000 (1981). The virtual extinction of the wool textile industry carried with it much of the unskilled labour in the minority ethnic communities. Bradford is not unique in suffering such a loss of its major industry. But it is unique among major UK conurbations in facing a precipitous de-industrialisation combined with population increase. The population is young by national comparisons, especially so in the minority ethnic communities, 50 per cent of whose population is estimated to be under 18. There are consequently more young people coming onto the labour market at precisely the moment when there are fewer jobs.
>
> (Bradford University 2002: 6)

The decline in the economy has been compounded by the failure to attract the type of new investment which other cities, for instance Leeds, have been able to achieve. The consequence is that the average income in Bradford is lower than the national figure, unemployment is higher, infant mortality is very high, and education has been deemed to be so poor that the government has required the Metropolitan District Council to contract out the educational provision. A more detailed view of these problems and the way they affect different areas within the Metropolitan District is provided by Professor James O'Connell, who knows Bradford well and has analysed the way deprivation affects four carefully selected wards: three largely white but reflecting the spectrum of privilege and deprivation across the district, and one largely populated by people of South Asian origin.

> A brief comparison of four wards – Ilkley, Tong, Wyke and University – in the Bradford Metropolitan area suggests the dimensions of social disparity (Table 11.1). Ilkley is in the top 19 per cent of wards of the country for positive advantage; Wyke is in the lowest 16 per cent ; and Tong is lower again. Ilkley is right at the top for education; Wyke is in the bottom 5 per cent. The contrast of the other statistics is equally striking: income, employment and health. Forty-two percent of Wyke families claim means-tested benefit, whereas less than 10 per cent of Ilkley families do. It is worth saying that Wyke – and the same is true of Tong – has very few Asian families, and this statistic is almost the only one that it shares with Ilkley. The contrast is between white poverty and white prosperity. When University ward is added in, the contrasts become even more striking. If the disparities between Ilkley and Wyke are between two white wards, the other contrast is between relatively poor white Wyke and Tong wards and an Asian University ward in which the latter is seen as even poorer. Tong is however much closer in poverty to University than even Wyke. University ward, which is more than half Asian, ranks among the poorest areas of the country in terms of multiple deprivation: it has one of the worst employment records, and its formal education achievement is miserable. Were we to take other criteria such as health and housing, University would still come towards the bottom of national tables. It seems worth adding that smaller Asian incomes have to be spread over larger families, and women have much lower levels of economic activity than the city or national average.
>
> (O'Connell 2002: 2–3)

Thus James O'Connell sets out the complex scene and difficult economic background in Bradford, against which faith schools have to assess and improve their contribution to social cohesion. His paper approaches the question of faith schools from a Catholic point of view but does so in a way that provides valuable data about Bradford, opening up the way for all three voluntary providers to consider the differences between each other's traditions and purposes, and then to look for common ground and common aims.

For Anglican school provision the picture looks as follows.

Primary schools

Bradford local education authority's (LEA) Office for Standards in Education (OFSTED) report (May 2000) notes that, 'some [areas of Bradford] are populated mainly by the minority ethnic groups and others have little, if any, minority ethnic population'. This

Table 11.1 Social disparity in four wards in the Bradford Metropolitan area

Ward	Index of multiple deprivation	Rank			
		% Income deprivation	% Employment deprivation	Employment	Education
Ilkley	7,627	10.93	5.27	6,515	8,185
University	104	52.11	25.73	292	7
Tong	247	48.13	22.08	560	475
Wyke	1,289	27.78	12.18	2,380	177

Source: O'Connell (2002).

means that many schools, rather than being multi-cultural, are becoming increasingly mono-cultural. Some schools have a population which is almost exclusively of bilingual minority ethnic origin, whereas others are almost entirely white. This raises concerns about the educational and cultural experiences offered to all Bradford children. The OFSTED report sees the answer as follows: 'the reorganisation [of schools] aims to raise standards of attainment, provide value for money and promote social harmony'. Statistics show that Church of England primary schools in Bradford district are playing their part in trying to achieve this aim. Aided schools, at present, are slightly more ethnically mixed on average than community schools. They have the opportunity to reserve a proportion of places for church families and a proportion for the local community and try to use their flexibility in admissions to ensure an ethnic and religious mix. However, despite the diocese's intentions, attempts to retain a policy of keeping an ethnic and faith balance are proving difficult, because of the continuing shift in the distribution of the city's population. Once a school has a significant majority of South Asian pupils, many white parents tend to see the area and the school as becoming 'Asian'. Recently Heaton and Riddlesdon, the parishes of the St Barnabus and St Mary Primary Schools – both parishes that lie outside the centre of the city – reported this tendency, and added that primary schools are increasingly being judged on the extent to which they can act as feeder schools to the more successful secondary schools.

This is a consequence of what is often called 'white flight': that is, a perceived tendency for white families, who can, to move from the inner city or poor housing estates to the outer suburbs. In practice there are further complexities. People from all ethnic backgrounds, who can afford it, seek to find locations with access to better schooling, particularly secondary schooling. However, in the prevailing social and economic conditions, it is the whites who are most aware and most able to seize this advantage.

Church aided and controlled schools achieve, on average, higher levels of attainment than community schools. There are 57 Church of England primary schools in Bradford Diocese. Twenty-seven of the primaries (11 aided, 14 controlled and 2 foundation) are in Bradford Metropolitan District, serving around 9,000 pupils. Eighteen of the 27 (67 per cent) gained higher than the LEA average point scores in the 2001 Key Stage 2 tests, and 37 per cent of the Church primaries exceeded the national average score, compared with 25 per cent of the community primaries. The EPP provider joint paper states:

> To be blunt, if social cohesion in Bradford is to be a reality, achievement levels in schools will have to increase dramatically. It does not seem sensible to undermine that part of the system where currently achievement levels are higher at a time when we are pressing for all schools to be more ambitious for their pupils.

Secondary schools

Primary schools are understandably limited in terms of intake by their relatively small catchment areas and consequently tend to draw largely from one ethnic group. Secondary schools draw from much wider areas; hence one would expect much more mixing. The pattern for Bradford presented below is complex but consequences are clear. Whilst no school wishes to serve one ethnic group, the majority do draw very heavily from one group and this points to serious segregation. However, matching schools to the neighbourhoods makes it clear that the way the population is housed is the key reason for this, along with government admission policies, which emphasise parental choice and steer clear of any strategy to balance ethnic origin, class or culture. Against this background the LEA and

Education Bradford have to try to provide high quality education at every school and to support what arrangements are possible for shared activities between schools. Plans being developed with the Learning and Skills Council to establish federated sixth-form provision could make a very valuable contribution to this approach.

Table 11.2 shows the ethnic proportions of Bradford's secondary school pupils. Table 11.3 shows the distribution by ethnic background for the LEA secondary schools and includes the 5 A–C scores as one measure of performance of which parents take particular note.

Only one school, Tong, comes anywhere near to the overall city ethnic distribution and few schools have a significant balance between white pupils and those of Pakistani or Bangladeshi origin. The results for 5 A–Cs show a marked skew in favour of the largely white outer-ring schools. The poorest results, below 20 per cent, are also found at largely white schools serving poorer areas although Wyke does not serve the poorest. Most of the schools serving largely South Asian areas have scores in the 20–30 per cent range. Amongst the faith schools, the two CofE schools are in the lowest category. The four Catholic schools range from 63 to 41 per cent and the Muslim aided girls' school, Feversham College, gained a 53 per cent score. There is, however, one interesting exception to the overall pattern not included in the LEA statistics: Dixon's City Technology College (CTC), which, following its own CTC admissions policy of drawing from different ability bands across the city, does produce a balance much closer to the overall city distribution. It also has the highest 5 A–C score of 94 per cent. The LEA average score is 37.3 per cent and the national average is 51.5 per cent. It is a measure of the overall problem that only four schools out of 26 scored above the national average, two of which were faith schools: one Catholic, one Muslim.

Within this pattern it is interesting to locate the CofE secondary schools. Bradford Cathedral Community College (CC) and Immanuel Community College are close to being totally white, but before jumping to any conclusions it is important to look at their history, location and condition. Prior to reorganisation one was an LEA upper school, the other replaced an LEA upper school. Both upper schools served some of the poorest white housing estates in the city. They were very poorly supported and resourced, and relied heavily on the efforts of key staff. One had recently come out of special measures and the other had serious weaknesses. Few parents of South Asian origin wished to send their children to either school.

In response to an LEA request prior to reorganisation that it take over two secondary schools, the Diocese recognised a duty to help in areas of hardship. The result was that the Diocese swapped a very popular beacon middle school in Shipley for possibly the two most hard-pressed upper schools in the city, each with very problematic catchment areas and backgrounds. Reorganisation involved the closure of middle schools and the transfer of pupils to upper schools to create complete secondary schools. This created

Table 11.2 Ethnic breakdown of secondary school pupils in Bradford, 2002

White	65%
Pakistan or Bangladesh origin	28%
Indian origin	3%
Black	1%
Other	1%

Source: Compiled from Bradford LEA (2002) and Performance Tables supplied by the Department for Education and Skills and Education Bradford (2002).

Table 11.3 Distribution by ethnic background of pupils in secondary schools in Bradford LEA

School	Pakistani/ Bangladeshi	White	Indian	Black	Other	5 A–C
Beckfoot	17%	80%	1%	1%	1%	42%
BelleVue B	92%	6%	1%	0%	1%	20%
BelleVue G	93%	4%	2%	0%	1%	30%
Bingley	2%	96%	1%	0%	1%	64%
Buttershaw	8%	87%	3%	2%	0%	14%
Carlton	81%	14%	4%	0%	1%	18%
Bolling Cathedral CofE	7%	91%	1%	1%	0%	16%
Challenge	72%	21%	5%	1%	1%	–
Feversham	96%	0%	2%	1%	1%	53%
Grange	86%	9%	3%	1%	1%	33%
Greenhead	65%	35%	0%	0%	0%	22%
Hanson	5%	86%	7%	1%	1%	42%
Holy Family	5%	94%	0%	0%	1%	48%
Ilkley	1%	97%	0%	1%	1%	73%
Immanuel CofE	1%	97%	0%	1%	1%	18%
Laisterdyke	88%	0%	10%	1%	1%	25%
Nab Wood	66%	27%	4%	1%	2%	21%
Oakbank	8%	92%	0%	0%	0%	46%
Parkside	1%	99%	0%	0%	0%	–
Queensbury	3%	92%	4%	1%	0%	43%
Rhodesway	56%	37%	4%	2%	1%	28%
Salt	2%	96%	1%	1%	0%	29%
St Bedes	1%	96%	1%	1%	1%	47%
St Joseph's	2%	95%	0%	2%	1%	63%
Thornton	13%	77%	8%	1%	1%	37%
Tong	23%	69%	3%	3%	2%	35%
Wyke	5%	92%	1%	1%	1%	16%
Yorkshire Martyrs	9%	82%	5%	3%	1%	41%

Source: Compiled from Bradford LEA (2002) and Performance Tables supplied by the Department for Education and Skills and Education Bradford (2002).

very serious problems for both schools. Hence the Diocese's intention to support educational improvement has, as yet, been difficult to achieve. However, with the help of Education Bradford and determined efforts by management and staff at both schools there is now clear evidence of improving provision and performance in examination and self-assessment tests (SATS) results. Yet given the very low base from which both started it is well recognised that there is a long way to go. Both schools seek to respond to the Diocese's aims to support cohesion and regeneration and to use their position as voluntary aided schools and their links to church primary schools to do this.

Cathedral CC has been involved in a very significant pioneering venture with Dixon's CTC to create an Academy with a new level of resources and an approach to using them that will give a much needed boost to the city's 14–19 provision. A key part of this is the priority the Diocese gives to retaining and developing the multi-faith, multi-ethnic pattern that Dixon's, as a CTC, has already been able to achieve. Immanuel CC is also seeking, as far as possible, to widen admission and increase integration through links with associated CofE primary schools in parishes serving largely South Asian communities. At the same time it is developing partnership activities with secondary schools with predominantly South Asian intakes. Whilst both church schools offer places for families who are members of the CofE and associated churches, both chose to be designated as Community Colleges with an aim to serve the wider community, meeting the needs of the less privileged pupils from all ethnic and faith groups.

Towards an understanding of the purposes of CofE schools

The Anglican tradition of service to society, modelled on the teaching of Jesus, is as important in the new millennium as ever. As the national church, the CofE set the scene for mass education by initiating elementary schooling to meet the needs of nineteenth-century industrialisation and urbanisation. At the same time, it was assumed that such education would instruct and lead pupils into the Anglican faith. Following the Forster Act of 1870, the government took increasing responsibility for the provision of education. Throughout the twentieth century, the church and state formed a 'partnership' in which the church became more and more the junior partner. Now, at the beginning of the twenty-first century, the old industries and with them much of the related way of life are declining, and 'education, education, education' rings out to meet the demands of new globalised 'knowledge economies' and societies. The CofE is therefore reconsidering its educational purposes and with the assistance of the government is extending provision, particularly in secondary education.

All schools have an important role to play in cementing social cohesion and providing opportunities for children from different religious, class, ethnic and cultural backgrounds to mix and learn about each other. Church schools cannot claim to be better at this, or to be 'more caring', than other forms of school. Claims to distinctiveness lie in the way commitment to achieving good practice is explicitly drawn from Christian beliefs and values. These include service to God, to the individual and to society. Church primary schools have served the community around them including such separate groups as travellers for many years. Some now extend this by developing links with schools in multi-ethnic areas: for instance, Horton in Ribblesdale with Keighley St Andew, and Richard Thornton in Burton in Lonsdale with St Mary in Riddlesden.

> Our vision is to ensure that all pupils develop to their full potential – academic, emotional, social and spiritual. We aim to achieve this through the quality of care and range of educational experiences we offer to all in our school community. We provide an environment that promotes a sympathetic understanding of the Christian faith, an appreciation of difference and diversity and acceptance of those from different faiths and cultures. Christian values are placed at the centre of our daily life and underpin all the relationships we try to develop. We attach high priority to strong links between school, home and the parish, welcoming and treasuring all children from the neighbourhood, whatever their background.
> (Mission Statement, Richard Thornton CofE [Voluntary Aided] School, Burton in Lonsdale)

Church schools are expected to make clear their Christian beliefs and values to all members of staff, pupils and parents, not with the expectation that all will share them, but to explain the basis of the school's purposes and the ethos it seeks to create. A Christian ethos is intended to inform school policies, providing the framework that enables children to work and play together and to learn to understand and respect each other. It relates Christian values to contemporary society as guidelines for learning and living. It seeks mutual respect between faiths, listens to non-religious viewpoints and guides all who enter the school to treat each other helpfully and sensitively. It is concerned with the educational development of pupils as individuals and also as members of a number of communities including: the school itself, the family, the neighbourhood, the church and, increasingly, the mosque, temple or other faith group to which a pupil may belong. In Bradford this involves trying to understand and sharing activities with a variety of faiths whose members have different levels and forms of commitment, and working with parents, religious and community leaders accordingly. The contribution such an ethos can play in school development is now the subject of research undertaken by the Grubb Institute and sponsored by the National College of School Leadership (Grubb Institute 2002).

Evidence of what is being achieved by the CofE primary schools in inner-city Bradford offers an interesting insight into the multi-faith dimension of school provision. 'The school is to be commended on the provision of a very caring Christian community in whose positive and sensitive ethos children of all backgrounds can develop spiritually and morally' (St Oswald's CofE [Voluntary Aided] Primary School, Great Horton, Section 23 Inspection Report).

Such success seems to turn on what Philip Lewis has identified as a process of developing 'religious literacy' that enables and encourages children and parents of different faiths to share understanding and build mutual respect in order to 'co-exist creatively and peace-fully'.[2] With the help of the city's Interfaith Education Centre schools can provide teaching that meets the requirements of each faith and also provide for multi-faith activities, including common religious assemblies. Several are steadily working towards 'the aim of promoting friendship by encouraging children to reflect on how those of fundamentally different beliefs can embark on joint action to create community in the context of plurality' (Cooling 1994).

Whilst Bradford emphasises the need for church schools to relate openly and positively to other faiths, by contrast it also emphasises the need to unpack what it means to have 'no faith'. For some children, parents may offer clear humanist beliefs; others may draw upon what might be called residual religious beliefs. However, as many teachers know, there is a vital need to understand and support pupils whose community and family experiences give them little sense of constructive belief and value. Even more urgent are the needs of pupils often left to their own devices and torn by tensions and loss as families strain or break. This issue cannot be taken further here other than to argue for a wider view which brings together all the major world faiths and concerned secular interests to consider a continuous 'crisis of valuation' and value formation or the lack of it as accelerating but uncertain change takes effect across the world (Mannheim 1943).

Nurture, service and inclusion

The Way Ahead, the report of the Church of England Review Group (2001), heralds the renewed commitment by the CofE to the expansion and improvement of education. It challenges the Church to think through its educational purposes and suggests two key concepts: 'nurture' and 'service'. As a religion, Christianity has to 'nurture' and develop followers, meeting their needs and concerns, telling them the stories of the faith, making clear its principles, and explaining its various forms. However, to be fully effective, 'nurture' must also provide for continued exploration, learning and reflection, as children and adults experience life and its impact on their faith and its development. At the same time 'service' involves providing high-quality education to enable all pupils who can, to benefit and contribute, constructively and critically, to a better quality of life for themselves and their 'neighbours'. Thus the Church sustains itself and demonstrates its capacity to serve others. This is a hasty attempt to summarise the position the CofE is now taking and to open the way to some of the questions and issues that might be raised in a multi-faith setting.

First, church schools face the longstanding educational dilemma between the social-isation effect of teaching and the freedom of the learner – especially where beliefs and values are concerned – to choose and adapt. Ideally, CofE schools offer nurture to children who seek it or discover an interest in it, giving them, as far as age, ability and readiness allow, the material, motivation and opportunity to think about what they have experienced, to investigate and come to conclusions for themselves. This is easy to propose but implementation poses deep educational challenges that require skill and sensitivity, especially in a multi-faith 'religious literacy' context.

Second, a related issue concerns the ways church schools provide all pupils with a general knowledge of religion and different faiths in a spirit of education that does not proselytise but is genuinely explorative and informative. How can the concept of 'religious literacy' be developed to provide for the nurture of one faith to its members' satisfaction whilst teaching respect for other faiths and engaging in discussion with them? Wider still, there is also the need for an understanding of and dialogue with well-considered non-religious beliefs and value positions, and the need for all to account sensitively and helpfully for those who have 'none' (see above). In passing it is important to note the recognition, even in secular humanist quarters, 'that some Church of England schools are doing a good job in deprived areas'. Could this be a pointer to better informed interaction on both sides (Wood 2003)?

Third, what does inclusiveness mean when different faiths meet in a school, particularly a church school? In Bradford Diocese parents of all faiths and no faith choose to send their children to CofE schools. They do so for a number of reasons: because it is their nearest school and part of the local community, in some cases because it offers education in a Christian setting, and in others because it respects religious beliefs and values in an environment where there are ' no strings attached'. In the present context, many Muslim parents choose CofE schools because they have an 'unapologetic religious ethos and actively encourage Muslim parents to involve themselves in school life'.[3] Most, if not all, try to engage sufficiently educated mothers or elder sisters as teaching assistants or to help in other ways. Where parish churches are conscious of educational need, they also try to respond, providing facilities and support for such activities as community meetings and literacy classes. The parish of St Philip's, Girlington, is a good example.

A fourth issue goes further. A school is one of the few places where young people, parents and extended families from different ethnic, faith and social backgrounds can meet, and talk about their concerns and goals. CofE schools with their links to parishes can help to consolidate community feeling. As schools become multi-faith this can extend to other denominations and faith communities and can lead to inter-faith dialogue where shared goals can be explored and shared action considered. All major religions contain a strong message of social respon-sibility. Members of all faiths can become involved in social provision, for instance: campaigning for recreational facilities and supporting hospices and adult literacy. Working together, faith communities can become a powerful source of regeneration.[4]

These questions point to the attempts CofE schools are making to balance their obligations to those of their own faith with those of 'other faiths and none' and through this their support for social cohesion. But they also indicate that these are early days, that what is being achieved is as yet fragile and limited and requires great commitment and sensitivity on the part of all who work within and support such schools. Further, they help to illuminate the limitations that all schools face when trying to tackle what in many aspects are social and economic problems conditioned by the circumstances in which pupils and their families live.

Poverty, dispossession and dignity

It is often argued that if religion is removed, secular society and its institutions will provide a better set of values, less divisive, more 'true' and effective than those developed from religious beliefs and experience. But can secular thinking be totally separated from religious antecedents, and has the record of secular thought and action so far been sufficiently successful to justify this argument? Surely throughout much of human history the major religions have been concerned about the segregating effect of poverty and dispossession. Surely, today, co-operation between state, secular and religious bodies makes good sense in trying to counter the growing division between rich and poor across the world, its causes and the consequences that now threaten.

The increasing gap between wealth and poverty, so clear in the countries of the 'Third World', is now more fully recognized in even the wealthiest Organization of Economic Co-operation and Development (OECD) members. But in emphasising poverty, care must be taken not to mask dispossession. Change brings people advantages and hope but it also brings fears that others may benefit whilst they lose. Arguably, technological and entre-preneurial change over the last 20 to 30 years has had this effect in Bradford, particularly for 'working-class' white and poorer South Asian communities. Those that could, have taken the opportunities that change afforded; those that could not, feel deeply the loss of hard-earned but outdated facilities, skills and prospects. Often this begins to threaten self-esteem and creates bitterness or hopelessness. Dispossession, whether real or perceived, thus leads to an erosion of identity and dignity. The antidote is commonly seen to be education but this is overoptimistic, for whilst education may help some it does not meet the needs of others. Increased diversity may improve this, but even so education is only one of the levers of social and economic improvement. Schools in Bradford reflect the problems this poses. The contribution which faith makes to education in all schools, including the different forms of faith school, should be evaluated carefully against this background – a full picture of what is happening in Bradford – and the wider issues this brings to light.

To counter dispossession and poverty the central requirement is to create and distribute wealth more effectively and fairly. But it is equally important to enable those for whom this process is designed to play an active part, to feel a sense of ownership and retain or reclaim their dignity. James O'Connell points to

> ... two groups in Bradford that are unlikely to make economic progress without success in education and that are presently failing within the system. The first are groups of Pakistani heritage, and the second are those white indigenous groups that are poor.[5]
> (O'Connell 2002: 3)

Both groups face very high levels of deprivation and dispossession but there is an important difference when it comes to their view of education.

The poor white community has had primary and secondary schooling for many years. Its members have seen others succeed, gain secure employment and eventually leave their neighbourhood. As a result, dogged by class-based thinking, and the rundown Bradford economy, a residual group remainS. Despite continual efforts to improve education and to offer second chance opportunities, some people see themselves failed by a form of schooling that has made them feel unwanted and has done little to help them find economic security. This process has been compounded by the continuing loss of ability and leadership from the poorer, more problematic housing estates as those who can, move out. Despite efforts by some to 'struggle on', for others, slowly but surely, 'working class' is becoming 'underclass', community and family bonds are falling apart, dignity is lost and atomised irresponsibility, bitterness or apathy are taking over, leaving those left behind vulnerable to commercialism, fascism, drugs and crime. This is the poverty and dispossession that education has failed to tackle or – worse – which, because of its inflexibility in relating to the realities it faces, it is helping to create. This might be seen as 'post-educational poverty'.

In contrast, people of South Asian origin have a different view. They came, and some are still coming, in hope of a better life. Many are used to much worse deprivation than the overcrowded housing of Girlington and Manningham. They recognise that they face poverty, at least in a relative form, but seek the answer to this, not for themselves but for their children, in good schooling. Initially they approach schooling with high aspirations and with none of the class-engendered fatalism to which poorer white people have become so accustomed. Many participate in a range of self-help activities not only to maintain and develop their own culture but also to provide adult education and literacy and to give considerable extra support to children in school. Their reference point is the advantages and success that a particular form of education appears to bring to prosperous whites. Their drive for such success comes largely from self-belief supported by values given to them by their Muslim faith. These enable many to maintain their dignity within the context of poverty they see around them and to seek the education to surmount it. Thus this might be seen as 'pre-educational poverty'.

Many have seen education succeed and, supported by their faith, most still hold out hope. But the signs of failure are becoming evident, particularly among boys who do not achieve and cannot find employment. Fatalism, irresponsibility and bitterness are beginning to show here too; a growing drugs trade and gang culture sadly exemplifies the consequences. The younger generation have good cause to feel that the opportunities they are prepared to work for are now being taken away. Many families want their children to have better education than that on offer. Thus some people of South Asian origin are now sadly beginning to have a sense of dispossession, at least in terms of fairness and equality of treatment, and are beginning to see 'pre-educational poverty' deteriorate into the even more worrying form of 'post-educational poverty'.

All are concerned with the breakdown of values, and growing tensions, particularly between young and old. Those in leadership positions are becoming less certain. They are deeply worried by what they see and the parallels this could have with the worst aspects of life on the poorest white estates. Do they continue to advocate education and adaptation, confident that the values they hold dear will support progress, will be respected, and not be eroded by commercialism, community breakdown and crime? Or do they join those already so concerned that they urge a more separatist, less integrated way of life, including separate schools, intended to protect communal structures, values and dignity, yet increasing isolation and thereby hindering progress towards the new advantages they seek?

The experience of residual white groups and the less successful groups of South Asian origin in Bradford, as they try to come to terms with being left behind, exposes the corrosive effects of dispossession, including the growing antagonism it creates between them. Immigrant communities naturally tend to live together and to that extent segregate. A multi-ethnic, multi-faith, multi-cultural society has to allow for this but at the same time encourage the overarching values and provide the structures, services and opportunities that enable all groups to live in harmony and work for the common good. Education is vital to all this. In particular it is vital to the key issue of economic development and employment for individuals and communities but it is not, in itself, sufficient. It can only be effective where it relates to the other necessary factors for wealth creation and personal development. Governments of all descriptions need to locate the improvement and expansion of education within more fully joined-up policies for social and economic progress. 'Teaching a person to fish' is of little use unless there are genuine opportunities to catch, process and trade.

Segregation, socialisation and selection

Ideally schools work for social cohesion by helping pupils to build their own sense of identity whilst they learn to understand and respect those who have different identities. But this process is subject to what happens in the wider community. The deeper divisions become, the harder it is for schools in any form to promote social cohesion, especially where division is fuelled by a continuing sense of injustice or fear. This is a growing worry in many parts of the world, so much so, that the United Nations Educational, Scientific and Cultural Organization (UNESCO) is now advocating a 'peace-building' approach that goes beyond the normal curriculum to engage directly with 'the structural causes' that are the issues that are really dividing people. Studies are being designed in seven countries, four of which, including Northern Ireland, have clear faith dimensions (International Bureau of Education [IBE] 2002).

But there is a second tension. On the one hand education is increasingly seen to be the key process whereby a society socialises its young to maintain social order and cohesion, emphasising equal rights and levels of provision. On the other it is seen to select and shape the talent that societies need to ensure effective leadership, organisation and economic progress, thereby allocating pupils to different levels of personal success and social mobility. This dichotomy has dominated educational thinking and planning for much of the last century. As citizens and neighbours, people tend to focus on the former; as parents, employers and potential employees, they tend to focus on the latter. In the United Kingdom (UK) this has left politicians and governments continually struggling to find a balance, most recently between comprehensive schools and parental choice, and teachers continually dealing with the 'fall out'.

Government admission requirements emphasise parental rights to choose and, in the light of experience, avoid 'social engineering'. It is argued that all schools can be managed and operated effectively and therefore Department for Education and Skills (DfES) policies require LEAs to ensure that every school offers high quality education. However, in areas where numbers make it possible, schools tend to separate along a fault line between those that draw heavily from, and therefore often seek to serve, poorer communities and those that attract wealthier families offering better access to social mobility. Consequently, notwithstanding 'value-added' success, parents are very conscious that schools differ, and that some by virtue of their local catchment areas and the cultural influence have become 'more equal than others' in the quality of the immediate learning environment and the long-term opportunities they offer their pupils. Strong evidence of this can be found regularly at the School Organisation Committee of every LEA.

Speaking recently in Bradford, Estelle Morris said that 'what worried her most' was that, despite all the efforts we have made, our education system is still failing the least advantaged children.[6] Attempts to understand and counter the persistent, indigenous class/

education problem have been a central concern since 1944. Now this concern must include the impact the class/education problem is having in the poorer urban areas of mixed ethnicity and faith. Moves are being instituted regularly, with increasing attention given to strengthening management, improving facilities and increasing inclusion and diversity. All these make good sense but do they really get to the core of the problem? How well do they meet dominating parental concerns about access to job prospects and social mobility in a school system differentiated in a number of ways and serving an increasingly competitive world? How well can they counter the sense of failure, exclusion or dispossession felt by some pupils and families this differentiation leaves in its wake?

These underlying tensions are part of education worldwide but come under a particularly telling spotlight in the schools of Bradford. Meanwhile, the high expectations of social mobility many parents currently have seem to be giving way to more limited prospects. The experience of Third World countries, which faced this problem much earlier, suggests that, as prospects decline, parents who can will press even harder for the schooling that leads to 'jobs' for their children and that the plight of those left without such schooling becomes worse.

Faith schools in support of social cohesion

This paper has focused on the role of CofE schools in relation to segregation in Bradford, explaining their aims, the social context in which they work, their achievements in the light of this and the deep educational tensions with which, along with all schools, they have to contend where social cohesion is concerned. Whilst it draws only on CofE experience it has also pointed to the links now developing between the Catholic, Muslim and Anglican providers of 'voluntary aided schools'.

Segregation is serious and, if it continues, very worrying for the future. In this respect the Ouseley and Cantle reports, which call for more integration in schools, need very careful attention (Cantle 2001; Ouseley 2001). The situation developing in Bradford and similarly placed cities and towns is confused, complex and contested but it is clear that there is a demographic pattern emerging which, in terms of housing and, therefore, schools, is leading to increasing ethnic and faith segregation. Closer links between the planning of housing and education could help but the emphasis on improved achievement must be strengthened, particularly for residual white pupils and the very significant group of pupils of South Asian origin who now, against all their hopes, are facing educational failure.

The major cause of division in Bradford is the debilitating form of poverty and dispossession threatening the poorest groups in both the white and South Asian communities and the way it bears upon the thinking of those that see it. All countries now need to develop 'the values that underpin a fair society' and the economic and social policies to put such values into practice. Islam and Christianity, both drawing upon the Abrahamic tradition, recognised much of the answer to this long ago, in particular controlling usury and its impact.[7] Arguably, Islam has been more careful in this regard, offering much clearer and more practical reminders of the importance of properly integrated social and economic development.[8] At their best, both faiths recognise the growing need for better, more healthy modes of entrepreneurship: showing concern for workers and others in business through 'a just wage, just price and just profits'. Both have serious concerns about the 'downside' of global market economics: overextended commercialism, the deteriorating moral context to which this seems to be contributing, the growing sense of dispossession and the consequences it brings. Within this broad sweep of concern both seek answers to what is happening in Bradford and efforts are being made to build mutual understanding and cooperation, but these need time and support.

The Archbishop of Canterbury, Rowan Williams, remembers a Welsh Muslim colleague suggesting 'a forum in Wales where Christians and Muslims could discuss together the nature and potential of faith schools to combat ... misunderstandings' (Williams 2002: 4). He used this comment to set a new more open scene for the understanding of faith and learning.

> Christians have nothing to gain from a Muslim population that feel their beliefs are seen by others with fear and ignorance. Everyone is the loser in such a situation. If we are properly confident in our faith, we shall be glad to venture it in the realm of statutory education and glad to encourage other faiths in the same task. We can work together to challenge mistaken secularism and to promote a lively interchange about faith in our society.
>
> (Ibid.)

There is certainly a need for the voices of the major religions to be heard where fairness, justice and humanity and using education to these ends are concerned. Where religions sponsor or provide education, care must always be taken to seek harmony and emphasise quality and opportunity for all. As this paper has tried to show, CofE schools are trying to develop the positive impact which, at its best, faith can have upon social cohesion and working with the other 'voluntary aided' schools and statutory agencies to achieve this. Arguably, however, there is a wider more comprehensive view developing, as 'community' and 'foundation' schools also face up to 'the post-Ouseley challenge'. To meet this in Bradford, all schools have to respond to the importance Muslim pupils and parents give to their faith, the bearing this has on relationships with others and the reactions it evokes.

Grange Technology College (a community school) is ensuring increasing success for Muslim pupils and has drawn upon this experience to establish an 'ethos of valuing faith' throughout the school. Now the principal and governors seek to distinguish between 'a single-faith school and a multi-faith school able to build on the common ground held by all the major religions, along with that of humanism', and argue that:

> Students of different faiths sharing experiences within the same school can provide the most secure foundation for meaningful and respectful relationships and doing so in the context of a school which self-consciously celebrates the importance of faith can only strengthen that foundation.[9]

From whatever position it is viewed the relationship between faith and learning poses a key challenge for our times. Its impact upon social cohesion is highlighted in Bradford and is clearly on the agendas of all the bodies that now share responsibility for education in the Metropolitan District. At the school level initiatives are developing: sharing good practice and resources, organising visits and exchanges, encouraging well-focused professional development and action research. The three 'voluntary aided school' providers now meet together to improve provision and extend interchange and, where possible, to consider rebalancing intakes. The relationship between faith and learning and the meaning of the term 'faith school' is increasingly being questioned and the need for opportunities for schools to discuss all this is becoming clear. The Interfaith Education Centre, now under review, has a vital part to play provided it receives the support needed. The prospect of an academy or possibly academies designed to include the growing multi-ethnic and faith dimensions of Bradford's demography opens a way to new flexibility. Better, fuller research into segregation, the educational problems it creates and practical ways of countering them would help greatly but more resources and commitment have to be found for this. With sensitivity, imagination and the right support, schools can play an important part in turning pluralism from being seen as a problem into being seen as an advantage (O'Connell 2002: Appendix 3).

But the use of schools to achieve cohesion can only go so far. Whilst education systems separate pupils, as they do in most countries, on a basis that is so strongly influenced by wealth and social and political standing, there will be educational differentiation that will advantage some but leave others, including large groups from ethnic and faith minorities, disadvantaged. Bradford reflects this strongly: witness Table 11.3. Efforts to improve school performance, extend diversity and increase inclusion are a key part of the answer but to be effective such moves must be related more sensitively to the demographic settings in which schools are placed. They must also be part of wider-ranging strategies designed to account for the full spectrum of social, economic, cultural and religious pressures, influenced by poverty and dispossession, now evident in Bradford but building up strongly in so many areas across the world.

Notes

1 The authors would like to acknowledge the help received from Philip Lewis and Jean Anderson, valuable comments by Mukhtar Ali and Mohammed Khan and the extensive use we have made of the paper by James O' Connell (2002).
2 Taken from helpful comments from Philip Lewis Peace Studies, Bradford University.
3 Comments by Philip Lewis.
4 A quick glance at the Bradford's *Telegraph & Argus*'s regular Yorkshire Observer section provides some interesting evidence.
5 A recent review of tax credits, showing a general improvement in tackling hardship, still points to 'concentrations of hardship ... among some ethnic minority groups, especially Pakistani and Bangladeshi families – three times higher than among white families'. Alan Marsh, 'Lifted out of the worst poverty', *The Guardian*, 5 August 2003.
6 Keynote speech at the launch of the Unit for Educational Research and Evaluation, the University of Bradford, 16 June 2003.
7 The underlying importance of Christian values to the search for a 'fair society' and their relationship to thinking from first principles is discussed in 'Onward Christian Citizens' by Will Hutton, *The Observer*, 9 February 2003.
8 See, for instance, the development in the north of England of the Muslim Investment and Mortgage Company, First Ethical, at http://www.1stethical.co.uk.
9 The key role which the Muslim faith plays in supporting the educational aspirations of many pupils of South Asian origin and the implications of this have been made clear by John Player and Donna Pankhurst, respectively Head and Chair of Governors of Grange Technology College. They argue in a preliminary draft paper for the term 'faith' school to be applied to a school that recognizes the role faith plays in education and provides for all the major faiths.

References

Bradford University (2002) *Bradford, One Year on: Programme for a Peaceful City*, Bradford: Bradford University.
Cantle, T. (2001) *Community Cohesion: A Report of an Independent Review Team*, London: Home Office.
Church of England Review Group (2001) *The Way Ahead: Church of England Schools in the New Millennium* London: Church House Publishing.

Cooling, T. (1994) *A Christian Vision for State Education*, London: SPCK.

Grubb Institute (2002) *Becoming Fit for Purpose: A Report to the Church of England Board of Education*, London: Grubb Institiute.

IBE (2002) *Curriculum Change and Social Cohesions in Conflicted-Affected Societies*, Educational Innovation and Information 112, Geneva: IBE.

Mannheim, K. (1943) *Diagnosis of Our Times*, London: Kegan Paul.

O'Connell, J. (2002) 'Reassembling communities: the role of schools in prosperity, cohesion and integration', Discussion paper for the Diocese of Leeds.

Ouseley, H. (2001) *Community Pride not Prejudice*, Bradford, Bradford Vision.

Williams, R. (2002) 'Faith schools', address to the Governing Body of the Church in Wales, University of Wales Lampeter, April.

Wood, K. (2003) 'Religions are divisive', letter to *The Independent*, 16 February 2003.

12 Through the looking glass: religion, identity and citizenship in a plural culture

From the viewpoint of the modern Orthodox Jewish school

Lynndy Levin

Greek mythology tells the story of Narcissus:

> At first he tried to embrace and kiss the beautiful boy who confronted him, but presently he recognized himself, and lay gazing enraptured into the pool hour after hour.
>
> (Graves 1955: 287)

> 'But was Narcissus beautiful?' said the pool.
> 'Who should know better than you?' answered the Oreads;
> 'Us did he ever pass by, but you he sought for,
> And he would lie on your banks and look down at you,
> And in the mirror of your waters he would mirror his own beauty.'
> And the pool answered: 'But I loved Narcissus because,
> As he lay on my banks and looked down at me,
> In the mirror of his eyes I saw ever my own beauty mirrored'.
>
> (Wilde, 1973)

I will continue in the style of children's books in which the reader is invited to take the story on in his/her own way and then create an ending:

> Narcissus looked deeply into the water and beyond his own reflection saw a myriad of multicoloured fish, bright as they swam amongst the mottled boulders beneath.
> He raised his eyes from the pool and gasped
> At the surrounding phantasmagoria of flora and fauna.
> He sat up, and saw people approaching,
> Some young, some old, some weeping, some laughing,
> Some poor, some wealthy, some worried, some tranquil,
> Some clearly at odds with others.
> He wondered at their endless diversity.
> Narcissus rose to greet them and as he rose looked up
> At the arc of sky above him from which shafts of sunlight spread,
> And in which a slice of pale moon hung, a silhouette in the ether.
>
> (Lynndy Levin)

In relation to the story I'd like to pose the following questions which I will attempt to address in this paper:

- If faith education is not about our unique 'selves' about whom then will it be?
- If faith education is only about our unique 'selves' then who will be for it?
- If now is not the time to address these issues then when is?

Faith schools and the liberal agenda

As the voice of one of the world's great civilisations, the Jewish voice has a place in the conversation of mankind. Amongst others it tells its own story of faith, culture, history and heritage; tradition, identity and effectiveness; justice, rights and responsibility. This civilisation could be described as 'aboriginal' in its authenticity. It provides the framework within which Jewish life is lived. It creates a faith norm. However, because Judaism has within it different plural ways of relating to and implementing this norm, tensions exist and strategies for problem-solving constantly need to be created, some of which are more successful than others. Thus within Judaism itself lie the seeds of both the conflictual and the dialogic. It is not the purpose of this paper to focus on the tensions internal to Judaism. However, the importance of drawing attention to them here is to highlight this dynamic as one with which Jews are familiar when interacting with people who have different attitudes, orientations and forms of lived practice.

From the current British liberal-democratic perspective Jews, and no doubt other minority groups, are seen as cognitive minorities. By cognitive minority I mean that we bring to the world a particular view, be it religious, cultural, social or political, which is shaped by our identity. It is crucial for us to understand the nature of the political culture in which we live because to a large extent it provides the parameters within which different ways of life can exist in this country. It seems reasonable to expect that a liberal state should strive to establish the conditions in which different lifestyles can proliferate and flourish. However, Spinner (1994) explains that it is not at all the case that liberals need to recognise specific cultures and work towards preserving them. The assumption that they would need to do this is to confuse '*pluralistic integration*' with '*cultural pluralism*.' Spinner explains:

> Pluralistic integration emphasises the protections of different cultures that are compatible with liberalism. Cultural pluralism, on the other hand, emphasizes the protection of different cultures regardless of the practices of these cultures. This emphasis ignores how cultures change and too blindly celebrates all cultures.
>
> (1994: 187)

The task of the liberal state is to establish the setting in which:

> Arguments over culture, discrimination, language policy and national identity take place; liberalism establishes the rules for these fights. Yet liberalism does not determine the victor. Liberalism depends on members of the liberal state to uphold liberal principles. Without this support, liberal theory will not be matched in practice.
>
> (1994: 187–8)

It must be recognised that, because liberalism does not reinforce different cultures, its impact on faith schooling in Britain could potentially be devastating. This is because through liberal eyes, the faith school is seen almost as an anti-liberal institution and one which is currently regarded as contributing to world divisiveness. As faith school representatives, the 'battle' is ours to fight – both separately and collectively, but our aim is probably the same – to prevent the erosion of our faith and ethnicity by the liberal-democratic state. To return in this regard to the story of Narcissus for a moment, it is the 'Pool' whose response is most chilling:

> 'But I loved Narcissus because,
> As he lay on my banks and looked down at me,
> In the mirror of his eyes I saw ever my own beauty mirrored'.
>
> (Wilde, op. cit.)

From this viewpoint it is clear to see how a liberal-democratic state can quite glibly suggest the imposition of other-faith pupils into a specific-faith school, and that in most cases the chances are that wherever liberalism gives its support, cultural boundaries will not remain 'taut'.

At this stage two questions will become the focus of this paper, each of which I will address in turn:

1   What is the *theoretical nature* of the interface between Jewish faith education and secular society as mediated by the conflictual and dialogic elements present in education for citizenship?
2   In what ways are the theoretical issues discussed in the question above useful in enlarging our *practical understanding* of and enhancing our relationship with faiths outside Judaism?

Let's address the first question:

> Though the modern state vastly increases the scope of individual rights and freedoms, it is not without its discontents. In particular the absence of a shared moral culture is experienced as a loss of personal meaning: anomie, as Durkheim called it. Instead of experiencing identity as something given by birth, tradition and community, individuals are thrown upon themselves, facing a vast choice of educational, career and relationship patterns.
>
> (Sacks 1993: 23)

Berger *et al.* (1974) corroborate this sense of loss of personal meaning:

> On the one hand, modern identity is open-ended, transitory, and liable to ongoing change. On the other hand, a subjective realm of identity is the individual's main foothold in reality. Something that is constantly changing is supposed to be the 'ens realissimum'. Consequently it should not be a surprise that modern man is afflicted with a permanent identity crisis.
>
> (Berger *et al.* 1974: 23)

It is here that religion enters contemporary society, for its great strength is that it offers content to personal identity: 'It provides a mode of belonging. It anchors life-cycle events in a scheme of traditional meanings. It offers community in the face of the often functional and faceless structures of the state' (Sacks 1993: 23–4).

This is the appeal of the faith school. Parents and their children who are pupils attending the school can reasonably expect its value orientations to be expressed through both religious codes and social, cultural and legal traditions, all of which ideally culminate in lived practice, and testify to the belief that (in the context of the modern Jewish Orthodox school which I will use as my example) a Jewish person who is both knowledgeable and practising will be a usefully contributing and valued member of his or her own community and of society in general. Thus, Sacks (1991) suggests, the task of the modern Jewish Orthodox school, existing in a cultural climate which has become deeply secularised, is to encourage in its pupils the belief that the embers of faith still glow and that the choices within a society are not open-ended. The message of the school is that religious values are active within its moral framework and that they lie at the heart of its deepest moral commitments.

Citizenship education as transformational

Any effective education for a citizenship programme will aim at enabling the pupil to transfer, to the context of civic engagement and public discourse, the skills, knowledge and understanding gained in the classroom. An important addition to developing these abilities is that schools must encourage the development of feeling and outlook – a democratic *disposition* within the pupil *out of which she acts*. This is because a viable democracy requires citizens to be committed to its core values, not just as a form of government, not just in the school which may have a democratic ethos, or in the family which may have democratic values, but by way of what Dewey conceptualises as a mode of associated living, of conjoint communicated experience which extends to the public socio-civic forum of public interaction.

The process of education is at best a transformational one which facilitates the pupil's maximum self-development. It is here I think that we begin to see the nature of the interface between Jewish faith education and secular society as mediated by the conflictual and dialogic elements present in education for citizenship. The aim of addressing and developing the transformational self in education is to help pupils to recognise that they have the capacity through critical reflection to be powerful agents for change, both within themselves and within others. This must begin by their being encouraged to evaluate at depth their own physical, emotional, psychological, intellectual and religious position so as to establish their identity and traditions in terms of constraints and possibilities, and in terms of their effectiveness as individuals. This process will mark the beginning of a conscious personal and interpersonal journey which may very well be conflictual at certain points, through the six different types of community – usefully defined by Rowe (1992) – to which people might belong during the course of their lives: '… the family community, the kinship community, the affiliative community, the school community, the state community and the world community' (Rowe 1992: 179).

The conflictual crunch for citizenship education comes in the attempt to develop a workable trans-social ethic whilst realising that a pluralistic society is necessarily based on the principle that individuals have the right to their own values and beliefs, which as moral and political ideas will, in all likelihood, be essentially contested. Not only do these pluralisms spring from religion or culture, which as has been said may exert a crucial influence on how members of a particular group view their allegiance as citizens, but also, as Rowe suggests, from the natural differences of character, socialisation and maturity that we find throughout the population. Thus the positive effect of the transformational aspects within education for citizenship will be reflected in the degree to which the pupils learn to value the 'we' *as well as* the 'I' in each of the contexts with which they engage. The crucial importance of reaching this balance of perspective and depth of concern is that it will give pupils a clearer, stronger sense of their identity amongst other identities, and the confidence and vision to see themselves as a source of choice, agency and responsibility, whose actions and decisions make a difference.

A four term convenantal relationship

Let's turn now to the second question: in what ways are the theoretical issues discussed in answering the first question useful in enlarging our practical understanding of and enhancing our relationship with faiths outside Judaism?

If, as has been suggested above, the message of the modern Orthodox Jewish school is that religious values are active within its moral framework and lie at the heart of its deepest moral commitments, it is important to explore the broader contribution of this outlook. From the Biblical story of Adam, the first man, recounted in the Book of Genesis, we see that God thought it undesirable for a human being to live alone. Yet later in the same Book we see from (among others) the examples of Cain and Abel, the generation of Noah and the decline of social order, Abraham and Ishmael, Jacob and Esau how difficult it is for human beings to live with one another. By way of processing this text as a Judaic 'inner' text and linking it to the 'outer' text of society and other faiths, it is my suggestion that we may find ways in which to move from undesirable isolation to tolerable association.

The word 'tolerable' is a key word in the process of moving from isolation to association because in today's world both pluralism and the conflict of values call for toleration. However, there is an important distinction to be made between tolerance and indifference, particularly in looking at the demands of tolerant personal conduct apart from toleration as a political practice. It is hugely important for faith schools to understand these principles, for two reasons. First, difference should never be seen as a ghettoised factor outside ourselves, but as something which we share as part of the human race, for we are *all* different from one another. Second, in the protection, celebration and perpetuation of ethnic origins, there will necessarily be tension between ethnic groups and the constitutionally-political host culture, and tension between ethnic groups themselves. It is clear that, in order to thrive, toleration needs a conflictual setting in which we are required to address and act upon such issues as autonomy and the limits of toleration, intolerance and looking beyond the individual to her essential humanness. I suggest that the radical implication of this view for Judaism is that it necessitates a re-characterisation of the notion of 'covenant' to include not only what I will call a 'two-term' covenantal relationship between God and the individual Jew, or a 'three-term' covenantal relationship between God, the individual Jew and the Jewish community, but also a 'four-term' covenantal relationship between God, the individual Jew, the Jewish community and the wider multi-faith, multi-cultural, local and global community.

To reflect this line of thinking, modern Orthodox Jewish schools must strive to develop ways to re-characterise selected elements of the curriculum in order to encourage pupils to look more broadly and creatively 'through the looking glass': i.e. beyond the specific applications of the 'subject' *per se* to the wider possibilities of its application. This will provide the curricular space in which to create a new kind of Jewish consciousness which will make a deep and profound difference to the way in which pupils encounter the traditional texts of Judaism. Table 12.1 outlines a few examples, which will be brief because of the constraints of space but which will hopefully illustrate what I mean.

These and additional examples could perhaps be worked out further to become part of a transferable faith school curriculum development model in the areas of religious

Table 12.1 Examples of curricular extensions of traditional orthodox concepts

Mitzvah: Divine command	Conceptual understanding	Re-characterisation	Extension of conceptual understanding
Tzedaka – charity	The material resources we possess come to us as a Divine gift; we are required to share these with needy individuals or institutions within the Jewish community	Jurisprudence, distributive justice	Responsibility to society by financially supporting or voluntarily working for local, national and global charitable initiatives and institutions
G'milut chassadim – acts of kindness	One of the fundamental pillars of Judaism is to love your fellow as yourself; this takes into its ambit a plethora of examples which demonstrate caring in the Jewish community, including: hospitality to strangers, visiting the sick, dowering the bride, burying the dead with dignity	Justice and caring	To develop a positive attitude of compassion and caring for all humanity through being able to see God's image in a person who is not in our image, and carry out the concomitant actions which flow from such a view
Tikkun olam – bringing 'correction' or making a difference to the world	To live in the modern world as a Jew connected through generations to the chain of history and heritage in a felt and existential way is a powerful expression of Jewish identity, which shapes the vividness with which Jewish faith, culture and values are transmitted within the local and world Jewish community; to live as Jews with passion will enable us to withstand outside de-legitimising pressures	Social action	To be active as members of an ethnic minority in making positive contributions to public debate and discourse and in social and political action affecting other world minorities; the attitude that lies behind this view is that a world that has no room for difference has no room for humanity

education, personal, social and health education, and education for citizenship. In their extension as informal curriculum activities based in the wider community outside the school they could provide a fruitful basis for multi-faith school cooperation.

Conclusion

In conclusion, it seems to me then that the issue of faith schools is neither one of conflict nor of consensus but of both, and as faith schools representatives we share the collective responsibility to ensure the continued flourishing of our institutions in the context of the British liberal democracy in which we live.

References

Berger, P.L., Berger, B. and Kellner, H. (1974) *The Homeless Mind: Modernizaton and Consciousness*, London: Pelican.

Dewey, J. (1916) *Democracy and Education*, New York: Macmillan (1963 edition).

Graves, R. (1955) *The Greek Myths*, Harmondsworth: Penguin.

Rowe, D. (1992) 'The citizen as a moral agent: the development of a continuous and progressive conflict-based citizenship curriculum', *Curriculum*, 13(3): 178–87.

Sacks, J. (1991) 'The fragile family', in *The Persistence of Faith, Religion, Morality and Society in a Secular Age*, New York: Weidenfeld and Nicolson.

—— (1993) *One People?: Traditions, Modernity and Jewish Unity*, Oxford: The Littman Library of Jewish Civilization.

Spinner, J. (1994) *The Boundaries of Citizenship: Race, Ethnicity and Nationality in the Liberal State*, Baltimore, MA, and London: The Johns Hopkins University Press.

Wilde, O. (1973) 'The disciple', *Prose Poems*, SLIII, Dublin: Crannog Press.

Part IV

Faith schools

The experience elsewhere

13 Measuring Catholic school performance

An international perspective

James Arthur

On a world basis Catholic schools continue to expand and they represent the world's largest non-governmental school system. There are over 50 million children attending Roman Catholic schools around the world. This number would be trebled if the Church had the resources to fund new schools. Nevertheless, new Catholic schools continue to open in Vietnam, India, Africa and in Eastern Europe. Thousands of religious schools have been founded since the collapse of communism in Poland, Hungary, Slovakia, Croatia and many other Eastern European countries. Catholic schools, whilst few in number, were also extremely popular under communist governments. In some countries the state relies almost entirely upon the voluntary efforts of the main religious groups in providing schools – this is particularly the case in some African countries. The perceived effectiveness of these schools among parents is one significant factor in explaining this continued expansion.

In Britain, the academic success of Catholic schools has been highlighted, in recent years, by Office for Standards in Education (OFSTED) Reports and by examination league tables. Andrew Morris (1994, 1997, 1998a and 1998b) has demonstrated that levels of academic achievement in Catholic schools are higher than those in local education authority (LEA) schools. Academic results in Catholic schools are well above LEA and national averages. Earlier studies during the 1960s also indicated that Catholic school academic performance was greater than in comparable schools. The Catholic Education Council (1967) enquiry in 1963–4 found that a higher proportion of school leavers from Catholic schools compared to LEA schools entered full-time higher and further education. Michael Hornsby-Smith (1978: 87) also found evidence during the 1970s that Catholics had been more upwardly mobile than the general population. Even the research evidence compiled by John Marks *et al.* (2001), whilst revealing the wide variations of standards among church schools in England, still concluded that faith-based schools, on average, do better in academic terms. Early studies in the United States of America (USA) by Greeley and Rossi (1966) also found positive associations between Catholic schooling and academic achievement and future economic prosperity. In continental Europe there has not been a great deal of research in this area, but where such research studies have been conducted, such as in Holland, they indicate that Catholic schools have higher levels of achievement as measured by public tests, especially in primary mathematics and language (Hofman and Hofman 2001).

Differences in pupil admission policies are often perceived as the principal cause of achievement variations between different kinds of school (see Teddie and Reynolds 2000). Consequently, some have suggested that Catholic schools do better because they attract better-educated pupils from more economically stable families, that they are guilty of 'skimming the cream', that they exercise a degree of academic and social selectivity bias in admissions. The evidence in support of these arguments is often anecdotal and potentially unreliable; even the chapter by Schagen and Schagen in this collection goes beyond the evidence available to make unfounded generalisations. Indeed, since the social composition of the British Catholic community has largely been Irish urban working class with origins in poor immigrant families, the evidence would appear to point in the opposite direction. This would also seem to be the case in Australia, New Zealand and the USA, where there is little evidence to suggest that the income and occupation of parents sending their children to Catholic schools in inner-city areas are significantly different from parents who send their children to government or state schools. There is certainly evidence of greater parental involvement in Catholic schools (see Arthur 1994).

Comparisons between schools must be conducted carefully to be valid and would generally include a comparison of the following factors: socio-economic background, parental involvement and the innate ability of pupils. All three factors have the potential to interfere with measured academic outcomes. In addition, because of the diversity of Catholic schools, many of the indicators produced are complex and need to be interpreted with care. Only by understanding and comparing these complex factors can we arrive at a genuine sense of the value-added element of the school. We need to sound another cautionary note here, for there have been a very limited number of studies and data collections in Australia, New Zealand and South Africa, whilst the main studies have been conducted in the USA. Not all countries provide reliable information on the nature and performance of Catholic schools and not all facets of Catholic schooling are covered by the indicators. Together with the USA research evidence, the available statistics and information from the other countries discussed in this paper cover some of these areas of comparison and help us to measure some aspects of Catholic school performance. It provides us with perhaps what might be called evidence for the 'Catholic school effect'. The socio-economic perspective in school effectiveness studies has become dominant in recent years because it relies on quantifiable data that are accessible. It is easier to gain information about cognitive outcomes and socio-economic status than it is to assess the religious ethos of a school. In measuring the effectiveness of Catholic schools we need to measure the extent to which they accomplish what they set out to do. This must include questions about the integration of human learning with religious faith, but few studies have been sophisticated enough to achieve this aim (see Fahy 1992). There has also been no international study of Catholic school effectiveness in terms of academic performance or religious mission.

The Catholic school effect

USA

In the USA the research evidence shows that many Catholic schools in the inner cities take a large share of disadvantaged students. Also in the USA where Roman Catholic schools were once filled with students from poor ethnic families, mostly of European descent, those poor have been replaced by a new urban poor, primarily African-Americans, Hispanics and Asians. Indeed, Hispanics and Asians now have a larger percentage of students in Roman Catholic schools than in public schools (see Neal 1997a).

Given the social and ethnic variety of their intake, it is clear that Catholic schools are among the most successful. In the USA the dedication and commitment of staff is quite simply remarkable. If you work within a Roman Catholic school, your salary will most likely be two-thirds that of the teacher in the local public school. On average, if you are employed as a teacher in a Catholic school in America then you will earn the equivalent of £17,000 per annum, whilst if you were employed in a public school, your salary would be in the region of £27,000. You would also have larger classes to teach.

These Catholic schools do not have the same resources in buildings and teaching materials that public school teachers enjoy. James Coleman (1981; Coleman *et al.* 1982; Coleman and Hoffer 1987), the eminent American sociologist, conducted research into Catholic schools in the 1980s and found the following three things. First, on average, Catholic schools were more educationally effective than public schools. Second, Catholic schools were especially beneficial to students from less advantaged backgrounds. Third, there were strong indications that higher levels of discipline and academic demands accounted in large part for the success of these schools.

Compared to students in public schools, Catholic school students scored about two grade levels higher in mathematics, reading and vocabulary. Coleman found that Catholic schools produced better cognitive outcomes even after family background factors that predict achievement were controlled. The study found that factors that accounted for this were more effective school discipline, fewer student absences, higher enrolments in academic course work and about 50 per cent more homework.

Coleman's research was undertaken in 1980 and 1987. In 1997 Derek Neal (1997a, 1997b), an economics professor at Chicago University, repeated Coleman's surveys. Whilst confirming Coleman's earlier results, Neal found that attendance at Catholic schools increased the chances of graduation by 26 per cent. No less than 97 per cent of students graduated from Catholic schools and 94 per cent went on to College. He also found that African and Hispanic Americans who attended city Catholic schools had a higher graduation rate than whites in city public schools. Attendance at Catholic schools also improved future economic prospects. His research demonstrated that immigrant, minority and disadvantaged children all did better in Catholic schools. The main reason he gives for these findings is the poor quality of alternative public schools in urban areas. In fact, Neal (1997a) concludes that urban minorities are the greatest beneficiaries of Catholic schooling. He says: 'In sum, these results do not indicate that Catholic schools are superior to public schools in general. Rather, they suggest that Catholic schools are similar in quality to suburban public schools, slightly better that the urban public schools that white students usually attend, and much better than the urban public schools that many minorities attend.' On this evidence, Catholic schools might be seen as more inclusive.

Similar studies to Neal's had been conducted previously in various states in the USA. Paul Hill *et al.* (1990) conducted a study of Catholic and public schools in New York with between 85 and 95 per cent intakes of black pupils for the Rand Corporation that revealed the following:

- Catholic schools graduated 95 per cent of their students each year whilst public schools graduated 50 per cent;
- 65 per cent of Catholic school graduates received the New York Regents diploma whilst only 5 per cent of public school students received this distinction;
- Catholic school students achieved an average combined standard assessment test (SAT) 1 score of 803 whilst the average combined SAT 1 score for public school students was 642;
- 60 per cent of African-American Catholic school students scored above the national average for African-American students on the SAT 1 whilst less than 30 per cent of public school African American students scored above the average.

It would seem that in SAT scores, high school completions and college entry Catholic schools are more successful, often strikingly so. This is achieved against a backdrop of difficulties with tight finances, shifting demographics and teacher retention. Catholic schools not only pay teachers considerably less, they also spend much less on pupils. Byrk *et al.* (1993) offer a useful interpretation of Catholic school success by focusing on community influences and the social and cognitive climates in USA Catholic schools.

Australia

There is much more limited evidence for the academic performance of Catholic schools in Australia. Nevertheless, there is the research of Marcellin Flynn (1985) who studied 2,041 pupils in 23 schools in 1982 who sat the Higher School Certificate of that year. He discovered that Catholic school pupils were more highly represented in the top 1 per cent of overall Higher School Certificate pupils. His research concluded that Catholic schools have unique positive effects upon the academic results of pupils. His explanation for this was that academic achievement in Catholic schools bears a distinct relation to the pervading values of the school. In other words, the informal climate or ethos of achievement is the result of important characteristics; some of these he identified as:

- the pervasive values of the school;
- the morale and spirit of the pupils;
- the importance of the development of each pupil;
- the pastoral care of the school.

When pupils experience these characteristics in schools they do better in final public examinations.

There is one other source of data that can be employed to compare state and Catholic schools in the Sydney system of schools. The Basic Skills Tests are administered each year to over 10,000 students in Years 3 and 5 to assess pupils' literacy and numeracy skills in the context of learning in the Key Learning Areas of the Australian primary school curriculum. In March 2001 these tests demonstrated that pupils in Catholic primary schools had, on average, higher levels of writing, reading and language skills than did state school pupils (Catholic Education Office, Sydney, 2001). The performance of Sydney Archdiocesan schools has consistently shown higher levels of literacy and numeracy and unofficial tables produced by the press indicate that Catholic schools are extremely well represented on 'Distinguished Achievers Lists' (see *Daily Telegraph* (Australia) 23 December 2001).

In 2000 there were 1,701 Australian Catholic schools educating 355,623 pupils in primary schools and 279,989 pupils in secondary schools, representing 19.7 per cent of all pupils in Australian schools. Catholic schools in Australia have also become extremely popular with non-Catholics with the proportion of non-Catholics admitted to them rising in recent years from 8 per cent to over 21 per cent. In a survey conducted by Kelvin Canavan (1994) it was found that parents ranked the attractiveness of Catholic schools in the following order: first, school discipline, second, quality of teachers, third, the school's value system and fourth, the academic reputation of the school. Consequently, the main reasons for selecting a Catholic school were value related, i.e disciplinary standards, religious education, better student behaviour, instilling of values and character. This was only then followed by academic reasons, i.e. a higher academic standard of education and academic achievement. The tentative evidence that exists in Australia would indicate that the higher the value-related aims of the school, the higher the academic performance. Research has also indicated that satisfaction and morale levels among teachers in Australian Catholic schools are high (see Ellyn 2001). In a recent longitudinal study of pupils in Catholics schools for the years 1972, 1982, 1990 and 1998 by Flynn and Mok (2002: 11) it was also found that pupils attending Catholic schools were generally happy.

New Zealand

In New Zealand there is a system that rates each school by the parents' jobs/incomes. A school in a wealthy area might get a decile rating of 9 whilst in a poor area this could fall to as low as 1 or 2. This system provides a good method of comparing the academic success of schools and on this basis Catholic schools, which are integrated into the State system, are on average between 10 per cent and 20 per cent more successful in public examinations. Several of these schools are also leaders in academic results (source: New Zealand Catholic Education Office).

However, the New Zealand government has a careful policy of not releasing any statistics which could be interpreted as supporting the idea of league tables, or, for that matter, setting Catholic and other state schools up in comparison with each other. Whilst the government is fully supportive of Catholic schools, there is great sensitivity about providing interpretations of school achievement statistics both by government and Church authorities.

South Africa

Government support for Catholic schools in South Africa is regularly stated in public. However, this has not prevented government subsidy to Catholic schools being substantially reduced in recent years. Nevertheless, parental demand for Catholic schools has been unaffected, despite increased fees levied on poor parents. This can be accounted for by the reputation for high-quality provision that Catholic schools enjoy in South Africa.

For example, St Martin De Porres Roman Catholic Primary School is one of at least nine diocesan Catholic schools situated in Soweto. The annual fee charged by the school in 1999 was R596 whilst the school's annual cost per pupil was R2,676. The government provides a maximum subsidy of 60 per cent of the annual cost per pupil. In comparison, the amount the government pays for each pupil in public primary schools is R3,173 per annum. St Martin's therefore must survive on a combination of government subsidy, ,church subsidy and pupil fees. Crucially, the school also has the active support and involvement of parents that ranges from painting school buildings to clearing ground for a football pitch. It was Coleman and Hoffer (1987) who drew attention to the social resources available in the functional communities that surround schools: such a community is characterised by a social network with structural consistency, a network of active parents that shapes the social norms and structure within the school community. Through a homogeneous system of norms, a functional community provides a consistent environment for socialisation to take place, and it protects against influences of conflicting values. This kind of community, according to Coleman and Hoffer, influences the outcomes of schooling, especially academic achievement. It could be said that the community represented by the pupils, parents and staff of St Martin's is exactly this kind of community. Teachers are committed and work longer hours for less salary, parents not only pay fees from their extremely modest incomes, but offer their services to the school, and pupils respond by achieving higher scores in public tests than pupils in state schools.

Many schools in South Africa face similar problems to schools in Third World contexts where a great deal of education time is lost due to weather, large classes, crop harvesting, teenage pregnancy, hunger and disease. There is often little homework and low morale among teachers. Evidence (Christie and Potterton 1997) indicates that Catholic schools, particularly in rural settings, seem to ride these problems and spend substantial time on task. There is an ethic of care in Catholic schools where teachers know their pupils, even in large classes. There is also an ideal that motivates staff and pupils that is often absent in state schools.

Commentary

The research studies and data reviewed in this paper offer different explanations for their results. A number of commentators on Catholic schools provide a range of possible reasons for this persistent and positive association between Catholic schools and academic achievement. Many focus on the shared values or ethos of Catholic schooling. Andrew Morris (1997) has suggested that Catholic schools that have a more holistic ethos – a greater proportion of Catholic school pupils and staff who focus on the primary aim of Catholic education (see Arthur 1995) – are even more academically successful. In other words, Catholic schools that have higher levels of agreement about the mission of the school and the degree to which all concerned ensure that the values, attitudes and pedagogical practices, together with parental expectations and support, are consistent with its generally accepted purpose, the more effective the school is likely to be. Flynn's (1985) research would also appear to confirm this. Shokraii (1997) found that in the USA, Catholic schools have fewer vocational courses on offer and more academic-orientated programmes. Catholic schools are also often characterised by a strong sense of community. John Marks *et al.* (2001) has suggested that we should look at teaching methods in Church schools, as opposed to their religious ethos, for an account of their academic success.

But the question remains, how does the Catholic philosophical world and life view influence educational practices in Catholic schools? Catholic Church teaching provides a set of 'givens' in terms of what Catholic education should be about and these givens could be summarised as primarily about developing the theological virtues of faith, hope and love. Academic performance is not neglected, but it is a secondary consideration. Catholic schools will also commonly develop particular core values, often referred to as 'gospel values', which they actively promote. Community and the promotion of the common good are also central, but what kind of community do they perceive themselves to be? Are Catholic schools theological communities of believers or are they more sociological communities of care? Gerald Grace's (2002: 125ff) major study of Catholic head teachers in England indicates that Catholic schools still see their mission in terms of promoting faith, community and the social dimension. However, Grace acknowledged that Catholic schools in England had given greater attention to academic performance in school prospectuses and that this development had been largely driven by government legislation. Grace (2002: 125) concluded that this emphasis on academic performance was viewed by the head teachers in the sample as an education for service.

Whatever kind of ideological inspiration Catholic schools offer, few would say that academic success is the primary aim of a Catholic school. Examination success is not the measure of a child in a Catholic school. The danger is that to focus on examination success is to view only one element of schooling that may lead many to take this one measurement as evidence of the overall standard of performance in the wider, more diffuse process of Catholic schooling. Whilst a measurable performance indicator is a useful tool, it is not in itself evidence of achieving the aims of Catholic schooling – which is to provide a Catholic educational experience and formation. Grace (2002: 142) found some evidence in his study of a stated resistance among head teachers to 'the domination of technical performativity' in English Catholic schools. There appear to me to be two main levels of explanation for the effectiveness of Catholic schools in public examinations that could be briefly raised or characterised under the more diffuse headings of the *religio-philosophical* and the *pedagogical*.

The religio-philosophical

The goals, purposes, values and ideals of the Catholic school are largely predetermined by the Catholic philosophy of life. There is a sense in which all Catholic schools are committed to shared values and beliefs within an authoritative teaching church. This tradition of theological, moral, spiritual, social and intellectual ideas forms the backdrop to Catholic schooling. From this tradition certain premises are derived about human nature and James Hunter (2000) maintains that Catholicism, whilst not hermetically closed to developments in psychology and the social sciences, nevertheless offers resistance to whole-scale absorption of 'child-centred' and 'development' theories into educational practice. Catholicism promotes the dignity of human life and the active duty and service we owe to others, and encourages pupils to give their best with an emphasis on civil duty and obligation to the common good. Consequently, are Catholic schools more able to motivate pupils to a greater extent and strengthen their will so that they give of their best both in and outside of the classroom? What are the effects of Catholic belief systems on academic study? Much of this religio-philosophical level has simply not been researched, but if Andrew Morris (1997) is right then pupils professing and sharing the Catholic faith or world view in a holistic faith environment will do better in public examinations.

The pedagogical

In all the countries discussed in this paper it appears that teaching methods in Catholic schools emphasise more structured learning and regular homework. There appears to be emphasis on academic performance and high standards of pupil behaviour. Absenteeism appears lower and there is strong parental involvement. Teaching methods are often more traditional and there is a hierarchy of authority that is clear, unambiguous and understood by all in the school community. There is perhaps less 'child-centred' learning and greater emphasis on the authority of the teacher. In some countries the Catholic school day is longer than in state schools and it appears that there are more extra-curricular activities on offer to pupils. Again, the research evidence for this pedagogical effect is fragmented and incomplete, but if Marks *et al.* (2001) are right then it is this area which accounts most for the success of some Catholic schools.

Nevertheless, there appear to be some critical features that help explain Catholic school academic success, particularly among the increasing numbers of ethnic-minority and low-income children admitted to Catholic schools. It is also important to add that the number of non-Catholic children, in all the countries mentioned in this paper, admitted to Catholic schools has increased rapidly in recent years. Nevertheless, priority is still given to Catholics in admissions policies with the justification that Catholic schools offer 'an education in the faith for those of the faith'. Catholic schools constitute a small to large, relatively homogeneous sector of schooling in each of these countries. Whilst more research is needed, the following tentative list of features might help explain the greater academic performance of Catholic schools:

- An ideological stance that is shared, celebrated and motivates the school community to respect and honour the innate abilities of self and others;
- A greater sense of vocational commitment on the part of teachers to sustain a Catholic ethos at some cost to themselves;
- Greater parental involvement and commitment to the school, including provision of financial support;
- An emphasis on the pastoral activities of the school with a marked focus on building community with high expectations of behaviour and attendance;
- An emphasis on a wide range of pedagogical methods, less emphasis on wholesale 'child-centred' approaches and a stronger atmosphere of order;
- Greater emphasis on academic as opposed to vocational courses, particularly a strong focus on religious education and the humanities;
- An atmosphere of success and belonging with strong parental support – on average, providing a more homogeneous school system of norms and values.

However, perhaps the most overlooked factor is the quality of available public schools, especially in urban areas as compared to Catholic school provision.

The review of evidence presented here suggests that pupils, on average, in Catholic schools, irrespective of their 'faith orientation', learn more, as measured by public achievement tests, than pupils in State schools – that is, in comparison to pupils of similar social backgrounds and ability levels. There appears to be a persistent and positive association between Catholic schooling and academic achievement that seems to be demonstrated on an international level. However, the evidence is fragmentary and there is therefore a need for an international study of Catholic schools to determine what combination of 'Catholic' and 'school' factors influences academic effectiveness and accounts for the comparative educational achievement of these schools. Most studies at local and national levels have focused on what can be measured in terms of outcomes. Few have addressed the religio-philosophical level which is a much more diffuse area, but such a study is necessary to understand and show how the Catholic Church's teaching on education is both realised within Catholic schools and how it influences, if at all, academic outcomes. A focus on academic success by itself is both narrow and reductionist and is not what Catholic schooling principally sets out to achieve.

References

Arthur, J. (1994) 'Parental involvement in Catholic schools: an increasing case of conflict', *British Journal of Educational Studies*, 42(2): 174–90.

Arthur, J., (1995) *The Ebbing Tide: Policy and Principles of Catholic Education*, Leominster: Gracewing.

Byrk, A.S., Lee, V.E. and Holland, P.B. (1993) *Catholic Schools and the Common Good*, Cambridge, MA: Harvard University Press.

Canavan, K. (ed.) (1994) *Why do Parents Choose a Catholic School?*, Sydney: Catholic Education Office.

Catholic Education Council (1967) *News Bulletin*, 14: 23–9.

Catholic Education Office, Sydney (2001) *Basic Skills Testing Program Report 2001*.

Christie, P. and Potterton, M. (1997) *School Development in South Africa: A Research Project to Investigate Strategic Interventions for Quality Improvement in South African Schools*, Johannesburg: University of the Witwatersand.

Coleman, J. (1981) 'Public schools, private schools, and the public interest', *The Public Interest*, 64, Summer.

Coleman, J., Hoffer, T. and Kilgore, S. (1982) *High School Achievement: Public, Catholic and Private Schools Compared*, New York: Basic Books.

Coleman, J. and Hoffer, T. (1987) *Public, Catholic and Private Schools: The Importance of Community*, New York: Basic Books.

Ellyn, G. (2001) 'Commitment and satisfaction among parochial teachers', *Catholic Education Journal* (Australia), Spring.

Fahy, P.S. (1992) *Faith in Catholic Schools*, Homebush: St Paul Publications.

Flynn, M. (1985) *The Effectiveness of Catholic Schools*, Homebush: St Paul Publications.

Flynn, M. and Mok, M. (2002) *Catholic Schools 2000: A Longitudinal Study of Year 12 Students in Catholic Schools*, Sydney: Sydney Catholic Education Commission.

Grace, G. (2002) *Catholic Schools: Mission, Markets and Morality*, London: Routledge.

Greely, A.M. and Rossi, P.H. (1966) *The Education of American Catholics*, Chicago, IL: Aldine.

Hill, P.T., Foster, G.E. and Gendler, T. (1990) *High Schools with Character*, Santa Monica, CA: Rand Corporation.

Hofman, R.H. and Hofman, A. (2001) 'School choice, religious traditions and school effectiveness in public and private schools', *International Journal of Education and Religion*, 2(2): 144–64.

Honrnsby-Smith, M. (1978) *Catholic Education: The Unobtrusive Partner*, London: Sheed and Ward.

Hunter, J.D. (2000) *The Death of Character*, New York: Basic Books.

Marks, J., Burn, J. and Pilkington, P. (2001) *Faith in Education: The Role of the Churches in Education*, London: Civitas.

Morris, A. (1994) 'The academic performance of Catholic schools', *School Organisation*, 14(1): 81–9.

Morris, A. (1997) 'Same mission, same methods, same results? Academic and religious outcomes from different models of Catholic schools', *British Journal of Educational Studies*, 45(4): 378–91.

Morris, A. (1998a) 'So far, so good: levels of academic achievement in Catholic schools', *Educational Studies*, 24(1): 83–94.

Morris, A. (1998b) 'Catholic and other secondary schools: an analysis of OFSTED inspection reports 1993–1995', *Educational Research*, 40(2): 181–90.

Neal, D. (1997a) 'The effects of Catholic secondary schooling on educational attainment', *Journal of Labour Economics*, 15(1): 98–123.

Neal, D. (1997b) 'Measuring Catholic school performance', *Public Interest*, (Spring) 127: 81–7.

New Zealand Catholic Education Office (2001) *Catholic Schools in New Zealand*, Wellington: The Catholic Bishops Conference of New Zealand.

Shokraii, N.H. (1997) 'Why Catholic schools spell success for America's inner-city children', *Heritage Foundation*, 1128, June.

Teddie, C. and Reynolds, R. (2000) *The International Handbook of School Effectiveness Research*, London: Falmer Press.

14 Faith schools and Northern Ireland

A review of research

Tony Gallagher

Northern Ireland has lived through 30 years of political violence in which some 3,700 people have been killed. When the violence began in the late 1960s many pointed to the existence of separate schools for Protestants and Catholics, and wondered whether this had contributed to community divisions and violence. Many at the time suggested that the rapid development of integrated schools, where all children could be educated together, could provide a ready solution to the escalating violence (Fraser 1973; Heskin 1980). Plans to encourage more faith schools in England have generated much opposition, largely on the grounds that they would be divisive, and faith schools in Northern Ireland are often cited as a negative example. This chapter will examine the Northern Ireland experience under a number of different themes, including the historical background to the development of separate schools, debates on the role of education after the outbreak of violence and a consideration of measures that were taken within schools to promote reconciliation and tolerance. The final part of the chapter will consider the impact of these efforts, locate them within the broader peace process of recent years and offer some general conclusions on the lessons from Northern Ireland on the issue of faith schools.

Historical background

Ireland developed a national system of elementary schools in the first half of the nineteenth century. The intention was that a common multi-denominational system should develop, but there were few examples of shared provision (Akenson 1970) and schools became denominationally divided. Political unrest throughout the nineteenth and early twentieth centuries reflected the divergent interests of Catholics and Protestants with regard to leaving or staying in the United Kingdom. The island was partitioned in 1921 and the Southern part of the island opted for independence. The parliament in Northern Ireland opted to stay, but was left with a substantial Catholic and nationalist minority who were reluctant members of the new polity (Darby 1997).

The first Minister of Education, Lord Londonderry, sought to lay the legislative basis for a non-denominational system through the 1923 Education Act by establishing three new categories of school: county schools, to be wholly owned and managed by local authorities; voluntary schools, to be owned and managed by private or church interests, but which would receive limited public funds; and 'four and two' schools which would receive higher levels of public subsidy, as public representatives would have minority representation on school committees. Londonderry's aspiration was for a unified system. Clergy of all denominations would have access to the schools to provide religious instruction, but only outside the normal school day and on the basis of the voluntary participation of pupils. The expectation was that the Protestant Churches would transfer their schools to county status. It was assumed, correctly, that the Catholic Church would opt for voluntary status. The hope was that the Catholics might, in time, be attracted by the 'four and two' option.

However, the Protestant Churches refused to act, concerned that the traditional character of their schools would be lost if they were transferred under the 1923 conditions. A campaign by the Protestant Churches resulted in a series of amendments to the 1923 Act and the resignation of Lord Londonderry (Akenson 1973; Buckland 1979; Dunn 1990). The amendments had three effects. First, religious education, defined as 'simple Bible teaching', was enshrined as a statutory requirement of the curriculum of county schools, thereby subverting Londonderry's intention for non-denominationalism. Second, local school committees were empowered to establish the short-list of candidates for teaching posts in county schools, virtually guaranteeing that all those appointed were Protestant. And third, the Protestant Churches were allowed to nominate representatives to the school committees of transferred schools.

The goal sought by the Protestant churches meant that the state-controlled school system, which was, in theory, open to all, adopted a Protestant character in ethos and practice. Catholics could attend the schools as pupils, but their identity would not be recognised. On the other hand, the Catholic authorities were so wedded to clerical control of their own schools that they would not consider any dilution of that authority, even to lay members of their own community. Thus were the parallel religious school systems established (Akenson 1973).

It was not until 1968 that rapprochement between the Catholic Church and the government was reached when the former, belatedly, accepted a version of the 'four and two' offer. Voluntary schools were now re-categorised as voluntary maintained schools and received higher public subsidy. As a quid pro quo county schools were re-designated as controlled and the Protestant Churches were accorded transferors' rights on all new controlled schools, as if they had all once belonged to the Churches and had been transferred. The fact that it took so long for a deal to be struck between the Catholic authorities and the state is indicative of the suspicion and mistrust that existed between them. For years Catholics had faced discrimination and felt that aspects of their culture and identity were denied legitimacy in public space. Separate schools were important as they provided the only significant social institution over which the community exercised any degree of control, space within which it was possible to celebrate and declare a distinctive identity and culture, and an important source of middle-class jobs. That a balancing deal had to be struck with the Protestant Churches highlights the ubiquity of denominationalism in Northern Irish politics.

The entire historical period highlights another important theme. In conditions of religious and political tension it is easier for the communities to develop institutions which enhance the degree of separation between them. This is, almost, the default condition, whatever the avowed intentions of policy-makers at different points. This implies that change in another direction will only happen if people strive to make it happen.

The years of conflict

In situations of conflict people often look to schools to contribute towards the amelioration of violence. In Northern Ireland people also asked whether the separate schools had contributed to social division and conflict. What the outbreak of violence revealed was an astonishing lack of information into what was happening within schools. When Akenson

(1973) published his history of education in Northern Ireland he reflected in the final chapter on the emerging conflict and the role of schools within it, but noted the virtual absence of information on the consequences of separate schooling. He pointed to some anecdotal evidence on differences in the curriculum provided by the schools and expressed the hope that some experiments in integrated education might help ameliorate community tensions (Akenson 1973: 199–200).

A series of studies was carried out by the Centre for the Study of Conflict to try and plug this gap (Darby *et al.* 1977; Dunn *et al.* 1984; Murray 1985) and a number of themes emerged. First, schools appeared to be as segregated as ever. The last official data on the denominations of pupils in schools had been published in the mid 1960s and some seemed to think that a significant degree of mixing had taken place. Darby *et al.* (1977) suggested that there was little evidence for this claim. A second theme was that while there were many similarities in the curriculum and practice within the schools, there were also some important differences to be found in the balance and content of the curriculum, and in their cultural and sporting activities. A third theme was that there was little or no organised contact between pupils in the separate schools and little evident enthusiasm for initiatives in this area. Finally, there was little evidence that contact between teachers from the separate schools provided opportunities for them to explore issues related to social division or conflict, or the role schools might play in contributing towards an amelioration of the conflict.

Two main explanatory frameworks emerged on the impact of separate schools (Darby and Dunn 1987). The 'cultural hypothesis' argued that the overt curriculum of the schools socialised young people into distinctive worlds, creating a sense of difference which, under certain circumstances, could easily translate into antagonism. The 'social hypothesis' argued that the mere fact of attending different schools provided implicit messages that were sufficient to establish a sense of distinctiveness, which also, under certain circumstances, could translate into antagonism. A third view, largely promoted by the Catholic authorities, argued that the violence was rooted in injustice and inequality, and that material difference, not ignorance, was the key factor.

Research evidence could be adduced to support the cultural hypothesis, as in, for example, the work of Magee (1970) and Darby (1974) on the teaching of history, and suggested that curriculum-based initiatives might be helpful. Murray's (1985) ethno-graphic research in two primary schools highlighted the role of symbols and images as markers of identity and offered support for the social hypothesis. Perceptions by teachers of these symbols as antagonistic remained unchallenged due to the 'social grammar' of polite conversation which discouraged the discussion of difficult or contentious issues in religiously mixed company (Burton 1978; Harris 1972). From this perspective a curriculum focus dealt with surface issues and failed to address the deeper consequence of separate schools. Rather, the way forward should be to encourage contact programmes to bring Protestant and Catholic young people together, or to work towards common integrated schools. The third view suggested that society should address issues related to equality and justice. Indeed, advocates of this view occasionally went further to suggest that a focus on schools was sometimes used to blame the Catholic minority for the problem on the basis that they refused to integrate into the state school system.

There was never any clear consensus on what constituted the most likely explanation of the consequences of separate schools and educational activists got on with developing a range of interventions. Most can be seen to fall under three broad headings. First, curriculum initiatives, aimed at developing common programmes in specific areas (Skilbeck 1973; Malone 1973) and, somewhat later, developing specific programmes related to community relations. Second, contact programmes to bring young Protestants and Catholics together through holiday programmes and occasionally work between two schools. And third, pressure to develop new integrated schools or to allow existing schools to change status (Moffat 1993).

Limited work was achieved in the 1970s, in part because of the high levels of violence in this period. In such a climate it is perhaps ambitious to expect that schools could have reversed the tide. The predominant approach in schools at that time was that they should operate as oases of peace and calm, places where pupils could leave the conflict and violence on the outside. While the motivation for this is understandable, it looks, in retrospect, like a strategy of avoidance. Nevertheless, there were major curriculum initiatives implemented and limited numbers of contact programmes.

During the 1980s more active measures, including new curriculum initiatives, were put in place to address conflict issues through schools. In 1981 the first integrated school was opened after parents grew frustrated at the mismatch between the rhetorical commitment of authorities towards the idea of integrated education and their apparent unwillingness to do anything concrete to make it happen. By 1989 they had been joined by 11 integrated schools, all started by parents, often with crucial support from charitable trusts in England. The Department of Education had issued a circular in 1982 (Circular 82/21) to all teachers indicating the responsibility they had to address issues related to community relations and established a cross-community contact programme in 1987 to provide funding support for teachers who wished to established contact programmes between Protestant and Catholic schools.

The 1990s was a period when government provided more explicit support for initiatives aimed at promoting better community relations. The basis was provided by the 1989 Education Reform Order. In addition to the creation of an educational market, with parental choice and competition between schools, the legislation also committed government to support developments in integrated education and placed Education for Mutual Understanding and Cultural Heritage (EMU/CH) as educational themes on the statutory curriculum. The commitment on integrated education was advanced by providing funds for the Northern Ireland Council for Integrated Education (NICIE) so that it could help parents and others who wished to consider establishing new integrated schools, and introducing a procedure through which the parents of pupils at an existing school could vote to transform it to an integrated school.

A key factor in the evolution of this policy was the increased cooperation between the British and Irish governments following the 1985 Anglo–Irish Agreement. One consequence was the development of a reinvigorated community relations policy by the government in Northern Ireland, with three core objectives of encouraging more opportunities for Protestant/Catholic contact; encouraging greater tolerance of cultural diversity; and promoting equality of opportunity (Gallagher 1995). The first two policy aims link directly to the 1989 Education Reform Order. The third issue of equality was addressed more indirectly, but did result in the opening of two new Catholic grammar schools, the allocation of 100 per cent capital grant to Catholic schools and a commitment to monitor the impact of policy and practice on the religious school systems (Gallagher *et al.* 1994).

This highlights an important feature of the political environment since the mid-1980s. While the government had taken a proactive role in regard to the promotion of better community relations, this included a legitimation of key aspects of the identity and culture of the Catholic minority. The commitment to expand opportunities for integrated education was in response to claims that parents ought to have the right to choose this option for their children. In the same vein, government accepted the right of parents to choose to send their children to Catholic schools. However, the recognition of this right also involved the acceptance by government that equity considerations would influence the way in which policy more generally impacted on the Catholic schools.

The impact of community relations measures

In various ways the consequence of this legislative and financial support is clear. For example, the rate of increase in the opening of new integrated schools accelerated as a consequence of the 1989 Education Reform Order and, over time, the proportion of post-primary schools has steadily grown. The money available to reconciliation bodies and the contact programmes has led to the growth of a host of organisations which provide support for EMU/CH work in schools. This includes statutory and voluntary organisations which produce materials, including videos, games, books, pamphlets and worksheets, on EMU/CH-related themes. In addition, the local authorities and higher education institutions have run training courses on aspects of EMU/CH. Over time, a considerable body of expertise has developed and, while some of these resources and support would have been available even without an overarching government policy on community relations initiatives in schools, it is likely that the sheer amount of support available has been enhanced by the policy climate and the underpinning support of public money.

Despite this creditable amount of activity, there remain some difficulties regarding the quality of the activity and its direct impact on community relations objectives. Three main reports have provided a picture of work in schools: Smith and Robinson (1992) suggested that the EMU/CH work lacked clear definition, thus leaving open the danger that the 'cutting edge' of the initiative could be lost if people focused on its less controversial and 'safe' aspects. There is reason to suppose this might occur: we noted above that a 'social grammar' exists in Northern Ireland such that people tend to avoid talking about the issues of religion and politics in (religiously) mixed company (Gallagher, 1994). While broaching these issues can be considered 'impolite', this unwritten social rule means that people can engage in cross-community contact while remaining largely ignorant of the views of members of the 'other' community on the fundamental social divisions that exist within the society. Smith and Robinson (1992) went on to suggest that there was a lack of coordination between the various statutory bodies with a responsibility for EMU/CH, concerns about an overemphasis on contact, as opposed to curricular, work within EMU/CH, and that schools tended to accord the policy a relatively low priority. These patterns were confirmed by Leitch and Kilpatrick (1999).

The difficulty with the overemphasis on contact work is that a significant proportion of these programmes appears to be of limited value and, all too often, fails to address issues of division and conflict. In the worst cases the programmes merely reproduce the degree of 'polite' contact, characterised by avoidance, that exists in the wider society. More generally, it can lead to a diminution of curricular work within schools and encourage a perception that community relations is the responsibility of only those teachers involved in contact programmes. Smith and Robinson (1996) argued that a refocusing of EMU/CH work was needed to emphasise its whole-school dimensions, to highlight the implications for teaching and learning, to encourage teachers to address more controversial issues and to reduce the focus on contact work (see also Council for the Curriculum, Examinations and Assessment [CCEA] 1997).

This has been affected by the recent, and ongoing, review of the statutory curriculum. Change will probably not start until 2004, but it seems likely that a citizenship education programme will be part of the new arrangements. Of course, developing a citizenship education programme in a contested territory is something of a challenge. It has been addressed through a pilot programme working along three themes, including, first, forms of democracy, second, rights and responsibilities, and third, issues of justice and equality. The intention is to give young people the conceptual tools and skills to enable them to become critical and reflective participants in Northern Irish society. The concern is that space on the timetable for an innovative citizenship programme might be squeezed in favour of more traditional subjects.

Research on the integrated schools has focused on a number of different aspects. Parents have a variety of motives in sending their children to integrated schools (Morgan *et al.* 1992), but claims that the integrated schools have a largely middle-class intake are unfounded. Research on one school suggested that friendship networks did cut across religious boundaries (Irwin 1993), while Gallagher *et al.* (1995) found in another that it had developed innovative approaches to the curriculum and teaching, and that staff were using the opportunity provided by an integrated setting to address issues related to social division and conflict. There is other evidence on innovative developments in curriculum and pedagogy in the schools to address issues related to a divided and conflicted society (see Moffatt 1993, and the NICIE website at http://www.nicie.org).

However, some recent research suggests that this aspect of the schools is being constrained, in part due to turnover of staff and limited training for teachers wishing to work in integrated settings (Johnston 2001). Other pressure arises from the enhanced accountability systems, the pressure of benchmarking and other performance-driven initiatives that draw time and energy from other activities, while other research suggests that the integrated schools sector may be characterised by weak systemic links, and a consequent limited consistency in their internal organisation and practice (Milliken and Gallagher, 1998). The emergent problems are being addressed by the integrated schools movement, but they serve as a reminder that simply changing the structure of the schools does not, in itself, solve all the problems of a divided society – a more proactive approach is not only needed, but arguably the problems of a divided society will only be addressed if they are constantly and explicitly being addressed.

Table 14.1 provides another sanguine note, in that despite two decades of growth only 4 per cent of the pupil population is in integrated schools. Opinion poll evidence over many years shows a consistent pattern such that a majority of respondents believe that integrated schools are a good idea and would contribute to improved community relations (Gallagher and Smith 2002). Most of the existing integrated schools developed as entirely new schools, but the government's preferred route of expansion is through the transformation of existing schools, as it is less expensive and there is already significant

Table 14.1 Denominations of pupils by school type in 2001/2, primary, secondary and grammar schools only

	Catholic	*Protestant and other*	*Not recorded*	*Total*
Protestant schools (%)	4	94	89	48
Catholic schools (%)	92	1	2	47
Integrated schools (%)	4	5	8	4
All schools (%)	100	100	100	100
All schools (n)	165,082	144,729	16,245	326,056

Source: Calculated from Department of Education data.

surplus capacity in schools. This raises a number of problems, however, as transformation schools have to develop a new character while casting off an existing ethos and character. Perhaps more important, in order to ensure that transformation represents a genuine process of change, the legislation requires that a school has a minimum 10 per cent minority enrolment at the point of transformation and achieves a minimum minority enrolment of 30 per cent within 10 years. At the moment, however, only about 40 of the existing 1,000 schools meet this starting criterion and not all of them are interested in considering the option of transformation.

Table 14.2 shows that between 1998/9 and 2001/2 there was an increase of over 5,000 in the number of pupils in integrated schools, but a change in the denominational proportions of pupils. This is explained by the fact that all of the transformed schools began as Protestant schools and hence continue to have a majority Protestant enrolment. This might create a political problem if a perception grows within the Protestant community that it is 'their' schools that are being 'taken over' through transformation. This is perhaps even more likely in a context where many Protestants feel that the peace process has worked largely to the advantage of nationalists.

The peace process of recent years provides the next most significant backdrop to educational developments. This process began in the early 1990s, but significant progress was delayed until after elections in 1997, before the signing of the Good Friday Agreement in 1998. The political institutions established by the Agreement remain fragile (at the time of writing they had just collapsed), but, thus far, politicians have managed to find some way to maintain progress. The present view is that the community relations strategy developed from the mid 1980s onwards helped to create an environment within which these developments were more likely to occur than not, and within which a generally supportive environment for negotiations was created. For all the problems that are evident in the specific contribution of schools to this community relations environment, they nevertheless made some contribution that should be acknowledged.

Following the Good Friday Agreement the Department of Education established a working group to consider ways in which the education system could contribute to the promotion of tolerance and a more integrated education system. This did initiate some interesting and critical discussion and provided a forum within which representatives of different schooling interests could explore areas of agreement. The Catholic Bishops in Northern Ireland established their own working group to explore the distinctive contribution the Catholic sector could play in this positive political environment and, while much of its deliberations were inward looking and defensive, it did publish one paper that provided evidence of new thinking about what has traditionally been one of the more conservative hierarchies in the Catholic Church (Catholic Bishops of Northern Ireland 2001).

Table 14.2 Denominations of pupils in integrated schools in 1998/9 and 2001/1 (number and percentages)

	Catholic	Protestant and other	Not recorded	Total
1998/9 (n)	4,644	4,023	789	9,456
1998/9 (%)	49	43	8	100
2001/2 (n)	5,901	7,367	1,358	14,626
2001/2 (%)	40	50	9	100

Source: Calculated from Department of Education data.

Specifically, the Bishops seemed to acknowledge that Catholic schools had a social and moral role that extended beyond their traditional role of maintaining the faith community, and that the schools had a responsibility to proactively promote reconciliation and justice as part of their purpose. Even more recently and as part of the review of post-primary education in Northern Ireland, the Catholic Bishops have surprised many by breaking with their traditional orientation and criticising the maintenance of academic selection at age 11, particularly on the grounds of the social injustices that the continuation of academic selection at that age involves (see http://www.deni.gov.uk/pprb/mr/index_doc.htm for the views of a range of organisations, including the Catholic Bishops).

Conclusion

This chapter has examined the development of separate religious schools in Ireland, the maintenance of this after partition, and how debates on the role of separate schools were conducted after the outbreak of violence in the late 1960s. When we consider the complex political and social dimensions to the divided society in Northern Ireland, it seems overly simplistic to attempt to explain the conflict purely on the grounds of separate schools, or to argue that the conflict would be solved merely by forcing all young people to attend the same schools. A characteristic of Northern Ireland before the conflict erupted was that it was a plural society, but one with a monocultural political and public space. Official space was cast as representing a general will, but operated in terms of the culture and ethos of the dominant community. In this context separate Catholic schools represented limited space within which the minority could celebrate its own identity and culture.

A key part of the way to peace in Northern Ireland has been to acknowledge the legitimacy of minority identity and culture, and there is a general acceptance of the right of all communities to run their own schools. Importantly, this right extends to the right of parents to choose an integrated school for their children if this is their wish and it remains a challenge to government to extend this opportunity to all who want it. Choice extends also to the right to choose a denominational school, but with the right of choice comes a responsibility on those who run the separate schools to acknowledge the social consequences (never mind the economic consequences) that arise and proactively to do something to mitigate any potential negative effects. This responsibility, of course, applies to all school authorities, not just to the representatives of minority communities.

Plural societies are faced with a dilemma on whether they should operate plural schools, within which all or most identities are acknowledged and recognised, or a plurality of schools, in which minorities are accorded the right to their own schools. Given the historical role of mass education as a vehicle for social integration, there has often been a state preference for a public school system within which most people should participate. All too often, however, public school systems are based on assimilationist principles in which minority identities are either denied or discouraged in favour of a fictive cultural homogeneity.

Faith schools ought to be places where a values base is explicit and within which values can be discussed and considered, and in this respect all schools in Northern Ireland, including integrated schools, can be described as faith schools. At their worst, faith schools can be introverted places, where the ethos and practice discourages critical reflection and imposes its own homogeneity on pupils. It is the case that schools in Northern Ireland, perhaps many of them, have exhibited some of these characteristics. But secular institutions are no different in their potential to promote intolerance, perhaps especially when they claim to represent a general interest in society, while actually privileging a particular interest.

In Northern Ireland the operation of separate schools is constrained in that classrooms lack diversity in terms of experience and perspective, and there is no doubt that this imposes a responsibility on teachers and school authorities. But the existence of an explicit values base in education has provided the basis for a discourse to challenge traditional practice, and to encourage a different sense of what can be achieved through education, as part of a wider strategy towards the promotion of a society that is characterised by inclusion, equality and social justice. This has not yet been achieved, because achieving such a goal is difficult, particularly in the context of a society which has undergone such extensive political violence. It is also the case that while schools have contributed to this process, they could and should do more. But to suggest that the problem was caused simply because of separate schools, or could be cured by the removal of separate schools, seems to oversimplify the situation. Life, unfortunately, is more complex than that.

References

Akenson, D.H. (1970) *The Irish Educational Experiment: The National School System in the Nineteenth Century*, London: Routledge.

Akenson, D.H. (1973) *Education and Enmity: The Control of Schooling in Northern Ireland*, London: David and Charles.

Buckland, P. (1979) *The Factory of Grievances: Devolved Government in Northern Ireland 1921–1939*, Dublin: Gill and Macmillan.

Burton, F. (1978) *The Politics of Legitimacy: Struggles in a Belfast Community*, London: Routledge and Kegan Paul.

Catholic Bishops of Northern Ireland (2001) *Building Peace, Shaping the Future*, Armagh: Catholic Bishops of Northern Ireland.

CCEA (1997) *Mutual Understanding and Cultural Understanding: Cross-curricular Guidance Material*, Belfast: CCEA.

Darby, J. (1974) 'History in the schools: a review article', *Community Forum*, 4(2): 37–42.

Darby, J. (1997) *Scorpions in a Bottle: Conflicting Cultures in Northern Ireland*, London: Minority Rights Group.

Darby, J. and Dunn, S. (1987) 'Segregated schools: the research evidence', in Osborne, R.D., Cormack, R.J. and Miller, R.L. (eds) *Education and Policy in Northern Ireland*, Belfast: Policy Research Institute.

Darby, J, Murray, D., Batts, D., Dunn, S., Farren, S. and Harris, J. (1977) *Education and Community in Northern Ireland: Schools Apart?* Coleraine: the New University of Ulster.

Dunn, S. (1990) *A Short History of Education in Northern Ireland, 1920–1990*, Annex B, Fifteenth Report of the Standing Advisory Commission on Human Rights. House of Commons Paper 459. London: HMSO.

Dunn, S., Darby, J. and Mullan, K. (1984) *Schools Together?* Coleraine: University of Ulster.

Fraser, R.M. (1973) *Children in Conflict*, London: Secker and Warburg.

Gallagher, A (1994) 'Dealing with conflict: schools in Northern Ireland', *Multicultural Teaching*, 13(1): 10–13.

Gallagher, A.M. (1995) 'The approach of government: community relations and equity', in Dunn, S. (ed.) *Facets of the Conflict in Northern Ireland*, London/New York: Macmillan/St Martin's Press.

Gallagher, A.M., Cormack, R.J. and Osborne, R.D. (1994) 'Religion, equity and education in Northern Ireland', *British Educational Research Journal*, 20(5): 507–18.

Gallagher, A.M., Osborne, R.D., Cormack, R.J., McKay, I. and Peover, S. (1995) 'Hazelwood Integrated College', in National Commission for Education (ed.) *Success Against the Odds: Effective Schools in Disadvantaged Areas*, London: Routledge

Gallagher, T. and Smith, A. (2002) 'Attitudes to academic selection, integrated education and diversity within the curriculum', in Gray, A.M., Lloyd, K., Devine, P., Robinson, G. and Heenan, D. (eds) *Social Attitudes in Northern Ireland: The Eighth Report*, London: Pluto Press.

Harris, R. (1972) *Prejudice and Tolerance in Ulster*, Manchester: Manchester University Press.

Heskin, K. (1980) *Northern Ireland: A Psychological Analysis*, Dublin: Gill and Macmillan.

Irwin, C. (1993) 'Making integrated education work for pupils', in Moffat, C. (ed.) *Education Together for a Change*, Belfast: Fortnight Educational Trust.

Johnston, L. (2001) *The Practice of Integrated Education in Northern Ireland: The Teachers' Perspective*, Research Report, Hofstra University, NY/Graduate School of Education, Queen's University Belfast.

Leitch, R. and Kilpatrick, R. (1999) *Inside the Gate: Schools and the Troubles*, Belfast: Save the Children Fund.

Magee, J. (1970) 'The teaching of Irish history in Irish schools', *The Northern Teacher*, 10(1): 15–21.

Malone, J. (1973) 'Schools and community relations', *The Northern Teacher*, 11(1): 19–30.

Milliken, J. and Gallagher, T. (1998) 'Three Rs – religion, ritual and rivalry: strategic planning for integrated education in Northern Ireland', *Educational Management and Administration*, 26(4): 443–56.

Moffat, C. (ed.) (1993) *Education Together for a Change*, Belfast: Fortnight Educational Trust.

Morgan, V., Dunn, S., Cairns, E. and Fraser, G. (1992) *Breaking the Mould: The Roles of Teachers and Parents in the Integrated Schools in Northern Ireland*, Coleraine: Centre for the Study of Conflict, University of Ulster.

Murray, D. (1985) *Worlds Apart: Segregated Schools in Northern Ireland*, Belfast: Appletree Press.

Skilbeck, M. (1973) 'The school and cultural development', *The Northern Teacher*, 11(1): 13–18.

Smith, A. and Robinson, A. (1992) *Education for Mutual Understanding: Perceptions and Policy*, Coleraine: University of Ulster.

Smith, A. and Robinson, A. (1996) *EMU: The Initial Statutory Years*, Coleraine: University of Ulster.

15 Exclusion or embrace?

Faith, social ideals and 'common schooling' in America's public education

Michael Totterdell

Religion and American culture has always seemed a conundrum to those on the outside looking in. Paradoxically, the American public arena is pervasively religious yet simultaneously thoroughly secular in structure (Madsen *et al.* 2002). This chapter explores four distinguishing forces in the American experience that might help explain America's apparently ambivalent attitude towards religion in the public realm. The intention is to trace the impact of such distinguishing forces on the realm of public education. In doing so we hope to illumine how the realm of public education has functioned to open a fissure in American cultural politics and conceals a democratic deficit in the edifice of American pluralism.

Religion and America: foundations and the meaning of America

It has been said that the 'discovery' of America was the cause of the greatest liberation of the European imagination. Thomas More's *Utopia* was the first mature reflection in the Old World on the potential of the New. The general idealism in Europe that mankind could begin again was widely shared, in both secular and religious circles (Evans 1979). America was to be more than a nation; it was to be an experiment in the possibilities of humankind, both the religious and secular hope of the world (cf. de Tocqueville 1835).

Ironically, it was largely this idealism that was to eventuate in the peculiarity of the American church–state tradition, which arises from the fact that it embraces two ideals which are, and always have been, essentially adversarial. One is what might be called the custodial model (Lindar 1975). It assumes that society is organic and that civil authorities have a custodial responsibility for the spiritual and moral, as well as the physical, well-being of the organism. This ideal was articulated with timeless eloquence in John Winthrop's sermon, *A Modell of Christian Charity*, which he wrote in 1630 aboard the *Arabella*. It offers one interpretative paradigm for American history: the meaning of America was to consist in 'building the city on the hill', in which the light to the Gentiles would shine and in respect of which all would one day turn and be converted (Smith *et al.* 1960, Vol. I: 97–102).

This sense of corporate liability would in time become the basis of the peculiarly American idea – that America was exceptional in the history of the world and on its fate hung the fate of humankind. This 'new Eden' or 'new Israel' ideology represents one dominant strand in construing early American development. Its custodial ideal stems from the belief that America was founded on certain covenantal principles and that these were deeply enmeshed in America's roots, involving even those who did not share full-blooded theistic convictions and sentiments (Evans 1994). Consequently, even in the nineteenth century in the wake of disestablishment, the great tradition of the American churches was what Hudson (1970) arrestingly calls 'the coercion of voluntarism', the compulsion to fulfil a distinctive and specific vocation in society, to nurture the common and enduring spiritual values of the life of the republic. Indeed, well into the twentieth century, the call for a transcendent civil religion can plausibly be interpreted as a contemporary contextualisation of Winthrop's conviction that in a healthy society the cultivation of private and public virtue is the legitimate concern of government (Lindar 1975).

Yet this is not the whole story. For always yoked to the custodial ideal has been another tradition, which has been called the plural ideal. This notion assumes that there is a critical difference between public interests and private concerns, and religion, for the most part, is a matter of private concern. The roots of the plural tradition stab just as deeply into the subsoil of American culture (Marty 1979). The primitive documents of Massachusetts are instructive in this respect. In the *Cambridge Platform* of 1648 the ecclesiastical and civil jurisdictions of the Commonwealth were separated (Smith *et al.* 1960, Vol. I: 128–39). While it is certainly true that the clergy influenced civil affairs, it is also the case that the civil foundations of the colony were set not in Scripture but in the common law, which was notoriously susceptible to the ferment of cultural and religious pluralism.

America's historic conception of government grew out of this natural law tradition, and it was a mixture of Locke's theory of social compact and Puritan covenantal views of civil society that came to underlie the American republican experiment (Noll, Hatch and Marsden, 1983). With the Constitution and Ten Amendments gaining normative status over the Declaration of Independence as the charter of the land in 1791, the custodial ideal was formally subordinated within the plural ideal. Nevertheless, both traditions have persisted as dynamic forces and integral parts of American civilisation. As Grant Wacker (1984) observes, this point is critical for understanding the present American scene. The duality of the church–state tradition has pre-structured the relationship between conservative religionists who embrace the custodial legacy and modern secular society, making the relationship inherently adversarial.

This custodial–plural duality is a cogent interpretive schema, but it must by implication be extended to incorporate parallel developments among liberal religionists, and ultimately even secularists. Both groups ostensibly belong within the plural tradition, but exhibit 'custodial' predilections towards their notion of non-sectarian religion or of liberal visions of 'the American Way'. In this respect, the representation needs refining to become more sensitive to the nuances and ironic subtleties highlighted by the postmodern critique of the way the Enlightenment came to regard human reason. In the process of searching for some more compatible adjustment to late modernity, it now needs to be recognised that champions of the pluralist ideal have frequently spawned their own custodial shibboleths. The boundary between the custodial and plural ideals cannot be drawn so conveniently as to demarcate the forces of conventional religion from the intellectual heirs of the Enlightenment. The spread of cultural disparity in the age of modernity brought with it ever-increasing efforts to influence and control schooling through a public philosophy of culture – viz., an officially sanctioned version of 'the forms of things that people have in mind; their models of perceiving, relating and otherwise interpreting them' (Goodenough 1964: 36). Consequently the fusion or perhaps confusion of the custodial and plural ideals has been particularly marked in the realm of public schooling where, as we shall see, an educational perspective was subtly subordinated to regarding education primarily as a social, economic and cultural force.

Educators and religion: two voices and the echo of a third in public education

The common religion legacy of Horace Mann

It has been claimed, with some legitimacy, that the direction of America's education system can be seen as a linear development from Jonathan Edwards (1703–58) and the Christian influence, through Horace Mann (1796–1859) and the Unitarian influence, to John Dewey (1859–1952) and the Humanistic influence. While Edwards has recently attracted a good deal of critical appreciation (Bremer 1996), his influence on contemporary American education has been all but eclipsed by the other two luminaries and therefore it is they who will occupy our attention.

In the early years of the new republic, schooling remained a local affair and was channelled largely through religious establishments. With the move towards what was to become known as the 'common school', which gained impetus in the 1830s as a tax-supported state-wide system of education, the question of religion would once again come to the fore. No one who reads the writings of Horace Mann, one of the main spokespersons and the chief architect for the common school reforms, can miss the humanitarian impetus for free public education or the moral fervour and democratic idealism that informed his programme. The *raison d'être* of the common school movement was an essentially civilising one of providing common ground for assimilation into the virtues of democratic Americanism, part of which included the concept of a 'common' or non-sectarian Christian religion.

Although the common schools offered free education to all children regardless of social class or religious affiliation, they were by no means free from religious influence. Mann, who enjoyed a lengthy and influential tenure as Superintendent of Schools in Massachusetts, argued in the spirit of Thomas Jefferson that religious establishment had always led to persecution and tyranny. Yet he also believed in the importance of 'inculcating all Christian morals' (quoted in Gaddy *et al.* 1996: 11). Opposed to religious dogma though he was, he still thought it was vital to use the Bible to teach moral values. Consistent with his self-professed non-sectarian philosophy, he permitted use only of those portions of the Bible that were agreeable to all sects.

It might be argued that Mann's actions demonstrate wisdom insofar as he attempted to accommodate the religious views of all those represented in the classrooms. He anticipated doctrinal neutrality as the watchword of American public education. Of course, Mann's enculturation of this principle of religious non-offence was projected in the Protestant context of his times; he still wanted the public schools to be seen as the official vehicle for promoting Christian values, but in a way that would be non-divisive. Nevertheless, upon closer scrutiny, it soon becomes clear that there are some serious flaws in Mann's programme, which in certain respects persist to this day. The failing in his recipe for public schooling lies in the fact that it reflects an overriding predisposition to avoid controversy. This led him to advocate a pedagogical strategy that targeted the lowest common denominator so as to diminish the potency of particular loyalties that could give rise to factions and ensure social convergence. This pedagogic strategy in turn promulgated a schema for religion study and education that was inherently disingenuous by refusing to recognise another person's or group of people's right to be different and distinctive.

This did not mean that the public schools should not teach religion; it only meant that they should teach the religion that was deemed to be common to all Christians. The Bible should be read in school, on the assumption that it could 'speak for itself', without doctrinal gloss or denominational commentary that might give rise to disagreement (Mann 1838–

48, Vol. XII: 117). However, it was soon objected that the resulting mixture, which reflects a conception of religion based on the suppression of doctrinal issues, constitutes a reductive deposit that eviscerates religion and substitutes blandness, which is ultimately counter-educational. Orestes Brownson (1839), perhaps the most incisive of Mann's contemporary critics, pointed out that Mann's system, by suppressing everything divisive in religion, would leave only innocuous residue bereft of the capacity to inspire feelings of awe and wonder. Children brought up in a mild and non-denominational 'Christianity ending in nothingness', in schools where 'much was to be taught in general, but nothing in particular', would be deprived of their birthright, as Brownson (1839: 404) saw it. They might be taught to 'respect and preserve what is'; they would be cautioned against the 'licentiousness of the people' but they would never learn a 'love of liberty' under such a system (ibid.: 411). This was the nub of the issue for Brownson: the impossibility of teaching people to stand fast in their freedom unless they were first brought up in a particular tradition. Brownson's conclusion, after extensive discussion, was that people were most likely to develop a love of liberty through exposure to wide-ranging public controversy, the 'free action of mind on mind' (ibid.: 434).

A second objection to Mann's programme is the disingenuous nature of its claim to be non-sectarian. The claim is stultified by the fact that Mann and his fellow reformers were Unitarian Whigs, committed to the promotion of natural religion, which they understood to be 'a liberal religion of moral duty and enlightenment' (Nord 1995: 72) that would underpin the ambitious programme of 'improvement' embraced by reformers and serve as the main source of social morality (Lasch 1991: 187). Once one sets aside their contentious use of 'sectarian', the depth of their hostility to revealed religion, which they took to be divisive and socially dangerous, is readily apparent and it is difficult to see how Mann can evade the barbs of his own invective. In the eyes of conservative religionists, his purveyance of a superficial Biblicism, shorn of doctrinal referents, as the exclusive belief structure for public education was neither 'non-offensive' nor educationally appropriate, as he was wont to claim (Glenn 1987).

Eventually most Protestants united behind the common school movement on pragmatic grounds in the face of growing immigration and a belief that it would provide the necessary socialisation to assimilate these newcomers into American ways. Warren Nord (1995: 72) quotes the assessment made by Robert Michaelsen (1970) in his study of the history of religion in America:

> By 1870 Protestants generally had arrived at the conclusion that the public school system was best for America, that sectarianism – as they understood it – had no place in that system, but that religion– 'non-sectarian', 'common' religion – was essential to the school.

For Protestants, by and large, a secular purpose had emerged to replace the influence of religious nurture – education was to create an educated electorate and loyal citizenry. Indeed, common schooling in America deliberately sought to break the ties that bound children to their natural communities (Coleman 1990: xiv). It is clear that 'America's public school system was conceived as an agent of the state, not the family' (Kane 1995: 2). This brought the state into direct opposition with regard to the education of the children of immigrants as it sought to integrate these children into American society, a predominantly Protestant one, thereby threatening the culture and religion of the immigrants.

The overall legacy of Horace Mann needs to be assessed differentially. His reputation, as the founding father of the public school system, is well deserved. Nevertheless, in relation to the place of religion in education, he was instrumental in implanting certain suppositions deep in the psyche of the public schooling system that have constrained it through to the twenty-first century. In institutionalising his particular conception of the pluralist ideal in the common schools, he set in motion the logic of secularisation as a characteristic dynamic of public education. As Nord (1995: 74) says: 'In a religiously plural culture, peace is achieved by eliminating what is divisive – that is religion – from public institutions.' In the twentieth century, even the residual tokens of Bible reading and 'inclusive' prayer became increasingly tenuous as the schools attempted to become truly common schools, acceptable to all religious and secular communities. Nord (ibid.: 74) makes the pertinent observation that, 'in eliminating all religion from schools it may be that a new sectarianism – a secular sectarianism – has been established in the place of the old Protestant hegemony'. Mann bequeathed to the American system an abiding suspicion of religion *per se* and a predilection to subordinate its doctrinal and spiritual force to its instrumental function in reinforcing moral values and democratic loyalties supportive of the 'American way'.

The legacy of John Dewey: from common religion to 'religious' non-religion

If Horace Mann serves as a cultural index of nineteenth-century education in America, John Dewey's credentials as a leading indicant of twentieth-century educational trends are equally well attested: 'no one had more influence over the theory and practice of public education in the United States in the twentieth century than John Dewey' (Gaddy *et al.* 1996: 152). Dewey, of course, is primarily associated with pragmatism as a philosophy. He anticipated later twentieth-century philosophical appreciation that knowledge includes a social dimension reflecting conceptual expectations. He appreciated that democracy requires vigorous public debate; that information, usually seen as the precondition of debate, is better seen as its by-product. Through debate we become avid seekers of information, otherwise we take it in passively; he saw the relationship between information and argument as complementary, not antagonistic (Dewey 1927). In educational terms, it is only by subjecting our preferences and projects to the test of debate that we come to understand what we know and what we still need to learn.

For Dewey, then, argument is risky and unpredictable, therefore educational. It is not properly construed as a clash of rival dogmas, but as respectful hearing of opposing arguments. This required the cultivation of certain vital habits: the ability to follow an argument, grasp the point of view of another, expand the boundaries of understanding and debate the alternative purposes that might be pursued. One might anticipate from the foregoing that, contrary to Mann, Dewey would at least countenance the rehearsal of public controversy, not only in politics but also in religion – what Brownson (1839: 393–434) had referred to as the 'two great concernments of human beings' – in the public schools. Unfortunately, however, Dewey's educational philosophy manages to be both egalitarian and elitist. It recognises the contingency of rationality together with the need for access to a common tradition of inquiry into inquiry, and it claims to eschew 'spiritual aristocracy'. Yet, because of his faith in the experimental method of science as the master metaphor for learning generally, it also appears to elevate the perspective of a progressive elite as the sole means of 'transformative action' or 'constructive social engineering' (Dewey 1916: 820–30). Consequently, it fails to address adequately the deeper questions of particularism and shared understandings in democratic pluralism, especially as these bear on religion.

What led Dewey to this impasse? He certainly appreciated that in its deepest and richest sense, a community must always remain a matter of face-to-face intercourse – vital and thorough attachments are bred only in the intimacy of an intercourse that is of necessity restricted in range. What Dewey could not explain was how this loyalty and responsibility could thrive in a world of mass production, mass communications and mass consumerism. He took for granted the disintegration of the family, church and neighbourhood. What was to fill the resulting void? How could the belief in the possibility of a return to the local homes of mankind be defended? Dewey recognised the importance of the question, noting that the significant thing in modern times is that loyalties, which once held individuals, which gave them support, direction, and unity of outlook on life, have well nigh disappeared. But his commitment to the idea of progress and his belief that present experience must anticipate the future rather than find its moorings in the past seems to have beguiled him.

His response was to promote a social philosophy which was oriented to the pursuit of the active relation between ideal ends and actual reality, and as a concomitant, to regard democratising the students of the public education system as attaining 'an explicit and articulated consciousness of the religious significance of democracy in education, and of education in democracy' (Dewey 1908: 175). It is in this respect that he spoke of 'a common faith' as an immanent humanistic and secular inspiration, and of 'God' as 'the unity of all ideal ends arousing us to desire and actions' (Dewey 1934: 29). Dewey saw no final Good or Truth as the *end* product of valuational activity, but rather as the *process* by which various specific goods do emerge and begin to operate. The criterion of value, for Dewey, of present experience was its future significance in experiential terms.

Dewey's (1934) mature thoughts on religion are expressed in *A Common Faith*, which represents his most transparent search for a basis for unity in a religious substitute, an absolute perspective that transcends the conflict between competing loyalties. In it he lamented the divisive effects of religion. He distinguishes between the terms 'religion' and 'religious'. He reserves the former as a strictly collective term for supernatural myths, while maintaining the term 'religious' for the world of the natural, especially as it involves human relations, welfare and progress. In contrast to 'religion', the 'religious' does not exist as an institution or any form of social organisation:

> ... a religion ... always signifies a special body of beliefs and practices having some kind of institutional organisation ... In contrast, the adjective 'religious' denotes nothing in the way of a specifiable entity, either institutional or as a system of beliefs ... it does not denote anything that can exist by itself ... it denotes attitudes that can be taken toward every proposed end or ideal.
>
> (Dewey 1934: 9ff)

Concerning such 'religious' attitudes, Dewey further explains:

> The sense of the dignity of human nature is as religious as is the sense of awed reverence when it rests upon a sense of human nature as a co-operating part of a larger whole. ... Any activity pursued in behalf of an ideal end against obstacles and in spite of threats of personal loss because of the conviction of its general enduring value is religious in quality.
>
> (ibid.: 25 and 27)

A distinctive feature of Dewey's 'religious' domain is that it is putatively transformative in promoting firmly established changes in ourselves (ibid.: 12). As Rosenow (1997: 429) describes it, 'This transformation occurs when our creative imagination challenges us to get involved in an active and constructive way in our world.' In this fashion a faith emerges which Dewey (ibid.: 23) characterises as 'the unification of the self through allegiance to inclusive ideal ends, which the imagination presents to us and to which the human will responds as worthy of controlling our desires and choices'.

The implication for education in the public schools is not without irony. Dewey addresses the issue directly in an essay (Dewey 1908), entitled 'Religion and our schools'. Dewey sees 'religion' as such as having little or nothing of enduring worth to contribute to science, morality or democratic ideals; the obverse of this, for Dewey at least, is that certain ideals and values do have lasting 'religious' significance worthy of educational attention (cf. Rockefeller 1991: 73–5). Education becomes, for Dewey, 'the modern universal purveyor' which fosters our moral and spiritual life, and consequently it is the responsibility of the common schools to see to it 'that we recover our threatened religious heritage' (Dewey 1908: 166). However, such a purpose cannot be achieved by the teaching of religion, since it is impossible to cultivate 'the religious' in this way (ibid.: 173). Traditional 'education in religion' forms 'habits of mind which are at war with the habits of mind congruous with democracy and science' (ibid. 168). The schools should therefore provide a *cordon sanitaire* protecting students from contagion by any such pathology and, if they are prudent, 'keep their hands off' the supernatural side of religion altogether (ibid.: 167ff). But giving up on teaching religion does not imply a loss of genuine religious heritage, in Dewey's view. He claims, 'Our schools are performing an infinitely significant religious work,' since they are engaged in promoting social unity, a solidarity of demo-cratic citizenship 'out of which in the end genuine religious unity must grow' (ibid.: 175) in turn inaugurating 'that type of religion which will be the fine flower of the modern spirit's achievement' (ibid.: 177).

Among the more perceptive of Dewey's contemporary critics was Reinhold Niebuhr (1892–1971), perhaps America's foremost social theologian and, like Dewey, an educator in his own right. Anticipating many elements of the communitarian and postmodernist critique of humanistic liberalism, he was convinced that Dewey not only misrepresented myth, but that his surrogate religion was an example of a misguided search for unity. Niebuhr considered Dewey's plea for an 'inclusivist' religious faith as an attempt to eliminate conflict and unite men of goodwill everywhere by stripping their spiritual life of all historic, traditional and supposedly anachronistic accretions. Dewey's position exemplified the faith of modern rationalism in the ability of reason to transcend the partial perspectives of the natural world in which reason is rooted. Dewey failed to appreciate that competing loyalties were rooted in something more vital and immediate than anachronistic religious traditions. The fervour they evoked could not be modified or resolved by the parochialism of the modern nor by experimenting with the rhetoric of its uncommitted environment; no amount of education will ever eliminate the inverse ratio between the potency of love and the breadth and expansion in which it is applied (Niebuhr 1934).

Prophetic religion, Niebuhr maintained, managed to sustain an intolerable tension between the absolute and the contingent and was not blind to the perennial force and the qualified virtue of less rational human relations. The value of mythology consisted, in part, of its understanding of the organic aspects of life which rationalistic morality frequently fails to appreciate. Particularism remained a source of 'virtue' as well as 'demonic fervour' (ibid.: xi–xii). Niebuhr (1932) believed that only 'myths' had the power to inspire effective political action. He saw desiccation, in effect, as a greater menace than superstition and fanaticism. Indeed, far from being outmoded, religion plays a crucial role in life in modern society: 'Whatever may be said of specific religions and religious forms, it is difficult to imagine man without religion; for religion is the champion of personality in a seemingly impersonal world' (Niebuhr 1928: 4).

Other critiques of Dewey's account of common faith (Mott-Thornton 1997: 51–60; Rosenow 1997: 434–7) suggest that the sustained attempt to discredit traditional forms of religion on the back of an adherence to a reductive naturalism, and to suggest that the future value of the religious function rests solely upon the extent to which it might be liberated from religion, turn out, upon reflection, to be misguided. For they involve a depreciatory caricature of religion clearly built upon an evaluation that excludes traditional religious views. A negative account is imported into the logic of any use of the term 'religion' on the grounds of a question begging naturalistic *a priori*, together with *ad hominem* representations and an unsubstantiated psychologism that educated practitioners of religion would regard with deep suspicion. In parallel fashion, in suggesting religious experience is one '... having the force of bringing about a better, deeper and enduring adjustment in life', and that 'whatever introduces genuine perspective is religious', Dewey (1934: 15 and 25) then builds a positive evaluation into the logic of his revisionist use of the term 'religious' as being non-derivative of the social practice of religion. It is also highly questionable whether Dewey's 'religious' way really is rational in a way which religionists' way of 'religion' is not. As Mott-Thornton (1997: 58) concludes:

> Dewey's account of the alleged contrast between 'religion' and the 'religious' appears not to take account of the extent to which any truth generating methodology is dependent upon a set of non-negotiable presuppositions that are embedded in a tradition and therefore born in the past. Science is but one historically contingent mode of experience. Scientific method does not provide the complete 'view from nowhere' that Dewey's account of religion appears to suppose.

Dewey's legacy to social and political philosophy generally may well be beyond dispute and like Horace Mann a century earlier he was surely right in thinking that what people need in public space and in the character of public life is not primarily fragmentation and difference but a sense of what they have in common – a sense of 'centredness'. However, like Mann he erred egregiously in thinking that a sense of 'centredness' or common patterns of understandings can be achieved bereft of the particularities by which truth, belief and knowledge of the difference between right and wrong are transmitted. These cannot be passed on without a structure, a system of belief, to sustain them. Indeed, without these, as Niebuhr and Brownson before him recognised, the American idea – tolerance, openness, opportunity, self-creation – is insufficient even to sustain itself. Dewey's 'common faith' inevitably rests on the notion of 'religious' consensus, which, as history testifies, is a dangerous fantasy. Moreover, in retrospect it is clear that his metaphysical naturalism was at times too tightly held for someone who claimed to be at ease with contingency. Religious thinkers who were his contemporaries, such as Niebuhr and Jacques Maritain (1938), addressed the same malady that concerned Dewey with a call to rediscover the eloquence of things in their particularity, to recognise the things that command our respect and grace our life, and help us to find the depth of the world.

American public schooling and the travail of religion

We have seen how both Mann and Dewey, in their respective centuries, regarded public schools as the best way to achieve a democratic society (cf. Gaddy *et al.* 1996: 150ff). This translated into the desire to prefigure education in a way that reflected their central concern with the moral and social development of society and of individuals. As they were greatly enamoured of scientist images of social intelligence and anxious to cement democracy in the fabric of public education, and as they harboured suspicions about the encumbrances of religion in both respects, they sought to dissociate religion from the ethos of the common school. Instead, they tried to fashion an officially non-sectarian civic religion as a common structure providing a kernel of consensual valuation that would complement a stable foundation for education, based in practical reason, and thus, as they supposed, be compatible with the pluralist ideal. For Mann this entailed appropriating plurality by advocating a point of lowest common denominator agreement in a 'basic' Bible suitably censored and abridged. For Dewey it entailed a notion of 'common faith' that predicates the unity of ideal ends and endeavours on the use of scientific methodology by the social community of teachers and students who will actualise this ideal. In articulating what he calls, 'My pedagogic creed', Dewey (1897: 95) declares the teacher's calling is to be 'the prophet of the true God and the usherer in of the true kingdom of God'. The 'religious' mission he confers on the teacher is to mobilise and channel spiritual energies of self-realisation or self-actualisation in the service of current social needs and a fervent commitment to democracy. Sidney Hook (1973: 116), one of Dewey's disciples, proposed that, 'Where churches and sects and nations divide ... the schools can unite by becoming the temples and laboratories of a common democratic faith'.

The combined impact of Mann and Dewey on the philosophy of public schooling in America has been great. Regarding religion, its conceptual frame has fused with the historical trajectory of the 'pluralist' tradition in America and also reinforced that particular configuration of structural pluralism that typifies church–state separation. At the same time, the practical outworking in public education maintains continuity with the 'custodial' tradition's sense of society as an organism: democracy is 'a spiritual fact' (Dewey 1893: 8), a moral imperative of which education is the custodian. But such an approach allied to religious revisionism constrains what is acceptable and bestows official sanction on an ideology implacably opposed to institutionalised religion. The physiognomy of hostility to traditional religion symptomatic of this – at the levels of policy, curriculum and the 'foregrounding of experience and cultivation of desire' (Usher and Edwards 1994: 196) in the prevailing pedagogy – has become virtually unassailable. It has occasioned programmes of study that arbitrarily endorse approaches which either dilute or exclude exposure to religious traditions in their wholeness and, in the process, de-legitimise religiously informed points of view from the educational mainstream. So the public school system continues to offer a supposedly neutral curriculum which disguises the importance of the religious dimension in American life and culture (cf. Nord 1995).

However, whilst archetypically modern, the contingency of these developments has been revealed in part by our attending not only to proponent opinion, but also to the countervailing critique voiced by articulate detractors. In Brownson and Niebuhr we hear prophetic warnings. They argue that the 'spirit' of educational reform entertained by the likes of Mann and Dewey, if taken to its logical terminus, would create a modern form of priesthood by setting up an educational establishment empowered to impose dominant opinion on the common schools; the power exercised over the mind by such a 'sacerdotal corporation', as Brownson (1841: ix) termed it, would serve, like all priestly hierarchies, to efface traditions of argument and undermine the cultural diffusion of education throughout the whole community. This correctly identifies the main problem with public education's treatment of religion in America, which lies not so much in its failure to represent facts, events and phenomena objectively and impartially, as in its failure to see itself as an agency for carrying on the cultural conversation about a quest that is constitutive of human life: the search for intelligibility and meaning. As a consequence, public educators have been unsuccessful in representing conflicts of culture, ideology and ideals through educating for 'living with our deepest differences' (Cassity *et al.* 1990). This symbolises a significant deficit limiting plural democracy and diminishing freedom. It also issues in a peculiar reductionism whereby education may too readily limit its attention to the *surfaces* of reality rather than engage with its deeper dimensions in all their rich particularity. Hence it may inadvertently neglect issues of spiritual or immaterial equity and weaken anti-material values. Yet, as Fogel (2000: 38ff) persuasively argues, it is precisely these issues and values, not the old ones, which will be the centre for the struggle for egalitarian reform during the next generation.

The American republican experiment, then, remains a work in progress with problems to overcome as well as achievements to celebrate. The doubts raised by the 'faith schools' are fundamentally those of the stranger or outsider who fears spiritual exclusion rather than embrace. By way of response, under the rubric of 'inclusivity', common schools may yet manage to foster an extravagant hospitality that draws people together without obliterating their differences. They would then perhaps recognise that the uniqueness of each person is necessary so that there will be a fuller abundance, a genuine giving to another and receiving what they do not already have. There would cease to be a 'null' curriculum that consigned religion to the margins of the modern world along with the assumption that religious discourse has nothing to add to secular descriptions. Rather, there would be a pedagogical acknowledgement of religion's continued relevance as a *cultural resource* with significant discursive reserves without disregarding the question of religion's truth content (see Haynes and Thomas 1998).

To achieve this, however, would necessitate public education adopting as one of its core purposes the humanisation of difference by sketching out a phenomenology of embrace that goes beyond de-differentiation. Embrace would become what Miroslav Volf (1996: 140) terms 'a metonymy for the whole realm of human relations in which the interplay between self and the other takes place' so that 'the negotiation of difference' which can 'never produce a final settlement' may be continued (Walzer 1994: 83). Moreover, as Volf (ibid. 146) avers, embrace should be seen not only as a metaphor for the 'merging' and 'diverging' of various streams that take place in every self and every community, but because we live in overlapping social territories it describes also a moral stance of the selves inserted into a permanent struggle for power and recognition. As a metaphor, embrace implies 'togetherness' in mutual alterity; integral to its structure is a 'multifinality' that rests on the undetermination of the outcome.

References

Bremer, F.J. (1996) *The Puritan Experiment: New England Society from Bradford to Edwards*, Cambridge, MA: University Press of New England.

Brownson, O. (1839) 'Review of Horace Mann's second annual report', *Boston Quarterly Review*, 2: 393–434.

—— (1841) 'Our future policy', in H.F. Brownson (ed.) (1883) *The Works of Orestes A. Brownson*, Detroit, MI: Ann Arbor Press.

Cassity, M.D., Guiness, O., Haynes, C.C., Seel, J., Smith, T.L. and Thomas, O.G. (1990) *Living with our Deepest Differences: Religious Liberty in a Pluralistic Society*, Boston, MA: Learning Connections Publishers.

Coleman, J. S. (1990) 'Choice, community and future schools', in W.H. Clune and J.F. Witte (eds) *Choice and Control in American Education: Volume 1. The Theory of Choice and Control in Education*, Bristol, PA: Palmer Press.

de Tocqueville, A. (1835) *Democracy in America*, Volume 1 (reprint, P. Bradley ed., 1958), New York: Vintage Books.

Dewey, J. (1893) 'Christianity and democracy', in J.A. Boydston (ed.) *John Dewey: The Early Works*, Volume 1. Carbondale, IL: Southern Illinois University Press: 90–2.

——— (1897) 'My pedagogic creed', in J.A. Boydston (ed.) *John Dewey: The Early Works*, Volume 5, Carbondale and Edwardsville, IL: Southern Illinois University Press: 84–95.

——— (1908) 'Religion and our schools', in J.A. Boydston (ed.) *John Dewey: The Middle Works*, Volume 4, Carbondale and Edwardsville, IL: Southern Illinois University Press: 165–77.

——— (1916) 'Progress', *Characters and Events*, 2: 820–30.

——— (1927) *The Public and Its Problems*, New York: League for Industrial Democracy.

——— (1934) *A Common Faith*, New Haven, CT: Yale University Press.

Evans, J.M. (1979) *America: The View from Europe*, New York: Norton.

Evans, M.S. (1994) *The Theme is Freedom: Religion, Politics and the American Tradition*, Washington, DC: Regnery Publishing.

Fogel, R.W. (2000) *The Fourth Great Awakening and the Future of Egalitarianism*, Chicago, IL: University of Chicago Press.

Gaddy, B.B., Hall, T.W. and Marzano, R.J. (1996) *School Wars: Resolving Our Conflicts over Religion and Values*, San Francisco, CA: Jossey-Bass.

Glenn, C.L. (1987) 'Moulding citizens', in R.J. Neuhaus (ed.) *Democracy and the Renewal of Public Education*, Grand Rapids, MI: Eerdmans.

Goodenough, W.H. (1964) 'Cultural anthropology and linguistics', in D. Hymes (ed.) *Language in Culture and Society: A Reader in Linguistics and Anthropology*, New York: Harper & Row.

Haynes, C. and Thomas, O. (1998) *Finding Common Ground: A First Amendment Guide to Religion and Public Education* (third revised edition), Nashville, TN: The Freedom Forum First Amendment Center.

Hook, S. (1973) *Education for Modern Man: A New Perspective*, New York: Humanities Press.

Hudson, W.S. (ed.) (1970) *Nationalism and Religion in America: Concepts of American Identity and Mission*, New York: Harper & Row.

Kane, P.R. (1995) 'Privatization in American education', *Private School Monitor*, 17(1): 1–12.

Lasch, C. (1991) *The True and Only Heaven: Progress and Its Critics*, New York: Norton.

Lindar, R.D. (1975) 'Civil religion in historical perspective: the reality that underlies the concept', *Journal of Church and State*, 17: 399–421.

Madsen, R., Sullivan, W.M., Swidler, A. and Tipton, S.M. (eds) (2002) *Meaning and Modernity: Religion, Polity and Self*, Berkeley, CA: University of California Press.

Mann, H. (1838–48) Annual Report of the Board of Education, together with the Annual Report of the Secretary of the Board (Volumes I–XII), Boston, MA: Dutton & Wentworth.

Maritain, J. (1938) *Integral Humanism* [trans. J. W. Evans], New York: Scribner's.

Marty, M.E. (1979) 'Interpreting American pluralism', in J.W. Carroll, D.W. Johnson and M.E. Marty (eds) *Religion in America: 1950 to the Present*, San Francisco, CA: Harper & Row.

Michaelsen, R. (1970) *Piety in the Public School*, London: Macmillan.

Mott-Thornton, K. (1997) *A Common Faith? Personal Development, Spirituality and State Education*, PhD Thesis. London: Institute of Education, University of London.

Niebuhr, R. (1928) *Does Civilization Need Religion?* New York: Macmillan.

——— (1932) *Moral Man and Immoral Society*, New York: Scribner's.

——— (1934) 'A footnote on religion' (a review of John Dewey's *A Common Faith*), *Nation*, 26 (September): 358–9.

Noll, M.A., Hatch, N. and Marsden, G. (1983) *The Search for Christian America*, Westchester, IL: Crossway Books.

Nord, W.A. (1995) *Religion and American Education: Rethinking a National Dilemma*, Chapel Hill, NC: The University of North Carolina Press.

Rockefeller, S.C. (1991) *John Dewey, Religious Faith and Democratic Humanism*, New York: Columbia University Press.

Rosenow, E. (1997) 'The teacher as prophet of the true God: Dewey's religious faith and its problems', *Journal of Philosophy of Education*, 31(3): 427–37.

Smith, H.S., Handy, R.T. and Loetscher, L.A. (eds) (1960) *American Christianity*, Volume 1, New York: Scribner's.

Usher, R. and Edwards, R. (1994) *Postmodernism and Education*, London: Routledge.

Volf, M. (1996) *Exclusion and Embrace: A Theological Exploration of Identity, Otherness, and Reconciliation,* Nashville, TN: Abingdon Press.

Wacker, G. (1984) 'Uneasy in Zion: evangelicals in postmodern society', in G. Marsden (ed.) *Evangelicalism and Modern America,* Grand Rapids, MI: Eerdmans.

Walzer, M. (1994) *Thick and Thin: Moral Arguments at Home and Abroad,* Notre Dame: University of Notre Dame Press.

16 Faith schools in France

From conflict to consensus?

Cécile Deer

This chapter describes how the French educational system has evolved in relation to faith schooling in recent years. It shows that from a historically-grounded, 'culturally' specific situation of antagonism, the secular state sector and the religious private sector have developed – or more precisely have been politically, legally and socially encouraged to develop – forms of complementarities which have led to an unprecedented level of mutual tolerance. Whether this may be deemed to be a consensual situation remains a point of debate.

Conflict: objectively symbolic writings and dates

Any attempt to give a brief but meaningful account and explanation of the evolution of an educational system is a difficult task. In order to emphasise certain points it is common to resort to objectively symbolic dates and events. This is, of course, not entirely satisfactory for we know that the meaning of historical events, and, in particular, the meaning of educational policies and practice, may be related and interpreted in very different ways (Durkheim 1995: 1922; Bourdieu and Passeron 1964; Boudon 1973; Archer 1979; Prost 1992; Bourdieu 1996).

The questions of faith and religion, agnosticism and atheism have played a central role in the intellectual and political shaping of the state, of society and of thought in France. Examples in French literary records range from Montaigne's essays or Rabelais' writing to Descartes' classical rationalism, Voltaire's fight against religious intolerance, Rousseau's deism, Diderot and d'Alembert's encyclopaedia project, Hugo's premonitory statements, Flaubert's scandals or Camus and Sartre's reflective thinking, while historical accounts would most likely include the revocation of the Edict of Nantes, the constitutional Church and the cult of the Supreme Being during the Revolution and the 1905 official separation of Church and State in the wake of the Dreyfus Affair (Baubérot *et al.* 1994; Minois, G. 1998). It must be added that France should not be considered as a monolithic entity where religion is concerned. Her various constituent regions make for different types of historical narratives, experiences and practices, bringing into the picture regional specificities which are difficult to pin down in one homogeneous national account. This is an important factor to bear in mind when considering the faith schools issue in France even if it will not be possible to develop the idea within the space of this chapter.

Ever since the Revolution of 1789, the religious and the secular forces in France have fought for political and social domination. This struggle was originally epitomised by decisions such as those that created the *état civil*, managed by the city councils, gave full citizenship to Protestants and Jews, secularised the calendar (albeit temporarily) and, more importantly, abolished public funding for the Church (1794). The last of these measures may be understood as a first step towards the separation between the Church and the State. This has been an all-pervasive ideological conflict in which the control and domination of education and schools has featured prominently. Some extreme revolutionary propositions recommended that children should be taken out of their family circle (and therefore away from the influence of the Church through the mother and the community) at the earliest possible stage to be publicly educated together. A more liberal approach was developed by Condorcet in the *Rapport et projet de décret sur l'instruction publique*, which he presented to the legislative assembly in 1792. This report, which still merits close examination today, was the first text to express a secular conception of education, expounding rational and enlightened forms of learning and teaching (Condorcet, 1994 ed.). Condorcet's project was not formally adopted as a decree but the text provided a frame of reference and may be said to do so even today.

Ten years later, the Napoleonic episode saw an acceleration of the secularisation of the public sphere,[1] driven by and achieved as a result of the quest for personal power (Concordat 1802–4). Catholic, Protestant and Jewish preachers became salaried and therefore dependent on the political power, whilst secondary and higher education remained the sole preserve of the State. This last point is important to note because the question of faith schools or, for that matter, religious schooling, has often been discussed without referring to the educational level at which the discussion is pitched, when this is an important dimension of the debate.

One could not expect the restored monarchy to pursue the secularisation of public affairs and indeed it did not. However, the monarchy also thought it wiser not to reverse the process entirely and, as far as education was concerned, it eventually maintained and even increased the educational momentum that was to be a salient characteristic of the nineteenth century in Germany, Britain and France alike. The Guizot Reforms (1833) may be said to have paved the way for a State-founded nationwide system of education (see below). However, the educational reforms undertaken at the end of the nineteenth century by Third Republic governments are by far the most symbolically significant in relation to schooling in general and consequently to faith schooling in particular. Not only do they still form the basis of the definition of state schooling in constitutional terms but they also inform today's debates, actions and decisions and, in this way, organise the politics of faith in French education (e.g. the Islamic veil affair). Throughout the 1880s and 1890s, the 'school war' (*guerre scolaire*) was part of the broader political conflict that opposed Republicans and Monarchists. Léon Gambetta summed this up well when he declared in Parliament in 1877: 'Clericalism, here is the enemy'. After 20 years of imperial rule, defeat against the Prussians in 1870 and the uprising of the Commune, Republican governments set out to create the free, compulsory, secular state education they knew would be so important in enlightening and shaping the minds of future Republican citizens. Anti-clericalism was the cohesive force that kept the Republican political forces fighting together against the Church and, by extension, against the Monarchists. Apart from the historical milestone of the formal separation between the Church and the State in 1905, the anti-clerical zeal of the Republicans has been greatest in and has almost been defined by its passion in educational matters. For Republicans, if schooling was to transform the mind of the nation it had to be a rational, secular business available to all, rather than a socially hierarchical activity in the hands of the Divine temporal order.

The main problem they faced in their enterprise was that of justification and definition: how could they formally define and morally justify the ultimate aims of a secular education?

Intellectual empowerment *a minima* of the people is the phrase that springs to mind to describe early Republicans' achievements in spreading not only basic knowledge but also the methods of acquiring knowledge. This was illustrated by the *leçons de choses* under Jules Ferry's ministry which upheld science and inductive scientific methodology as the best way to train the minds of future citizens. On this point, it is interesting to find that a number of prominent figures who were at the origins of secular schooling in France were of Protestant creed (e.g. F. Guizot, F. Buisson, Pécaud). *A minima* refers to the fact that universal access to primary education at this time did not aim to level social inequalities. There was a clear separation between the offspring of the bourgeoisie who would continue studying at a higher level and the remainder.

It should be clear from the previous section, where the historical background was outlined, that the position of faith schools in France was in conflict with that of government schools from the outset of the setting-up of the educational system in France. This conflict was part of a broader ideological confrontation in the national political arena, in the highest spheres of the State and across post-Revolution French society. When, after the First World War, the Republic finally became the established and accepted form of democratic government, the dichotomy between faith/private schools and secular/public schools became established not only as one aspect of the educational system but as one of its defining elements. Today, non-governmental schools in France are mostly faith schools and faith schools are mostly Catholic (95 per cent). This is well illustrated by a somewhat idiosyncratic semantic classification according to which faith schools could be referred to in the national debate as '*écoles libres*' (free schools) or '*écoles privées*' (private schools) rather than directly as '*écoles confessionnelles*' (denominational schools). The first term, which is slightly dated now given the type of evolution that will be described later, has been used by those who have sought to emphasise the fact that faith schools were independent and therefore free from state injunctions and governmental pressure. The second term has been increasingly used by protagonists on all sides and reflects the evolution of the situation and of the debate. It is used for different purposes by the two camps; on the one hand, there are those who see in the use of the term 'private' the values and advantages of an economic liberal approach to education; on the other hand, there are those who consider that the use of the word 'private' is more a reflection of the reluctance of schools in this sector to abide by the national, Republican, egalitarian agenda that should be part of the brief of any educational institution worthy of its name.

From conflict to consensus?

An account which charts the shift from conflict to consensus of faith schooling in France could start in 1984, or perhaps in the second half of the 1970s, when the left-wing coalition in opposition drafted its manifesto for an all-encompassing national public service of education. Elected to power in 1981, the Socialist–Communist government set out to put its unifying pledge into action. However, when Alain Savary, the Education Minister, announced his plans for reform in 1984, his propositions met with staunch opposition from a coalition of members of the teaching profession and parents which culminated in massive demonstrations in Paris and in regional towns and cities and similarly massive counter-demonstrations by the opposite camp (it is estimated that approximately one million people took to the street on both sides). In a generally unfavourable political and economic climate, with a three-year Keynesian attempt to relaunch the economy having reached its limits, the Minister had to resign and since then, the question of faith schooling has yet to be tackled directly again by a left-wing majority. This episode provided a perfect illustration

– and was in some ways the culmination – of the persistently strong feelings in matters of educational principles in relation to religion towards the end of the twentieth century in France. In 1994, a centre-right government tried to tackle the issue from another angle by proposing to enlarge the possibilities for local and regional authorities to increase their financial participation in non-government schools. But the Education Minister François Bayrou failed to drive through his reform towards even greater availability of public money for private schools when, once again, over 600,000 people took to the street to defend the secular principle of publicly funded education.

When considering the evolution of the situation of faith schools in France, several legislative milestones need to be taken into account: the Guizot Law in 1833, the Falloux Law passed in 1850, the 1905 law that enshrined the separation between the State and the Church and the 1959 Debré Law. The Guizot Law (28 June 1833) was the first wide-ranging intervention by the public authorities at national level concerning elementary schooling since the 1789 Revolution. Each town with more than 500 inhabitants was to have one school for boys and each *département* one teacher-training college. The financial burden which this decision placed on the local authorities meant that the decision was only partially implemented. However, the number of schools funded by public money increased significantly. In 1850, the Falloux Law allowed 'free schools' to have up to 10 per cent of their expenditure (physical assets) funded by local, regional and even national authorities. Furthermore, it gave parish priests the power to check on the activities of primary school teachers, enabling the second Imperial power to reinstate a form of control of education by the Church which even the July Monarchy had refrained from reintroducing. It also provided the Church with the means of opening more schools by making it no longer necessary for ecclesiastics to hold the certificate of aptitude for teaching (*brevet de capacité*). In December 1905, under the Third Republic and at a time when the Republic ensured freedom of belief (*liberté de conscience*) while anti-clericalism was running high, a law was passed which clearly stated that, while guaranteeing the unhindered exercise of any religion (*exercice des cultes*), in the interest of public order it also neither recognised nor financed any religion. The direct effect was that no public money was to be used to subsidise religious activities. This was – and remains – a key piece of legislation which helps to understand the situation of faith schools in France and the tight restrictions imposed on any form of partnership the public authorities may want to establish with religious interests. The 1905 law, for example, was recently quoted by a number of associations in their protest against the use of public money to cater for the visit of the Pope in France. This explains why the passing of the Debré Law in 1959, followed by the Guermeur Law in 1977, was so controversial.

The 1959 law allowed contractual agreements to be passed between the central public authorities and non-government schools. The subtlety of this law lies in the fact that it did not refer specifically to denominational schools but to any private school that might wish to avail itself of government subsidies in exchange for greater control by public authorities on its activities. Like the 1905 law, it was an unusual piece of legislation referring only to 'private schools' in the plural when it was in fact private schooling in the singular which it sought to reorganise. Given the configuration of private schooling in France, essentially religious and essentially Catholic, there was no mystery for the supporters of a secular public-funded education as to what the government was trying to achieve in the guise of neutrality and equality: it was reintroducing 'through the back door' the public financing of Catholic schools, hence the controversy.

Forty years later, now that the dust has settled, we may say that the Debré Law has proved to be a most significant step towards the normalisation and integration of faith schools within the national system of education. The original aim was to enter into formal agreements with private schools on a voluntary basis so as to ensure that in exchange for substantial public subsidies their teachers would be trained and would operate in the same way and share the same pedagogical practices and professional background as their colleagues in the public sector. With this configuration already in place, the passing of the Guermeur Law in 1977, which reinforced public subsidies and catered for teacher training for private schools whilst guaranteeing their 'specific' (i.e. religious) characteristics, resulted in the formal recognition of a national structure for Catholic schooling. Today a majority of private primary and secondary schools have entered into a 'strong version' of contractual agreement with the State whereby they adopt the official programmes, syllabuses and timetables applicable to secular state schools in exchange for their general overheads (*dépenses de fonctionnement*) and teaching costs being fully met by public funding. It must be noted that a weaker type of contractual agreement does exist where the school remains more autonomous in its organisation, but, according to its terms, school expenditure is only partially met by the public purse. There are few non-contractual private schools. These have to conform only to administrative regulations. They do not receive any public subsidy and information about them is hard to obtain.

The picture would not be complete if the effects of the Debré/Guermeur Laws were not combined with those of the reforms which have been introduced since the mid 1980s. For besides its failure to reform the private school sector, the left-leaning majority in power throughout most of the 1980s and 1990s also introduced significant changes in the organisa-tion of secular public education. Decentralisation laws have meant that the whole sector has become less monolithic (Charlot 1994) as funding responsibilities have been redistributed (although this does not concern the two key areas of staff salaries and national curricula).[2] Schools have been encouraged to be more autonomous in a pluralistic perspective with an emphasis on the fact that the unity of the public service of national education should not be synonymous with uniformity. New regulations have been introduced whereby each school contributes to the public service by having a degree of institutional responsibility in the form of a mission statement which determines the spiritual, pedagogical or cultural identity of the school.

The Debré Law was an ambiguous law which brought closer together the two separate and antagonistic major parts of the French educational system. The ensuing reforms introduced by the Socialists in power aimed at diversifying the mission of the public sector. The final picture is that of a unified but pluralistic school system where different religious and political traditions cohabit. On the one hand, it is no longer a case of defining the specificity of Catholic schools, as their pedagogical practice has been largely secularised and they must welcome all children regardless of their creed and respect their religious or non-religious beliefs. On the other hand, as faith schools have been gradually recognised both *de facto* and (indirectly) *de jure* as an integral part of the national system of education, traditional anti-faith school feelings have been watered down, the symbol of which was the 1992 Lang–Couplet agreement which agreed on public subsidies of FF1.8 billion to the private sector, fixed new modalities for collaboration between the State and contractual private schools and which established parity between teaching staff in the private and the public sectors as recognition of the contribution of private schools to the national educational effort. In fact, public subsidies to private schools are now largely accepted by taxpayers, including those on the centre-left. For parents, being able to choose a school and even an area for their children to be educated has become increasingly important.

One last concluding remark to this section would be to note that so far we have spoken of secular/State schools and of faith/private schools with regard to their evolution and their interactions. We have even spoken of the secularisation of faith schools. However, we have not spoken of faith within State schools. Those with some knowledge of the French educational landscape will probably be aware of the highly publicised problem this last remark refers to – the problem of the Islamic veil – but it also concerns, more generally, the place of faith within a secular education. It is worth remembering that both the Education Ministry and the State Council (Conseil d'Etat) have encouraged neutrality, but the affair of the Islamic veil, which extended the neutrality required from staff to the pupils, is clearly a case of secular schooling being possible but a strict secular education (secularism) denying the possibility of faith. This may also be an argument for Muslims to demand their own contractual schools. Alternatively, we could paraphrase Daniel Cohn-Bendit, one of the leaders of the 1968 riots, commenting upon the affair of the veil: 'Let these girls come into school. Let them take advantage of an education and hopefully they will come in with the veil and leave dressed in a ragged pair of jeans'. This could be labelled and dismissed as social engineering by the self-righteously liberal. One way or another, the question of the place of faith within secular public schools remains (Baumard 2001) and is well illustrated by Régis Debray, one of the staunchest atheist Republican intellectuals in France who was once a guerrilla fighter in Latin America and special advisor to François Mitterrand, but who has now published a book on God (Debray 2001) and has led a commission of inquiry into the teaching of religions in secular State schools (Debray 2002).

Consensus? A critical understanding of change

Having described the various laws and evolutions that have taken place in relation to faith schools in France over the last 20 years, how are we to explain and interpret them? Should we remain factual or should we propose a critical understanding? By being factual, the illusion is that of being consensual. By being critical, the illusion is that of being conflictual. However, we should not forget the potential long-term benefits of an ongoing critical/ conflictual approach to change in modern democratic societies. This trust in the Habermasian paradigm of social change can be usefully applied to educational change.

The conflict between secular and religious education has often been a battle between two differing visions of what the meaning of society – and the meaning of life more generally – should be. One hundred years ago, the question was: why secular schools? Today, with the growing secularisation of modern societies, the question is arguably: why faith schools? From a parental perspective, there might be two possible answers: 'by choice' or 'by default'. If the answer is 'by choice', it implies that religious education cannot be separated from the schooling process. Then, in a sense, the responsibility of explaining why and how the type of education and knowledge imparted in religious schools may differ from that imparted in a secular school is the onus of those who wish to avail themselves of a denominational type of education for their offspring through specific schools.

Do faith schools confer special and indispensable social skills (i.e. greater morality) on their pupils? Answering this question does not fall within the remit of this chapter. However, it is interesting to note that this whole debate echoes the debates that surrounded the secularisation of society, and of schooling in particular, at the turn of the nineteenth century in France. As an answer to this type of ontological questioning, Auguste Comte in *Discours sur l'esprit positif* (1844) provided many of the guiding principles of secular Republican thought by systematising Condorcet's philosophy through a three-stage rule: in the first stage, humanity in its infancy is in a state of mental unity and social balance through religion, and monotheist religions organise themselves and organise societies; in the second stage, a metaphysical critique of the established religious order which runs contrary to the unifying theological spirit appears and develops; finally, the mental consensus which is necessary to the smooth working of society is ruined and individualism triumphs. For Comte, the hope is that the scientific approach at all levels will provide the next mentally unifying principle of humanity, thereby replacing religion. In this picture, formal education takes up a central role. However, in *Discours sur l'ensemble du positivime* (1848), the same Auguste Comte also acknowledged the importance of feelings as opposed to reason, that of the heart as opposed to the mind. For this reason, he considered as indispensable the educational input from the family and the community. For radical positivists, on the contrary, the power of the Church on the minds had to be neutralised and for this purpose education had to be a secular public matter taking place as soon as possible to take the children out of the influence of their families. As far as morality was concerned, a form of patriotism could even advantageously replace a form of spiritualism.

Durkheim's sociology was also in its way an answer to the question concerning education and faith, secularism and morality. The debate on faith education versus secular education has been rehearsed. The heart of the matter is that, in contrast to a religious set of morals, a secular one has no theological grounding, so the responsibility of explaining why and how a secular education may be as morally justifiable as a religious one is the onus of those who want to see institutional education devoid of any religious references. A secular set of morals implies a Kantian notion of ethics. In areas such as politeness or probity, it does not differ much from a religious one, but when one starts to discuss science (e.g. evolutionism versus creationism, bioethics), history and its interpretation or literature (e.g. a generation ago Voltaire was placed on the Index of Forbidden Books in some Catholic schools), value judgments may become divisive. Moral certitudes are needed in the face of the uncertainty of action but within a framework of personal freedom and responsibility. Only the rational approach is critical and collective. Reason leads as much to religion, scepticism or materialism but any imposed truth is not accepted as Truth. As Jean Jaurès once said in parliament: 'There is no sacred truth … if God himself were to stand up and to make himself visible above the multitudes, the first duty of man would be to refuse to obey, to treat him as an equal with whom one enters into debate, but not as a master to whom one should submit' (my translation).

These sorts of high-grounded considerations only partially provide a genuine sociological understanding of the situation of faith schools in France today. For many parents, the choice to send their children to a faith/private school is a question of opting out of the State system of education, to what was referred to earlier as the 'by default' option. This means that private/faith schooling becomes a viable and preferable option when the type of schooling on offer in secular public schools becomes unsatisfactory. What has happened to faith schools in France may be interpreted as a certifying evolution, whereby the gradual integration of faith schooling within the national system of education through the harmonisation of its staff conditions and teaching activities with those in secular public schools has been a way to guarantee that by attending a private school at some time in one's school career one did not find oneself disqualified from continuing at a later stage in the state sector. Parents are 'shopping around' for what they perceive to be better offers. The next question is, in what sense may the public educational provision appear unsatisfactory? The answer is a multi-faceted picture of personal and sometimes localised reasons that may not be generalised. In fact, past and recent surveys have shown that a large majority of the public (70 per cent to 80 per cent) is satisfied with the secular state system of education. However, there has been an increase in social segregation through catchment areas, the very principle of which was designed to diminish this effect (the equivalent of the postcode logic in Britain). Traditional pedagogical practices have been called into question (children repeating years, the availability of staff on a personal basis). Many reasons for dissatisfaction may be summarised under a heading that would be the degree of access and input the family circles and traditions can and should have in the institutional educational process. Religion is only one dimension – even if it is the most salient in the light of past practices – of this broader evolution (Bronner 2001).

In France today the choice to send a child to a faith school or to a secular government school follows a logic of consumption rather than one of ideological or religious beliefs (Baumier 1999). In a sense, this has been partly a way to introduce a degree of choice in education, turning parents into choosers or consumers of educational school services (Ballion 1982) and allowing forms of parental 'zapping' and even parental strategies (Ballion 1991). But in order to be fully understood, the evolution which has taken place over the last 20 years or so needs to be placed in its broader social context. From the outset, formal education in France has been at the heart of the conception of Republican meritocracy, organising and legitimising forms of social mobility. Paradoxically, and this will appear familiar to readers from other horizons for it is not specific to France, the democratisation of education in the forms of higher success rates in national examinations and greater access to all levels of the educational system has resulted in a reinforcement of the advantages conferred to social capital, with the effect that the last 20 years have seen not an end to but a slowing down of the 'social elevator' that education had represented for previous generations (Rochex 1995). Several examples may serve to illustrate this evolution, which sociologists, politicians and general commentators have testified to and discussed at length. The perceived failure of the '*college unique*', which is the French version of the comprehensive school ethos, has encouraged parents to opt for types of lower secondary schools which could diminish the negative effects of this 'comprehensiveness' through their recruitment and pedagogical practice (Kepel 1987). On the part of the public sector, this has been matched by an unwritten weakening of catchment area rules and a proliferation of the options on offer. The result has been an increase in selective academic practices that have objectified practices that are socially selective. The setting up of *Zones d'éducation prioritaires* (ZEP), the French version of Education Action Zones, was the official acknowledgement that not all government schools were equal. While the myth of equality of access, provision and therefore life chances has been exposed, external demands for more say and rights in the delivery of educational services have become more apparent and pressing as they have been, in a sense, increasingly justified (Derouet 1992). This has clashed with those in the teaching profession in the public sector who consider national education to be an institution rather than a fully fledged public service (Prost 1981). Successive governments have tried to fend off this type of approach to teaching duties by officially encouraging (even by law) child-centred pedagogical practice ('*la centration sur l'apprenant*') and by setting up parental school councils. However, as recruitment practices and employment legislation and regulations safeguarding the independence of the profession have remained largely untouched, the effects have been limited. Notions such as the British *in loco parentis* or pastoral care remain alien to the formal organisation of public teaching and learning in France, which is essentially perceived and practised as a knowledge transmission activity, pedagogy being a means to an end rather than an end in itself for fear it might turn into forms of demagogy (Forquin 1993). Faith/private schools rightly or wrongly may therefore be perceived by certain dissatisfied parents as educational establishments where their children will receive closer attention and where they, as parents, will receive a more sympathetic hearing. It is not rare for parents of children who have been told to repeat a year to take them away from their school and place him or her in a faith/private school (the reverse is not an unknown occurrence either).

Conclusion

The final conclusion is that faith schools in the form of 'private' schools may bring a salutary degree of diversity to centralised and unified state school systems such as the French one. Condorcet foresaw exactly this, adding that it was the best impetus for a strong public sector to perform to its highest potential. However, this adds weight to the contrasting proposition that in an atomised school system such as the English one, faith schools constitute yet another layer of differentiation and specialisation which further reinforces the system's academic and social divisions.

Notes

1 In 1804, the civil code did not make reference to religion but to natural reason while the penal code recognised only secular weddings as legal weddings by forbidding priests to marry couples who produced proof of their having wed through a civil union.
2 The regions were made responsible for the building and maintenance of upper-secondary schools (*lycées*) and given considerable powers regarding vocational training. The *départements* were made responsible for the maintenance and building of lower-secondary schools (*collèges*). The *municipalités* are responsible for the building, maintenance and administrative control of elementary schools.

References

Archer, M.S. (1979) *Social Origins of Educational Systems*, London: Sage.
Ballion, R. (1982) *Les consommateurs d'école*, Paris: Stock.
Ballion, R. (1991) *La bonne école: évaluation et choix du collège et du lycée*, Paris: Hatier.
Baubérot, J., Gauthier, G., Legrand, L., Ognier, P. (1994) *Histoire de la laïcité*, Besançon: Cerf-CRDP de Franche Comté.
Baumard, M. (2001) 'Petits arrangements laïques', *Le Monde de L'Education* (298): 24–7.
Baumier, A. (1999) 'Le privé, privé de religion', *Le Monde de L'Education* (270): 42–3.
Boudon, R. (1973) *L'inégalité des chances*, Paris: Colin.
Bourdieu, P. and J.-C. Passeron (1964) *Les Héritiers: les étudiants et la culture*, Paris: Editions de Minuit.
Bourdieu, P. (1996) *The State Nobility: Elite Schools in the Field of Power*, Cambridge: Polity Press.
Bronner, L. (2001) 'La leçon faite au public', *Le Monde de L'Education* (292): 22–4.
Careil, Y. (1998) *De l'école publique à l'école libérale: sociologie d'un changement*, Rennes: Presses Universitaires de Rennes.
Charlot, B. (ed.) (1994) *L'école et le territoire: nouveaux espaces, nouveaux enjeux*, Paris: Armand Colin.
Comte, A. (1844) *Discours sur l'esprit positif*, Paris: Carilian-Goeury et V. Dalmont.
Comte, A. (1848 : 1909) *A General View of Positivism*, J.H. Bridges, trans. London: Routledge.
Condorcet (Marquis de) M.J.A.C. (1994 : 1790/1791) *Cinq mémoires sur l'instruction publique*, Paris: Flammarion. Foreword by Coutel, C. and Kintzler, C.
Debray, R. (2001) *Dieu, un itinéraire*, Paris: Odile Jacob.
Debray, R. (2002) *L'enseignement du fait religieux dans l'école laïque*, Paris: Odile Jacob.
Derouet, J.L. (1992) *Ecole et justice: de l'égalité des chances aux compromis locaux*, Paris: Métailié.
Durkheim, E. (1995 : 1922) *Education et sociologie*, Paris: Presses Universitaires de France.
Forquin, J.C. (1993) 'Savoirs et pédagogies: faux dilemmes et vraies questions', *Recherche et formation* (13): 2–24.

Jaurès, J. (1895) Déclaration à la Chambre, 11 February, in Baubérot, J., Gauthier, G., Legrand, L. and Ognier, P. (1994) *Histoire de la Laïcité*, Besançon: Cerf-CRDP de Franche Comté.

Kepel, G. (1987) *Les banlieues de l'Islam*, Seuil: Paris.

(2001) *La loi Debré: Paradoxes de l'état éducateur*, Amiens: CRDP d'Amiens.

Minois, G. (1998) *Histoire de l'athéisme*, Paris: Fayard.

Prost, A. (1981) *L'enseignement et l'éducation en France, l'école et la famille dans une société en mutation*, Paris: Nouvelle Librairie de France.

Prost, A. (1992) *Education, société et politiques: une histoire de l'enseignement en France de 1945 à nos jours*, Paris: Seuil.

Rochex, J.Y. (1995) *Le sens de l'expérience scolaire*, Paris: Presses Universitaires de France.

Part V

Faith schools

The way forward

17 Faith schools and communities

Communitarianism, social capital and citizenship

John Annette

One of the interesting aspects of the policies of New Labour has been the increased recognition of the role of faith communities in education and community development.

I want to consider how the government's support for faith communities' role in regeneration activities in inner cities has influenced their policy of supporting an increase in faith schools. The new policy is stated in the Department for Education and Skills (DfES) publication *Schools: Achieving Success* (DfES 2001) where it is written:

> Over the last four years, we have increased the range of faith schools in the maintained sector, including the first Muslim, Sikh and Greek Orthodox schools. There are also many independent faith schools and we know that some faith groups are interested in extending their contribution to state education. We wish to welcome faith schools, with their distinctive ethos and character, into the maintained sector where there is clear local agreement.
>
> (DfES 2001: 45)

I will argue that this policy development reflects the 'communitarianism' of both Tony Blair and David Blunkett, which has been influenced by the emergence of an influential communitarianism in the United Kingdom (UK) and the United States of America (USA), which has both liberal and conservative orientations. This communitarianism has a distinctive view of civic religion which sees religion as contributing to a democratic political culture. This policy development is also based on a realisation of the role that faith communities can play in developing 'social capital' in the inner cities. Following Robert Putnam (2000) this assumes that such social capital will lead to increases in active citizenship, although I want to critically examine this claim.

I would like to finally examine the models of social capital being utilised in this policy development concerning faith schools and then consider how these models result in varying conceptions of citizenship education. The approach of faith schools towards citizenship education also raises questions about whether or not this policy development of increasing faith schools is based more on the recognition of the role of religion in producing a democratic political culture rather than an appreciation of their distinctive traditions of faith and theological frameworks.

Faith and civil society

At a time when traditional faith communities (e.g. the Roman Catholic Church and the Anglican Church) are experiencing a decline in membership, this recent emphasis on faith communities and schools recognises the importance of the black British evangelical churches, Muslim mosques and other non-Christian black and ethnic minority faith communities, whose numbers are increasing. In the 2001 Census, according to the Office of National Statistics, some 37.3 million people identified themselves as Christian (71.7 per cent) while some 1.5 million identified themselves as Muslims (2.7 per cent). There were 1 per cent of the population identifying themselves as Hindu, 0.6 per cent as Sikhs, 0.5 per cent as Jewish and 0.3 per cent as Buddhist. Overall 76.8 per cent of the population identified themselves as 'religious' with 15.5 per cent of the population saying they had no religion and 7.3 per cent not answering the question. The black and minority ethnic communities rose from 6 per cent of the population in 1991 to 9 per cent in 2001. The increase in the black and ethnic minority communities in the UK, and a related increase in evangelical churches and Muslim faith communities in the inner cities of England, has led government ministers to revitalise the Inner Cities Religious Council of the Office of the Deputy Prime Minister, which was established in 1992, to facilitate this increased recognition of the importance of faith communities within civil society.

To what extent, however, is it true to say that it is only with the New Labour government that there has been recognition of the role of faith communities in civil society? Historians of British politics, for example, have long since recognised the importance of dissenting Christianity in reform politics from the Levellers in the English Civil War to the eighteenth-century radicalism seen by E.P. Thompson as central to the making of the English working class and then to the Christian ethical socialism of John Ruskin and later R.H. Tawney. In many respects the political thinking of both Tony Blair and David Blunkett are a mixture of dissenting Christian ethical socialism, communitarianism and think-tank new think. In the USA, Robert Bellah and colleagues diagnosed the fragmentation of contemporary society and the growth of a narcissistic individualism (Bellah *et al.* 1996) In this work, and also in an earlier work, Bellah (1992) considers the role of 'public religion' , a phrase taken from the work of Martin Marty, in helping to counter the rise of individualism and the breakdown of community. In the UK, Tony Blair has recognised the influence of John MacMurray on his views of community and spirituality. His conception of a 'Third Way' politics is not just based on the theory of Anthony Giddens and other proponents of a new way beyond neo-liberalism and socialism but it is also based on an ethical and religious vision of the importance of community in contemporary society (Driver and Martell 1997). The political language of both the New Democrats in the USA and New Labour in the UK is about restoring the broken covenant and revitalising communities, including faith communities, within civil society. Robert Wuthnow has analysed extensively the role of faith communities in the maintenance of civil society and has called for the 'reassembling of the civic church' (Wuthnow 1996 and 2002).

It is also true to say that for many neo-liberal conservatives, civil society and the active role of religious congregations within it has provided a means to limit the power of the welfare state. Peter Berger and Rev. Richard John Neuhaus published an influential essay entitled *To Empower People* which called for 'mediating structures' in civil society (Berger and Neuhaus 2002). These are organisations and associations like churches and congregations that 'mediate' between the individual and the state and provide for the realisation of social justice within civil society and independently of the welfare state. The Berger–Neuhaus thesis has been very influential among neo-liberal conservatives in the USA in their criticisms of the welfare state and in developing a contemporary 'compassionate conservatism'. This criticism also influenced the faith politics of Iain Duncan Smith, for whom community was a key feature of his social policy (Streeter 2002). To what extent, therefore, has this emphasis on civil society signalled a retreat from maintaining the importance of the 'political' and a criticism of the social democratic welfare state? This is an important issue in the contemporary debate about the role of public religion in civil society and its relationship to the state (cf. Elshtain 1995; Beem 1999). It is important therefore to consider the difference between a conservative or neo-liberal communitarianism and a civic republican conception of communitarianism, for an understanding of the role of religion in civil society.

Faith-based community action in the UK and the USA

There is considerable evidence of an increase in faith-based community action in both the UK and the USA since the 1980s. It was in 1985 that the Archbishop of Canterbury's Commission on Urban Priority Areas published its report *Faith in the City* (Archbishop of Canterbury 1985). This report followed on from the Brixton race riots and the report of Lord Scarman's inquiry and it emphasised the social responsibility of the church for its poor inner city communities. Subsequently the Church Urban League was established (Lawless *et al.* 1998) and the Urban Theology Group was formed in 1990 and has continued to reflect on the theological implications of urban poverty (Northcott 1998). More recently there has been a growing number of studies of the role of faith communities in urban regeneration in the UK (Lukka and Locke 2000; Farnell 2001; Smith 2002). One study has examined the role of faith-based groups in the government's recent 'New Deal for Communities' programme (Musgrave, 1999) and another more generally in urban regeneration (Smith 2000). Meanwhile the Church Urban Fund, which is part of the Church of England, in partnership with the New Economic Foundation has produced a review of the role of faith groups in neighbourhood renewal activities (Lewis 2001).

There are no hard data of the nature and extent of faith-based community action in the UK although Richard Farnell was at the time of writing engaged in a qualitative analysis of its influence for the Joseph Rowntree Foundation (Farnell *et al.* 2003). In London, however, the London Churches Group for Social Action has attempted to analyse the nature of faith-based community and social action in the New Labour government's Neighbourhood Renewal Strategy (London Churches Group for Social Action 2002). This study estimates that there is extensive faith-based community activity in London and that the newly established Local Strategic Partnerships are beginning to include and support the work of faith communities. While the Anglican and Roman Catholic Churches continue to provide important faith community work the biggest increase in activity has been among the black and ethic minority faith communities. An important issue raised by this report is the sometimes problematic relationship between local government and the faith-based voluntary and community sector. Too often, it is claimed, local government officers are sceptical of the claims of these faith-based groups to represent their local faith communities. This could be significant, because according to the DfES publication *Schools: Achieving Success* it is stated:

> Guidance to School Organisation Committees will require them to give proposals from faith groups to establish schools the same consideration as those from others, including LEAs. Decisions to establish faith schools should take account of the interests of all sections of the community.
>
> (DfES 2001: 45)

There is limited evaluation available concerning the operation of School Organisation Committees and based on my own experience of being on one the views of the local authority often prevail. The issue of the failure of some local authorities to recognise the role of faith communities has led the Local Government Association (LGA) to publish a guide entitled 'Faith and community: a good practice guide for local authorities'. In the foreword, signed by the member of parliament (MP) Sally Keeble (Undersecretary of State, Department of Transport, Local Authorities and the Regions [DTLR], now the Office of the Deputy Prime Minister [ODPM]), Angela Eagle, MP (Undersecretary of State, Home Office) and Sir Jeremy Beecham (Chairman, LGA), it is written:

> Most of our towns and cities are places of great diversity – that is one of their great strengths. Faith is an element of this diversity. But the benefits of this diversity cannot just be taken for granted. This guide points to the fundamental importance of community cohesion, in building a prosperous and fair society where people from diverse backgrounds can flourish. Relations between faith communities – and in turn between faith communities and local government – can make a significant contribution to promoting community cohesion.
>
> (LGA 2002)

This emphasis on the role of faith communities representing diverse communities is also advocated by the Inner Cities Religious Council which has become a focus within the ODPM for advocating a role for faith groups in urban regeneration and community cohesion. The range of recent government statements about the importance of faith communities in regeneration and community cohesion also reflects the language of social capital which will be explored in more detail.

Government thinking on this matter has also been influenced by liberal ideas of 'new covenants' (Wallis 1994 and 2000), the 'politics of meaning' (Lerner 1997) and 'compassionate conservatism' (Olasky 2000) from the USA, which emphasise the role of religious organisations within civil society. This is made more complicated in the USA by the constitutional principle of separation of church and state. The recent governments of Bill Clinton and now George W. Bush, Jr. have explored ways to avoid this constitutional block on giving government support to faith-based community organisations. This includes the 'charitable choice' legislation which has enabled the US federal government to fund faith groups that provide social services as part of a new compact with the voluntary and community sectors. When George W. Bush, Jr. became President in 2000 he soon established the White House Office for Faith-Based Community Action to work across government departments to facilitate support for faith-based communities. Jim Wallis and his liberal Christian movement called the 'Sojourners' and Michael Lerner and his liberal Jewish organisation 'Tikkun' advocate the role of faith groups in providing for the urban poor, but they also recognise the importance of working in partnership with the welfare state (Wallis 2000). The ideas of 'compassionate conservatism', which George W. Bush used in his 2000 election campaign under the influence of Marvin Olasky, emphasises the role of faith communities in providing social services as a neo-liberal policy of cutting back welfare state spending and limiting the power of the state (Olasky 2000). This ideological division between a civic republican communitarianism and a conservative (neo-liberal) communitarianism is not always clear cut and there is often an elision between the two positions in popular political discourse. Both New Democrat and New Labour policy statements often elide both ideological positions, where voluntary and community sectors involvement is seen as both limiting the sphere of the state while seen also as a way of working in partnership with the state. This has led conservative critics like Bruce Frohnen to view communitarianism as inherently a cover for community-based social democratic politics (Frohnen 1996) while some left critics view communitarianism as inherently neo-liberal.

The influence of faith-based community action and religious communitarianism in the USA have affected both the communitarian views of Tony Blair and New Labour and the 'compassionate conservatism' of both William Hague and Iain Duncan Smith. The criticism of social-democratic Labour Party writers, like Polly Toynbee in the *Guardian*, is that the views of Tony Blair and David Blunkett on faith politics are dangerous and reflect a move to the right politically. It is my interpretation, however, that their political and religious communitarianism remains civic republican and social democratic. This is because it emphasises the role of faith communities within civil society but still recognises the essential role of the state in educational and social provision. It also emphasises the civic republican role of active citizenship in democratic politics. The more serious question, however, is whether these schools are socially divisive or promote wider social cohesion.

Faith-based community action and social capital

Recent studies of faith-based community action in the USA (Warren 2001; Warren and Wood 2001; Wood, 2002) and in the UK (Farnell 2001; Farnell *et al.* 2003 and Smith 2002) have emphasised its importance for the development of social capital. There are of course major differences between the conceptions of social capital in the work of James Coleman, Pierre Bourdieu and more recently Robert Putnam. The work of Coleman sees social capital as a resource for members of a community while Robert Putnam in his neo-Tocquevillian version emphasises how forms of associations with their norms and values can lead to greater citizenship and political participation. While I agree with the view of social capital as a useful and primarily heuristic tool for social science (cf. Baron *et al.* 2000) I believe that we need to consider the 'political' implications of our use of the concept. The version of Putnam is based on the correlation between levels of association and levels of civic engagement and political participation and this has come under criticism from other political scientists (Edwards *et al.* 2001). For some social scientists, Coleman's view of social capital more clearly illustrates the strengths and weaknesses of the concept, especially in analysing the position of socially excluded poor communities. In this analysis, while bonding social capital does provide benefits to communities and bridging social capital can provide useful access to more influential social and political networks as resources for the community, they cannot replace the importance of capital in providing for the well being of the community (Saegert *et al.* 2001).

The work of Mark Warren (2001) entitled *Dry Bones Rattling* studies the role of faith alliances in San Antonio, Texas and the activities of Ernesto Cortes, a remarkable Hispanic American community organiser and a protégé of Saul Alinsky. Warren shows convincingly the role of faith communities in producing both bonding and bridging social capital and critically examines their role in civic engagement. His research, however, does not provide evidence of a causal link between social capital and civic engagement but his work does reveal the importance of faith-based community action in developing both bonding as well as bridging social capital. Richard L. Wood, in his study entitled *Faith in Action* (2002), which analyses faith-based community organising in California, has also emphasised the importance of social capital. He advances the view that we also need the concept of 'political culture' to explain how community action may lead to political participation. In this way a model of 'political culture', which involves both bridging social capital and also 'political' or 'civic' engagement, is seen as essential for creating a more democratic political culture.

Recent government policy in the UK on community cohesion, given the ethnic and religious violence in northern towns in the summer of 2001, also emphasises the necessity of bridging social capital through inter-faith dialogue as well as addressing the fundamental inequalities or social exclusion that exists between communities. What these policies do not do is address the questions of how, 'politically', community groups can engage in the process of addressing these key problems facing neighbourhood renewal. Too often the need to develop the capacity for 'community leadership' is seen in the community development literature as a technocratic problem of dealing with the mechanics of 'partnership working' and fails to consider the political or citizenship knowledge, skills and understanding that are necessary for citizen action. The Neighbourhood Renewal unit has recently published *The Learning Curve* (Neighbourhood Renewal Unit 2002) which is its learning strategy for capacity building for neighbourhood renewal. While this document is excellent, especially with its recognition of the importance of experiential learning, I believe that it fails to provide a basis for learning active citizenship.

In the USA, even Robert Putnam (2000) in his book on the decline of social capital in the USA has now realised the importance of bridging social capital for community cohesion and for the development of political participation. It is this type of bridging social capital linked to 'political' or 'civic' engagement which can best correlate to increased levels of citizenship and political participation. Contrary to Putnam, however, it is argued that by itself it does not necessarily lead to active citizenship and democratic politics. Putnam is not clear how the norms and values associated with the social capital of a community are linked to 'political engagement'. This could be linked to the study of civic or political cultures to be found in the established literature on political participation, and the creation or not of a civic culture can be viewed as the means by which social capital is seen as producing increased active citizenship. The important studies of Warren and Wood provide evidence of how faith-based community action can not only produce bridging social capital based in interfaith social and political networks but that they can provide the basis for developing a political culture that is fundamentally democratic (Warren and Wood 2001).

An alternative view of religious communities in relationship to social capital is that they are potentially exclusive and will actually reduce bridging social capital and wider community cohesion. The race and religious disturbances in northern cities in 2001 and the findings of the Cantle Report (Cantle 2001) raise important issues about how bridging social capital can be brought about through the necessary actions of public policy. These same concerns are being raised about faith schools where their religious identity can be seen as undermining the wider community cohesion. What is needed is a framework of civic engagement in which faith schools can work together for the common good and contribute to a civic culture which will transcend particular religious and cultural identities.

Faith schools, communitarianism and social capital

I have tried to illustrate the context for the New Labour government's policies for faith-based community action and I believe that this is the same context for the policy of increasing the number of faith schools, especially for evangelical Christian and Muslim faith communities in inner-city areas.

One of the main reasons given for developing faith schools is that they produce higher levels of social capital. This is particularly true for the literature concerning Roman Catholic schools (Bryk *et al.* 1993; Grace 2002). This analysis has been influenced by the work of James Coleman, who in a number of studies examined Catholic schools in the USA. In his studies, Coleman discovered that young people from disadvantaged backgrounds did better if they attended a Catholic school and he developed the concept of social capital to explain this. He argued that Catholic schools did well because of the norms and values of the faith communities which supported them. Gamarnikow and Green have recently examined the research claims of Coleman (including the issue of selectivity bias) as part of their critique of the use of the concept of social capital which obscures social class inequalities in education (Gamarnikow and Green 2003, 2000; also cf. Fine 2001). Anthony Bryk and his colleagues in their definitive study of Catholic schooling in the USA (Bryk *et al.* 1993) argued that, in addition to the external social capital provided by the local faith community, the Catholic school itself represented a type of internal social capital. What is not clear is how the external social capital of the local faith community produces the internal social capital of the faith school, which makes it so distinctive. For Robert Putnam the social capital of a community is also to be found in its norms and values which, as I have indicated earlier, should be linked to the study of civic or political cultures. It is this aspect of bridging social capital in faith communities that has been studied by Warren and Wood, who have linked social capital in faith communities to the development of distinctive democratic political cultures.

Faith schools, religious communitarianism and citizenship

Bryk *et al.* (1993) argued that one of the strengths of Catholic schools is their 'inspirational ideology' and that more research is needed to consider in what ways this can impact on faith schools. Gerald Grace (2002) in his comprehensive study of Catholic schools in the UK also discusses, for example, tensions between the church and its teachings on social justice and the common good and the realities of the competitive educational marketplace faced by head teachers. More research is needed to consider how faith traditions actually influence the 'ethos' or 'inspirational ideology' of faith schools. This is particularly true concerning the approach of faith schools towards the teaching of the new citizenship education curriculum in schools and community involvement, which is part of this new citizenship curriculum. As part of some preliminary research undertaken in this area I have been struck how interviews with teachers responsible for personal, social and health education (PSHE) and citizenship in faith schools (Church of England, Roman Catholic, Jewish and Muslim) have varied considerably in indicating their knowledge and understanding of theological writings concerning the relationship between their schools, faith communities and the wider issues relating to rights and responsibilities and community involvement. To what extent do teachers in faith schools have knowledge of some of the key contemporary theological and religious texts relating to their faiths and community (e.g. Sacks 2000, 2002; Catholic Education Service 1997; Vallely 1998; Northcott 1998; Dalacoura, 2003; etc.)?

James Arthur, in his important study of communitarian agenda in education, argues that many faith schools are based on a 'religious communitarianism'. He also argues that this is particularly true of Catholic schools given the Catholic Church's 'social teachings' (Arthur 2000) and following Paul Vallely that this social teaching is inherently communitarian (Vallely 1998). It is interesting to note that the Muslim Council of Great Britain in its inaugural meeting in 1997 used the theme 'Seeking the Common Good', which was based on the document produced by the Catholic Bishops of England and Wales, *The Common Good and the Catholic Church's Social Teachings*, published a year earlier. The impressive book *The Politics of Hope* of the Chief Rabbi Jonathan Sacks, first published in 1997, also represents a religious communitarianism. This religious communitarianism poses challenges for faith schools in their teaching of human rights and also conflicting moral and social values. It also poses the challenge of how learning through community involvement will be structured in either an apolitical or political context. Too often, student volunteering or community involvement is taught primarily as doing 'good' in community and not as political or civic engagement (Annette 2000, 2003). James Arthur also argues that there are some key distinctions that can be made between secular communitarianism and a religious one and that for many faith schools it is impossible for them to be based on a secular communitarianism. Referring to the work of Robert Bellah, with its references to religions as 'communities of memory', Arthur argues that the secular communitarian advocacy of a 'civic religion' has an instrumental view of religion as serving the public good which takes priority over the transcendent purpose of religion. It is clearly this civic role of religion which has influenced New Labour's policy of supporting faith-based community action and the encouragement for the development of faith schools.

In their study of community service for young people in the USA, James Youniss and Miranda Yates (1997) provide evidence that volunteering positively influences their moral and political development. What is particularly interesting is that their main case study was a Catholic secondary school which had established a 'service learning programme' on the social teachings of the Catholic Church and especially its ideas on 'social justice'. This is typical of many Catholic schools in the USA and also many Catholic universities with their service learning programmes based on social justice. Thus the ethos of the school can be seen as representing a set of norms of values developed through activities in the school and in the local community which are also based on a faith tradition of the common good or social justice. This ethos, however, also encourages students to become more active citizens and to develop civic engagement. To what extent, however, are there potential conflicts between the faith traditions or religious communitarianism of faith schools, which is also based on the social capital of local neighbourhoods, and the conflicting claims of active citizenship in a multicultural and multifaith society? In what ways will faith schools be distinctive in their approach to citizenship education and community involvement?

Conclusion

I hope that I have shown how the New Labour policies for increasing both faith-based community action and faith schools is based on certain assumptions from communitarian theory and social capital theory. To what extent are these assumptions in accord with the actual role of faith schools and faith-based community action in providing social capital, community cohesion and active citizenship?

Is it the case that claims made for faith schools are largely based on their functional contribution to bonding social capital in their communities, which is seen as providing a basis for neighbourhood renewal? If so, then to what extent will faith schools also provide bridging social capital and wider community cohesion? How distinctive will their approach be to citizenship education and how will they encourage community involvement and civic engagement as compared to secular schools? To what extent is their ethos based on a religious communitarianism that is compatible, or not, with a wider civic republicanism? There is evidence concerning faith-based community action that their bridging type of social capital can also be compatible with a civic republican form of communitarianism, which also recognises the important role of the state in providing educational and community services. I have argued elsewhere that civic republicanism had an important influence on the idea of citizenship that Bernard Crick and his colleagues deployed in their commission report on citizenship education (cf. Annette 2000; the Qualifications and Curriculum Authority (QCA)1998; Crick 2000, 2003). Will citizenship education in faith schools raise serious problems for them in reconciling the claims of faith and also deliberative democracy? It may be that while faith schools will be based on absolutist faith traditions they will also need to be pluralist in the teaching of PSHE and active citizenship.

References

Annette, J. (2000) 'Education for citizenship, civic participation and experiential service learning in the community', in R. Gardner, J. Cairns and D. Lawton (eds) *Education for Citizenship*, London: Continuum.

Annette, J. (2003) 'Community and citizenship education', in J. Annette, Sir B. Crick and A. Lockyer (eds) *Education for Democratic Citizenship*, Aldershot: Ashgate.

Archbishop of Canterbury's Commission on Urban Priority Areas (1985) *Faith in the City*, London: Church House Publishing.

Arthur, J. with R. Bailey (2000) *Schools and Community: The Communitarian Agenda in Education*, London: Falmer Press.

Baron, S., J. Field and T. Schuller (eds) (2000) *Social Capital*, Oxford: Oxford University Press.

Beem, C. (1999) *The Necessity of Politics*, Chicago: University of Chicago Press.

Bellah, R. (1992) 'The broken covenant: American civil religion', in *Time of Trial*, Chicago: University of Chicago Press, 2nd edition.

Bellah, R., R. Madsen, W. Sullivan, A. Swidler and S. Tipton (eds) (1996) *Habits of the Heart*, Berkeley: University of California Press, 2nd edition.

Berger, P. and R.J. Neuhaus (2002) *To Empower the People*, Washington, DC: American Enterprise Institute Press, 2nd edition with Novack, M.

Bryk, A., V. Lee and P. Holland (1993) *Catholic Schools and the Common Good*, Cambridge: Harvard University Press.

Cantle, T. (2001) *Community Cohesion: A Report of the Independent Review Team* (The Cantle Report), London: Home Office.

Catholic Bishops of England and Wales (1996) *The Common Good and the Catholic Church's Social Teachings*, Manchester: Gabriel Communications.

Catholic Education Service (1997) *The Common Good in Education*, London: Catholic Education Service.

Crick, B. (2000) *In Defence of Politics*, London: Continuum, 5th edition.

Crick, B (2003) *Democracy*, Oxford: Oxford University Press.

Dalacoura, K. (2003) *Islam, Liberalism and Human Rights*, London: I.B. Tauris.

Dee, T.S. (2003) 'The effect of Catholic schooling on civic participation', CIRCLE (Circle for Information and Research on Civic Learning and Engagement), University of Maryland. Working Paper, 9 July, available online at http://www.cf.www.civicyouth.org.

DfES (2001) *Schools: Achieving Success*, Cm 5230, London: Stationery Office.

Driver, S. and L. Martell (1997) 'New Labour's communitarianisms', *Critical Social Policy*, 7(3): 27–46.

Edwards, R., M. Foly and M. Diani (2001) *Beyond Tocqueville: Civil Society and the Social Capital Debate in Comparative Perspective*, Hanover: Tufts University Press.

Elshtain, J. (1995) *Democracy on Trial*, New York: Basic Books.

Grace, G. (2002) *Catholic Schools*, London: RoutledgeFalmer.

Farnell, R. (2001) 'Faith communities, regeneration and social exclusion', *Community Development Journal* 36(4): 95–107.

Farnell, R., R. Furbey, S. Hills, M. Macey and G. Smith (2003) *'Faith' in Urban Regeneration?*, Bristol: JRF/The Policy Press.

Fine, B. (2001) *Social Capital versus Social Theory*, London: RoutledgeFalmer.

Frohnen, B. (1996) *The New Communitarians and the Crisis of Modern Liberalism*, Lawrence, KS: University of Kansas Press.

Gamarnikow, E. and A. Green (2003) 'Keeping the faith with social capital: from Coleman to New Labour on social justice, religion and education', unpublished paper.

Gamarnikow, E. and A. Green (2000) 'Citizenship, education and social capital', in R. Gardner, J. Cairns and D. Lawton (eds) *Education for Citizenship*, London: Continuum.

Lawless, P., P. Else, R. Farnell, R. Furbey, S. Lund and B. Wishart (1998) 'Community-based initiative and state urban policy: the Church Urban Fund', *Regional Studies*, 32(2): 43–56.

Lerner, M. (1997) *The Politics of Meaning*, Reading: Addison-Wesley.

Lewis, J. with E. Randolph-Horn (2001) *Faith, Hope and Participation*, London: New Economics Foundation and the Church Urban League.

LGA (2002) *Faith and Community: A Good Practice Guide for Local Authorities*, London: LGA Publishers.

London Churches Group for Social Action (2002) *Regenerating London: Faith Communities and Social Action*, London: Greater London Enterprises.

Lukka, P. and M. Locke (2000) 'Faith, voluntary action and social policy: a review of research', *Voluntary Action*, 3(1): 25–40.

Northcott, M. (1998) *Urban Theology: A Reader*, London: Cassell.

Musgrave, P. (1999) *Flourishing Communities: Engaging Church Communities with Government in the New Deal for Communities*, London: Church Urban Fund.

Neighbourhood Renewal Unit (2002) *The Learning Curve*, London: Neighbourhood Renewal Unit/ ODPM.

Olasky, M. (2000) *Compassionate Conservatism* (foreword by George W. Bush), New York: Free Press.

Putnam, R. (2000) *Bowling Alone: The Collapse and Revival of American Democracy*, New York: Simon and Schuster.

QCA (1998) *Education for Citizenship and the Teaching of Democracy in Schools* (Crick Report), London: QCA.

Sacks, J. (2000) *The Politics of Hope*, London: Vintage.

Sacks, J. (2002) *The Dignity of Difference*, London: Continuum.

Saegert, S., J.P. Thompson and M. Warren (eds) (2001) *Social Capital and Poor Communities*, New York: Russell Sage Foundation.

Smith, G. (2000) *Faith Makes Community Work*, London: Shaftesbury Society and the DETR.

Smith, G. (2002) 'Religion and the rise of social capitalism: the faith communities in community development and urban regeneration in England', *Community Development Journal*, 37(2): 167–77.

Streeter, G. (ed.) (2002) *There is Such a Thing as Society*, London: Politico's.

Vallely, P. (1998) *The New Politics*, London: SCM Press.

Wallis, J. (1994) *The Soul of Politics*, London: Fount.

Wallis, J. (2000) *Faith Works*, New York: Random House.

Warren, M. (2001) *Dry Bones Rattling: Community Building to Revitalise American Democracy*, Princeton: Princeton University Press.

Warren, M. and R.L. Wood (2001) *Faith-Based Community Organising: The State of the Field*, Jericho, NY: Interfaith Funders.

Wood, R.L. (2002) *Faith in Action: Religion, Race and Democratic Organising in America*, Chicago: University of Chicago Press.

Wuthnow, R. (1996) *Christianity and Civil Society: The Contemporary Debate*, Philadelphia: Trinity Press.

Wuthnow, R. (2002) 'Reassembling the civic church: the changing role of congregations in American civil society', in R. Madsen, W. Sullivan, A. Swidler and S. Tipton (eds) *Meaning and Modernity: Religion, Polity and the Self*, Berkeley: University of California Press.

Youniss, J. and M. Yates (1997) *Community Service and Social Responsibility in Youth*, Chicago: University of Chicago Press.

Other sources consulted

Charles, R. (1999) *An Introduction to Catholic Social Teaching*, Oxford: Family Publications.

Cnaan, R. (1999) *The Newer Deal: Social work and Religion in Partnership*, New York: Columbia University Press.

Coleman, J.S. (1997) 'Social capital in the creation of human capital', in A.H. Halsey, H. Lauder, P. Brown and A. Stuart Wells (eds) *Education, Culture, Economy and Society*, Oxford: Oxford University Press.

Coleman, S.J. and A. John (2002) 'A limited state and a vibrant society: christianity and civil society', in N. Rosenblum and R. Post (eds) *Civil Society and Government*, Princeton: Princeton University Press.

Dearing, R. (2001) *The Way Ahead: Church of England Schools in the New Millennium*, Report of the Church Schools Review Group, London: Church House Publishing.

Dionne, Jr, E.J. and J. Dilulio (eds) (2000) *What's God Got to do with the American Experiment?*, Washington, DC: Brookings Institution Press.

Hall, P. (2002) 'Great Britain: the role of government and the distribution of social capital', in R. Putnam (ed.) *Democracies in Flux*, Oxford: Oxford University Press.

Lewis, P. (2002) *Islamic Britain*, London: I.B. Tauris.

Siranni, C. and L. Friedland (2001) *Civic Innovation in America*, Berkeley: University of California Press.

Wineburg, R. (2001) *A Limited Partnership: The Politics of Religion, Welfare and Social Service*, New York: Columbia University Press.

18 The impact of faith schools on pupil performance

Ian Schagen and Sandie Schagen[1]

Faith schools are currently popular, both with parents and with the government. They are often oversubscribed, and parents may fight hard to gain a place for their child. Faith schools can be seen as part of the Blair government's drive to raise standards and promote diversity. The recent White Paper *Schools Achieving Success* (DfES, 2001) advocated an expansion in their number, although this suggestion has met strong opposition, usually on the grounds that segregated education could damage race relations and increase divisions in a community.

Why, then, are faith schools so popular? Evidently they are perceived by some to be 'better' than other state-funded schools, but in what sense? A poll reported in the *Times Educational Supplement* (30 November 2001) indicated that support among the general population for church schools was focused mainly on good discipline and religious ethos. Good examination results were cited by only 10 per cent, although academic excellence is one reason for the government's support for expansion.

This chapter explores the relative performance of faith and non-religious[2] schools in terms of General Certificate in Secondary Education (GCSE) and Key Stage 3 test results. This should not be understood to mean that we consider academic achievement to be more important than the other good qualities associated with faith schools. Moreover, we recognise that academic performance may be linked with non-academic factors; one could argue, for example, that good discipline and behaviour are prerequisites for effective teaching and learning which lead to good examination results.

Nevertheless, there is a need for objective research into the claims that faith schools achieve higher levels of pupil performance. It is true that they tend to obtain good academic results, and often appear at the top of local education authority (LEA) league tables. The crucial question is whether these good results mean that faith schools are particularly effective, or whether they merely reflect a more select, privileged intake.[3] To answer this question, it is necessary to undertake a full-scale value-added analysis of pupil data – something which, to our knowledge, has never previously been undertaken for this purpose.

National value-added datasets

The introduction of national testing at the end of every key stage has made it possible to measure pupil progress over time. National value-added datasets (NVADs) provide the matched pupil-level information to facilitate effective value-added analysis. However, test results were only collected in this form from 1996 onwards, so the first NVAD linking Key Stage 2 and GCSE results (1996–2001) was not available until 2002. When the research reported here was conducted (at the end of 2001), it was necessary to look at Key Stages 3 and 4 separately, using data from two different cohorts: Key Stage 2 1997 to Key Stage 3 2000, and Key Stage 3 1998 to GCSE 2000.[4]

The sizes of the datasets are set out in Table 18.1, in terms of cases with usable matched data across the key stages. Each dataset covers the large majority of schools and pupils in the appropriate cohort in England.

The basic datasets as supplied by the Department for Education and Skills (DfES)/ Qualifications and Curriculum Authority (QCA) contained the following information:

- pupil identifier (anonymised)
- school identifier (DfES number)
- male/female indicator
- date of birth
- prior attainment data (for KS2–3: KS2 levels in English, maths and science; for KS3–GCSE: KS3 levels in English, maths and science)
- outcome data (for KS2–3: KS3 levels in English, maths and science; for KS3–GCSE: grades achieved in each subject at GCSE or General National Vocational Qualification [GNVQ]).

On matching to the National Foundation for Educational Research's (NFER) Schools Database, via DfES number, the following school-level information could be added:

- type of school
- LEA identifier
- measure of the percentage eligible for free school meals.

The main statistical techniques employed in the analysis were linear regression and multilevel modelling.[5] At both key stages, we aimed to discover

- how the various types of faith schools performed, in value-added terms, relative to non-religious schools;
- whether the impact of attendance at a faith school was the same throughout the ability range;
- the impact (if any) of faith schools on the other schools within an LEA.

Key Stage 3 to GCSE

Table 18.2 shows the distributions of pupils and schools between the various categories in the dataset linking Key Stage 3 1998 to GCSE 2000. As would be expected, the two largest categories of faith schools are Roman Catholic (RC) (338 schools) and Church of England (C of E) (141 schools). Five Jewish schools are identified and treated here as a separate group (no Sikh or Muslim schools are included in the NVAD). The 'other Christian'

Table 18.1 National value-added datasets

	KS2 1998 to KS3 2000	*KS3 1997 to GCSE 2000*
Number of students	387,595	482,399
Number of schools	3,034	3,124
Number of LEAs	149	149

Table 18.2 Pupils and schools with different religious affiliations in KS3–GCSE dataset

Religious affiliation	Number of schools	% of schools	Number of pupils	% of pupils
Non-religious	2,632	84.3	412,088	85.4
Church of England	141	4.5	21,336	4.4
Roman Catholic	338	10.8	47,365	9.8
Other Christian	8	0.3	937	0.2
Jewish	5	0.2	673	0.1
Total	3,124		482,399	

category includes joint RC/C of E schools as well as schools belonging to other Christian traditions (e.g. Seventh Day Adventist). We acknowledge that this is not an entirely satisfactory grouping, but it is not feasible to further subdivide a category which is already very small. In total, nearly 15 per cent of pupils are in faith schools at this stage; more than two-thirds of these are in Catholic schools, and most of the others are in C of E schools.

The GCSE outcomes investigated were:

- total GCSE point score[6]
- average GCSE point score
- mathematics point score
- English point score
- science point score.

The following background variables were taken into account in all of the analyses:

Pupil-level

- sex (girl or boy)
- age (in years and months)
- prior attainment (average level achieved at Key Stage 3).

School-level

- type of LEA (i.e. metropolitan or non-metropolitan)
- percentage of pupils eligible for free school meals
- type of religious affiliation (if any).

Overall impact of faith schools

A multiple regression analysis was undertaken in order to compare GCSE performance in faith and other schools, controlling for the background variables, most importantly Key Stage 3 performance. Table 18.3 indicates the number of GCSE points gained (or lost) by pupils in faith schools compared with the norm represented by non-religious schools.

Faith schools in all four categories obtained significantly better results in terms of GCSE English and total point score. For other subjects, the picture is less clear. RC schools were above average for mathematics, but below average for science; Jewish schools were above

Table 18.3 The impact of faith schools at GCSE

Outcome	Significant coefficients (GCSE score difference) relative to non-religious schools			
	Church of England	Roman Catholic	Other Christian	Jewish
GCSE total score	1.117	1.454	2.161	4.604
GCSE average score	–	0.030	–	0.552
GCSE mathematics	–	0.031	−0.129	0.522
GCSE English	0.056	0.150	0.062	0.307
GCSE science	–	−0.017	−0.080	0.507

average for both; 'other Christian' schools were below average for both; C of E schools were not significantly better or worse for either subject.

Although all four groups were ahead of non-religious schools in terms of total point score, only two (Jewish and RC) were significantly above the norm in terms of average score. Moreover, although the advantage of RC schools is significant, it is very slight relative to their advantage in total score. This suggests that church schools may enter pupils for more GCSEs, which would increase their total score but not necessarily their average score. GCSE in religious education (RE) is often compulsory in church schools, and if it is taken as an extra subject (rather than an option) this could help to explain our findings.

Overall, it is the Jewish schools which produced by far the best results. They are the only group to be significantly ahead on all five outcome measures. Moreover, for each outcome measure they have by far the highest coefficient. In terms of total score, they are nearly five points ahead (equivalent to an additional grade C) and on most other measures they are half a point/grade ahead. For English, the advantage is only 0.3, but this is still double that achieved by any other category of school.

On the whole, it seems that church schools – whether C of E, RC or 'other Christian' – outperformed non-religious schools on some measures, but only to a very slight degree.

Impact on different ability groups

Multilevel models were set up for each of the five outcome measures, incorporating all of the background variables listed above. The results confirmed that faith schools tend to have a slight positive impact, and indicated further where this impact was experienced. This is illustrated in the Figures 18.1 and 18.2, for GCSE total and average scores respectively. The lines illustrate 'expected' GCSE performance for pupils across the range of prior attainment, taking average values for the other background factors. Only the three main school categories are illustrated; the Jewish and 'other Christian' categories are very small, and two extra lines would make the graphs more difficult to read. In each graph, the thick black line represents the performance of pupils in non-religious schools; the thin line represents pupils in C of E schools, and the broken line pupils in RC schools.

In Figure 18.1, illustrating total scores, the three lines overlap at the low-ability end, but gradually diverge. It appears that pupils with below-average attainment at Key Stage 3 (levels 3–4) attained, on average, the same total score regardless of school type, but the positive impact of being in a church school was experienced more strongly as we move up the ability range; pupils who had achieved level 7 (for example) at Key Stage 3 obtained significantly better total GCSE scores in a church school (particularly an RC school). In

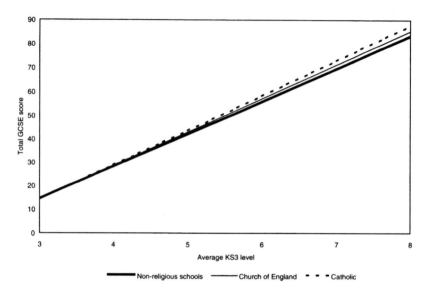

Figure 18.1 Total GCSE score vs KS3: religious and non-religious schools

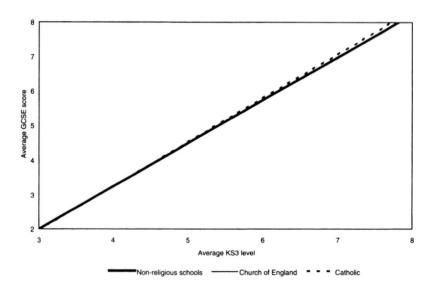

Figure 18.2 Average GCSE score vs KS3: religious and non-religious schools

the light of the foregoing discussion, this may mean that church schools encourage their most able pupils to take additional GCSE subjects.

This hypothesis is confirmed by looking at Figure 18.2, illustrating average GCSE scores. Here the line representing C of E schools is indistinguishable from that representing non-religious schools, and the RC line is only barely distinguishable towards the top of the ability range. Church schools therefore seem to have less impact in terms of average score, which again suggests that their advantage in total score is due to taking extra GCSE subjects.

In mathematics and science, there was hardly any difference between church schools and other schools. In English, however, church schools clearly outperformed non-religious schools (see Figure 18.3). In C of E schools, the advantage appeared to be focused on lower-attaining pupils, while in RC schools, it was experienced across the ability range.

Impact of faith schools on performance, by LEA

Because faith schools have good results and good reputations, informed parents may be keen to obtain places for their children, even if they are not adherents of the religion concerned. This could further improve the results of faith schools, and thus contribute to an increasing polarisation between faith schools and other schools.

To test this hypothesis, we considered performance results in an LEA context, taking into account the proportion of pupils in faith schools. Schools were divided into five categories:

* faith schools in LEAs where up to 20 per cent of the pupils in that LEA were in faith schools;
* other schools in that type of LEA;
* faith schools in LEAs where over 20 per cent of the pupils were in faith schools;

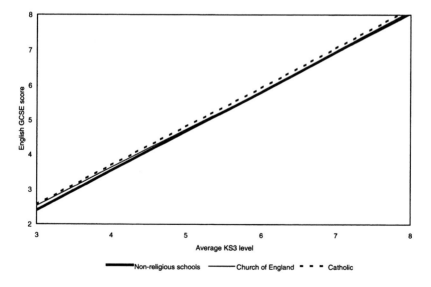

Figure 18.3 English GCSE scores vs KS3: religious and non-religious schools

- other schools in that type of LEA;
- LEAs with no faith schools.

A regression analysis was carried out, taking schools in LEAs with no faith schools as the norm. Table 18.4 lists the significant coefficients of the other school types. The figures in the table indicate the number of extra GCSE points gained (or lost) by pupils in faith schools and those in schools 'competing' with faith schools.

Faith schools had mainly positive outcomes (five, against two negative); again, they seemed to perform particularly well in terms of total GCSE point score. By contrast, 'competing' non-religious schools were below the norm for all outcomes except mathematics. This provides some confirmation for the hypothesis that faith schools are succeeding to some extent at the expense of neighbouring schools.

To explore the issue further, the analysis was rerun combining all schools within the three types of LEA: high percentage in faith schools, low percentage in faith schools and no faith schools. Taking the latter as the default, the coefficients (differences in GCSE scores) for the other types of LEAs are shown in Table 18.5.

LEAs with a high proportion of pupils in faith schools achieved better than average results in terms of total point score (again, possibly due to compulsory RE GCSE) and mathematics (though the difference here is very slight). In terms of average score and science, these LEAs were below the norm, and for English there was no significant difference. In general, they performed a little better than LEAs with a low proportion of pupils in faith schools, which achieved at or slightly below the norm in all outcomes.[7]

Table 18.4 Faith schools in context at GCSE

Outcome	Significant coefficients (GCSE score difference) relative to LEAs without faith schools			
	Non-religious (low % in faith schools)	*Non-religious (high % in faith schools)*	*Religious (low % in faith schools)*	*Religious (high % in faith schools)*
GCSE total score	−0.224	−0.325	1.074	1.253
GCSE average score	−0.061	−0.042	−0.047	–
GCSE mathematics	–	0.019	–	0.058
GCSE English	−0.053	−0.032	0.055	0.101
GCSE science	−0.051	−0.027	−0.084	–

Table 18.5 The impact of faith schools on GCSE results, by LEA

Outcome	Significant coefficients (GCSE score difference) relative to LEAs without faith schools	
	Low % in faith schools	High % in faith schools
GCSE total score	–	0.230
GCSE average score	−0.060	−0.030
GCSE mathematics	–	0.031
GCSE English	−0.048	–
GCSE science	−0.065	0.032

Key Stage 2 to Key Stage 3

Value-added analyses tend to be based on GCSE performance, using Key Stage 3 attainment as a baseline. However, secondary schools cover Key Stage 3 as well as Key Stage 4, and we wished to examine what impact (if any) faith schools had in the early years of secondary education.

The analyses reported above were therefore repeated for Key Stage 2–3. The NVAD for Key Stage 2 1997 to Key Stage 3 2000 was used,[8] and the background variables were the same as for the Key Stage 3–GCSE analysis (except that prior attainment was the average level for Key Stage 2). In this case, there were four outcome variables:

- average Key Stage 3 level
- mathematics level
- English level
- science level.

Once again, a multiple regression analysis was undertaken, and Table 18.6 shows the significant coefficients of faith schools' impact at Key Stage 3. Numbers in the table indicate the difference (in levels) between the outcomes of pupils in faith schools and the norm represented by non-religious schools.

As at GCSE level, the Jewish schools performed best, although at this stage their science outcomes were not significantly different from non-religious schools. However, their performance in mathematics and English was strong, and their average score was 0.11 levels above the norm. If a level equates to approximately two years' work, then pupils in Jewish schools were more than two-and-a-half months ahead of others at Key Stage 3.

Christian schools of all types were ahead in English, and Church of England schools were also ahead (but only marginally) in science. RC schools had significantly lower levels in mathematics and science, and therefore lower average levels. Average levels were significantly above the norm in C of E and 'other Christian' schools, but not as far above as in Jewish schools; using the same formula (one level = two years), pupils in 'other Christian' schools were about five weeks ahead of pupils in non-religious schools, while those in C of E schools were two to three weeks ahead.

Impact on different ability groups

The results of multilevel modelling for Key Stages 2–3 showed little variation across the ability range between RC, C of E and non-religious schools in terms of average Key

Table 18.6 The impact of faith schools at Key Stage 3

Outcome	Significant coefficients (KS3 score difference) relative to non-religious schools			
	Roman Catholic	Church of England	Other Christian	Jewish
KS3 average level	−0.011	0.029	0.055	0.110
KS3 mathematics	−0.045	–	–	0.132
KS3 English	0.066	0.062	0.162	0.146
KS3 science	−0.057	0.033	–	–

Stage 3 level. In mathematics and science, RC schools appeared to achieve slightly poorer outcomes with their lower-attaining pupils. In science, C of E schools added slightly more value at the top end of the ability range. In English, lower-attaining pupils in both types of church school outperformed their peers in non-religious schools. However, none of these differences were large enough to show very clearly on graphs similar to Figures 18.1–18.3, and they are therefore not reproduced in this paper.

Impact of faith schools on performance, by LEA

Again, we considered performance results in an LEA context, taking into account the proportion of pupils in faith schools. Schools were divided into the five categories identified above, and a regression analysis was carried out, taking schools in LEAs with no faith schools (nine, in this case) as the norm.

Faith schools in 'high faith' areas had three significantly positive outcomes, English being the most striking. Other schools in the same areas were at or below the norm for every outcome except mathematics. This might seem to suggest that the faith schools are taking 'better' pupils. However, in the 'low faith' areas, non-religious schools performed better than faith schools.

A further analysis was undertaken in order to compare the overall results of the three types of LEA: high percentage faith schools, low percentage faith schools and no faith schools. Mathematics was the only subject in which LEAs with faith schools outperformed others. In English, LEAs with a low percentage of pupils in faith schools were marginally below the norm; for all other outcomes, the difference was not significant.

Conclusion

The analyses aimed to discover whether faith schools were more successful than other schools, in value-added terms. The findings have not yielded clear answers, but they have raised issues worthy of further exploration. The first question is why Jewish schools were so successful in value-added terms. The analysis has shown that they obtained much better results than other schools (Christian and non-religious) for all of the outcomes investigated except Key Stage 3 science. However, there were only five schools in this category, so it is open to question whether their success was due to the inherent nature of Jewish schools, or to other shared characteristics.

For Christian schools, the picture is much more varied and complex. A slight advantage in terms of GCSE total score could be due to taking an extra GCSE subject (perhaps RE). Beyond this, different types of church school obtained results above or below the norm in different subjects at different key stages. For example, RC schools were negative for most Key Stage 3 outcomes, but positive for all GCSE outcomes except science. There is no obvious way to balance these differences, which are in any case very slight. We must therefore say that, overall, RC schools do not seem to perform better or worse than non-religious schools.

C of E schools, on the other hand, had some significantly positive outcomes (and no significantly negative outcomes) at both key stages. Overall, then, they seem to perform marginally better than non-religious schools, but again, we must stress that the differences were very slight.[9] It seems likely therefore that the good 'raw' results achieved by many church schools reflect the nature and quality of their intake.

One point worthy of note is that faith schools of all types outperformed non-religious schools at both key stages in English. Again, the difference is small, but it is consistent, and it would be interesting to explore whether there is something in the nature of faith schools which encourages development of literacy skills, or whether other factors are involved. Our analyses took into account prior attainment (the chief determinant of performance) and other important pupil- and school-level factors. However, other relevant variables for data were not available, such as ethnicity, English as an additional language (EAL) and level of parental support. It could be, for example, that faith schools have a lower average proportion of children with EAL, and this could have an impact on English results.

The aims of faith schools are broader than simply raising academic attainment, important though that is. Nevertheless, one might hypothesise that creating a caring, supportive and well-ordered environment would provide a climate in which teaching and learning would flourish, and that this would lead in turn to high achievement. We have not found any clear evidence to support this view (except possibly in the case of Jewish schools).

A further hypothesis is that faith schools do well because the families represented are part of a recognisable community, and that as a consequence there would be shared values, a high degree of parental support and good home–school relations. None of these factors could be included in our models, but all could contribute to good results and indeed could help to explain the highly positive outcomes achieved by Jewish schools. However, one might expect the same factors to enhance results in RC schools (and less so in C of E schools); yet our findings show that overall, C of E schools have a positive (albeit very slight) impact, while for RC schools, mainly positive outcomes at GCSE are balanced by largely negative outcomes at Key Stage 3.

Notes

1 The research project was funded by the Local Government Association. The authors wish to thank Christine Boateng-Asumadu and her colleagues at QCA and DfES for supplying the matched value-added datasets used. Thanks are also due to NFER colleagues, especially Peter Rudd, Deborah Davies and Tom Benton, who worked on the project.

2 There is no obvious or agreed designation for schools which are not faith schools. We have used non-religious, acknowledging that some would regard schools without religious affiliation as multi-faith rather than non-faith.

3 A recent analysis of Welsh data (NAfW 2001) showed that church schools obtained better GCSE results than non-religious schools; however, when varying free school meals (FSM) levels were taken into account, the difference was not statistically significant.

4 Since this paper was presented at the conference on Faith Schools: Consensus or Conflict?, we have repeated the analysis using the 1996–2001 dataset. The findings present a broadly consistent picture, with some minor variations.

5 Multilevel modelling is a recent development of regression analysis which takes account of data which is grouped into similar clusters at different levels. For example, individual pupils are grouped into year groups or cohorts, and those cohorts are grouped within schools. There may be more in common between pupils within the same cohort than with other cohorts, and there may be elements of similarity between different cohorts in the same school. Multilevel modelling allows us to take account of this hierarchical structure of the data and produce more accurate predictions, as well as estimates of the differences between pupils, between cohorts, and between schools.

6 Points were derived from subject grades in the standard manner, i.e. A*=8, A=7, B=6 ... G=1.

7 It should be noted that only eight LEAs have no faith schools at all included in the 1998–2000 NVAD, and as those LEAs may not be entirely representative, it would be unwise to conclude that having a low percentage of pupils in faith schools results in below average performance. It

is more instructive to compare results for the 'high' and 'low' categories, and these consistently favour the former, although the differences are small.

8 This has more gaps than the Key Stage 3–4 database, but still includes a large majority of English schools.

9 It should be noted that, because of the large numbers of schools and pupils in these analyses, quite small differences will be flagged as statistically significant.

References

DfES (Department for Education and Skills) (2001) *Schools Achieving Success*, London, DfES.

19 Faith schools, religious education and citizenship

John Keast

Curriculum change 1988–97

Since 1988 the curriculum of maintained schools in England has been required to be broad and balanced, and to promote pupils' 'spiritual, moral, social and cultural development and to prepare them for the opportunities, responsibilities and experiences of adult life.'[1] A basic curriculum consisting of religious education (RE) and the National Curriculum (NC) was introduced to all maintained schools. Despite these explicit references to the higher purposes and areas concerning values in education, there was, during the 1990s, rising concern about the actual values young people were growing up with, highlighted by tragic and well publicised murders involving young people, for example the murder of James Bulger in Merseyside by two boys of early secondary school age, and the murder of a head teacher, Philip Lawrence, whilst carrying out his duties in London. This concern was eventually to contribute to a more explicit statement of the values that education should promote.

Among the responses to this concern was an initiative taken by Sir Ron (later Lord) Dearing and Dr Nicholas Tate, Chairman and Chief Executive of the Schools Curriculum and Assessment Authority (SCAA)[2] in 1996. They established the Forum on Values in Education and the Community. The 'Values Forum', as it was popularly known, consisted of about 150 people from many walks of life, charged with producing a statement of the values commonly held by most people. The Forum produced a statement of values in early 1997.[3] The number of dissenting voices was small, mainly because the statements of values held to be common were very general ones, and the agreed statement was sent to the main religious groups in England, who also endorsed it. The work of the Values Forum helped to shape the review of the National Curriculum by the Qualifications and Curriculum Authority (QCA) in 1999.

Development of citizenship

In May 1997 the first Labour government since 1979 was elected, with a slogan 'Education, education, education'. Its social inclusion initiatives soon began to impact on education and take this work on values in a quite different and significant direction. A white paper published in July (HMSO 1997) pointed the way forward – more emphasis on citizenship and personal, social and health education (PSHE). In the autumn of 1998, the Crick Report (HMSO 1998) recommended that citizenship be introduced into the National Curriculum, given 5 per cent of curriculum time and accompanied by a range of support mechanisms. In this context, citizenship was deemed to comprise social and moral responsibility, community involvement and political literacy. Key concepts, skills, attitudes and dispositions, as well as knowledge and understanding, were identified for each key stage. A PSHE group (HMSO 1999) reported the following year and made complementary recommendations for the review of the National Curriculum.

There were many reasons for the development of citizenship (and PSHE). In addition to reflecting the general concern mentioned above, they included a growing anxiety about the disengagement of young people from the political process. The 1997 General Election saw fewer young people vote than in previous elections. Enabling young people to become part of the democratic process of decision-making was a government priority. Introducing citizenship into the National Curriculum could reduce woeful ignorance about politics – national and local – and also help stimulate the involvement of young people more generally and more positively in society and community affairs.

But this was only one aspect of the wider social inclusion agenda that impacted on education. Another was the development of a legally binding statement of educational inclusion,[4] This required all National Curriculum subjects to put greater emphasis on removing the barriers to learning faced by some pupils, through disability, special educational needs or membership of some ethnic minority groups. This inclusive approach to education would help schools do what the wider social inclusion policies of the government were intended to do for the unemployed, single mothers, and those disadvantaged by class or race, in society generally. There were other related initiatives as well, such as sex and relationship education, and the National Healthy Schools Standard. 'Education, education, education' were clearly regarded as the keys to social reconstruction and transformation of society after nearly 20 years of Tory rule.

The inclusion statement was not the only key statement at the beginning of the new National Curriculum. Another was the first ever statement of the aims, values and purposes of the school curriculum.[5] England had had a National Curriculum for over 10 years but nobody had stated why or what it was intended to do. In addition to the references to the value of and values necessarily found within education that were largely influenced by the Values Forum, the statement contains two aims for the school curriculum. They are to enable all pupils to learn and achieve, and to promote pupils' spiritual, moral, social and cultural development and prepare them for opportunities, responsibilities and experiences in adult life. The statement on inclusion also reflected the value and importance attached by both government and educationalists generally to ensuring that all children should have access to good education and benefit from it.

To help fulfil these aims, the new subject of citizenship was introduced into the National Curriculum for all secondary school pupils to take effect from August 2002.[6] A non-statutory framework for PSHE[7] was also introduced for all key stages with links to citizenship. The contents of these curriculum developments may be briefly characterised as personal development, citizenship, health and safety, and relationships. Citizenship consists of three elements: knowledge and understanding about become informed citizens; the skill of enquiry and communication (of contemporary issues); and the skill of participation and taking responsible action. This last is the most innovative and is intended to ensure that citizenship is not dry, boring civics or simply political education. All this new material was in addition to existing requirements for RE and, in secondary schools, careers education and guidance, and sex education. Thus the school curriculum came to include a clear and pronounced social dimension, and schools were explicitly put in the frontline of the social inclusion agenda.

At the same time as tackling curriculum reform the government changed the structural framework of the school system (HMSO, 1998). Grant-maintained schools were abolished and new community and foundation schools were introduced, in addition to aided schools.

Some foundation schools were designated as having a religious character. Together with most aided schools, they have become popularly known as 'faith' schools, though this terminology does not do justice to the wide variety of such schools. Far from abolishing faith schools, which some of its supporters wanted, the government encouraged them, driven by the priority of its standards agenda. Faith schools achieved proportionally higher standards than other schools, in terms of examination results. There also developed the view that it was better to have faith schools within the maintained system where some control could be exercised over them through the National Curriculum and funding mechanisms than have them outside as fully independent where their potentially socially divisive effect could not be mitigated.

Changes in religious education

RE had also been developing as a subject alongside the events described above. A combination of national initiatives and local activities by many emerging and some quite effective Standing Advisory Councils on Religious Education (SACREs) had brought about something of a renaissance for RE. National model syllabuses (SCAA 1994) for use by local agreed syllabus conferences were devised, which invigorated curriculum development locally and improved the quality of many agreed syllabuses. Office for Standards in Education (OFSTED) inspections of RE enabled national agencies and local SACREs to gain a fuller and more consistent picture of standards and quality of teaching and learning in RE for the first time. This enabled SACREs to implement development plans in many areas. Although RE was not reviewed as part of the review of the National Curriculum, non-statutory guidance (QCA 2000a) was produced alongside it and sent to all LEAs. This provided national expectations in the form of an eight-level scale, parallel to such scales in use in National Curriculum subjects, and other material that matched the revised curriculum subject booklets. Schemes of work for RE at Key Stages 1, 2 and 3 were also published alongside other subjects.

One of the most important events was the introduction, from 1996, of the new General Certificate in Secondary Education (GCSE) (short course) in religious education (renamed religious studies in 2001 when revised criteria were introduced). Together with the full course, GCSE entries rose from approximately 110,000 in 1995 to 325,000 in 2002, transforming the provision, nature, quality and effectiveness of RE at Key Stage 4, and putting religious studies among the major entry subjects for the first time ever. Some variations within these figures are worth noting. The pattern of full course entries has remained largely the same throughout this period, with the majority of such entries coming from faith schools or independent schools. This reflects the continuing commitment to RE found in faith schools. The growth in the short-course entries has come from non-faith schools. Such a trend is confirmed by AS- and A-Level religious studies entries. These have also increased, though not at the same rate, but faith and independent schools remain the core sector for such study. At the same time, then, as the curriculum and structural reform was being carried out, RE was growing and improving, albeit patchily in non-faith schools, but remained a strong feature in faith schools.

Changing and developing the school curriculum in the ways described above can be described as enhancing and emphasising the 'social curriculum': that is, adapting what schools teach and how they educate pupils to relate more specifically to the personal and social needs of the pupils, their families, communities and society generally. Education was regarded as a means of social improvement and schools were the agencies. All maintained schools, including faith schools, were involved in this development of the social curriculum, contained in the statements at the beginning of the National Curriculum, by the introduction of citizenship into it, the publication of a non-statutory framework for PSHE for the first time, and the re-energising of RE as a discrete subject. The greater emphasis on values and ethos that is also a necessary part of inclusion, citizenship, PSHE and RE in schools has very important implications for faith schools that have developed specific forms of these based on the religious tradition within or by which they were founded. Such schools have traditionally included a clear and strong emphasis on RE, being required to provide this according to their trust deed, unlike other maintained schools whose RE is to be taught according to locally agreed syllabuses. The relationship of the increased emphasis on values and the social curriculum to faith generally, and therefore with faith schools and with religious education in particular, became and still is an important question.

Faith and values

What people believe is a crucial element in their sense of identity, sense of meaning (or otherwise) in life, their attitudes and actions. Their faith (for this is what their beliefs constitute) is closely linked to other similar identifiers and motivators, like opinions, assumptions, values and cultures. Nobody believes nothing. Even non-religious believers have outlooks on life. If human beings are to be taken seriously, their beliefs (or faith) have to be taken seriously. As beliefs have deep roots and powerful origins in being closely connected with people's upbringing, family, communities, society, religion and culture, they inevitably affect how and why children are to be educated. Education therefore is not value free or neutral, for it is about transmitting and receiving the values that are the beliefs of those whose examples people are presented with and which affect how they make their choices. All schools then are places of certain values and of value, and so they are places dependent on beliefs and believing. The Chief Rabbi, Dr Jonathan Sacks, argues that, as armies are needed to defend a country, so schools are needed to defend a civilisation.[8] Articulating the values, aims and purposes of schools becomes an exercise in what people believe about themselves, the world and each other.

An education that is provided by a religious group, and schools owned and organised by religious communities, will inevitably have fundamental and even more profound interest in the values and beliefs that underpin that education and those schools. Such values and beliefs will be determined by the beliefs, teachings and practices of the religious communities that own faith schools. The ethos of the school, the values enshrined and articulated in the school and the purposes of the education provided will be based on the faith that inspired the foundation of the school. What religious beliefs and faith are held and how they are practised do inevitably vary. Some forms of religion are more socially inclusive than others; some religious communities are more open than others. Religion may promote an inclusive or a separatist mentality; its practice may be outreaching or it may be serving the established community only.

Such diversity in the ways in which a religious faith may influence the kind of education provision it offers has particular relevance for any religious education offered by a faith school. The social curriculum – citizenship and RE in particular – are therefore of more than passing interest to faith schools. If based on the values and beliefs of the foundation of the school they will be powerful means of promoting those values and influencing the personal and social development of the pupils. If the social curriculum is at odds with the values of a faith school, or if the values of a faith school are not compatible with the aims and purposes of the social curriculum, then a fundamental contradiction arises, and a complex set of tensions emerges that will blunt the effectiveness of both the social curriculum and the school itself.

Social inclusion and faith schools

Two of the most crucial areas where such tensions may arise are in the areas of social inclusion and the role of religious education. The social curriculum is based on a clearly inclusive approach to education, both in the curriculum and in the school generally. But here lies a tension, for faith schools draw their pupil population largely from children of followers of their faith, leading to the allegation that they are socially and religiously exclusive of other faiths. If this is actually the case, how can the purposes of the new social curriculum be effectively fulfilled? If faith schools cease to be exclusive in this alleged way and promote social inclusion by taking children from different religious communities and serving the diversity of faiths now found in Britain, how can they fulfil their original purpose in providing an education and religious nurture for the children of their faith community? This dilemma is particularly acute for faith schools that conceive their role primarily as faith nurture in this way. Many faith schools are oversubscribed, so have to choose the pupils they admit, adding to the dilemma. Others include large numbers of pupils not from the faith community that runs the school. This too adds a different dimension to the inclusive/exclusive dilemma.

The culture of success promoted by the government through performance tables in which faith schools did proportionately very well adds another layer of complication to the issue of inclusion, because many critics of some faith schools allege that their existence and admission processes are not just religiously divisive but socially exclusive as well. They serve middle-class interests under the guise of religion. When the government supported the proposal of the Church of England to expand its secondary schools (Archbishops' Council 2001) it was accused of undermining its own inclusion agenda. Various ways are being proposed to try to ensure that faith schools can continue to fulfil their specific purpose but without becoming religiously divisive or exclusive by ensuring their admission policies are more inclusive.

The dilemma referred to above can be exemplified specifically through the citizenship curriculum and the RE curriculum. A compulsory part of the citizenship programmes of study for maintained secondary schools is to teach pupils about the diversity of identities found in the UK, including religious identities.[9] Many faith schools will find it quite new to embrace such an approach and openly teach about other religious identities. How will they do this? Will it be part of citizenship lessons that are separate from RE or become part of their RE provision? The citizenship requirement in the National Curriculum matches the RE requirement for locally agreed syllabuses. These have to take account of the beliefs and teachings of the principal religions other than Christianity that are represented in Britain (HMSO 1996). But faith schools do not have to use agreed syllabuses for RE. They are required to teach RE according to their trust deed, so in some faith schools a multi-faith RE is not taught. Whilst some faith schools have not taught (about) religions other than the one that founded the school, others have been doing this for a long time. Those faith schools that have drawn their pupils from multi-ethnic and multi-faith communities have embraced a multi-faith RE to reflect their diverse pupil populations, in spite of the trust deed. There is thus a diversity of practice and approach to the teaching of RE in faith schools that may or may not link with the citizenship requirements.

The development of a non-statutory national framework for RE was proposed to the Secretary of State in May 2002, following a feasibility study. Such a development would raise the question, 'If there was a non-statutory framework for RE for non-faith schools, would it become an expectation or a norm for faith schools?' Such a framework would inevitably need to reflect the government's commitment to an inclusive religious education that helped pupils live in a religiously plural society. It would be part of the community cohesion initiative that has become so important since 11 September 2001. The existence of such a framework would have repercussions on expectations and standards in RE that faith schools could not ignore, if only because all schools share a common qualifications system in GCSE and AS/A-Level (now) RS. The development of a national statement of RE would condition any other statements of the purpose and content of RE, faith schools included. A framework of this kind could offer a way of ensuring that the RE taught in faith schools did not become exclusive, even if the school itself was attached to promulgating a particular religious point of view. In short, faith schools' RE could be profoundly influenced by a non-statutory national framework if it reduced the difference between the types of RE found in them. In the eyes of those who feel that RE in faith schools should specifically perform the role of religious nurture or instruction in a particular faith, this would, however, be regarded as a retrograde step. It is almost inevitable that, if a non-statutory framework were to be developed, its use by faith schools would be entirely voluntary and be followed in different ways.

In May 2003 a statutory national syllabus for RE was proposed by the churches, by suggesting extending the work needed to develop a non-statutory framework into developing what might eventually become a statutory syllabus. This proposal throws into even sharper relief some particular aspects of the dilemma noted above. There is no agreement on the desirability of this course of action among the various constituents of the RE community, which has been proposed by the main Christian churches in England. Among the many issues such a course of action would raise is whether such a syllabus would apply to faith schools. If it were, the contention above, concerning the possible influence of a national view of RE on faith schools' RE, would be even more explicit. If it were not, then the notion of a statutory national syllabus for RE would be gravely weakened. All these issues are currently being considered by the Secretary of State, along with another crucial area of values in schools, especially faith schools, i.e. collective worship.

Issues of collective worship

The tension for faith schools between social inclusion and faith nurture noted above can also be seen in the more contentious issue of collective worship. The law requires all pupils in non-faith schools to take part in an act of collective worship daily, which should be of a wholly or mainly Christian character, but provides opt outs for schools to have other forms of collective worship where appropriate for non-Christian pupils. Faith schools can hold collective worship of their own kind, again influenced by the trust deed or founding community of the school. Such worship is an important part of the mission of the faith school. It not only articulates the religious tradition within which the school and its education lie, it articulates the values and the beliefs that underpin the ethos of the school. The relationships and practices of the school are informed by and exemplify such an ethos. In faith schools where the pupils are not from the religious tradition that owns the school, most children are not withdrawn from collective worship, despite the parental withdrawal clause, so may take part in activities that are not part of their own faith background. This raises questions of the integrity of the collective worship, the integrity of the school and the motives of the parents who send their children to such schools.

Issues in religious education and citizenship

There are also philosophical issues concerning the concepts of citizenship and religion (and so of RE) in faith schools that need exploration. These issues depend in part on how far faith schools perceive and exploit the flexibility and breadth in the citizenship curriculum, both in terms of its meaning and purpose and in terms of what it requires to be taught. Flexibility for schools to develop a citizenship curriculum that related to their pupils' and communities' needs was a key message that accompanied the publication of the citizenship programmes of study in 1999–2000 (QCA 2000b). How discrete should citizenship and PSHE be in the curriculum provision? What links with other subjects should be identified, and how extensively should they be promoted? In faith schools, how religious concepts of citizenship relate to these and other questions could be important issues.

The various religious traditions are united in regarding human beings as under a greater authority or truth than the state. For example, Jews are 'Bar mitzvah', sons of the covenant, and under the authority of the Torah; Christians live in God's kingdom and are citizens of a celestial city as well as being part of human societies; Muslims are members of a universal 'ummah', subject to the will of Allah as revealed through the Prophet and the Qur'an. In faith schools, then, what kind of citizenship is to be taught? Questions of conformity with accepted laws and practices may clash or vie with questions of challenge to this world order. Acceptance of current social norms may conflict with the prophetic edge of religious teachings, which critique secular society. Faith schools have their own take on citizenship because of their faith perspective. This conceptual set of questions was particularly important for RE, many of whose supporters in faith schools felt that the introduction of statutory citizenship might be the beginning of the end for statutory RE. This concern was expressed at a conference at Lambeth Palace in the autumn of 2000, at which the Minister for School Standards made clear that RE had a distinctive, continuing and important role in the school curriculum alongside the new subject of citizenship and PSHE.[10]

There were also practical issues for schools, such as the advice on teaching and learning that teachers should be given, and how they could be helped with issues of bias and balance. How much material supplied by organisations keen to support these areas should be available? There is a challenge here for faith schools who may want to ensure that the materials they use for teaching citizenship represent the faith tradition in which they participate. There are obvious examples of moral and social dilemmas where religious communities have particular perspectives that would need to be reflected in teaching and learning materials.

There were also issues of assessment. Citizenship became a National Curriculum subject, yet it is more than a subject. It involved promoting moral responsibility, active involvement in community and dealing with contemporary issues. Should, or could, such a thing be assessed? If no assessment and accreditation regime was attached to it, schools would too easily be able to ignore or devalue citizenship. After all, it was argued with some justification, RE had been statutorily taught at Key Stage 4 since 1944 but many schools had not really taken it seriously until a GCSE (short course) had been introduced. The suitability of a GCSE examination approach for all pupils was clearly an important issue. What about pupils for whom GCSE was not a suitable form of assessment? How could a written GCSE examination deal with active citizenship? Would not GCSE stifle the involvement of pupils in the process of decision-making at school and in society? What message would be sent to young people themselves and to our society at large if pupils were shown only to get a grade G (or even ungraded) in citizenship? Was not this the first step on a slippery slope that not only undermined the social inclusion agenda but also threatened the very concept of a free society? Would those who 'failed' citizenship be second-class citizens, or worse? These issues also have a particular bearing on faith schools who perceive their role as developing the whole child, and providing excellence in spiritual, moral, social and cultural development.

Issues of effectiveness

The introduction of citizenship (and PSHE) into the national curriculum, alongside RE, is undoubtedly very significant. This is partly because it recognises the work schools have been doing in these areas in relatively haphazard ways for many years, and thus not only legitimises this provision but also regularises it through a more progressive and coherent structure. It is also partly because it embodies an even more explicit role for schools in promoting the personal and social development of their pupils and in contributing to the formation of healthier communities, through inclusion and involvement. It is thus a bold move, given a (somewhat guarded) welcome, whose effectiveness is already put to the test.

First, whether or not schools have the capacity to take these matters seriously is tested by the requirements of other aspects of government education policy, especially the drive to raise standards in the core subjects. There is evidence that this drive has been squeezing the time and energy primary schools (especially non-faith) give to planning and delivering a broad and balanced curriculum, including their provision for RE, citizenship and PSHE, even though they value these areas of the curriculum. For example, much primary RE is relegated to being taught only in afternoons, often reduced in time to allow other things to be fitted in also. The Key Stage 3 strategy is trying to avoid the same effect by having a foundation subjects strand and focussing on thinking skills. The changes that are being discussed for post-14 education and training may also affect the place and nature of citizenship in the future.

Second, forces and changes in society are already testing the ability of schools to teach citizenship effectively. The immense influence of the media, even though it is an element of the programme of study for citizenship, is far from conducive to the values, aims and nature of much of the citizenship and RE curricula. The public perception of politics and politicians, religions and some religious leaders, can sap the willingness and energy of teachers and others to give citizenship and RE their best shot. There are, however, big differences between faith and non-faith schools here as far as RE is concerned. Perceptions of religion and the roles religion and religions play in society change. There is evidence that religions are less marginalised than in the past, particularly in discussions of public policy-making concerning social inclusion and cohesion. The roles therefore that RE and citizenship play in education may mirror the increased attention paid to religions in the community generally. Perceptions of religion vary, of course. For some they are positive contributors of social capital; for others religions are regressive and extreme. So RE in schools will need to equip pupils to deal with the varying faces and roles of religions, and could act as a moderating influence on the more extreme tendencies of some proponents of RE in faith schools.

Third, the capacity for promoting effective citizenship and RE in schools to be muddled with and distracted by questions of citizenship, nationality, religion and identity in our country more generally is very real, especially for some groups within society, both religious and secular. Divisions among our communities along social, ethnic, political or religious lines exert tensions that may make schools feel daunted by the task of promoting citizenship and RE in some areas, and may make teachers feel they are engaging in risky pursuits.

Handling in schools the changing roles and the varying perceptions of religions will require teachers skilled in techniques of dialogue and valuing diversity. Such skills can be acquired but the training implications are enormous. The issues here are being faced on the European level by the Council of Europe's new project on Intercultural Education and the Challenge of Religious Diversity and Dialogue.

Faith schools have their own contribution to make towards the ultimate success or failure of citizenship and RE, and, more generally, the social curriculum and inclusion. In addition to the general pressures and tensions noted, the ways in which issues of faith and citizenship, faith and inclusion, and faith and education interact with the increased emphasis put on the role of schools to help promote community cohesion and inclusion will become increasingly important. If citizenship and RE in schools is to work as hoped by many politicians and faith community leaders, the media, politicians, parents and faith community groups have to play an even more significant, consistent and positive role in supporting schools in these endeavours.

Notes

1 Education Reform Act of 1988, consolidated in Education Act 1996.
2 SCAA was the successor body to the National Curriculum Council (NCC), which itself became the Qualifications and Curriculum Authority (QCA) on its merger with the National Council for Vocational Qualifications in 1997.
3 This is attached as an appendix to the *National Curriculum Handbooks* for teachers published by HMSO in 2000.
4 To be found in the *National Curriculum Handbooks*.
5 This is also found at the beginning of the *National Curriculum Handbooks*.
6 Published by in the *National Curriculum Handbook for Secondary Teachers*.
7 Published by in the *National Curriculum Handbooks*.
8 Various lectures, e.g. 'The Future of the Teaching Profession' to the Institute of Public Policy Research, September 2001.
9 See programmes of study for Citizenship, strand 1b.
10 Correspondence took place between Estelle Morris and Dr John Gay, Director of the St Gabriel's Programme, on this matter in October 2000.

References

Archbishops' Council (2001) *The Way Ahead: Church of England Schools in the New Millennium*, London: Church Publishing House.
HMSO (1996) *Education Act*, London: HMSO.
HMSO (1997) *Excellence in Schools* London: HMSO.
HMSO (1998) *Schools Standards and Framework Act*, London: HMSO.
HMSO (1999) *Preparing Young People for Adult Life*, London: HMSO.
HMSO (2000) *National Curriculum Handbook for Secondary Teachers* and *National Curriculum Handbook for Primary Teachers*, London: HMSO
QCA (1998) *Education for Citizenship and Democracy in Schools*, London: QCA.
QCA (2000a) *Non-statutory Guidance in Religious Education*, London: QCA.
QCA (2000b) *Citizenship at Key Stages 3 and 4: Initial Guidance*, London: QCA.
SCAA (1994) *Model Syllabuses for Religious Education*, available online at http://www.qca.org.uk, London: QCA.

20 Continuing personal and professional development and faith schools

Roy Gardner and Jo Cairns

> A school does not belong to its leaders or managers. As a teacher I do not own the classroom, the pupils, the resources or the learning ... We are stewards of public resources that are put into our hands for particular purposes, on behalf of the wider community. We can rightly be held to account for what we do in school with time, people, buildings, resources and knowledge. These are given to us in order to be given away by us; we are expected to maximise their effectiveness in the service of education.
>
> (Sullivan 2002: 92)

John Sullivan's statement encapsulates our personal and professional responsibilities as teachers, leaders and managers in schools. Our experience in carrying them out leads to a continuous cycle; that of planning our work within the overall purposes of the school, putting it into practice, reflecting on its impact and evaluating its contribution to the learning of our students. As a result, we return time and again to the key question, 'What best informs me about how to teach and lead and manage to good purpose?' Our personal and professional development continues as a result of our work as both teachers and learners. The question which this chapter wishes to pose is, 'To what extent should I as a teacher, leader or manager in a faith school expect to be offered and to participate in continuing personal and professional development (CPPD), which is different or additional to that engaged in by my colleagues in non faith schools?' Its purpose is to discuss the possibilities which CPPD opportunities might afford to all who work in faith schools and to argue that to ignore them could imperil the continuing existence of such schools in our increasingly secular and economically driven society.

All schools in Britain at present are called to give an account of how they deliver the two overall aims set out for schools in *The School Curriculum and the National Curriculum* (DfEE and QCA 1999: 10–11).

> Aim 1: The school curriculum should aim to provide opportunities for all children to learn and to achieve.

> Aim 2: The school curriculum should aim to promote pupils' spiritual, moral, social and cultural development and prepare all pupils for the opportunities, responsibilities and experiences of life.

Equally all schools will have had to face, in some form or other, the following questions set out by Stewart Sutherland (in Sacks and Sutherland 1996: 49) about issues connected with inclusion and the individual school which recent legislation has posed for schools:

When a pupil is excluded from a school what is it that is lacking? Is it a capacity within the pupil? Is there a structural problem within the school community which makes it impossible for this individual to be part of the community? Or is there no conceivable education community which could encompass this and other non-excluded pupils?

What distinguishes each school in its response both to achieving the aims of the National Curriculum and in working with issues related to inclusion matters is the manner in which it is able to speak for itself to the wider community outside; how it internally organises itself so that its overall purpose can be tested not only in relation to the external guidance and constraints of national education policy but also in line with its individual purpose and values; and to what extent giving account of itself will be strategically planned and underpinned by internal and external principles. This is so because of the nature of each school's culture or ethos and these, as we are reminded by Busher (2001: 76) are 'dynamic and created through the interactions of people. They are a nexus of shared norms and values that express how people make sense of the organisation in which they work and the other people with whom they work' and there follows a warning:

> ... organisational culture is often taken for granted by current participants who may be unaware how a particular culture has been constructed, how it might or can be changed or how it is sustained by those in positions of power and authority.

CPPD for teaching and non-teaching staff defines its purpose from how those working in schools make real the overall purpose of education as defined nationally for each of the pupils in their care within each individual culture. It therefore becomes urgent for each school to be able to identify, describe and evaluate its individual identity, purpose and organisation both for itself internally and for the wider community in which it is situated.

So far in our discussion there is no justification for a separate discussion of the CPPD needs of faith schools. Their explicit task is to share in the raising of standards in education, make proper provision for the social, moral, spiritual and cultural development of their pupils and thereby prepare them to meet the challenges and opportunities of adult life. Central initiatives in curriculum and testing, governance, inclusion, attendance and citizenship have all brought about the need for what Hamilton (1996) has called, 'targeted INSET [in-service training] therapy'.

Schools are changing, moving targets, however, for ever-increasing educational initiatives and calls for transparent accounting and they therefore require an increasing level of sophistication in how they differentiate for themselves and for external stakeholders their approach, purpose and outcome. This is true, of course, of faith schools, also.

Do faith schools require a different approach to CPPD?

As previous chapters have indicated, there are over 7,000 faith schools currently in the maintained community sector of England. The vast majority belong to the Church of England and the Roman Catholics but there are around 50 Jewish schools, and some Methodist, Muslim and Hindu owned. Nor, of course, do all children and young people of a religious persuasion follow their education in a faith school. As a result, all of these faith groups offer a variety of informal alternative education opportunities for their children and young people outside of the formal state education system.

Yet the White Paper, *Schools Achieving Success* (DfES 2001), pays little if no attention to the fact of the many differences and distinguishing features of the faith schools currently in existence. Government policy may choose to speak about the desirability of an expanded dual system in global terms but the policy, and very importantly, the schools themselves, will suffer if no attempt is made to define and categorise groups or clusters of schools which comprise faith schools. Calling for accountability from each school in a system increasingly characterised by centralised resourcing, curriculum reform, league tables and external reporting demands attention to the individual school and its particular characteristics and culture. As Gerald Grace, writing in *The Guardian* (8 November 2003), recently reminded us: 'Thoughtful debate about faith schooling must recognise that faith schools constitute a great variety of educational cultures, principles and practices.' This was in response to Francis Beckett's article in *The Guardian* (14 October 2003) in which he argued that faith schools 'breed only intolerance and isolation'.

This chapter will therefore attempt to outline a policy for the support and guidance of CPPD in faith schools which will, first, seek to ensure that blanket judgments and evaluations of faith schools, as in Francis Beckett's article, will be increasingly regarded as unacceptable in relation to the general category of faith schools. Second, it will seek to evaluate the contribution which faith schools might make to a genuine public debate about the role of faith, faith communities and faith schools to our plural late modern, and some would now argue post secular, society in working with the three categories of aims established for all schools in the state sector by the 'Introduction' to the National Curriculum (DfEE 1999). This will be considered most particularly through consideration of the role of reflexive CPPD programmes within and across schools. Third, it will seek to encourage purposeful engagement with CPPD within faith schools through a reflective description of CPPD activities undertaken by the author and others in partnership with faith communities within faith schools, leading to the establishment of core values and outcomes for CPPD within the sector.

The chapter starts from the recognition of the present diversity of CPPD provision for faith schools and the fact that a number of faith communities have very sophisticated models for such provision. As yet, however, we have no overview of the state of the provision, its aims, costs or outcomes. The chapter will therefore raise questions about how present and future provision may be shaped and evaluated both within each faith community and across the education service. Its purpose will be to prompt those responsible within each community and those responsible nationally for quality of provision to examine and evaluate different philosophies and practices in provision. Examples of good and interesting practice and philosophical approaches in past and present provision are employed not to highlight any one particular value or significance in one community's practice over and against another but to point to the richness and appropriateness of the current national picture among the faith communities with which we worked. They are offered with the hope that these and many others not included here will be further investigated and act as a catalyst for future strategic and successful CPPD provision for faith schools.

Profiling faith communities and their schools

For any reasoned discussion about the continuing personal and professional needs of teachers and non-teaching staff in faith schools and the ability to meet them, we must first differentiate between different types of faith community involvement in education. (For a fuller discussion of this matter, please refer to Chapter 2.) Such typologies might be developed by asking each of the communities sponsoring a faith school in compulsory education the following questions:

- Do you have within your community a central planning body responsible for overseeing the establishment of your faith schools in Britain? If so, is its authority recognised across the community? Are there several bodies?
- For how many nurseries and faith schools are you responsible? In which age-phases are they? Are you responsible for any joint or interfaith nurseries or schools?
- Do you have support mechanisms and/or informal education opportunities for those children and young people who do not attend full-time education in a faith community school?
- Do you require teachers in your schools to hold a specific qualification related to their faith?
- Have you undertaken, or are you currently undertaking, a national/local needs analysis of the viability of faith schools sponsored by your community?
- What funding arrangements does your community have in place to support your faith schools?
- Do you have higher education institutions within your community?
- Do your members have access to higher level study about their tradition?
- Are your members able to gain Qualified Teacher Status through accredited community institutions?
- Do you have partnerships with higher education institutions in this country and/or overseas for the benefit of teachers' professional development?
- Do you have national and/or local advisors working in your faith schools? Do these advisors parallel the work of local authority, DfES or special initiatives advisers?
- Does your community develop its own resources for use in your schools, for teachers, pupils, managers, governors?
- Do you have national and/or local resource centres for schools?
- Do you support local/national networks and associations of your schools, teachers and students?

In addition, each community, individual or cluster group of faith schools would evaluate their specific needs in CPPD for particular time periods, ranging from immediate one-off sets of academic term-specific programmes or consultancies to long-term strategic plans related to:

- Pre-service training of teachers, nursery assistants, classroom assistants, governors;
- CPPD needs analysis provision for all employees in faith schools;
- In-service induction for all teachers in faith schools and regular in-service support for school staff and governors in relation to community ethos, values and education for the personal, moral, spiritual and social development of pupils in the schools;
- Accredited in-service provision for specific curriculum post-holders, school leaders, classroom assistants and community and/or informal educators attached to the school or community;
- Learning resources development and distribution.

Strategies for supporting the CPPD of those involved in faith schools will inevitably involve a balance between responding to national and local educational initiatives, raising the question of to what extent we as a community, on the one hand, need to contribute something additionally to this new initiative and, on the other, to take part in the continuous support, guidance and research required to support the community's schools. Additionally, each community might choose to work independently of other providers or communities in some areas and collectively in others. Responses to the above questions would elicit a series of typologies of existing provision, raise questions about the levels of CPPD support necessary for faith school communities and provide a framework for discussion about strategic pooling of planning tools, personnel and teaching and learning resources.

For the present it is possible to identify three types of faith community in relation to their existing CPPD provision. There are those which are seemingly resource rich in relation to present CPPD provision, in terms of owning higher education institutions, having access to teacher training provision and holding together a network of support personnel and resource centres. There are those which are not rich in such institutional provision for the support of CPPD provision but are already committed to partnerships with state and secular pre- and in-service providers to support the continuing professional development needs of their teachers. Included in this type will be those communities which have traditionally relied on overseas institutions to offer higher-level religious studies but which are now anxious to enrich the knowledge status of their followers and teachers. There will be a further type which is resource poor in relation to CPPD provision, in terms of supporting their young people in state or faith schools, but anxious to give access to full-time education for those parents and children of their faith who see education as a means of protecting their identities and securing the handing on of knowledge in a stable environment.

As members of one of the major national providers of CPPD in the south east, the Institute of Education, University of London, entered into a number of partnerships with faith communities from each of the three types described above. In the resource-poor category, we looked to devising a strategy for building local expertise through relationships with overseas providers, offering consultancy services in terms of community planning and supporting small-scale research projects developed by our research students. In the middle category we were able to contribute to community planning exercises, working to put together a cascade model for building teacher training and resource and curriculum developers for the community across the world, build a strategic partnership with the newly developing community university and participate in conferences and workshops which were held regularly to update and upgrade the personnel who originally attended our specialist courses.

With the resource-rich community a partnership was established at a number of levels. On one level, the university department agreed a policy of interviewing all members of the community who applied for pre-service teacher training courses, master's level courses and research degrees. It also worked with the community to provide trial programmes for initiatives set up by the Teacher Training Agency and OFSTED, which eventually became free-standing community-based programmes. At master's level, students received scholarships to study at that level first in education and then in their own religious studies. At another level, we formed the nucleus for a research initiative which brought together scholars and students from across the world to examine the pedagogical and curriculum needs of that community's schools in Britain. Finally we added an additional dimension to a community which included several branches, each of which had its own resource centres and teachers. As a secular provider we were able to offer a safe and public space in which all the resources could be pooled and teachers and schools from across the community could benefit.

Each of these initiatives brought our secular institution into a rich and varied conversation with the faith communities involved. Yet, at their heart, all of our conversations were rooted in the following questions: 'What do we understand by education in our community?'; 'How might this be applicable in faith-based schools?'; How is it applicable in state community schools?'; 'How is it applicable in weekend or after-school settings?';

'What is its purpose in each of these settings?'; and ' What religious input and values can faith communities offer in terms of pedagogies and educational outcomes?' In other words, we as secular educators, in partnership with the faith communities, were sympathetic towards both the liberal educational agenda and to the faith tradition's agenda. That is also the nature of the dual system of full-time education in Britain. Faith schools are situated in a state system which through its funding, curriculum and assessment and inspection agencies already sets the agenda and standards for faith schools. It is of the utmost importance, therefore, that any discussion about the purposes and practices of faith schools is rooted in an education framework.

So we need now to ask what the minimum level of CPPD activity in faith schools would be which would support the schools in responding to those questions, which we originally developed with our colleagues from the faith communities, internally and in a wider public conversation.

To begin to answer this question it is profitable to consider how a faith school and its staff would tackle the following exercise as part of a CPPD initiative.

Faith schools speaking for themselves

The following extract is taken from an article (written by Stephen Pollard, who claimed he is 'not a Christian and thinks creationism is nonsense', 28 April 2003) which appeared in *The Times*:

> Imagine a school where 98 per cent of the pupils, not one of whom had been selected by academic ability, gained five or more A* to C passes at GCSE. With the average school managing to achieve these grades with only 52 per cent of pupils you'd think the school must be doing something right and it would be worth replicating. There is such a school in Gateshead. The people behind it should be lauded as heroes.
>
> Except that to many in the liberal establishment they are not heroes but villains because they are Christians who believe in creationism, and the literal truth of the Bible. Ignore for the moment Emmanuel's exam results. Ignore the fact they are a state school which teaches the National Curriculum. Ignore that it passes its OFSTED inspection with flying colours. Ignore that it is always heavily over-subscribed. And ignore that many of its pupils are Muslim.
>
> Just think about this. Is there a more narrow-minded group than the liberal secularists and the old Labour left who demand the abolition of such schools?

In a school-organised CPPD session, how would you and your colleagues set about responding to

1   Stephen Pollard
2   liberal secularists?

We raise these questions for our experience has shown that it is within such whole-school sessions that the acquired wisdom and intelligence of the school community can be retrieved and articulated. Morrison (2002:19) quoted by Wrigley (2003: 33) would agree for he writes:

> Schools are storehouses of distributed knowledge: it frequently governs the micro-politics of the organization …The collective memory of this institution is located

everywhere in it; there is then a need for careful storage, access to and retrieval of this collective memory. This respects the person-centredness of schools; all participants in the school can make a knowledge contribution to the school; leadership equates with dispersed, distributed leadership. The notion of distributed intelligence and information has huge implications, for it argues against hierarchical and bureaucratic command-and-control approaches to management and leadership and, instead, argues for the realization that systems are more fittingly conceived to be networks (just as the brain is a series of neural networks) – loosely coupled or more tightly coupled.

MacBeath (1999: 1) has warned us too that schools should not hand over this collective ability to evaluate and reflect on their aims and performance to outsiders:

> In healthy systems there is sharing and networking of good practice within and among schools on a collegial basis. It is an unhealthy system which relies on the constant routine attentions of an external body to police its schools ... In such a system there is an important role for an Inspectorate or Office of Standards to make itself as redundant as possible.

There is a very real need to foster then the kind of CPPD exercise outlined above. Inter- and intra-school discussion, reflection and evaluation can foster the continuous development of school staff in their professional lives as members of a faith-based institution; can prompt holistic school policies in relation to curriculum development and pedagogical practice; and facilitate schools in setting their own quality and standards in line with both national standards and the school's mission. Indeed, Grace (2002: 99) has argued that if the climate or culture of Catholic schools is to be better understood, then 'the concept of the self-researching school' will need to be developed. OFSTED inspections and PANDA (Performance and Assessment Data for Schools) data have inevitably and in many ways rightly focused schools on particular modes of identifying their school cultures and school outcomes for themselves and for those interested outside the school. Macbeath, on the other hand, has reminded us that self evaluation rather than external inspection creates a culture of understanding the interconnectedness of school life, as well as supporting a disposition to share information and network both within and across schools.

To encourage the conditions which would support each school in self evaluation and research there needs to be commitment from within and outside the school, both to the development of systems which can collect, retrieve and analyse data and be accessed and used by all the staff in the school, and to an articulation of the purposes of the school and their relation to individual pupils, teachers, curriculum areas and personal and social education. As Wrigley (2003: 7) has written:

> We have devoted such energy to developing a sophisticated knowledge of change management, planning, assessment, school cultures, leadership. Now, in this new century, the question is unavoidably – to what end is all this? Where is the vision?

Information systems, staff expertise in data analysis and each teacher committed to reflective self-evaluation are, however, not a substitute for fundamental questioning at strategic points in a school's planning about its aims and practices. They are supportive of it. If the schools see it as their responsibility to work in this way, then they will be ready and able to enter into the wider discussion about the place of faith schools in our plural and fragmented community.

Relating the culture of CPPD in faith schools to the wider educational and social culture

The wider educational culture

Wrigley (2003: 2–3) has reminded us that:

> It is over ten years now since Jean Rudduck said we should talk less about the management of change and more about the meaning of change. This neatly encapsulates much of the present difficulty. Improvement should be an ethical project, not just a technical one. This is frequently signalled by the use of words such as 'mission', 'vision', and 'values' in the (school improvement) literature, yet somehow a discourse has been constructed which hollows out these words.

The demand for improved educational standards has indeed led to an avalanche of change in our schools, not least through a heavy emphasis on targeted CPPD. Standards have been 'talked up', 'driven up' and re-established in a multifaceted series of initiatives and concentration on assessment through school improvement and the development of the effective and intelligent school. Nonetheless, perhaps the most striking feature of the culture of CPPD in the last five years has been a gradual realisation that the kind characterised as 'school improvement' must be subject to scrutiny and evaluation. Such a critique at its most searching can be clearly seen in the words of David Hamilton (1996: 55), in his review of Sammons, Hillman and Mortimore (1995) *Key Characteristics of Effective Schools* in *FORUM:*

> In short schools have become sick institutions. They are a threat to the health of the economic order. Their decline must be countered with potent remedies. Emergency and invasive treatment are called for. Schools need shock therapy administered by outside agencies. Terminal cases merit organ transplants (viz. new heads or governing bodies). And above all, each school requires targeted INSET therapy. Senior management teams deserve booster steroids to strengthen their macho leadership, while their rank and file colleagues should receive regular appraisal-administered HRT (human resource technology) to attenuate their classroom excesses.

Wrigley (ibid.: 35) highlights a further aspect of the school effectiveness initiatives which did not do justice to the complexities of school change. In writing about school cultures he has argued that they are highly contested and thus:

> School improvement cannot be understood by focusing on internal processes alone but require us to look at the interaction between internal and external cultures. The dominant ideas and values within a wider society, the principles which permeate the macro-political culture are not only transmitted downwards through a management hierarchy, but permeate our general consciousness as discourse, thus entering into our assumptive worlds … It is time for school improvement research to develop a more contextual and critical sense of the dynamism and contradictions of culture formation in schools. Whereas the dominant version sees cultural leadership as an homogenising force, effectively co-opting teachers into the government's view of successful schooling, creative and responsive school development requires a vision forged out of the many voices of staff, students and communities.

Faith schools cannot afford to ignore the social and political culture in which they are placed and which are the home of their parents, teachers, students and governors. At the same time, now that some of the dominant motifs in improving schools and their standards through CPPD have been challenged, it is worthwhile to ask whether there are certain conditions which might be promoted in faith schools which ensure that the purpose of school development lies not wholly in central government's hands but in 'the many voices of staff, students and communities'? In raising the question we might take very seriously the comment of one researcher into faith schools, Treston (1997: 15), who pointed out that: 'The dissonance between the official rhetoric about Catholic schools and the world views of students and parents (and some staff) is a very serious issue confronting the movement to authenticate Catholic schools.'

Here we are alerted to the dilemma faced by faith schools: for whom and to whom do they speak? They are responsible to their faith community sponsors, as well as to the wider community which supports them financially. Without adequate evidence from within and across similar schools, they have little but anecdotal evidence to add to that of official league tables, OFSTED and Adult Learning Inspectorate (ALI) reports. Just as crucially, they are dependent on such external means of describing and explaining themselves when faced with asking basic questions about how they use such external data to inform their own missions, pedagogies, learning outcomes and overall impact on the lives, beliefs and values of their pupils.

We might well therefore refer to the work of Gerald Grace (1995: Chapter 9) as one possible response to our question. He sets out the results of his research with Catholic head teachers, who voice their understanding of their moral and spiritual leadership but say that they are often unprepared for working with moral and spiritual issues in the contemporary world. In a later book, Grace (2002) sets out his research with Catholic schools in which he argues that Catholic leaders face fundamental conflicts between the commitments of their distinctive educational mission and current educational cultural requirements for school 'success', 'effectiveness' and survival. Again, as in the 1995 research, Grace clearly defines the management-leadership dilemma experienced in a range of schools.

The wider social culture

It is incumbent, however, for those who support and work in faith schools to find means of engaging in a conversation explaining (and justifying?) what they are about. To do this they will wish to take into account the culture and society in which they work. Varieties of labels have been used to characterise our present culture, ranging from post-Christian through to secular, from post-modern to post-secular and from multi-faith to plural. Certainly it is a time of uncertainty in a whole spectrum of human affairs, not least in how to handle personal and communal faith. Some years ago Clifford Longley (1995: xiii), as a shrewd commentator on religious affairs, wrote very directly about such matters:

> Democracy will have to outgrow its silly habit of rejecting all that is old and wise simply because it is not new and startling. All those with something to offer the moral debate will have to be allowed, and, if necessary, invited to put their contribution forward. The faith communities in Britain, including the Christian churches, the Jewish community, and the religions of the sub-continent now amply represented among us, will have to be treated not as anachronisms but as among our most vital national assets. They are our spiritual gold reserves.

Stewart Sutherland (Sacks and Sutherland 1996: 38) put the present predicament succinctly when he argued that there are three 'faultlines' running through our society. These are 'cultural pluralism, fragmentation of knowledge and moral atomism which has followed from this'.

This very brief and inadequate outline of the cultural map which forms the backcloth for how decisions are taken about the purpose of education, the role of religion within it and its support for the place of individual identities in promoting the moral, physical, spiritual and social development of our young people suggests a very particular task for CPPD and research within faith schools and faith communities.

In order to establish this particular task, we need to set our reflection within the political context in which the continuing survival and expansion of faith schooling is being allowed to take place. In a speech made shortly before his government came to power, Tony Blair (1996), as a committed communitarian, argued in Southwark Cathedral:

> People increasingly recognize that to move forward as individuals we need to move forward as a community ... We are social beings, nurtured in families and communities and human only because we develop the moral power of personal responsibility for ourselves and for each other. Britain is simply stronger as a team than as a collection of selfish players.

How do communities support individuals 'to move forward'? How can human beings flourish, to pose a further question set by Stewart Sutherland, in a time of 'cultural pluralism, the fragmentation of knowledge and moral atomism'? Since all schools face the same questions and challenges, in what ways might faith schools differ in the way they respond?

Excavating the culture and identity of the faith school through CPPD

In 1988, the then Archbishop of Canterbury wrote:

> Church schools are as concerned as any other school to equip pupils for lives marked by rapid change, global competition and insecurity. But church schools know in their viscera that this is not just about acquiring skills and good examination results ... It is about forming people who, however academically and technically skilful, are not reduced to inarticulate embarrassment by the great questions of life and death, meaning and truth. Church schools themselves embody the truth that a context of firm principles suffused by faith and love is the best and right basis for learning and growing.
>
> (1988: 9–10)

The *Way Ahead* publication of the Archbishops' Council (Church of England) Church Schools Review Group (2001: 15) upheld this argument for the differences between church schools and others and refers to one diocese which sees as the aspiration of all schools that Christian values will 'run through every area of school life as the writing runs through a stick of rock'. Further, taking up the communitarian theme echoed in Tony Blair's words, the Jesuit general superior, Fr Arrupe (1994: 32), in addressing alumni of Jesuit schools, said:

Today our prime educational objective must be to form men and women for others: men and women who cannot even conceive of love of God which does not include love for the least of their neighbours; men and women completely convinced that love of God which does not issue in justice for men and women is a farce.

The director of the Scottish Catholic Education Service, Michael McGrath, recently emphasised in addition to the above that a distinctive Catholic philosophy of education 'can only be fully delivered by teachers who are themselves committed to it' (*The Times*, 14 November 2003). This emphasis is important; a mission which involves religious, spiritual and moral values must involve a particular kind of teacher. For he argues: 'Catholic schooling involves developing Catholic values, religious education, spiritual and moral formation and a commitment to serve the common good, all within a supportive climate that affirms the life and dignity of every person.'

Within the United Kingdom (UK), the thinking of Professor Ali Ashraf about Muslim education has been seminal. One of his major concerns has been that western liberal education is at heart both secular and undermining of religion. In his work, particularly at Cambridge and in conjunction with the eminent liberal philosopher of education, Paul Hirst, he set about exploring the significant relationship between religious values and the aims, purpose and organisation of education. He thus established a particularly fruitful pathway for genuine discussion about the nature of Islamic, and indeed other faith, education, within a state-supported education system. Further, within that particular pathway, in an article entitled, 'Post-modern education and the missing dimension', M. Bari (2000: 46) a local education adviser, argues that he sees the main objective of education in most western countries as 'creating citizens of a successful democratic society', whereas the alternate Islamic aim is to familiarise the individual with a number of concepts, which he lists as:

- Responsibility in life
- Relationship to other creatures
- Responsibility to the human community
- Social relations
- Relationship to the universe and universal phenomena and to the exploration of natural laws in order to utilise and exploit them
- God's creative wisdom apparent in creation.

In conclusion he (ibid.: 48) makes the case that 'all subject areas could be re-shaped with the principle at their core that human beings are to be responsible managers of the earth and its belongings ... Only a moral framework in the school environment can produce generations of people bonded together with purpose and a sense of responsibility.'

Since educational activity has as its central purpose the development of human beings, then it demands a moral framework for all of its activities. What is important is that the whole school, including the leaders, the teachers and the parents, are aware of the particular moral framework employed by the school and the part which it plays in the school life of each of these groups. To return to a theme already underlined in this chapter, Wrigley (2001) wrote in an Editorial following 11 September 2001:

Much of the high level government interest in school improvement has led to an intensification of teaching, accountability, league tables, teachers feeling deprofessionalized and disenchanted (or leaving), a relentless drive for more though not always better – and silence on the question of educational purpose. What really matters: new targets to meet? Higher maths grades perhaps? Or caring and creative learners, a future, a sense of justice, the welfare of the planet and its people?

The moral purpose of the school and its consequences need careful examination and evaluation through CPPD. For use in such work, it will be helpful to make the distinction about which Richard Pring (1984: 21) has written:

> It would seem important therefore to distinguish between those qualities which are essential to development *as a person* and those qualities and powers which, however important they seem to us, are not essential but depend upon particular values which some people hold but many certainly don't ... There are qualities that are important because they are intimately connected with what we mean by someone being a person, and there are qualities which we cherish because of specific values which we hold.

Pring (1984: 23–4) then breaks down the different kinds of values and knowledge which are relevant to 'this or that sort of person' in order to search out the implications for the curriculum of the distinction which he has drawn. These fall into:

- Intellectual virtues (for example, 'concern for getting at the truth').
- Moral virtues (for example, 'dispositions such as modesty, kindness, generosity, which govern the emotion').
- Character traits (for example, 'those qualities of the will such as perseverance or courage).
- Social competencies (for example, 'the ability to deal with certain kinds of social situation ... but it could also include basic good manners').
- Practical knowledge ('No doubt a particular kind of school ethos, de-valuing practical know-how and skills will generate the sort of expectancies which will push children in a particular direction').
- Theoretical knowledge (for example, 'religious or political concepts and understandings', since 'being a person presupposes some developed form of consciousness').
- Personal values (for example, 'the value of pacifism' or 'the value of private property').

In judging my personal role as a teacher and the institutional role of the school in working with and developing the personal values of each student, there will need to be a consideration of what is understood by the autonomy of each pupil by the school. Questions such as, 'What is the moral tradition and content on offer in our school by which our pupils judge what is right and wrong?' and, 'To what extent and in what ways are our pupils encouraged to set out to each other and the school what their values are?' and, 'What other traditions and sets of values, apart from those commended by my school, do I use in order to make up my own mind about my own values?'

In short, schools will wish to know for themselves how each teacher individually and the school collectively responds, with real knowledge and understanding of their own students and the school's own culture, to those questions posed by Stewart Sutherland (Sacks and Sutherland 1996: 48):

- What are the conditions of human flourishing?
- What are the conditions of flourishing within a pluralistic society?

What should faith schools speak out about to the wider community?

Any debate about the nature and outcomes of faith schooling is extremely limited in Britain due to a lack of national research projects related to faith schools and an absence of faith community interpretations of data sets held at national level by the DfES and OFSTED. The result is that much of the precise and specific work of faith schools is ignored and through a lack of information faith schools themselves are ill equipped to take part in informed debates about the aims and practices of education at the national and international level. In his book, *The Reflective Practitioner: How Professionals Think in Action*, Schon (1983) argues decisively for the importance of professionals reflecting on their practice. Only from this, he says, can real professional growth and development take place. Faith schools, therefore, despite the lack of national research about them, must not abdicate their responsibility to promote the professional growth of their staff and provide worthwhile information to their parents and governors and the wider community. This theme is taken up by Catherine Lacey (1996: 259): 'Teachers begin the process of creating rather than reproducing culture when they bring their own professional knowledge into articulate form and interpret its meaning with others in a community of inquiry.'

The values and priorities which shape our faith schools and their purposes require exposure, particularly at this time of uncertainty and instability in our wider culture, and it is the teachers and managers in them who will be the first-line exponents of their particularities and outcomes.

Equally, if faith schools are to encourage children and young people to participate in an environment which takes faith and the spiritual seriously at a time of increasing plurality, instability and growth in knowledge, it follows that teachers in those schools will need time to consider their own role in that process. Encouragement in this form of reflection has several consequences at this time of increasing responsibilities for teachers in all classrooms in terms of curriculum and assessment changes, inclusion matters and continuous demands on their ongoing professional development in relation to professional accountability and their personal concerns for promotion.

In particular, teachers in faith schools will need both to be aware and to make each other and the wider community aware of the specific conditions in which they teach their curriculum areas and act as tutors, subject heads and managers in faith schools. Some of these conditions will be related to the explicit mission statement of their school; others will be innate to the 'hidden' or implicit curriculum embedded in their school. How do these impact on their ways of working with their pupils in terms of pedagogy, advice and guidance and professional expectations? In what ways do their professional ethics overlay, interplay and underplay the ethics of belief at work in the school? For, as Hobson and Edwards (1999: 85) argue:

> Principles and values from an ethics of belief complement democratic values to provide ethical and epistemological norms which should inform the teaching of religion and act as a guide to how religious differences should be handled in the curriculum.

Is a faith school working with or towards a particular theological understanding of education? Or is it working in a post-modern, plural and post-secular environment with an uncertainty of how best to proceed but willing to experiment with models of school cultures which can embrace and support the diversity of teachers, pupils and parents as they seek to educate the young for an uncertain future? Which are the points in school life and culture where faith and education meet?

Thus CPPD in faith schools, in order to be able to speak out to the wider community, might set an agenda from the above discussion which might include some or all of the following.

The mission and culture of the faith school

Although the aims for state-funded education have now been set out purposefully in the 'Introduction' to the National Curriculum (DfEE 1999), each school is encouraged through its mission statement to set out its own identity in the spectrum of schools participating in state education. There is the opportunity for each to set the school's prime purpose of educating the child or young person within a particular spectrum of values and traditions (the school culture) within which the pupil's interest and achievement in learning is rooted. Some faith schools would not divert too far from the reference given in Wrigley (ibid.: 6) quoting Francis Bacon, who saw knowledge as 'a rich storehouse, for the glory of the Creator and the relief of man's estate'. At its best a school mission can articulate, for those both in and outside the school, the wider purposes it sets for education and the traditions, practices and values through which it seeks to achieve its aims.

Sammons *et al.* (1995) identified 'shared visions and goals' as one of the key characteristics of effective schools. Yet in some ways, the emphasis placed on effectiveness and school improvement over the last 10 years or so has led to a diminution of the importance of clarity in aims and values in each school. Comments can be found in recent research literature, published by authors such as Morley, Macbeath and Wrigley, of the kind found in Slee and Weiner (1998: 111): 'Effective schooling and the school improvement movement is blind to a searching interrogation of outcome. Test scores become ends ... Explicit discussions of values and the types of society to which schools articulate/adhere are ignored.'

There are as many school mission statements as there are faith schools but in some way, no doubt, all will reflect some of the ideals and vision encompassed in the ethos statement offered recently to all Church of England schools (Archbishops' Council 2001: 14), although using language and terms apposite to each faith:

> The school will preserve and develop its religious character in accordance with the principles of the Church at parish and diocesan level.
>
> The school aims to serve its community by providing education of the highest quality within the context of Christian belief and practice. It encourages an understanding of the meaning and significance of faith and promotes Christian values through the experience it offers all its pupils.

Each school within its own faith tradition will reflect on the impact of its promotion of the spiritual development of the young people in its care and develop sensitive ways of evaluating its work. There is little doubt that such activities within the context of CPPD will increasingly involve the trialling of new forms of pedagogy, thus bringing together the mission, faith base and learning of the school into greater coherence.

Also as a result of the complexities of each faith school's culture and ethos as well as the wide variation in each school's educational practices it is important that each school is able to describe, reflect upon and evaluate the following constituents of its ethos and practice and how these impact upon the pupils' development and learning:

The spiritual

Andrew Wright (1998: 97–8) writes persuasively about the difficulties facing schools as they fulfil their duty to promote the spiritual development of their pupils, arguing that:

> Since there is no universal understanding of the nature of spirituality ... it becomes the responsibility of the school to make decisions regarding the spiritual tradition that informs the whole curriculum. A school with spiritual integrity must take this responsibility seriously.

In some non-faith school spiritual education, the emphasis has been to employ those areas of the curriculum and school communal life which the school judges to help children and young people find and make meaning in their lives. 'Purposeful humanistic concern' can possibly be best used to characterise this form of curriculum implementation. In other schools, the spiritual is centred on a particular faith tradition, with its accompanying rituals and practices which seek to engage the learner in perceiving the world through this particular spiritual dimension. School teachers and leaders will wish for time to reflect upon and evaluate in which part of such a spectrum their individual classroom and tutorial activities place them and whether these align with the school's mission in this area. Those involved with citizenship education will no doubt wish to discuss this question in the light of the further opportunities afforded the school for promoting the spiritual and values development of their pupils, since the QCA (1999) stated that citizenship education provides opportunities for: 'spiritual development, through fostering pupil's awareness and understanding of meaning and purpose in life and of differing values in human society'.

Who am I that educates?

The faith school teacher and leader might also wish to reflect on the above question posed during a discussion on spirituality and religious education by Colleen Griffith (2003: 60). The professional competences and standards of teachers and their individual curriculum areas have been established with varying degrees of rigour over the last few years. Teachers in faith schools will wish for the opportunity to reflect on how their own story in the profession and in a particular faith school have been influenced by such developments and whether these are adequate either to their experience or in some cases (cf. the head teachers in Gerald Grace's research) predicament. The fundamental questions would seem to be, 'To what extent am I as a teacher a learner?' and 'To what extent am I influenced by the faith tradition in whose school I work?'

Listening to the student voice

We need mechanisms to know and understand who our pupils are and how they perceive themselves at particular times. We need also to find a way of accepting each pupil as a whole person against the concept which lies at the heart of the developmental theories which have underpinned much of our curricular thinking, namely that young people are 'becoming' and 'developing' rather than 'being'.

It is important as well that we make these efforts to know our students' voices so that we can actively pursue in our classrooms the concept of school as a 'community of persons' which is set out in *The Way Ahead* (Archbishops' Council 2001: 15) when it quotes the Archbishop of York as saying:

To stress that the school is a community of persons is to emphasise relationships: the personal is thus prior to the institutional; the institutional exists not for its own sake but purely for the purpose of nurturing and sustaining the relationships of the persons who comprise any particular community or organization.

Knowing our pupils as individual persons, whatever their ethnicity or belief system, answers Richard Pring's concern (1984: 30), too, when he says:

> To teach without coming to grips with how the learner understands things, or to provide a particular course of studies without relating it to the students' consuming interests, would be to impose a system of ideas or a set of values that disrespect the learner as a person ... as someone with a conscious view of things and of what is of value.

The school as community

James Coleman (2001: 90–2) develops the concept of social capital alongside human, economic, etc. He argues that all social relations and social structures facilitate some forms of social capital but certain kinds of social structure are, however, particularly important in facilitating some forms of social capital; the school is one of them. Since he argues that organisational and intergenerational relationships (as, for example, those found in faith schools), have unexpected consequences, it is profitable to ask whether different forms of human capital emerge in a faith school as opposed to a non-faith school.

For this reason, and the better to diagnose the holistic or fragmented nature of their schools, CPPD sessions may seek to work towards a methodology, through, perhaps, the use of a template which can be the basis for an examination of the content and impact of the culture of faith schools. The following such template was introduced by Susan Shevitz of Brandeis University and based upon the definition of culture by Edgar Schein (1992) to teachers from faith schools, supplementary schools and informal education activities in the RESQUJE (Research for Quality in Jewish Education) unit of the Institute of Education and involved collective sessions of staff working on each area in relation to their own circumstances:

Learned responses to external survival issues
- Shared definition of tasks, mission and strategy
- Shared goals and definitions of success and failure
- Shared sense of how to accomplish goals
- Shared measurement systems to detect errors or problems
- Shared sense of means to correct error.

Learned responses to the problems of internal integration
- Shared language and concepts
- Shared definition of group boundaries
- Shared criteria for acquiring status and power
- Shared rules of face and intimacy
- Shared criteria for rewards and punishment
- Shared ideology and looking at the world.

Higher order abstractions, which are shared assumptions about
- The nature of reality
- The nature of truth
- The nature of human nature
- The nature of human activity and purpose
- The nature of human relations and the role of schooling.

Working together on such a template would permit shared conversations within each school as well as conversations across schools. It would also contribute to an analysis by each faith community's Section 24 inspectors of the critical factors that contribute to an understanding of how a school's culture contributes to the spiritual, moral, social and cultural elements of a pupil's development and help to identify the types of evidence required in these areas to make judgements.

An education in faith: religious education and citizenship education

It is important for the wider community to know from faith schools what the school understands a faith education to be. RE is the only formal curriculum area in which the state, in its Education Acts (1988, 1992 and 1996), has opted out of formal responsibility. There are a wide variety of practices in RE. In some Christian schools, for example, distinctions are made between 'formative' and 'critical' RE. Jeff Astley (1994: 84–107) provides a most informative commentary on this debate. It will suffice here simply to adopt the position of McKenzie towards this distinction, which is quoted by Astley (1994: 84):

> McKenzie concentrates on cognitive learning outcomes and distinguishes within that category between those that result from formative education and those that are the products of critical education ... He places knowledge (as measured by recall), comprehension, application of learning in the category of formative learning outcomes. Critical education, McKenzie claims, results in analysis and synthesis of what has been taught, and its evaluation using internal evidence and external criteria.

Astley (1994: 89) also provides a helpful summary of what he calls 'political critical religious education'. Here educators adopt Freire's rejection of the 'banking' model of education which is seen as the most passive form of a formative education. They adopt instead Freire's 'problem solving' which strives for 'the emergence of critical conscience or conscientization, involving reflection on the learner's own historical experience', which leads to action in the community by the learner. A faith school would, no doubt, wish to articulate how its religious education curriculum chimed with its mission and its moral framework for the purposeful development of human beings. The values which schools wish to promote and the means by which they seek to educate for values development are increasingly set within centralised government initiatives. As Leslie Francis (2001: 12) has commented: 'The question of values has remained at the centre of government initiatives to regenerate aspects of the education system for the twenty-first century.'

Francis points specifically to two examples of this: drug education and sex education. It is precisely in such areas that each school, faith or otherwise, will wish to establish and clarify its own policies for the better understanding of its teachers, pupils and parents. In a similar way, the school would wish to set out its compliance with the curriculum for citizenship education.

McLaughlin has argued (1995: 244) that if society is to educate for citizenship what is needed is a wide-ranging and informed national debate to establish some degree of agreement about 'public virtues', the 'common good' and citizenship. Faith schools must take a real part in this debate because if faith schools see their mission to be that of developing a particular kind of person and conducting education in such a way that their pupils have the opportunity to live out a particular set of values and ideals in the community of the school, then the wider public needs to know what kinds of people are valued by particular faiths. The public also needs to know whether such schools are successful in influencing the intellectual, spiritual and values development of their pupils and to what extent faith schools look to their graduating pupils ultimately to be responsible for and autonomous in their choice of life stance and its accompanying values. Since McLaughlin's comments the citizenship curriculum has been introduced into schools but the debate continues as to what constitutes 'public virtues' and the common good. As a result, it is crucial that faith schools are able to evaluate the contribution of their own thinking and mission on the development of the values and attitudes of their pupils and to assess the amount of freedom which the pupils believe they have in making up their own minds on such contested questions.

Conclusion

The question must be raised as to what the optimum conditions are in which ongoing personal and professional development of the kind outlined here can take place. Muriel Robinson (2002: 154) speaks of the need for a 'flexible programme of renewal for all staff, with short courses and study opportunities (including action learning and school-based research)'. She adds that for the (Catholic) faith school it should be the normal part of the 'school development plan to include in-service for all staff in the central area' of religious studies and faith schools, which links with award-bearing work and 'which values the achievement of colleagues who undertake such awards and the contribution they can make to school-based professional development'.

Along with many of us who have worked with faith schools and faith communities in CPPD, Robinson emphasises the need for any such programmes and courses to be centred on action learning and school-based research. In this way, teachers working in faith schools will be able both fully to reflect on and make explicit the tacit knowledge which they are acquiring daily in teaching and learning in a sector whose boundaries are fluid and permeable as a result of its situation within the wider national compulsory educational context, yet built on long-standing and revered traditions. There will also need to be discussion with the DfES and faith sponsoring bodies about funding for an important mixture of CPPD activities other than accredited courses in order to develop and support networks of schools, teachers, parents and governors from within each faith community and across faith communities. These might take the form of workshops, conferences, websites and other internet links. A further question to be discussed at a national level will be concerned with which authorities will oversee the quality and standards of such provision.

The expectation is that from such focused school-based work in CPPD, individual teachers, leaders, faith schools and faith communities sponsoring state-aided schools will be able to contribute to an informed discussion and evaluation of the work of faith schools in their mission, culture and outcomes in our present plural and possibly post-secular society. This chapter has argued that such a discussion can only take place if it is rooted in the following principles and values: a concern at all times to question and articulate the role of faith in education within a liberal democratic, plural and, possibly, post-secular framework; a commitment by each school and the wider community to articulate the kinds of human beings which they are seeking to develop through education, in addition to setting targets for attainment in tests and examinations for them; and continuing school- and community-based research, supported in future by independent and nationally sponsored long-term research projects, to evaluate the consequences and impact of faith-based practices and cultures in education on social, economic and cultural patterns in society and the academic and values development of children and young people and their families.

References

Archbishop of Canterbury (1988) 'The importance of church schools', in *A Christian Voice in Education: Distinctiveness in Church Schools*, London: The National Society.

Archbishops' Council (Church of England) Church Schools Review Group (2001) *The Way Ahead*, London: Church house Publishing.

Arrupe, Fr (1994) 'Men for others', in C. Melrose (ed.) *Foundations*, Washington, DC: The Jesuit Secondary Education Association.

Astley, J. (1994) *The Philosophy of Christian Religious Education*, Birmingham, AL: Religious Education Press.

Bari, M. (2000) 'Post-modern education and the missing dimension', in *Muslim Education Quarterly*, 17(2): 45–6.

Beckett, F. (2003) *The Guardian*, 14 October.

Blair, A. (1996) 'Faith in the city – ten years on', lecture in Southwark Cathedral, 29 January.

Busher, H. (2001) 'The micro-politics of change, improvement and effectiveness in schools', in A. Harris and N. Bennett (eds) *School Effectiveness and School Improvement: Alternative Perspectives*, London: Continuum.

Coleman, J. (2001) 'Social capital in the creation of human capital', in A.H. Halsey, H. Lauder, P. Brown and A.S. Wells (eds) *Education: Culture, Economy and Society*, Oxford: Oxford University Press.

DfEE (1999) 'Introduction', *National Curriculum Review*, London: DfEE.

DfEE and QCA (1999) *The National Curriculum: Handbook for Primary Teachers in England, Key Stages 1 and 2*, Norwich: HMSO

DfES (2001) *Schools Achieving Success*, White Paper, Norwich: HMSO.

Francis, L.J. (2001) *The Values Debate: A Voice from the Pupils*, London: Woburn Press.

Grace, G. (1995) *School Leadership: Beyond Education Management*, London: Falmer Press.

Grace, G. (2002) *Catholic Schools: Mission, Markets and Morality*, London: RoutledgeFalmer.

Grace, G. (2003) *The Guardian*, 8 November.

Griffith, C. (2003) 'Spirituality and religious education: fostering a closer connection', in T.H. Groome and H.D. Horell (eds) *Horizons and Hopes: The Future of Religious Education*, Mahwah, NJ: Paulist Press.

Hamilton, D. (1996) Book review in *FORUM*, 38(2): 54–6.

Hobson, P.R. and Edwards, J.S. (1999) *Religious Education in a Pluralist Society*, London: Woburn Press.

Lacey, C. (1996) 'Renewing teaching: building professional communities of hope and inquiry', in T.H. McLaughlin, J. O'Keefe and B. O'Keeffe (eds) *The Contemporary Catholic School*, London, Falmer Press.

Longley, C. 'Introduction', in J. Sacks (1995) *Faith in the Future*, London: Darton, Longman and Todd.

MacBeath, J. (1999) *Schools Must Speak for Themselves: The Case for School Self-Evaluation*, London: RoutledgeFalmer.

McGrath, M. (2003) *The Times*, 14 November.

McLaughlin, T.H. (1995) ' Liberalism, education and the common school', *Journal of the Philosophy of Education* 29(2): 239–55.

McLaughlin, T.H., O'Keefe, J. and O'Keeffe, B. (eds) (1996) *The Contemporary Catholic School*, London: Falmer Press.

Morrison, K. (2002) *School Leadership and Complexity Theory*, London: RoutledgeFalmer.

Pollard, S. (2003) *The Times*, 28 April.

Pring, R. (1984) *Personal and Social Education in the Curriculum*, London: Hodder and Stoughton.

QCA (1999) *Citizenship: The National Curriculum for England*, London: DfEE and QCA.

Robinson, M. (2002) 'Continuing professional development', in M.A. Hayes and L. Gearon (eds) *Contemporary Catholic Education*, Leominster: Gracewing.

Sacks, J. and Sutherland, S. (1996) *Education, Values and Religion* (Victor Cook Memorial Lectures), St Andrews: St Andrews University Press.

Sammons, P., Hillman, D. and Mortimore, P. (1995) *Key Characteristics of Effective Schools: A Review of School Effectiveness Research*, London: OFSTED.

Schein, E. (1992) *Organizational Culture and Leadership*, 2nd edn, San Francisco, CA: Jossey-Bass.

Schon, D. (1983) *The Reflective Practitioner: How Professionals Think in Action*, New York: Basic Books.

Slee, R. and Weiner, G. (eds) (1998) *School Effectiveness for Whom? Challenges to the School Effectiveness and School Improvement Movements*, London: Falmer Press.

Sullivan, J. (2002) 'Leadership and management', in M.A. Hayes and L. Gearon (eds) *Contemporary Catholic Education*, Leominster: Gracewing.

Treston, K. (1997) 'Ethos and identity: foundational concerns for Catholic schools', in R. Keane and D. Riley (eds) *Quality Catholic Schools*, Brisbane: Catholic Education Office.

Wright, A. (1998) *Spiritual Pedagogy*, Abingdon: Culham College Institute.

Wrigley, T. (2001) 'Editorial', *Improving Schools*, Autumn.

Wrigley, T. (2003) *Schools of Hope*, Stoke on Trent: Trentham Books.

21 Faith schools

Some political issues and an agenda for research

Denis Lawton and Jo Cairns

In 1992 John Smith took over from Neil Kinnock as Leader of the Labour Party. In 1994 Smith died and Tony Blair was elected Leader. It may well be that either Kinnock or Smith would have led the Labour Party into a very different future after the 1997 General Election. All three Leaders were of the ethical socialist kind rather than belonging to the economic efficiency wing of the Party. Blair was a member of the Christian Socialist group but he wanted to modernise the Party in such a way as both to make it more electable, appealing to the middle classes, and to produce a country that would be more competitive internationally. He wanted to combine both ethics and efficiency. His support for faith schools has two motives. First, he believes that they provide a moral and religious basis for the young that most state schools do not; second, he believes that faith schools generally are likely to be more effective academically than 'bog standard' comprehensive schools. (That unfortunate phrase was not used by Blair himself but by his press officer; Blair seems, however, to share the opinion that the typical comprehensive school is likely to be sub-standard.)

In the period from 1994 to the Election in 1997, there were several important changes in Labour Party education policies that affected not only the Party but also the whole of the country. First, comprehensive schools would be 'modernised'; second, selection of various kinds would be quietly encouraged. Grammar schools were not to be abolished without local ballots of a kind that were almost impossible to organise; specialist schools would be encouraged; and faith schools would also be supported in general, and for minority faiths in particular. Specialist schools and faith schools were seen by many educationists as a form of selection, even if only by schools interviewing parents. Faith schools were also increasingly seen by parents as a superior tier of the secondary school system.

All of this was opposed by 'old Labour' members who complained that the comprehensive 'modernisation' was a betrayal of Labour values, and that the modernisation process involving specialist and faith schools was really developing into a completely different secondary education policy. The Blair line on faith schools was a major shift in British politics. Traditionally, the Labour Party, like the Liberal Party before it, was in favour of secular state education, in contrast to the nineteenth-century Conservative Party view that the state should keep out of education as much as possible and leave schools to religious bodies, preferably Church of England. That tradition of opposing support for denominational schools was sometimes uncomfortable for the Labour Party, especially in those constituencies where there were large numbers of Roman Catholic voters who might argue that if public money could be spent on Church of England schools, why should the same principle not apply to Roman Catholic institutions?

This contradiction has resulted in the official Labour Party line becoming one of reluctant acceptance of the dual system. Many prominent Labour Party members retained a strong preference for a policy of secular schools, but after the 1944 Education Act it ceased to be a major controversy within the Labour Party. This minor division of opinion within Labour, however, was quite different from what developed into the New Labour policy of encouraging all kinds of communities (for example, Islamic groups, Sikhs, Hindus, as well as evangelical Christians) not only to be on a level footing with Church of England schools but also to regard faith schools as intrinsically superior to state comprehensive schools.

This added a new dimension to the faith schools debate at the beginning of the new millennium. The superiority claim was, of course, disputed, and it was soon alleged that there was little evidence to support the assertion that faith schools should be encouraged because they were academically more successful. (When social class and other variables were taken into account, the difference was very small and not statistically significant.) This did not prevent Blair from persisting with his policy. The political twist to the faith school narrative further complicated an already complex set of arguments about education in England. Many had assumed that faith schools would eventually fade away in an increasingly secularised society, or would at least remain unobtrusive within the complex English education system. Instead, faith schools have become a major area of debate for a variety of reasons.

It may be useful to summarise the issues at this stage. First, in a multicultural, multifaith society, would it be better for the state to keep out of any religious issues in education? Or, could it be argued that it is part of every future citizen's essential education to learn something about the Christian faith and to respect and tolerate alternative faiths? A second issue is the Roy Hattersley question: how can the state refuse to grant faith school maintained status to Islamic schools when Church of England and other denominations have a well-established right to run their own schools? On the other hand, it has been argued that whereas Church of England schools are firmly part of English culture and Roman Catholics have, even if only in the last century, become acceptable to British society, with the Roman Catholic churches no longer being regarded as a permanent threat to the English state, the same acceptance could not be guaranteed for some groups who might now wish to assert their claim to have a right to have faith schools on the same basis as Church of England and Roman Catholic schools.

This argument is not simply British ethno-centrism; there is a serious cultural point here that might have been thought out before the gates of maintained status were opened apparently to any religious group that wanted to establish their own schools. First of all, there are problems of definition. Some years ago there was litigation in the courts about whether Scientology should be accepted for charitable purposes as a religion. It was difficult to define what was meant by 'religion'. (The case for Scientology failed but it was not totally conclusive.) Would we be happy if such organisations claimed the right to establish a faith school? Where to draw the line could be a serious difficulty for a liberal society. Democratic states sometimes have to guard against the illiberalism of others, including some of its own parents. There is an even more problematic area. Church of England, Roman Catholic and Jewish schools have been accepted in a largely secular society because they now share the dominant form of the rationality of the host community – that is a form of reasoning which respects evidence, including scientific evidence, as extremely important. That form of rationality does not rule out 'faith' (that is, a belief which does not rely on evidence) but allows for, and tolerates, different interpretations of such evidence as sacred texts (the Bible). (It was not always so, of course; the Reformation and religious wars of the fifteenth, sixteenth and seventeenth centuries did involve different attitudes to the Bible, but such differences were eventually superseded by a common acceptance of scientific rationality – the Enlightenment.) Today the important difference between societies and religious groups is not between religious and secularised belief systems but between rationally maintained faith and tolerance on the one hand, and fundamentalist intolerance on the other.

Many English non-believers would happily accept the subsidising of Roman Catholic schools and even admit that there might be evidence which indicated that some of these schools did give something extra to its students, over and above the academic curriculum. But the same sceptics would be unwilling for the state to subsidise a school which teaches (or even indoctrinates) its pupils into 'creationist science', denying them any understanding of Darwin's theory of evolution. There was a scandal on precisely that issue in 2000–2 which was not resolved to everyone's satisfaction.

So, how would the New Labour government respond to a request from a Christian sect that was sufficiently 'fundamentalist' to want to deviate from National Curriculum science in that way? Would this count as 'modernisation'? Or how would the Department for Education and Skills (DfES) deal with an Islamic school that denied the importance of science as part of a pupil's entitlement to an understanding of the world? The clash is not simply one of beliefs about evidence and rationality, it is a clash between the parents' rights to educate their children in the way that they want (even if that is mis-education) and the state's right to insist on certain educational entitlements for every future citizen.

The state permits parents a good deal of discretion in how to bring up their children but parents' rights in this respect are by no means absolute. Limitations include, for example, the right of the state to intervene on questions of health: for example, in the case of Plymouth Brethren parents who refuse to give consent for a vital operation. But should the Plymouth Brethren be allowed to run their own schools? Similarly, some minority groups would like to practise female circumcision, but this is forbidden by the state. Should such groups be allowed to run their own schools? Freedom includes the right to educate but is not absolute. The state has a duty to intervene where necessary. This was one of the justifications for the National Curriculum – that is, the 'entitlement of the child' argument.

The state recognises parents' rights but also recognises the need to limit those rights. The suggestion that any group of parents has a right to set up their own school could be a dangerous step away from the protection of children's rights. Future citizens sometimes take precedence over the wishes of the parents – hence compulsory schooling between the ages of five and 16. Most democratic societies have taken on the responsibility for educating the young, including inspecting schools to ensure that children are not mis-educated. This task becomes more difficult where there are schools run by groups who do not share important aspects of the mainstream national culture.

We are now committed not only to the dual system but to an extension of it. A few of the problems have been outlined here if the faith school idea is stretched too far. It is almost certainly true that Blair has not considered all the possible difficulties. They may not be insuperable but they should have been carefully considered before so many promises were made. All politicians should be aware of unintended consequences. In order to mitigate possible dangers and to make the most of potential advantages of faith schools, a considerable research programme will be essential.

Research and faith schools

Heelas (1996: 4) has argued that our society contains 'a fragmented, variegated range of beliefs and values'. How is education, which itself is so intimately connected with beliefs and values, to respond? So far we have argued that the best way is without the intervention of politicians. That being said, what can the education community do to examine what kinds of schooling, in terms of its aims, culture and practices, best fit the conditions in which educators and learners now find themselves? It must first ask questions of itself and then not only share the information it finds but also encourage reflection and response to it from the wider community in a genuine conversation about the place of faith and religion, beliefs and values in our education system.

Those who seek to persuade us that we currently live in a postmodern age have alerted us to some of the conditions in which we live in the twenty-first century; namely, that it is time to speculate about what the modern age is and has been all about. Flanagan (1999: 7), for example, is of the opinion that precisely because our community shares this 'fragmented, variegated range of beliefs and values', 'spirituality has unexpectedly entered the soul of sociology as an analytical consideration'. He speculates further:

> Perhaps the primary reason (for this) is the dawning sociological realisation that, in the words of the Irish poet Seamus Heaney, 'a search for images and symbols adequate to our predicament' in present culture necessitates the recognition of spiritual considerations.

The argument here is that postmodernity has overturned the conventions of modernity, one of which was to consign tradition to the past since it was incompatible with the modern age. Again Flanagan (1999: 6) makes the point well: 'This suggests that if postmodernity is about postsecularity, it also represents a revolt against apparently settled notions of indifference which secularisation cultivated in its marriage with modernity.'

In cultural terms there can no longer be indifference to matters of faith and belief. If the abstractions of postmodernity and postsecularity are perhaps ultimately unconvincing about this matter of indifference, the events of 11 September 2001 and subsequent occurrences leave us in no doubt. In practice, for the purposes of this chapter, this means that the prevailing philosophical and social culture, combined with the historic dual settlement in British education, demand a conversation about the continuing and growing presence of faith schools, which is grounded in research evidence, both of a theoretical and empirical nature.

Faith schools, as we have noted, have won their current strong position as a result of their relatively easy alignment with favourable political dispositions towards communitarianism, the reemphasis of the need for moral principles to be taught in an explicitly moral environment and their strong showings in government-sponsored league tables of test results. The extent to which faith schools do offer significantly different models of education, both theoretical and practical, which are able to impact on individual pupil attainment or their spiritual, moral, social and cultural development, or on overall school outcomes, is for the most part untested. We need, therefore, to work towards developing an agenda for research into faith schools. Much of the territory is at present uncharted and any such research will need to take its place in a research context recently described by the Methodist Conference (1999: 4.9) in the following way: 'There is an increasing and worrying tendency for that which is easily measurable to assume importance rather than finding ways of making that which is truly important in terms of individual personality and community measurable.'

As the government works towards increasing the number of specialist schools and city technical colleges, it is important that a strategy is developed. At a national level, it might first examine the role of mission, focus and specialisation across schools and their impact on specific areas of school communities. These would include such matters as their organisation, governance and standards; leadership and values; culture and ethos; pupils' attainment and their personal and social values; home-school and intergenerational relationships; the curriculum, both formal and informal; the ecologies of schools and their local communities; and their continuing personal and professional development needs. It will then be appropriate to look to ways of researching those aspects of faith schooling which current theoretical and empirical studies suggest create the differences which characterise faith schools. In order to pursue this policy, faith schools, at least, would need to be encouraged, and supported financially, to 'speak for themselves' alongside external inspection and 'self-researching'. How this might be achieved has been set out in the previous chapter, where it was argued that continuing personal and professional development policies in faith schools had a significant part to play in creating 'self-researching schools'.

This chapter seeks to outline external forms of research and evaluation which are independent of the faith communities involved in supporting schools and calls for a coordinated strategy for specialist and faith school research planning. This in turn would form the basis for the development of interdisciplinary and methodological partnerships. Such an independent research policy, in conjunction with a commitment by faith schools to becoming 'self-researching', could yield rich data sets capable of excavation at national, local, communal and individual levels. Without such a strategy, national education policy, at this critical stage in our social and cultural development, will be much the poorer in depending for its future planning on data culled mainly from test and assessment results and external inspection. The current paucity in research approaches does not do justice to the present government policy of support for specialist and faith schools and their concern for inclusion, access and justice.

We need to know what differences occur in the graduates of different kinds of schools, in their identities, values, academic and cultural attainment and social attitudes and relationships, rather than, as now, where differences are recorded by test scores. Equally we need to know what elements in a school's constitution, while making it different from other schools, also contribute to individual and communal satisfaction with their education policies. With a purposeful national strategy for research in faith and specialist schools, data and methodologies would be available to form part of an international approach to measuring the effectiveness and impact of faith schools in local and national education systems. Similarly, comparative approaches might also be developed for comparing characteristics and cultures of effective faith schools (as outlined in James Arthur's chapter in this volume) and their pedagogies and outcomes.

The following agenda for a national research policy to examine faith schools is, therefore, offered tentatively as a basis for further discussion.

An agenda for research into faith schools

Mapping current and proposed provision

There is a need to know what precise forms of faith-based schooling are offered and where, in order to establish different types and clusters of provision. Part of this mapping exercise could be achieved through working with existing data sets at faith community, local authority and national level. A nationally available data base of faith school provision in relation to gender, ethnic and religious distribution of pupils, social and economic status of parents and school–community partnership initiatives would provide an essential and valuable tool for some immediate research needs. Criteria for establishing 'typologies of faith school provision' will be a matter for vigorous debate and there will also be the need to examine current DfES and Office for Standards in Education (OFSTED) matching of schools on a national scale in relation to faith school research. Faith communities themselves will no doubt wish to enter into discussions about the current methods which they employ for comparative analysis of data from within and across communities.

Typologies of provision will also require situating within typologies of faith communities. For example, there will need to be an examination of the theological and philosophical bases for each community's (and possibly individual branches in communities) rationale for supporting and expanding its own provision within compulsory education. Typologies based on resource provision, discussed in the previous chapter by Roy Gardner and Jo Cairns, might also be used here. Certainly, an assessment will need to be made of pre-service and in-service teacher education needs within faith communities and appropriate partnerships considered with local and national education bodies to support any necessary supplementary provision.

How faith school provision fits with local and national education planning needs will be the final part of the mapping initiative. Recently, there have been two examples of faith communities' contribution to the planning process. The first was the publication of the Archbishops' Council (2001), *The Way Ahead: Church of England Schools in the New Millennium*, in which the Church offered an analysis of its rationale for contributing to compulsory education at the present time, an examination of its mission, educational resources and present provision and its estimate of the number of new Anglican secondary schools it believed were needed to fulfil current needs. Very different kinds of publications have emerged from the Institute for Jewish Policy Research (JPR) (2001 and 2003); first, there was 'The future of Jewish schooling in the United kingdom: a strategic assessment of a faith-based provision of primary and secondary school education' and secondly, 'The Jewish day school marketplace: the attitudes of Jewish parents in London and the south-east towards formal education'. This latter JPR survey importantly provides detailed attitudinal data on what Jewish parents want for their children. The authors write that their research 'has sought to access their voices' in order to gain a clearer picture of how community planners can best meet the needs and wants of current and potential clients. These reports highlight a key aspect of the proposed growing partnerships between the state and faith communities in compulsory education, namely the significance of 'choice' and 'market'. Any topography of faith schools will need to be able to map parents' ability, or lack of it, to choose to send their children to faith schools.

Finally, the JPR Report (Institute for JPR 2003: 32) alerts us to further reasons for mapping faith school provision as specifically as possible for it points out:

> Parents have to accept schools as an entire package, for, while, for example, they may be impressed by a school's academic record, they may be less sure about how it caters for children with special educational needs or the effectiveness of multicultural education. Nevertheless, parents cannot pick and choose different elements from schools and, as such, there may be parts of school policy that they do not like but have little power to change.

Not all parents in faith communities choose to send any or all their children to a faith school. The research which we have indicates that they make their choice often based on the specific needs and personality of each child. It is hoped that the more detailed picture which the proposed mapping exercise can offer, together with other elements of the research agenda to be discussed below, will begin to clarify aspects of faith schooling which are particularly important to parents in making their choice of where to send their children to school. They will also form a core knowledge base for community planners, in opting for developing certain kinds of school and not others for their communities.

The aims of education and the role of faith schools in the compulsory system

The recent concerns with standards in schools and the need for schools to improve continuously have resulted in the generally held view that the overriding purpose of education is to gain qualifications which are recognised and useful when the pupil leaves the school. Yet other purposes have been introduced into schools through their curricula, without any nationally focused discussion about their overall contribution to a child's or young person's general education; probably the two most important examples of this are the introduction of citizenship education and sex education. Such a view is consistent with that of Wrigley, who has described a situation in which the government has driven forward extensive change in schools, without raising fundamental questions among the public about what constitutes the significant purposes of education. Thus Wrigley (2003: 7) writes:

> Much of the high level government interest in school improvement has led to an intensification of teaching, accountability, league tables, teachers feeling deprofessionalized and disenchanted (or leaving), a relentless drive for more though not always better – and silence on the question of educational purpose.

In that reference, Wrigley was at the beginning of making his case for a new direction in the theory and practice of improving schools. His case is that 'school improvement' has 'given little thought to the purpose of education and has largely neglected social justice'. He continues, 'how can we know if schools are improving unless we decide what they should be good for?'

Faith schools must not be ignored in this debate. Indeed, they might offer a distinctive contribution to it, if they were given a voice through which to reflect publicly on the principles and values in which their school missions are rooted and by which their day-to-day learning and teaching is ordered. In that way school outcomes, including but not exclusively concerned with pupils' examination performance, might be more easily matched with the distinctiveness of individual school cultures.

For schools and faith communities to engage in the wider community's development and understanding of the aims of education at the beginning of the twenty-first century, there will need to be an invitation for them to participate, even from those educators and policy makers who do not see a role for religion in education in a modern world. Secondly, the communities will need to be able to offer their educators facilities to study, at higher levels, the theology, history, philosophy and sociology of their beliefs, values and practices. In this way, schools will be aware of how their individual mission is rooted in their sponsoring community's principles and values and their proponents will be contributing and equal partners to the ongoing conversation about the critical aims for education in the new millennium in the wider fragmented and plural community.

The identity, culture and ethos of faith schools

At present our knowledge of faith schools is limited, and the task of setting an agenda for research into them must take care to tread a sensitive path between what the schools have to say about themselves, much as any other kind of school is able to do, and what we as the wider community need to know in order to make up our minds about their contribution to our compulsory education system. For some time, faith schools have been disadvantaged in what they have been encouraged to say about themselves. This has been the result of a wider cultural agenda at work in much of the western world. That agenda has been characterised by what might be called the Rawlsian approach to a just society. This approach, melded in the mode of liberal pluralism, suggested a political response to those matters of beliefs and values and beliefs which may give rise to conflict. For the common good they were to be avoided in public and sent packing to the private world of the individual. Carter (1993: 8) picked up on this privatising of belief and values when he argued that the liberalism practised in the United States encourages religious belief to become a private, and even a trivial, affair:

> We are trying, here in America, to strike an awkward but necessary balance, one that seems more and more difficult with each passing year. On the one hand, a magnificent respect for freedom of conscience, including freedom of religious belief, runs deep in our political ideology. On the other hand, our understandable fear of religious domination of politics presses us, in our public personas, to be wary of those who take their religion too seriously.

In many ways it has become convenient for those educators and politicians wedded to our liberal democracy to push the issue of faith schools under the carpet, since they too subscribe to the notion that religion's place is in the privacy of the individual believer's private life, not in the public arena. Nonetheless, we do have a significant number of faith schools in our midst, sponsored by public funding.

To what extent then can or do faith schools contribute a vital element to our common good? What are their principles on justice, inclusion and educational attainment? Indeed, we might ask, do these schools offer some models for how we might settle differences between individual rights and belief, on the one hand, and the protection of the values which underpin a liberal, tolerant society, on the other? If we were to do this, then our real conversation would be with members of faith schools who are not only citizens of our liberal democracy but also members of faith communities. We might be encouraged here by the argument advanced by Brian Stiltner (1999: 9) for he says: 'Since religion involves both belief and practice, as well as both cultural and institutional expressions, a focus on religion helps us to investigate the variety of pluralism – cultural, institutional, religious, and ideological – in modern society.'

Thus non-faith educators and researchers can usefully investigate whether such schools are in fact contributing to the human capital of living in a liberal democratic society. Such investigations might then form the backdrop to the question with which this section has been most particularly concerned: 'What should be the balance between all schools contributing to a politically driven understanding of the "common good" and each school's particular understanding of what constitutes the most effective culture for the development of "flourishing" individuals?' Here the word 'individuals' would embrace all with a sense of identity born from their individual histories, circumstances and communities.

If we can invite faith schools to define their cultures to the wider community, taking account perhaps of Stoll's definition (Stoll and Fink 1996: 82–3) of culture as being 'How things are ... in essence, it defines reality for those within a social organisation, gives them support and identity and creates a framework for occupational learning,' then our research agenda will have ensured that each school understands its place in the wider education context, has the means to be able to understand the similarities and differences of its own and other cultures and has a set of particularities in which to set out its aims and values.

Of course, this is not the whole story which we will wish to see emerge from investigation of the identities, cultures and ethos of faith schools. Being a faith school with an apparent underlying common world view does not necessarily ensure that each school easily shares its goals and unity of purpose. It is worth quoting at length here an introduction given in 1996 by the then Jewish headteacher of a new Jewish secondary school in east London to a conference of teachers of Jewish studies on 'Developing Ethos in Jewish Education' (unpublished), organised by the Research for Quality in Jewish Education Unit at the Institute of Education. It summarises succinctly some of the major difficulties faced by faith schools in coming to terms with developing a specific school mission and culture:

> It is my contention that beneath an apparently clear set of shared goals and unity of purpose, most Jewish secondary schools ... contain a number of conflicting goals which are exacerbated by conflicting external pressures. At its simplest level it is often expressed in the complaint from schools that families do not really care about Jewish Studies. In some schools, of course, the opposite may apply – families may appear to care too much – but they remain equally dissatisfied. It is in fact rare to find a harmonious relationship between many parents and schools with relation to Jewish Studies, outside of those schools which only serve particular communities (e.g. Chasidic schools) ... If we then add to the pot the differing understandings of Jewish identity and differing levels of commitment among Jewish staff in Jewish schools, the ratio of Jewish to non-Jewish staff in most secondary schools, the conflicting demands of governors and the conflicting demands on curriculum time, then we create an even more complex picture of ethos – or lack of it.

This was a brave and fine summary of the position which many believed that particular faith community's schools faced. What can be the ethos of such a school and how can each school manage to create and sustain a message that can be shared and absorbed by students, staff, parents and governors?

Bryk *et al.* (1993: 334–5) when discussing their own empirical study of Catholic schools in the United States have also drawn attention to tensions inherent in faith schools:

> Catholic educators must struggle to discern the valuable contributions of this larger secular culture, while maintaining fidelity to the religious ideals which have vitalized Catholic schools since the Second Vatican Council. Such openness with roots inevitably creates organizational tensions and dilemmas.

Thus our research agenda must ask whether the coherent school culture and ethos, which figured prominently in the lists of characteristics associated with 'effective schools' does exist in faith schools. In what form and to what effect?

And most importantly, 'Is this faith school different from non-faith schools?'; 'How does a faith school know it is different from neighbouring schools?'; and, 'What evidence does a faith school use to assure itself that it is functioning effectively as a faith school?'

Teachers' stories: who am I that educates? And who am I that leads?

What is the distinctive role of the teacher in a faith school? What do we know about teachers' professional and sometimes personal identities in faith schools in relation to the mission and culture of the school? What difference to the culture of a faith school does it make to have teachers from inside a particular faith and teachers of no faith, for example? There are schools where the only core staff involved in the faith identity of that school are the headteacher and members of the religious education department. To what extent is the specific mission of the school met by the teachers in their explicit curriculum areas and in their general participation in the school community?

In addition, we might wish to examine the identities of teachers working in religious education in faith schools. For example, in a piece of research undertaken by the Research for Quality in Jewish Education Unit (1995) in 56 Jewish primary schools, four classifications of respondents to the research questionnaire were identified among the Jewish studies teachers of those schools. Of these, the vast majority of Jewish studies teachers were not formally trained in pedagogic skills in contrast to their secular studies colleagues. Only a very small percentage had qualified teacher status (QTS).

Without a traditional pre-service QTS qualification and with varying forms of induction in faith schools, we must ask, to what extent are teachers in faith schools actively engaged in following a professional code of practice related to beliefs and values? And to what extent should faith schools continue to involve non-qualified teachers in the work of full-time schools?

Leadership in faith schools

We will also wish to add to our agenda the need to involve the headteachers of faith schools in telling their own stories. The fine work of Gerald Grace (2002) in this very particular area of leadership in a faith school's mission has identified helpful research models in this area.

The underlying question about school leadership in faith schools is, 'To what extent is leadership in a faith school a different process from leadership in a non-faith school? What are the values and concerns attached to it? To what extent is the headteacher a co-ordinator of a wide and disparate set of views about the purpose and nature of education or the leader who, infused with her/his own understanding of the tradition and its relation to education, sets a course and establishes an organisation within the limits laid down by the school's governors?

There is a need too to audit the practices of governors in relation to their formal duties and their application of the school's foundational principles, in order to map differing approaches to the governance and communal practices which distinguish different types of faith schools.

The student voice

To what extent does the view of the faith school on what constitutes 'human flourishing in a plural society' influence the pupil graduating from it? This might well be the key question to which an informed conversation about faith schools might generate valuable responses.

We need mechanisms to know and understand the pupils in faith schools, how they perceive themselves at particular times, what their values are and their attitudes to belonging to a faith school. Leslie Francis' recent work (2001) in developing a values profile of 33,982 13–15 year olds provides an important model for research in this area and identified 15 values areas in its questionnaire: personal well-being, worries, counselling, school, work, religious beliefs, church and society, the supernatural, politics, social concerns, sexual morality, substance use, right and wrong, leisure, and local area. Francis (2001: 3) offers it as a 'benchmark' for those teachers concerned with 'the delivery of values education to year nine and year ten pupils against which the values climate in their own classrooms can be assessed'. It also provides a significant landscape of beliefs and values of young people today against which data from a similar questionnaire for use in faith schools might be compared. For example, Francis (2001: 37) summarises the information gleaned from his research about young people's religious beliefs in the following way:

> The data provides a profile of a generation of young people who are divided between theists, agnostics and atheists. Large numbers have no real opinions to declare on issues like the resurrection, life after death and the exclusivist claims of Christianity. The danger is that young people who are not forming views on religious matters may become vulnerable to the persuasion of cults and quasi-religious systems. Values education needs to equip young people to think rationally and intelligently about contrasting and conflicting religious claims within a rapidly changing pluralist society.

A further part of Francis' analysis (2001: 166–70) involved mapping the relationship between church attendance and the 15 areas explored by the survey. The research shows, for example, that young churchgoers hold a significantly more positive attitude toward school than young people who never attend church. At the same time, these young churchgoers are more likely than non-churchgoers to worry about their school work and to worry about their exams at school. They are worried about being bullied at school and are slightly less likely to like the people with whom they go to school.

It would increase our knowledge and understanding of the relationship between different types of faith schools and the values of their pupils, if a similar survey were to be conducted among pupils from faith schools and non-faith schools, and data used to identify whether attendance at such schools might be a factor in predicting individual differences in the values held by young people.

Equally, there is need for research which can unfold students' views on the school culture and climate in which they are living and learning every day. Student questionnaires can systematically unfold such student views on the school culture and climate. Adopting a questionnaire used by Flynn (1993) in the Catholic schools of Australia, Paddy Walsh and Jo Cairns have administered these to cohorts of school leavers in Catholic schools in the United States, Ireland, Botswana, Indonesia and Grenada. Paddy Walsh has recorded the findings of a case study of a Jesuit school in the United States (in Cairns, Gardner and Lawton, 2000: 147–9). He reports that it is the results from the section of the questionnaire headed 'School Life and Climate' which 'yield sustained and dramatic evidence of strong school community'. The sample of students there used a five-point scale to respond to a series of 36 statements expressing feelings and views regarding their school, its ethos and its teachers. Their overall response was 'quite formidably positive' in response to the following themes:

- Perception of their own feelings
- Community spirit
- Evaluation of the school

- Discipline
- Catholicity of the school.

In response to life goals, the sample (ibid.: 149) gave 'pride of place to fulfilment and relationship goals over both success goals and religious-spiritual goals.'

The use of such a questionnaire can also help us to investigate a concern with faith schools which Richard Pring articulated in relation to all schools (1984: 30) when he wrote:

> To teach without coming to grips with how the learner understands things, or to provide a particular course of studies without relating it to the students' consuming interests, would be to impose a system of ideas or a set of values that disrespect the learner as a person ... as someone with a conscious view of things and of what is of value.

The questionnaire, which was designed to discover what the students thought about certain issues and to explore their experience of a Catholic school and its influence on their lives, also contained sections on students' home backgrounds, 'reasons for staying on at school', 'the curriculum' , 'religious education', 'religious beliefs and values', 'personal goals for the future', and 'expectations of Catholic schools'. In the section on 'curriculum' the students are asked how strongly they agreed or disagreed on a five-point scale to the following statements: 'The subjects offered in my school curriculum develop in me the capacity for independent and critical thinking,' and 'RE classes help me to form my own conscience'.

Through the use of the questionnaire and related strategies, it is possible first to articulate for the pupils the school's concern that they are ultimately free agents who have been offered an education which is designed to help them make up their minds about the purpose and usefulness of knowledge and the values and principles which they hold, and to collect feedback about the pupils' own perceptions of the curriculum they have studied. Has it contributed to the pupils' own sense of identity and personal worth? And to what extent do pupils feel autonomous in their personal values, choices and life-styles as they leave the school community?

Religious education, spiritual education and the students' philosophies of life

Barbara Wintersgill (2002), when leading a discussion on 'the spiritual dimension of the curriculum', recalled Wittgenstein's comment that 'the world of the happy man is an altogether different world from the world of the unhappy man'. She argued with Wittgenstein that we perceive the world in one of three ways: materially, morally and spiritually. We need to know how a school perceives the world in each of three ways and what efforts it makes to inculcate such views through its curriculum and culture in the lives of its pupils; how it chooses to employ these ways of seeing in developing the autonomy and critical faculties of its teachers and pupils; and how it judges it has been successful in its work. In relation to faith schools, we also need to know how much of its work in these areas has been related to an implicit approach in its culture and ethos or by an explicit rooting of the spiritual in its, and perhaps others', religious traditions. It is important that research can throw light on the argument recently put forward by Sandra Schneiders (2000: 13) who has concluded that, in this context of promoting the spiritual in education, 'religion is the optional context for spirituality'. She continued: 'The great religious traditions of the world are much more adequate matrices for spiritual development and practice than personally constructed amalgams of belief and practices.'

Since this particular view often lies at the heart of a faith school's rationale and is in direct opposition to the curriculum approach taken to the promotion of the spiritual in state community schools, it is worthy of serious investigation, despite the methodological problems involved.

A national research agenda should also focus on the religious and philosophical views of life held by pupils in schools. Without such knowledge it is difficult to assess the contribution of schools to the students' current and later attitudes and values to other people's religious and world views. Sven Hartman's (1994) research in this area makes a very interesting contribution to the work of examining the role of faith schools in the making of human capital or 'human flourishing in plural conditions'. He has argued for research into the religion of children and young people focusing primarily on their personal philosophy of life. He views children as human beings on their way through life, with their views changing in different ways but not towards a goal that is predefined by psychological developmental theories or educational policy. Hartman is therefore chiefly interested in the content of children's views of life (corresponding to a broad concept of religion) and how changes are made in their personal philosophy of life, which is in part a dynamic and complex process including questions about life, individual experience and established religious positions, and how this process is influenced by personal and social factors.

We would also wish to examine how different faith traditions employ religious education in their promotion of the social, moral and spiritual development of their students. For assistance here in devising methodologies, we might look at the following works already in progress. One Hindu educator, for example, is tackling the question of how religious education might contribute to the perpetuation of liberal pluralism. Desai (1997) has proposed the 'Interface Approach Towards a Liberal Indigenous Charter' (IATaLIC) model for religious education. The model respects justice but recognises the classroom educator's limitations in motivating young persons with a strong religious identity towards a liberal disposition. Equally, he argued, the communal guardians of religious identity may not care for justice. Hence the classroom educator, sympathetic towards both the liberal and the traditional community agenda, must work with the faith communities. He concluded that:

> Educators must encourage indigenous personnel to excavate liberal principles from religious texts, and then evangelise these principles throughout their community. Then justice will be met and communal integrity maintained. In England, opportunities do exist for education to establish a consensus across religious and liberal viewpoints. Such opportunities should not be neglected.
>
> (Desai 1997: Introduction)

In Israel, Alexander (2001) published his *Reclaiming Goodness: Education and the Spiritual Quest*, a critique of general education in liberal societies which, he argued, are failing to equip children with a sense of the 'higher good'. In the United States, Bryk *et al.* (1993: 335) argue that Catholic schooling is a form of defensible liberal education in a secular culture:

> An alternative conception ... envisions Catholic schools as a realization of the prophetic Church that critically engages common culture. Anything that even remotely smacks of 'indoctrination in the mind of the Church' can seriously undermine this more public function ... from this perspective, Catholic education represents an

invitation to students both to reflect on a systematic body of thought and to immerse themselves in a communal life that seeks to live out its basic principles.

Do all faith schools readily fit the model developed by McLaughlin, when discussing Catholic schools, which he envisages in their modern form as being characterised by 'openness with roots'? Thus he writes (1996: 147): 'Such schooling can be seen to be compatible with liberal, democratic principles, not least by providing a substantial starting point for the child's eventual development into autonomous agency and democratic citizenship.'

What is the role and impact of differing models of religious education found in faith schools at the present time?

Conclusion

Situating faith in an open, postmodern and democratic schooling system is a huge responsibility, challenge and opportunity both for the state and for the faith communities involved. We need to know the results from the schools themselves of this initiative, as well as from independent observers and research. Whatever those results, the context in which we the wider community will make sense of them and make our judgements about the place of faith schools in our compulsory education system has been astutely described by Roy Niblett (2001: 127) when writing about his understanding of the purposes which education might serve in the twenty-first century:

> The schools and the places of higher education to which the young will go, while still efficient at training the mind to reason and be critical, will need to recognise again, far more than now, the power of a loved community both to educate and to discipline its members. The young need help and human examples if they are to absorb the heritage freely offered by literature, music and the arts. Schools themselves need to see that insights of great importance to human development are given by failure as well as success and that hope – which has many dimensions – matters enormously.

We have referred earlier in the chapter to Terry Wrigley, who has recently argued for the introduction of new models of education to be provided for our wider community that are appropriate to the needs of our times. He proposes a model of hope (2003: 8) which might be one that fits Niblett's own vision:

> To examine school improvement using the touchstone of hope is not a vaguely utopian moralism but an attempt to reconnect to core issues. Hope is a principle which unites the actions and aspirations of teachers, parents, children and headteachers ... It articulates connections between the five key areas of school development, curriculum, pedagogy, ethos and the wider community which school leaders need to align in order to bring about significant change.

Our purpose has been to call for a reasoned, critical and informed conversation about the faith schools which are currently proliferating in our community. That conversation will be richer if the research agenda outlined here can provide information on a range of models of education from which we can choose, knowing that they are grounded in twenty-first century identities, values and communal perspectives. In this way we hope we will have followed Brenda Watson's (2000: 12) appeal in such conversation that:

Neither religious or secularist confessionalism should be our starting-point in education. We should neither assume that there is a God, nor that there is not, but rather convey the supreme importance of the question. We need to encourage pupils towards evaluation of all assumptions, secularist as well as religious, and to acknowledge that all positions are confessional. Instead of dogmatically instilling authoritative answers, emphasis needs placing on opening up issues.

References

Archbishops' Council (2001) *The Way Ahead: Church of England Schools in the New Millennium*, London: Church House Publishing.

Alexander, H. (2001) *Reclaiming Goodness: Education and the Spiritual Quest*, Chicago, IL: University of Notre Dame Press.

Bryk, A., Lee, V. and Holland, P. (1993) *Catholic Schools and the Common Good*, Cambridge, MA: Harvard University Press.

Cairns, J., Gardner, R. and Lawton, D. (eds) (2000) *Values and the Curriculum*, London: Woburn Press.

Carter, S. (1993) *The Culture of Disbelief*, New York: Basic Books.

Desai, A. (1997) 'Politics and religion: the need for an overlapping consensus', doctoral thesis, University of London.

Flanagan, K. (1999) 'Introduction', in K. Flanagan and P.C. Jupp (eds) *Postmodernity, Sociology and Religion*, Basingstoke: Macmillan Press.

Flynn, M. (1993) *The Culture of Catholic Schools*, Homebush, NSW: St Paul Publications.

Francis, L. (2001) *The Values Debate: A Voice From the Pupils*, London: Woburn Press.

Grace, G. (2002) *Catholic Schools: Mission, Markets and Morality*, London: RoutledgeFalmer.

Hartman, S. (1994) 'Children's personal philosophy of life as a basis for religious education', in *PANORAMA International Journal of Comparative Religious Education and Values*, 6(2): 104–28.

Heelas, P. (1996) 'Detraditionalisation and its rivals', in P. Heelas, S. Lash and P. Moros (eds) *Detraditionalisation: Critical Reflections on Authority and Identity*, Oxford: Blackwell.

Institute for Jewish Policy Research (2001) *The Future of Jewish Schooling in the United Kingdom: A Strategic Assessment of a Faith-Based Provision of Primary and Secondary School Education*, JPR Report No 2, London: JPR Publications.

Institute for Jewish Policy Research (2003) *The Jewish Day School Marketplace: The Attitudes of Jewish Parents in London and the South-east Towards Formal Education*, JPR Report No 1, London: JPR Publications.

McLaughlin, T. (1996) 'The distinctiveness of Catholic education', in T.H. McLaughlin, J. O'Keefe and B. O'Keeffe (eds) *The Contemporary Catholic School*, London: Falmer Press.

Methodist Conference (1999) *The Essence of Education: A Report of the Methodist Conference 1999*, Peterborough: Methodist Publishing House.

Niblett, R. (2001) *Life, Education, Discovery*, Bristol: Pomegranate Books.

Pring, R. (1984) *Personal and Social Education in the Curriculum*, Sevenoaks: Hodder and Stoughton.

Research for Quality in Jewish Education (1995) *Teachers' Stories*, RESQUJE, Institute of Education, University of London.

Schneiders, S.M. (2000) 'Religion and spirituality: strangers, rivals or partners?', *Santa Clara Lectures*, 6(2): 13.

Stiltner, B. (1999) *Religion and the Common Good: Catholic Contributions to Building Community in a Liberal Society*, Lanham, MD: Rowman and Littlefield.

Stoll, L. and Fink, D. (1996) *Changing Our Schools: Linking School Effectiveness with School Improvement*, Buckingham: Open University Press.

Walsh, P. (2000), 'New wine in renewed wineskin: a Jesuit school now', in J. Cairns, R. Gardner and D. Lawton (eds) *Values and the Curriculum*, London: Woburn Press.

Watson, B. (2000) in *Muslim Education Quarterly*, 17(2): 12.

Wintersgill, B. (2002) 'The spiritual dimension of the curriculum', unpublished.

Wrigley, T. (2003) *Schools of Hope: A New Agenda for School Improvement*, Stoke on Trent: Trentham Books.

Index

Note: tables and figures are indicated by the use of *Tables* or *Figures* after the page numbers, e.g. the entry 'achievement 202–11(*Tables 18.1–18.6* and *Figures 18.1–18.3*)' indicates that there are both Tables and Figures relating to achievement between page 202 and 211.

ability groups 205–7, 209–10
academic standards 52, 94–5, 149–50, 150–1, 152, 153–4
Academy Schools 84, 127
accountability 108
achievement: of Bradford schools 125, 126, 127; in Catholic schools 147, 148–9, 151; class and gender 97–9; economic and social conditions 147; and ethnicity 91; in faith schools 52, 147–54, 202–11(*Tables 18.1–18.6* and *Figures 18.1– 18.3*), 215, 217; in joint church schools 120
admissions policies: and achievement 147–8; in Catholic schools 153–4; in Christian schools 108, 111, 123; in faith-based schools 7; and humanist policy 75–6; in joint church schools 114, 117–18
Advisory Centre for Education (ACE) 39
Agreed Syllabus 22–3, 23–4, 27, 28, 30
aims *see* educational aims
Akenson, D.H. 158
Alexander, H. 66, 254
Amnesty International 77
Anglicanism *see* CofE; CofE schools
Anglo–Irish Agreement (1985) 159
anti-clericalism 179
Archbishops' Council 7, 38, 42, 76, 235, *see also* Canterbury, Archbishops of; *The Way Ahead* (Dearing Report); York, Archbishop of

Arrupe, Fr 231–2
Arthur, J. 120, 197, 198
Ashraf, Ali 232
Asian communities 122–3, 124, 125, 130, 131, 132
assemblies, inclusive 79
assessment 149–50, 219; SCAA 213
Astley, Jeff 238
atheists/atheism 15
attainment *see* achievement
attendance 149, 252
Australia 148, 150–1
autonomy: as aim of education 57, 59, 233; of Catholic schools 152–3; of the child 11, 42–3; rational autonomy and divisiveness 66; and secularisation 84–5

Bacon, Francis 235
Baker, John (Bishop of Salisbury) 115, 116
Bari, M. 232
Barrell, G.B. and Parington, J. 36
basics skills 150
Bayrou, François 181
Beckett, F. 224
Bel Geddes, J. 39
beliefs and attitudes: Catholic 115, 153–4; and divisiveness 64–5, 68, 84–5; humanist 74; and RE teaching 118–19, 253–5; of teachers 185, 197, 233, 234, 236, 251; and UK public culture 88–9, 244–6, *see also* ethos; faith traditions; religion; values
Bell, Andrew 17
Bellah, Robert 192, 198
Berger, P.L. 140, 192
A Better Way Forward (BHA) 74
BFSS (British and Foreign School Society) 16, 27

BHA (British Humanist Association) 29, 30; on parents' and child's rights 40, 41, 42–3, 44; policy on education 74–81
Bible 117, 243–4
Bills of Rights for Children (Canada and US) 39
Bishops' Conference of England and Wales 114
Blackstone, Tessa 8
Blair, Tony 192, 195, 231, 242
Blunkett, David 44, 192, 195
Bourdieu, P. 93, 99, 195
Bradford 122–36
Bradford District Race Review Team *see* Ouseley Report
Bradford University 123
Brownson, Orestes 169, 170, 173, 174
Bryk, A.S. *et al.* 67–8, 197, 250, 254–5
Budd, Christopher (Bishop of Plymouth) 115–16
Buddhists 192
Burton in Lonsdale school 128
Bush, George W. Jr 194
Busher, H. 223
Butler, R.A. 23

Cairns, Jo 252
Canada 39
Canavan, Kelvin 150
Canterbury, Archbishops of: Runcie, R. 231; Temple, W. 23; Williams, R. 8, 9, 11, 135, 193, *see also* Archbishops' Council
Cantle Report (*Community Cohesion*) 62, 67, 76, 122, 134, 196
Carter, S. 249
catechesis 118
Catechism of the Catholic Church 115
Cathedral CC (Bradford) 126, 127
Catholic Bishops of England and Wales 197
Catholic Bishops of Northern Ireland 162–3
Catholic Education Council 147
Catholic schools 147–54; in Bradford 122, 126; communitarianism and citizenship 197, 198; and divisiveness 67–8, 70; ethos of 150, 152, 154, 163, 198, 231–2; growth of 31, 243–4; joint Catholic–CofE school 113–21; mission and achievement 97–8(*Table 8.1*), 99, 230; in Northern Ireland 157; performance of 203, 204(*Table 18.2*),

205(*Table 18.3*), 210; research in 250, 252–3, 254–5; and social justice 91, 96; in the US 67–8, 91, 147, 148–50, 196–7; voluntary aided and controlled 23
Catholic training colleges 24, 25, 28
Catholics/Catholicism 15, 17, 19–20, 28, 156
Census (1851) 15(*Table 2.1*)
Census (2001) 7, 22, 51, 192
'centredness' 163
Central Society of Education 16
Centre for the Study of Conflict 158
Chanlett, E. and Morier, G.M. 38–9
'charitable choice' 194
children: as pupils 233, 236–7, 251–2; rights of 38–40, 40–4, 75–8, 77, 244
Children's Legal Centre 40
choice *see* parental choice
Choice and Diversity (DES) 52
Christian identity 22, 123, 192
Christian schools 105–12, 203–4(*Table 18.2*), 205(*Table 18.3*), 210; in 19th and 20th centuries 15–26, 156–60, 160–3, 167–73, 243–4; discrimination in favour of 76, 78; ethos of 108, 111, 114, 202, 231–3; inter-church RE proposal 218; USA non-sectarian 158–63, 168–73, *see also* Catholic schools; CofE schools; 'dual system'; interdenominational provision
Christian unity 115
Church of England (CofE) *see* Archbishops' Council; CofE
church schools *see* Catholic schools; Christian schools; CofE schools; joint faith schools
Church Schools Review Group *see The Way Ahead*
church and state *see* state systems; state–church relationships
Church Times 8
Church Urban League 193
Church in Wales 27
Circular 7/73 25
cities 68, 122–36, 148, 193
citizenship: and communitarianism 197–8; democratic citizenship and divisiveness 66, 69; education for 141–2, 160–1, 213–14, 220, 236; and RE 213–15, 217–18, 219–20, 238–9; and social capital 196
civic republicanism 194
civic values 68–70, 197–8

class issues 97–9, 133–4, 180
clothing 41, 80, 183
CofE 27; in 19th and 20th centuries 15, 19–20, 128, 243; *Consultation Report* 55; and education in Bradford 122–36; and faith-based community action 193
CofE schools: in Bradford 122, 123, 125, 126–31; and divisiveness 63, 71; ethos of 76, 95, 96, 128–9, 130, 231, 235; joint RC–CofE school 113–21; and New Labour policy 217, 243; performance of 203, 204(*Table 18.2*), 205(*Table 18.3*), 210; secondary schools 27; voluntary controlled schools 22, 38, *see also* Christian schools; joint faith schools
CofE training colleges 24–5, 26, 27
Cohn-Bendit, Daniel 183
Coleman, J. 149, 151, 195, 196, 237; (*Equality of Educational Opportunity* Coleman Report) 90–1, 96–7, 98–9
The Common Good (Catholic Bishops of England and Wales) 197
common religion/common faith 161–3, 168–70, 174
common schools 69–70, 77, 168–70, 172, 173–5
communitarianism 191, 193, 194–5, 196–8, 231
communities: and Catholic schools 151, 152; and citizenship 141; faith schools in 211, 230–1, 234–40; faith-based communities 106–8, 193–6, 224–7; joint church schools in 120, 130; in Northern Ireland 159; poverty and dispossession in 131–3, 134; schools as 106–8, 237–8; state policies 169
community colleges 126, 127–8
community relations measures 159, 160–3
community schools 125, 135, 214
community-based CPPD 226–7
compassionate conservatism 194, 195
complaints procedures 80
Comte, Auguste 183–4
Condorcet, M.J.A.C. 179, 186
Congregation for Catholic Education 114–15, 118
conscience clause 16–17, 18, 19, 218; in Catholic schools 28
conservative communitarianism 194
consultation, local 80
contact initiatives 158–9
continuing personal and professional development *see* CPPD

controlled schools 157
Convention on the Rights of the Child (CRC) 39–40, 41, 43, 75–6
Cooling, T. 129
Cosgrove, A. 28
county maintained schools 22
county schools 156, 157; link with churches 23–4
covenant (St Edward's school) 116
covenantal relationship 142–4
CPPD (continuing personal and professional development) 222–40; for faith schools 223–8, 238–9; identity and culture of faith schools 231–3; provision for 226; and the wider culture 229–31
Crick, Bernard 198
Crick Report 213
cultural factors: beliefs and attitudes 88–9, 243–6; and CPPD in faith schools 229–31; cultural pluralism 139; diversity 21–2; dress 41, 80, 183; relativism 70; USA public culture 167, 174–5; Western and Asian 123, 124–5, *see also* beliefs and attitudes; ethos
Cultural Heritage (CH) 159, 160
curricula: in Catholic schools 153–4, 182; changes in RE curriculum 215–16; in Christian schools 107, 108–9; for citizenship 197, 213–15, 236; French secularist 180; GCSE and Key Stage 3 tests 202–11(*Tables 18.1–18.6* and *Figures 18.1–18.3*); for independent schools 36; initiatives in Northern Ireland 158, 159, 160–1; and Jewish orthodox concepts 142–4(*Table 12.1*); LEA Agreed Syllabus 22–3, 23–4, 27, 28, 30; place of RE 24, 28; and role of faith education 11–12, 238–9, 248, 254; social curriculum 215–16, *see also* National Curriculum
custodial–plural duality 166–7, 174
CW (Collective Worship) 218; 1944–2002 22, 30; and BHA consultation document 79

Darby, J. *et al.* 158
datasets, national value-added 202–3 (*Tables 18.1 and 18.2*)
Davie, G. 22
Dawkins, R. 61
de Toqueville, A. 109
Dearing, Ron 213
Dearing Report *see The Way Ahead*

debate 170
Debray, Régis 183
Debré Law (1959) 181–2
Declaration of the Rights of Geneva
    (1924) 38–9
democracy *see* citizenship; liberal values;
    political process
denomination 122; of pupils in Northern
    Ireland 161(*Table 14.1*), *see also*
    Christian schools; interdenominational
    provision; non-denominational
    education
deprivation 123–4
Desai, A. 254
Dewey, John 162, 168, 170–3, 174
disadvantaged children 91, 94, 97–8; in
    the US 148, 149
discipline 149, 202
discrimination, in faith-based schools 75
dispossession 131–2
dissenters 15, 16–17, 192
distributive justice theory 91
diversity 21–2, 68
Divini illius magistri (1927 Encyclical) 20, 28
divisiveness 61–71; barriers to autonomy
    84–5; interpretations of 63, 64–5, 67
Dixon's CTC (Bradford) 126, 127
Dobson, Frank 52
dress 41, 80, 183
'dual system': changes in (1944–2002)
    21–6; and CPPD 227; and New
    Labour policy 244; state–church
    partnership (1870–1943) 18–21
Durham Report: The Fourth R (1970) 27
Durkheim, Emile 184

economic factors: and academic
    achievement 147; in Bradford 123–4,
    131–2; for faith schools 26, 113–14;
    parental wealth 151; and poverty 134
ecumenism 114–15, 119–20
education: and CPPD in faith schools
    229–30; Dewey's philosophy of 170–3;
    faith-based 106–7, 139; purposes of
    7–8, 133, *see also* educational aims
Education Acts (Northern Ireland) 156,
    157
Education Acts (UK) 7, 11, 19, 238; 1944
    Act 22–3, 51; 1996 Act 36; school
    provision 1944–2002 22–3, 24
Education for All (HMSO) (Swann Report)
    62
Education Policy Partnership (EPP)
    122–3, 125

Education Reform Order (1989) 159, 160
educational aims 55–9, 105, 106, 248,
    255–6; of Catholic schools 152–3; and
    divisiveness 63–4, 66; mission
    statements 116–17, 128, 182, 235; of
    the NC 214, 222–3, *see also* ethos;
    values-based education
Edwards, Jonathan 168
embrace 175
employment 123, 124(*Table 11.1*)
EMU (Education for Mutual
    Understanding) 159, 160
England 8–12, *see also* north of England
    riots 2001
equality 10, 53, 91, 92, 93
equity 96–9
ESTYN (Inspectorate for Education and
    Training in Wales) 23
ethnicity: Asian communities 122–3, 124,
    125, 130, 131, 132; and children's
    rights 42; and divisiveness of faith
    schools 64, 78; and educational
    achievement 91; ethnic distribution in
    Bradford schools 125–6(*Table 11.2*),
    127–8(*Table 11.3*); ethnic diversity
    21–2; minority faith groups 193; and
    student philosophies 253–5; and
    tolerance 41, 142
ethos 52–3, 95–9, 223, 231–9; in Catholic
    schools 150, 152, 154, 163, 198,
    231–2; in Christian schools 108, 111,
    114, 202, 231–3; and citizenship 197;
    in CofE schools 76, 95, 96, 128–9,
    130, 231, 235; of faith schools 231–3,
    235, 249–50; of Jewish Orthodox
    schools 141, 143(*Table 12.1*); Muslim
    education 232; and parental choice
    185, *see also* beliefs and attitudes; value
    systems; values-based education
eucharistic celebration 119–20
European Convention on Human Rights
    40
evaluations 224–5, 228, 246
excellence 94
Excellence in Schools (DfEE) 96
exclusivity 98–9, 175, *see also* inclusiveness

faith *see* beliefs and attitudes; faith
    traditions; religion
Faith in the City (Archbishop of
    Canterbury) 193
'Faith and community' (LGA) 194
faith schools: arguments against 42–4,
    54–6, 62; arguments for 11, 52–4, 62,

95–6, 196–7, 243; and autonomy
85–7; characteristics of 107–8;
contributions of and divisiveness
67–71; and CPPD 223–8, 238–9;
defence of 56–9; faith and
denomination 122; foundation schools
as 215; in France 180, 181–2, 185;
girls and single-faith schools 78, 86,
126; and liberal values 83–9, 139–41,
227–8; nature and variety of 65–6;
performance and achievement of 52,
147–54, 202–11(*Tables 18.1–18.6* and
Figures 18.1–18.3), 215; research into
244–55; role in compulsory system
248; and social cohesion 134–6, 218,
see also religious schools
faith traditions: in Christian schools 108,
109; and social cohesion 134–5; in
state education 41, 183; in the UK
26–31, *see also* religion
faith-based communities: community
action 193–7, 198; and CPPD 224–7
faith-based schools *see* faith schools;
religious schools
Falloux Law (1850) 181
Farnell, Richard 193
FC (Free Church) 15, 19, 23, 28–9
Feldman, Sandra 84
Ferry, Jules 180
financial contributions, legal frameworks
38
Flanagan, K. 245
Flynn, Marcellin 150, 151, 152
Fogel, R.W. 175
food 80, 97, 98(*Table 8.1*)
Forum on Values in Education and the
Community *see* Values Forum
Foster, H.H. and Freed, D.J. 39
foundation schools 37–8, 214–15
Four Faiths School 31, 44
four and two schools 156
France 41, 178–86
Francis, Leslie 238, 252
Free Church (FC) 15, 19, 23, 28–9
free school meals (FSM) 97, 98(*Table 8.1*)
freedom of religion 78, 84
Freeman, M.D.A. 39
Freire, P. 238
A Fresh Way Forward (BHA) 74–5
Frohnen, Bruce 194
fundamentalism 110, 244; Christian 86, 87
funding: and autonomy 86; for church
schools 55, 113–14; 'dual system'
1870–1943 18–20; 'dual system'

1943–2002 22–4; of French faith
schools 181, 182; legal frameworks for
37–8; and secularisation 83; in South
Africa 151; voluntary Christian
provision 1803–69 15–17

Gaddy, B.B. *et al.* 170
Gallagher, *et al.* A.M. 161
Gallagher, Tony 12
Gamarnikow, E. and Green, A. 197
Gambetta, Léon 179
GCSEs 202–11(*Tables 18.1–18.6* and
Figures 18.1–18.3); assessment of 219;
in RE 215
gender issues 78, 86, 98
Gibbons, W.J. 33
girls, and single-faith schools 78, 86, 126
globalisation 94, 110, 134
Godfrey, G. *et al.* 40
Gold, K. 97
Good Friday Agreement 162
good practice 80
Goodenough, W.H. 167
governing body, joint faith school 118
Grace, G. 96, 97–8(*Table 8.1*), 197, 224,
228; on heads' mission aims 152, 153,
230, 251
Grange Technology College 135
Graves, Robert 138
Grayling, A.C. 83, 84
Greeley, A.M. and Rossi, P.H. 67, 69, 70,
147
Greer, J. 1
Griffith, Colleen 236
Grubb Institute 129
The Guardian 7, 44, 52, 224
Guermeur Law (1977) 181, 182
guidance, legal 80
Guizot Law (1833) 179, 181
Gundara, J.S. 42

Halstead, J.M. 10, 65
Hamilton, D. 223
Hamilton, David 229
Hartman, Sven 254
Hastings, Michael 9
Heelas, P. 244
Heelas, P. and Woodhead, L. 9
Herbert, I. 72
Hewer, C. 36
Hill, Paul 149
Hindus 30–1, 192, 254
Hirst, P. and Peters, R. 11
Hirst, Paul 232

HMI (Her Majesty's Inspectorate),
    independent schools' inspections 37
Hobson, P.R. and Edwards, J.S. 234
holidays, religious and public 79
Hook, Sidney 174
Hornsby-Smith, Michael 147
Hudson, W.S 167
Human Rights Act 1998 (HRA) 41, 53–4,
    77
humanism: humanist beliefs 74; humanist
    traditions 29–30, 168; and multifaith
    education 130
Humanist Philosophers Group 42–3, 63,
    77–8
Hume, Cardinal Basil 115, 119
Humfrey, Peter 118
Hunter, James 153

identity: Christian 22, 123, 192; faith
    identity 9–10, 123, 140–1; of faith
    schools 231–3, 249–50; and faith-
    based education 70–1, 249–50; of
    minority groups 139; RE and
    citizenship curricula 217
ideologies: separationist in France 179,
    180; social in USA 166–75
Ilkley (Bradford) 124(*Table 11.1*)
Immanuel CC (Bradford) 126, 127–8
immigrant communities 148, 169, *see also*
    ethnicity; minority groups
inclusive community schooling 44
inclusiveness 78–81, 96, 109, 120, 130; in
    admissions policies 123; and exclusivity
    98–9, 175
income levels 123, 124(*Table 11.1*), 148–9,
    151
independent schools: legal framework for
    36–7; religious schools as 80–1
individual liberty 10
indoctrination: and arguments against
    faith schools 55–6; and children's
    rights 43; and defence of faith schools
    58–9; and rationality 56, 59
inequality *see* equality
Inner Cities Religious Council 192, 194
inner-city schools 68
inspections: of independent schools 37; in
    voluntary aided schools 23, 37
integrated school movement 54, 68, 113,
    159, 161–2
integration *see* social integration
interdenominational provision: new
    initiatives 31, 218; 19th century 16, 19,
    20

Interface Approach Towards a Liberal
    Indigenous Charter (IATaLIC) 254
Interfaith Education Centre 129, 135
interfaith initiatives 31, 128–31; multifaith
    provision 129, *see also* joint faith schools
International Bureau of Education (IBE)
    133
intolerance *see* tolerance
Investment for Reform (DfES) 96
Ireland *see* Northern Ireland
Islamic values 41, 134, 183, 232, *see also*
    Muslims

Jackson, R. 10, 62
James, David 123
James Report (1972) 25
Jaurès, Jean 184
Jebb, Eglantyne 38
Jesuit schools 231–2
Jewish schools: Orthodox 138–44, 243;
    performance of 203, 204(*Table 18.2*),
    205(*Table 18.3*), 210; strategies for 247,
    250, 251; voluntary aided and
    controlled 23
Jews/Judaism: educational traditions 30;
    identity 9–10, 192; in 19th century 15;
    and religious discrimination 75
joint faith schools 68, 109, 113–21, 120,
    130; Four Faiths School 31, 44, 68
JPR (Institute of Jewish Policy Research)
    9–10, 247
Judaism *see* Jews/Judaism
Judge, H. 8, 61

Key Stage 2 tests 209
Key Stage 3 tests 202–11(*Tables 18.1–18.6*
    and *Figures 18.1–18.3*)

Labour government (1997–): policy aims
    8–9, 90,
94–5, 213; support for faith schools 191,
    242–3; views of faith education 8–9,
    44, 51, 52
Lacey, Catherine 234
Lancaster, Joseph 16, 17
Lang–Couplet agreement (1992) 182
leadership: community 196; in schools
    230, 251
LEAs (Local Education Authorities) 19;
    Agreed Syllabus 22–3, 23–4, 27, 28,
    30; faith schools and performance
    207–9(*Table 18.4–18.5*), 210; and faith-
    based community action 193–4;
    support for training colleges 21, 24

legal frameworks: faith schools 36–8; of US government 167
legal guidance 80
Leitch, R. and Kirkpatrick, R. 160
Lerner, Michael 194
Levin, Lynndy 138
Lewis, Philip 129
liberal values 10, 56, 57; and divisiveness 65–6, 68–9; and faith schools 83–9, 139–41, 249, 254–5
literacy skills 210–11
local education authorities (UK) *see* LEAs
local consultation 80
London Churches Group for Social Action 193
Londonderry, Lord 156, 157
Longley, Clifford 230

MacBeath, J. 228
McGrath, Michael 232
McKenzie, R. 238
McLaughlin, T.H. 66, 239, 255
MacMurray, John 192
Magee, J. 158
maintained schools: county maintained schools 22; faith schools as 215, 243; grant-maintained schools abolished 214; and NC 215–16; voluntary maintained schools 156, 157, *see also* 'dual system'; joint faith schools
Mann, Horace 15, 168, 169–70, 174
Mannheim, K. 129
market forces 97, 185
Marks, John *et al.* 147, 152, 153
Marty, Martin 192
Mass 119–20
Mayall, B. 41
Methodist Conference 245
Methodists 29
Michaelsen, Robert 169
Middle East 105, 109
minority groups: black and ethnic faiths 193; Catholic 157, 158–9, 163; cognitive 139; and rights 41, *see also* ethnicity; Jews/Judaism
mission statements 116–17, 128, 182, 235
Mitzvahs (Divine commands) 143(*Table 12.1*)
Modood, T. *et al.* 44
Mok, M. 151
moral education: and RE 29–30, 232–3; in USA 168, *see also* values-based education

moral values 69–70, 232; and secularism 184
More, Thomas, *Utopia* 166
Morris, Andrew 147, 152, 153
Morris, Estelle 133
Morrison, K. 227–8
Mott-Thornton, K. 173
Mozart vs Hawkins 87
Mukadam, M.H. 40
multifaith provision 129, 217
multifaith schools *see* joint faith schools
Murray, D. 158
Muslim Council of Great Britain 197
Muslim schools, and autonomy 86
Muslims 30–1, 192; in Bradford 122–3, 130; in Christian schools 107; and divisiveness 67; Islamic values 41, 134, 183, 232, *see also* South Asian communities

National Council for Civil Liberties 39
National Curriculum (NC) 213–21, 222–3, 224, 244, *see also* curricula
national faith identity, England 9–10
natural religion 169
Neal, Derek 149
Neighbourhood Renewal Unit, *The Learning Curve* 196
neo-liberal conservatism 192, 194
networks 94
Neuhaus, R.J. 192
Neusmer, Jacob 57
New Labour 94–5, 97, 192, 195, 198, 243, *see also* Labour government
New York 149–50
New Zealand 148, 151
Newsome, D. 15
NFER (National Foundation for Educational Research) 52
Niblett, Roy 255
NICIE (Northern Ireland Council for Integrated Education) 159
Niebuhr, Reinhold 172, 173, 174
non-common educational environments 63, 64
non-contractual private schools 182
non-denominational education 20–1, 29, 156–7, 158–75
non-religious schools 204–8(*Tables 18.2, 18.4 and Figures 18.1–18.3*)
Nord, Warren 169, 170
north of England riots 2001 43, 62, 64, 67, 122, 195–6

Northern Ireland 156–64; divisiveness
and conflict in 64, 67, 157–60;
integrated school movement 54, 159,
161–2
NS (National Society) 16, 19, 27
nurture 129–30
NVADs (national value-added datasets)
202–3(*Tables 18.1 and 18.2*)

Oakeshott, M. 56–7
Observer 83
O'Connell, James 123–4, 131, 136
OFSTED inspections: in Bradford 124–5,
129; on Catholic schools 147; and
CPPD initiatives 226, 228; in joint
church school 116; of RE 215; in
voluntary aided schools 23, 118
Olasky, Martin 194
Ouseley Report (*Community Pride not
Prejudice*) 43, 54, 62, 76, 134

parental choice 52, 71; and child's needs
247–8; in France 182, 183; of
Muslims 123, 130; in South Africa
151; and state systems 96, 184–5
parents: and Catholic schools 148, 151,
154; and N. Ireland integrated schools
159, 163; support for faith schools 123,
130, 211, 218
parents rights: and admission
requirements 133; and children's rights
40–4, 77, 244; as justification for faith
schools 54; in Northern Ireland
159–60; and reform of faith schools 88
Parker-Jenkins, M. 75
particularism 162
partnership 8–9, 18–26, 227
peace 105
peace process 162
pedagogy *see* teaching methods
performance 52, 147–54, 202–11, 217, *see
also* achievement
personal development 56–7
Phillips, Trevor 53
Pinner, H. 10
pluralism: beliefs and attitudes 68, 71;
cultural pluralism 139; custodial–
plural duality 166–7, 174; and values
of faith education 12, 110, 163
pluralistic integration 139
policy making: BHA policy on education
74–81; of Christian schools 106; for
faith schools 225–7, 246–55; Labour
government (1997–) 8–9, 90, 94–5;

national strategies 1870–1843 18–19;
in Northern Ireland 159, 160–3; and
social justice 92
political process: faith and religion in 191,
231; and social capital 195, 196
Pollard, Stephen 227
postmodernity 245
poverty 123–4, 131–2, 134, 148
prayer 119
primary schools: in Bradford 124–5, 129;
Catholic 150; and curriculum 220; in
Northern Ireland 158; voluntary aided
and controlled 23
Pring, Richard 11, 233, 237, 253
private schools: and autonomy 85–6; in
France 180, 181–2, 185; in the US 84,
86, 87
private values 68–9, 167, 249
Protestants/Protestantism 156, 157, 169,
180
PSHE 213–14
public schools (USA) 83–4, 85–6, 166–9,
173–5; compared with Catholic
schools 149–50, 154, *see also* state
controlled schools
public values 69–70, 84–5, 239, 249;
and non-public domains 68–9, 167,
247
Puente, Archbishop Pablo 115
pupil-teachers 17
pupils 233, 236–7, 251–5; children's rights
38–40, 40–4, 75–8, 77, 244; pupil
performance 202–11, *see also*
achievement
Putnam, R.D. 93, 191, 195, 196

Quakers 17

Race Relations (Amendments) Act 2000
42, 78
rational autonomy 66
rationalism: consistent rationality 10;
Dewey 170–3; and indoctrination 56,
59; and secularism 184, 243–4
Rawls, J./Rawlsian theory 91, 92
RE (Religious Education): and BHA
consultation
document 79; in Christian schools 28,
107, 118–19; and citizenship 213–15,
217–18, 219–20, 238–9; curricular
changes 22–3, 24, 213–15, 215–16,
217–18, 219–20; humanist view of 74;
and Jewish education 30; and moral
education 29–30; and social inclusion

217–18; and student philosophies 253–5
Reeves, Marjorie 53
relationships 111, 142–4
relativism 70
religion: and civil society 191–3, 197–8, 220–1; common faith 161–3, 168–70, 171–3, 174; definitions of 243; 'religion' and the 'religious' 171, 173; and US public schooling 173–5, *see also* beliefs and attitudes; faith traditions
religious diversity 21–2
Religious Education Council of England and Wales 30
religious literacy 129, 130, 142–4
religious schools: and autonomy 85–6; defined 63; humanist views of 77, 78–81; 'old' and 'new' 65; and secularisation 87–8; in the US 67–8, 84, 86, 87, 91, *see also* faith schools
Republicans (France) 179–80
research strategies 244–55
resources for CPPD 226
respect 10, 68–9, 70
RI 22–3, *see also* RE
rights: of children 38–40, 40–4, 75–6, 77, 244; of parents 40–4, 54, 77, 88, 133, 159–60, 244
Robinson, Muriel 239
Roman Catholic *see* Catholic; Catholics
Rosenow, E. 171–2
Rowe, D. 141
RS (religious studies) 215
Rummery, R. 28
Runcie, R. (Archbishop of Canterbury) 231
Ruskin, John 192

Sacks, J. 57, 58, 140, 141, 197, 216; and Sutherland, S. 12, 222–3, 231, 232
St Cuthbert Mayne School (Torquay) 115
St Edwards School (Poole, Dorset) 113, 115–20
St Martin de Porres RC Primary School (Soweto) 151
Sammons, P. *et al.* 235
SATs (Standard Assessment Tests, USA) 149–50
Savary, Alain 180
Save the Children International Union 38–9
SCAA (Schools Curriculum and Assessment Authority) 213

Schagen, S. and Schagen, I. 52, 148
Schin, Edgar 237
Schneiders, Sandra 253–4
Schon, D. 234
The School Curriculum and the National Curriculum (DfEE and QCA) 222
School Organisation Committees 37, 193
School Standards and Framework Act 1998 37
Schools: Achieving Success (DfES) 1, 7, 191, 193, 202, 224
Schools: Building on Success (DfES) 7, 38, 51, 95
Schools Curriculum and Assessment Authority (SCAA) 213
Scotland 109
secondary schools: in Bradford 125–8; Catholic 150; CofE 27; ethos and access 96, 185; faith schools performance 202–11(*Figures 18.1– 18.3*); in France 185; joint church comprehensive 113, 115–20; voluntary aided and controlled 23
sectarianism 169–70
secularists/secularism 110; in 19th century 15, 178–9; in France 179–84; and multi-faith education 130; and non-sectarianism 169–70, 174; and tolerance 163; in the UK 21, 29–30, 83–5, 87–8
segregation 122, 125, 133–4; and N. Ireland contact initiatives 158–9; social, in France 180, 184–5
selective systems 185, 242
self-researching schools 228, 246
separationism 84–5, 87–8, 179
service (concept of) 129–30
services *see* worship
shared school *see* joint faith schools
Shevitz, Susan 237
Shokraii, N.H. 152
Short, G. 63
Sikhs/Sikhism 30–1, 192
single-faith schools *see* faith schools; religious schools
single-sex education 78, 80, 86, 98, 126
Skeie, G. 10
skills: basic 150; literacy 210–11
Slee, R. and Weiner, G. 235
Smith, A. and Robinson, A. 160
Smith, A.B. 41
Smith, David 123
Smith, Ian Duncan 192, 195

social capital 90–9, 92–3, 191, 237–8; and
    faith-based community action 195–7;
    and social policy 94
social cohesion 133, 134–6, 195–6, 218
social conditions: 1944–2002 21; and
    academic achievement 147; in
    Bradford 123–4(*Table 11.1*), 129–36;
    and CPPD in faith schools 230–1;
    loyalty and responsibility 170–1, *see
    also* communities
social curriculum 215–16, 216–17
social inclusion 214, 217–18, *see also*
    inclusiveness
social integration 76; integrated school
    movement 54, 68, 113, 159, 161–2
social justice 90–2
Socialist–Communist government
    (France) 180–1
'Sojourners' 194
South Africa 151–2
South Asia Solidarity Group and Asian
    Women Unite 78
South Asian communities 122–3, 124,
    125, 130, 131, 132
Soweto 151
Spinner, J. 139
Spinner-Halev, J. 69
spirituality 108, 109–10, 119, 236, 245,
    253–4
SRE (sex and relationships education) 80
staff *see* teachers
standards: academic 52, 94–5, 149–50,
    150–1, 152, 153–4; and CPPD in faith
    schools 229–31, *see also* achievement
Standing Advisory Councils on Religious
    Education (SACRE) 215
state controlled schools 22–3, 157; faith in
    183, *see also* public schools
state systems: autonomy and religious
    schools 84, 85–6, 87–8; and faith
    schools 7, 107, 109–10
state–church relationships: criticism of
    partnerships 54–6; 'dual system' 18–26,
    227; in France 178–83; in USA 166
Stiltner, Brian 249
Stoll, L. 250
strategies *see* policy making
student teachers 24, 25
students *see* pupils
subsidies 151
Sullivan, J. 222
Sutherland, Stewart 12, 222–3, 231, 232
Swann Report (*Education for All*, HMSO)
    62

syllabuses *see* curricula

Talbot, M. 86
Tate, Nicholas 213
Tawney, R.H. 192
teacher education and training: and BHA
    consultation document 80; and the
    'dual system' 20–1, 24–6, 227; in
    Northern Ireland 161; voluntary
    Christian provision 1803–69
    17–18
Teacher Training Agency 226
teachers 185, 197, 233, 234, 236, 251;
    appointments in voluntary aided
    schools 37; in Catholic schools 148–9,
    153, 154; Christian responsibilities
    107, 108, 111, 174; and CPPD 224–7,
    237–8; pupil-teachers 17; student
    teachers 24, 25
teaching methods: and indoctrination
    58–9; non- denominational 168–9;
    and school ethos 111, 153–4
Temple, William (Archbishop of
    Canterbury) 23
TES (*Times Educational Supplement*) 41, 52,
    97, 202
The Learning Curve (Neighbourhood
    Renewal Unit) 196
Third Way 94, 192
Thompson, E.P. 192
Thornton, Richard 128
'Tikkun' 194
The Times 8, 11, 227, 232
tolerance 68–9, 70, 110; and ethnic
    groups 41, 142; intolerance and
    secularism 163
Tomasi, J. 69
Tong (Bradford) 124(*Table 11.1*), 126
Toynbee, P. 61
traditions of thought 57, 59
training colleges 17, 20–1, 24–6; Catholic
    24, 25, 28; CofE 24–5, 26, 27; Free
    Church 29; Jewish 30
transformation schools 162
Treston, K. 119, 230
typologies: of provision 226, 247; of
    religion 9

unemployment 123, 124(*Table 11.1*)
UNESCO 133
United Nations, CRC 39–40, 41, 43,
    75–6
United States: American Bill of Rights for
    Children 39; autonomy and faith

schools 85–6; Catholic schools 67–8, 91, 147, 148–50, 196–7; faith schools versus common schooling 166–75; faith-based community action 193, 194–6, 198; secularisation and separationism 83–4, 87, 88–9, 194
unity 115, 119–20
University of London, Institute of Education 226
University Ward (Bradford) 124(*Table 11.1*)
Urban Theology Group 193
USA *see* United States

Valins, O. 30
value systems: Catholicism 153–4; and faith education 10, 68–70, 107, 108, 110, 253–5; poverty and dispossession 131–2, 134, *see also* beliefs and attitudes; ethos; values-based education
Values Forum 213, 214
values-based education 106, 107, 110, 163–4, 232–9; Catholic 152–4; and faith-based education 216–17, 238–9, 249, 252; Judaism's relationships with other faiths 142–4; and National Curriculum 213, 214, 216, 235, *see also* liberal values
veil, Islamic 41, 183
Volf, Miroslav 175
voluntary aided schools 22, 23, 122; financial contributions of 118; legal frameworks for 37, 38; Muslim schools 86
voluntary Christian schools (1803–69) 14–18
voluntary controlled schools 37, 38
voluntary schools/voluntary maintained schools 156, 157

Wacker, Grant 167

Wade, J. 15
Wales 18, 23, 27
Wallis, Jim 194
Walsh, Paddy 252
Walzer, M. 175
Warren, Mark 195, 196
Watson, Brenda 255–6
The Way Ahead (Dearing Report) 10, 97, 114, 129–30, 231, 236–7, 247
Wesleyan Methodists 29
White, John 56
white population: in Bradford 124, 125, 131–2; Irish immigrant 148
Wilde, Oscar 138, 140
Williams, Rowan (Archbishop of Canterbury) 8, 9, 11, 135
Wilson, H.B. 15
Wintersgill, Barbara 253
Winthrop, John 166
Wittgenstein, L. 253
women: income levels 124; opposition to religious schools 78; support for CofE schools 130
Wood, K. 130
Wood, Keith Porteous 54–5
Wood, Richard L. 195, 196
World Bank 93
worship: collective worship 22, 30, 79; joint school celebration 115–16, 119–20
Wright, Andrew 236
Wrigley, T. 228, 229, 232–3, 235, 248, 255
Wuthnow, Robert 192
Wyke 124 (Bradford) (*Table 11.1*), 126

York, Archbishop of 236–7
Youniss, James and Yates, Miranda 198

Zipfel, R. 28
Zones d'éducation prioritaires (ZEP) 185